Success in
COMMUNICATION

Success Studybooks

Accounting and Costing
Accounting and Costing: Problems and Projects
Book-keeping and Accounts
British History 1760–1914
British History since 1914
Business Calculations
Chemistry
Commerce
Commerce: West African Edition
Communication
Economic Geography
Economics
Economics: West African Edition
Electronics
Elements of Banking
European History 1815–1941
Geography: Human and Regional
Geography: Physical and Mapwork
Information Processing
Insurance
Investment
Law
Management: Personnel
Office Practice
Organic Chemistry
Physics
Principles of Accounting
Principles of Accounting: Answer Book
Principles of Catering
Statistics
Twentieth Century World Affairs
World History since 1945

Success in
COMMUNICATION

Stuart Sillars

JOHN MURRAY

For Elfryd Evans, Andre Morgan and my friends, colleagues
and former students in Aberystwyth

Cartoons by Colin Wheeler

© Stuart Sillars 1988

First published 1988
Reprinted with amendments 1991

Typeset in 9/11 pt and 8/10 pt Compugraphic English Times by Colset Private
Ltd.
Printed in Great Britain by Richard Clay Ltd, Bungay, Suffolk.

British Library Cataloguing in Publication Data

Sillars, Stuart
    Success in communication.
    1. Business practices. Communication
    I. Title
    651.7

ISBN 0-7195-4523-4

Contents

Foreword

It is not easy to avoid communication in today's world, however much we may be tempted to try. At times we all feel besieged by marauding telephone calls, junk mail and the report which has to be on the boss's desk first thing tomorrow morning. The vocabulary of electronic communication, let alone the machines themselves, can be baffling and intimidating.

This book is about making communication work for you instead of being frightened or enslaved by it. It is aimed at people who want to pass examinations in communication, including those of the RSA, LCCI, Pitman Examinations Institute, City and Guilds, and the leading relevant professional bodies, as well as students on BTEC courses in business and finance. But it is also aimed at people who want to make sense of communication in their everyday working lives – perhaps to help in running a small business, to improve their efficiency at work, or to make the administrative side of their job easier and clearer. *How* the book should be used will depend very much on the reason *why* it is being used – some suggestions are made on page xii, and advice on tackling examinations is given on pages xiii–xiv.

Written or spoken, verbal or non-verbal, pictorial or graphic, communication is an essential element of success in every field of contemporary activity. It is the purpose of this book to give guidance and encouragement in all these areas of communication, and also to show that clear, professional communication can be not only an instrument of achievement in other fields of activity but also a pleasure and source of fulfilment in itself.

S.J.S.

Acknowledgements

Many people have given generously of their time and expertise to help in the writing of this book. Anne Webster and Flair Kennett at John Murray provided boundless enthusiasm and practical help in the early stages, and Bob Davenport and Wendy Reed continued this process at a later stage of the book's growth. The list of others who have aided the gestation and delivery is long; to them all, whether they read an early draft and made helpful suggestions, or whether a chance remark of theirs suggested a way of solving a problem, I am sincerely grateful. Any errors or discrepancies which remain in the text despite the good offices of the above are, of course, the results of my personal intransigence.

Colin Wheeler's cartoons bring visual directness and a much-needed sense of satire to the text, and I am delighted to thank him here for his contribution to the book.

Illustrations have been reproduced by kind permission of the following organizations: MFI Furniture Centres Ltd (fig. 1.1), the Controller of Her Majesty's Stationery Office (figs 3.3, 14.14, 14.16 (from a COIC publication *Developing New Products*); 12.3 (top), 13.1, 14.11, and 15.2 – all Crown copyright), the Trustees of the Imperial War Museum, London (fig. 4.4), The Open University (fig. 10.4), Kwik-Fit-Euro Ltd (fig. 13.3), Girobank plc (fig. 13.5), British Railways Board (fig. 14.2), J Sainsbury plc (fig. 14.3), Amstrad Consumer Electronics plc (fig. 17.1), International Computers Ltd (fig. 17.2), Apple Computer UK Ltd (fig. 17.3), Siemens Ltd (fig. 17.4), Pitney Bowes plc (fig. 17.5), Thomas Cook Ltd (fig. 17.6), Bell & Howell Ltd (figs 18.1 and 18.2). Additional material is reproduced by courtesy of the London Chamber of Commerce and Industry Examinations Board (fig. 9.2(a)), *The Economist* (fig. 9.4(a)) and the Business & Technician Education Council (fig. 12.17(a)). The solutions given in figs 9.2(b) and 12.17(b) are the author's own and are not the responsibility of the examining bodies concerned.

Questions from past examination papers are reproduced by courtesy of the Association of Accounting Technicians (AAT), the Association of Business Executives (ABE), the Institute of Credit Management (ICM), the Institute of Purchasing and Supply (IPS), the London Chamber of Commerce and Industry Examinations Board (LCCI), the Royal Society of Arts Examinations Board (RSA), and the Southern Examining Group (SEG).

S.J.S.

How to use this book

This book covers all the kinds of communication, both written and spoken, that you will need for working in business and for taking business communication exams. It covers each topic in increasing depth, beginning with simple examples and moving to more complicated ones, so that you can work up to the level of difficulty which suits your own needs. You can work straight through it, starting at the beginning and completing the exercises as you go through each section; but other approaches might be more suitable. Some suggestions are given below.

To prepare for an exam

1 Read your syllabus carefully to see what you need to cover.
2 Look through past papers to gauge the level of difficulty.
3 Read through the contents pages of this book.
4 Work through topics in the order they appear in the book. Make sure that you cover each topic in the right depth – don't go on to the more advanced sections unless you really need to. Be sure, too, that you work through all the exercises and assignments.

To help at work

1 Think carefully about what your work involves.
2 Skim through the contents pages of this book and check which sections will be most useful to you.
3 Work through the necessary sections to the level of difficulty you think is appropriate to your needs.

Using the index

The book has a detailed index to help you find specific items quickly. Use it to:

● find the main entries on particular topics as and when you need;
● check that you have covered every aspect of a topic. Some may be covered in two or more units – like letters, for example, which are mentioned in Unit 17 as well as Units 11 and 12.
● check details quickly, as a reference guide.

All these points will help you to get the best from the book. Use it wisely!

Tackling exams

All of us tend to leave exam revision to the last minute. If you think about your exams throughout your studies, however, your preparation for them will be much more thorough, and you will be far more likely to succeed. For this reason, the following hints are included at the beginning of this book rather than later on.

During your studies

Take notes   Use the principles given in Unit 9 to take notes when studying. List:

- key points in each unit;
- points of layout and presentation;
- points about topics likely to come up in the exam (use past papers to help here).

Revise continuously   Keep your work fresh in your mind by reading over what you have done at regular intervals. When you finish a topic, revise it before going on to the next one.

Practise by doing   Use every opportunity to write letter, reports, memos – anything which will feature in the exam. This will fix the layouts in your mind and help you to write quickly and fluently.

Six to eight weeks before the exam

Try a past paper   Get someone to check it afterwards – this will tell you how much you know.

Know your weaknesses   Think about what topics need work – usually they are the ones you enjoy the least.

Make a timetable   Work out how much time you have and how you're going to use it. Give most time to your weak areas. Once you have a timetable, stick to it.

When revising

- use your own notes;
- read tutors' comments on your work, if you have any;
- study the sample letters, memos etc. in this book;
- take regular breaks to keep up concentration.

Test yourself   Tackle past papers against the clock when you have revised a topic. This will encourage you, as it will show you that your knowledge is improving.

Just before the exam

Vary your revision   Work in different places, like public libraries, or talk to friends who are also taking your exam.

Keep healthy   Go for walks, eat well and get plenty of rest.

Keep a sense of proportion   Exams aren't everything, even if they seem to be at the moment!

The nature of communication

1.1 What is communication?

Communication may be defined as

> the giving, receiving or exchange of information, opinions or ideas by writing, speech or visual means – or any combination of the three – so that the material communicated is completely understood by everyone concerned.

This may appear to be quite a straightforward process – after all, we communicate all the time, by talking to each other, writing letters, making telephone calls, and even by making signs and gestures when we are angry or upset. So why is there any need to study communication?

The answer is that, simply because we are all involved in communication for such a large amount of the time, we need to make sure that we get it right – that we really do put across ideas and information in a way that everyone involved can understand. The more complicated the activity, the harder it is to communicate about it. Think how often you have tried to explain something which you understand very well to someone who knows nothing about it – how to get by road to a local landmark through a system of one-way streets, for example. You will agree, I am sure, that communicating is sometimes not at all easy.

Thinking about what we have to say, working out the best way of saying it – in a letter, on the telephone, or in person, perhaps – finding the right words, making sure the other person understands, and understanding anything he or she says in reply are all vital stages in communicating, and at every stage things can go wrong.

1.2 Social communication

Humans are social beings and spend much of their time together. We first learn to communicate in a social setting, usually with parents and relations, and throughout life much of our time is spent in social communication. At every step – whether as child, adolescent, young adult, parent, relation or friend – we communicate socially with those around us. We learn what we can and cannot say to certain people, getting to know 'how far to go' in terms of what subjects and forms of expression are acceptable to different people. We develop our own languages in small groups – the word-games of schoolchildren, the slang of students, the specialist words used by jazz musicians, rugby players or accountants, for example.

As well as speaking in person and on the telephone, we may use other kinds of communication. When we are young we are encouraged to write thank-you letters for presents and to send postcards to friends when we are on holiday. When we are a little older, we may write love letters which, older still, we hope have been destroyed. We meet in groups to play games, and learn how to suggest that the referee's eyesight is not quite what it should be, and how to make an appeal for 'leg-before' so convincingly that only the sternest umpire can refuse. We meet in twos and threes, over coffee or at the bus-stop, and say what he said to her and what she did then, and as we get older we explain how we were never like that when we were that age.

All of this is social communication, which has its own codes of what is and is not acceptable. It is usually informal, and, even if it is not actually spoken, it will probably have a lot to do with spoken language in the words that are used and in their organization. Although we rarely realize it, communication of this sort is a highly skilled activity. If we can do it well, we may become very successful as social animals: if we do it badly, we may become isolated and lonely. But it is not just social communication that most of us have to think about: there is another area where successful communication is of very great importance.

1.3 Business communication

Anyone who works for a living is involved in business communication. It is not something which exists only in offices and big City institutions. Unlike social communication, which is relaxed, informal and (most of the time) friendly, business communication is carefully organized, formal and more concerned with getting things done than with exchanging pleasantries.

In social communication, the telephone is an instrument for having a chat: in business it is a way to convey information quickly and perhaps cheaply. Social letters are full of personal news and are informal in language and style: business letters contain only essential factual information, are much shorter and use a more formal – though not completely impersonal – style. Social talk is unhurried, uses slang and expressions understood only by small groups, and often does not follow grammatical sentence structure: business talk is carefully planned, carried out quickly as time is valuable, uses no slang – although it may well use specialized language – and should be grammatical in its construction. In short, business communication is planned in layout and expression and composed according to clear objectives, whereas social communication follows no rigid structure and may be quite spontaneous.

This difference is crucial and lies at the heart of the proper use of communication in business. It can be illustrated by considering some of the situations in which communication is used in the workplace.

At a very straightforward level, a mechanic who wants an exhaust held in place while she welds it together will ask a short, simple and clear question to get someone to help her. A nurse seeking help with a patient needing resuscitation will be similarly direct. If a solicitor writes a letter to a client about how the sale of a house is proceeding, or when the client is due to appear in court, she will not waste time on unnecessary personal comments. If a bank manager wants to know if you are able to repay a loan on a new car, he will not tell you about his holiday in the Bahamas. An accountant writing a report on possible company expansion will present the facts, and her own opinions of the scheme, concisely and directly. A personnel director placing an advertisement for staff in a newspaper will want to get as much information as possible into the space he can afford to buy.

All of these are situations in which communication plays a vital role. To fulfil the demands placed on it, communication in business must be clear, concise and direct, otherwise time and money will be wasted while those on the receiving end try to understand what is being said. And, as they are struggling, someone else may have won the contract or got the job – all because of inadequate communication.

1.4 Some problems and solutions

Adopting the appropriate form of communication and using it in the right way are crucial to both personal and business life. Unless friends and acquaintances know what we mean, relationships will become strained. Unless employees know what is expected of them, they will be unable to supply it. Unless clients are given precise details of costs and delivery dates, they will not order products. Unless the directors can conduct a meeting, they will be unable to run the company.

This will become clearer if we consider a few situations – some fictitious, but based on real life – and the role played by communication in each.

1.4.1 Beat it!

A learned British professor of music was asked to carry out some examinations for very young performers in the United States. For one of these tests, the candidate had to beat time to a piece of music played by the examiner on the piano. One young boy was very nervous when asked to do this and made no movement at all when the professor played. The professor stopped, explained again what was required, and began to play once more. Still the boy did nothing. In exasperation the professor shouted 'Well, go on then, beat it!' The boy stared for a moment, then shot out of the room and down the street.

The problem here is simple. The professor did not realize that, to the boy, 'beat it' was a forceful way of telling someone to go away. The story shows an essential rule of communicating: always make sure that a word or phrase means the same to the person you are talking to as it does to you. Common words can have widely different meanings to people from different backgrounds, and using them can have surprising and disruptive results.

1.4.2 Making cars by telephone

A major producer of sports cars took the decision to transfer production of one model to a different plant. Its administrative headquarters, however, remained at the plant where the car had first been made. In the assembly-line method of car building, each model is built up as it proceeds along the line, with the appropriate engine, body trim and mechanical components being used to match an order placed by a customer or dealer. In this way everyone gets the exact model variant ordered, and there are no cars which nobody wants. When the production was moved to the new plant in this particular case, little thought was given to how the specification for each car would be communicated to the workers actually assembling it.

The best that could be done was to telephone through the details. Since there were four different versions of the model, twelve different paint colours and countless variations in transmission, suspension and other mechanical details, each call took several minutes. There was no written record, and often the line was bad. Instructions were misheard, the wrong cars were made, customers cancelled their orders, garages changed to dealing in different cars and the plant closed.

This is a simple story of how a failure in communication might have disastrous effects on a company's activities. The use of a more effective way of communicating the model specifications would have solved the problem and perhaps saved the plant – and the jobs of all its workers.

1.4.3 Getting the right pictures

Furniture manufacture in the United Kingdom is dominated by firms which produce self-assembly items – pieces of furniture which the customer buys as a set of parts and then assembles at home. When the method was first introduced, people were not used to building their own furniture. They needed to be convinced that the furniture was good, solid and durable, and that it could be put together quickly by someone with no previous experience and only a minimal tool-kit.

The first problem was solved in the showroom, where the furniture was shown assembled, to make clear that it was just as good (in the manufacturer's view) as anything bought fully assembled. The second problem was more complicated. It was solved by providing clear, diagrammatic instructions with every piece of furniture, explaining in pictures how the furniture should be assembled. The diagrams used the minimum number of words – as much information as possible was conveyed by pictures. If the instructions had all been written, with no illustrations, very few people would have understood them (or would have been willing to try to understand them) and the firm might not have succeeded. Because of the clarity of the instructions, self-assembly furniture is now widely accepted and there are many firms with large showrooms in most major towns in the UK.

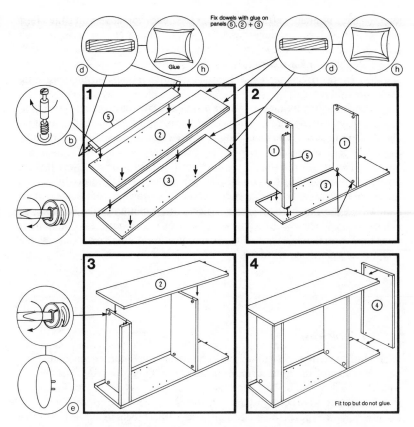

Fig. 1.1 An excerpt from an instruction booklet for self-assembly furniture

All of this is the result of finding the right solution to a communication problem: showing people how to convert pieces of veneered chipboard into a wardrobe which looks like a professionally made piece of furniture.

1.4.4 On the move

Imagine that a company manufacturing hazardous chemicals has to transport its goods from its factory through a town to a customer's factory. The police are concerned about safety; the manufacturer is concerned to get the goods delivered. The haulage contractor wants to know what kind of vehicle will be needed; the local shopkeepers and residents are alarmed about the risks involved.

This situation can be effectively resolved only by communication. Meetings must be held, with representatives of all the organizations involved, so that specialist knowledge can be pooled. They must work out the best route for the load, bearing in mind traffic flow (which the police can advise on), the safest vehicle to use (which the haulier can tell them), the real extent of the risks (which only the manufacturer knows), what precautions can be taken in case of spillage (in which police, manufacturer, haulier and local people will all be involved), and the best way of telling the local population what is going on and reassuring them of its safety.

As well as holding the meeting where people can talk the problem over face to face, there will be a need to exchange information by telephone, and to draw up plans for timing and route and notify all involved of them. Statements must be issued to local residents, perhaps as circular letters or advertisements in the press, and a safety-procedure document must be issued to make sure that all involved in transporting the goods are aware of the necessary procedures. The success of the whole venture depends on everyone knowing what is happening: it is, once again, a communication issue. If the communication is wrong or inadequate, residents will be angry (at best) or injury may result if spillage occurs (at worst). Using accurate communication of the right kind, which everyone understands, is crucial.

1.5 Conclusion

From the last section you will see that communication is not, as you might have been forgiven for thinking, a simple process of talking or writing. Neither is it something which can be kept separate from other areas of activity – a special skill which, like brain surgery or growing roses, is practised by only a few highly qualified or gifted people. It is a complicated, subtle process which affects every facet of our working and private lives, and which gives plenty of opportunities for mistakes. Yet this makes it exciting as well as daunting, as it shows that improved communication can in turn improve almost everything that we do.

Some aspects of communication are changing fast. The microchip revolution has not only altered the way in which we contact each other and the way we produce documents, it has also changed the language we use. People now 'access data' instead of 'finding information'; they talk of 'interfaces' instead of 'meetings'. Modern technology has perhaps even altered the way in which we think. Analogies to computers can be used to explain how the human memory works, while the stages involved in a complex process can be simplified by comparison with electronic data processing. The effect of information technology on the ways in which we communicate is discussed in Unit 17.

But however technology changes, one thing is certain: success in the world of business will depend increasingly on the ability to understand complex issues and to explain complex ideas clearly. Effective communication – whether using the most up-to-date electronics or the age-old language of gesture and touch – is the only way of making sure that this understanding and explanation are achieved.

1.6 Exercises

1 Think about a situation – at work, at college or in your personal life – where things have gone wrong because of poor communication. Write down:

(a) the information which should have been communicated;
(b) any details or points which should have been included but which were not;
(c) the way the information was communicated – by letter or on the telephone, for example;
(d) the way it should have been communicated;
(e) the results of poor communication.

2 Start a collection of pieces of written communication – letters, forms, sales leaflets, reports or any other documents. Consider how well they put across their message, and how they might be improved. Answer the following questions:

(a) What impression are you given of the writer (for example, is he or she considerate, tactless or business-like)?
(b) How good is the communication at getting you to do what it wants (for example, buy a product, use a service or simply write a reply)?
(c) What changes would you make to improve the document?

3 Keep a diary of the various people who communicate with you orally – in person or by telephone – during *one week*. Write down the person's name, the kind of communication he or she uses, and his or her reason for communicating. Then add some brief comments on how successful the communication was, and what could have been done to improve it.

Kinds of communication

2.1 Choosing the medium

As Unit 1 has made clear, the relationship between what is intended by a message and how that message is conveyed is one which is very close and very important. As a result, the communication medium – the form in which ideas, information or opinions are to be conveyed – must be selected with great care and only after considering all the factors involved. This unit will look at the main kinds of communication which are available to the business person, but we must first consider the factors which will help us to decide which method is the best for any particular situation.

2.1.1 Reliability

Reliability is of fundamental importance. Unless you know that the message will be received, it is pointless sending it. So, if you need to contact a company in a country where you know there is a postal strike, writing a letter is obviously not a good idea. Similarly, if you want to send a message to everyone in a building, it is not wise to put up a notice on a notice-board which is in a busy corridor, since no one will stop to read it. In these situations, an international telephone call or telex (or its electronic-mail equivalent if available) and a circular letter or a notice on a board which is more effectively sited would be far better choices for the respective needs.

As well as the reliability of the communication in terms of the message arriving at its destination, there is also the question of how reliable it is in getting across the ideas it contains. If you are communicating to someone whose command of English is poor, it may be better to talk in person so that anything not clear can be explained straightaway, rather than to write a letter which may contain phrases that the reader does not understand. This is something we shall return to when discussing style (see section 4.10) and the matching of your expression to the vocabulary and attitudes of the reader. Even before you get to the stage of wording your communication, however, you should consider whether the form you have chosen is reliable. Ask yourself this question: will the intended reader or readers be able to understand it and take the necessary action?

2.1.2 The receiver

In communication, 'the receiver' is the term used to refer to anyone who is given a message or communicated with. He, she or they must be considered when you are choosing the medium of communication. Would they be upset to receive a letter giving news which they would expect to be told in person? Would they prefer a written statement of whatever you have to tell them? Would they be happy to discuss matters in a group, or would a series of personal meetings be better? All these are points to consider when deciding on how best to communicate.

2.1.3 Your relationship with the receiver

In most business activities, you will work with people in a variety of relationships. Some people will be in authority over you, others will be subordinate to you, but many will be of the same level of seniority. Sometimes you will need to help and encourage people – new entrants or trainees, for example. At times you may need to issue warnings or take disciplinary measures – although this will happen only when you have achieved a post of some seniority.

The exact nature of the relationship you have with each member of the company will influence the kind of communication you use. For example, it would be inappropriate for a new trainee to telephone the managing director, but quite in order for the head of a department to telephone someone in his or her section. The same need to consider the relationship will apply when deciding how to communicate with someone in another organization. Do you know the person well enough to telephone or to write a letter addressed in person, or would a letter addressed simply to the company in general be more appropriate?

As well as these questions of relative seniority, the question of your personal relationship with the receiver needs to be remembered. Are you at ease with each other? Do you 'get on'? If you have just had an argument with someone, it might not be a good idea to write a memo to him or her about a pressing issue that has just come up – a better way of getting the message across, as well as patching up the disagreement, might be to go and see the person.

2.1.4 Formality

Some kinds of communication are very formal. They give the impression that everything is being done in an official way and they seem to overlook the personal touch which is so often needed to encourage people and make them feel that they are necessary members of the organization. An impersonal letter can often have a detrimental effect, even though it may be meant to congratulate or encourage someone. Here again, an informal meeting might be more suitable.

Some communication must be formal, however. Orders and requests for details about goods; letters about employment and promotion matters, including disciplinary procedures; advertisements for new staff; and records of what happened at meetings of committees – all these need to be produced with a certain formality.

2.1.5 Suitability to purpose

What do you want your communication to achieve? You must think about this before deciding which method to use, and you must also think about what kind of contact will encourage people to do what you want them to do. Will a formal letter be more effective than a personal visit in persuading someone not to resign in protest over a particular decision? Is a telephone call more likely than a simple written notice to encourage someone to attend a meeting? Will a form four pages long actually be completed by anyone? You should ask yourself questions like these when deciding on the type of communication to use in any situation.

2.1.6 Confidentiality

Some messages are confidential and should be read or heard only by the intended recipient. Others are less private. This difference can sometimes be important. Information about someone's pay, for example, will usually be confidential; the date and time of a meeting may not be. If something is confidential, it should be communicated in a letter or some other document which is seen only by those authorized to do so. If something is not confidential, then a telephone call about it may be made from a public place, a notice be displayed, an open memo or note be sent, or a message be delivered orally by a third party.

2.1.7 Cost

Short local telephone calls are usually cheaper than a letter, when the costs of writing, typing and stationery are considered in addition to the postage. Long-distance calls – especially long ones – are very much more expensive: perhaps a letter would do, unless the communication is urgent or requires an exchange of ideas which moves towards a firm conclusion and agreement. Personal visits are more costly still if they take place far away from the office. Is it really necessary to get together, or could the matter be dealt with on the telephone or in an exchange of letters? Cost is a consideration, like any other, which must be borne in mind when selecting the right kind of communication.

2.1.8 Speed

Some messages must be conveyed very quickly, in which case the telephone or a personal meeting will be necessary. Others are less urgent, and first- or second-class post may be more than adequate. Speed is usually linked with cost, too: messages which take longer to arrive are usually cheaper.

2.1.9 Conclusion

All of these factors influence the decision to use one kind of communication rather than another. Cost will always be important – but so will speed, and suitability to the receiver and to the nature of the message to be passed on.

Often there will be no single 'right' answer to a communication problem, and you will need to use your own judgement and experience when making the decision.

The units which follow discuss the major kinds of communication in detail but, before examining them in depth, we will first give an outline of each of them below, so that you have an idea of the nature, advantages and disadvantages of each and are familiar with the circumstances in which each one might be used.

2.2 Forms of oral communication

Oral communication is communication by word of mouth. It may be *direct*, when two or more people meet and talk, or *remote*, when the telephone is used. Notice that both forms are called 'oral communication' and not 'verbal communication' – verbal communication means 'communication through words' and is thus a description of written as well as spoken communication.

2.2.1 Unplanned exchange
This is simply a chance meeting at which a few words are exchanged by two or three people about a matter of common interest. The disadvantage is that, as the meeting is unplanned, it is easy to leave out important points. For example, you may meet the office manager in the lift and discuss the new photocopier which keeps breaking down, but forget to mention that the mechanic promised to replace it if it happened again. Such meetings are good for conveying information quickly, though, and for making people feel that they are part of the organization.

2.2.2 Planned informal talk
This has more formality but is still fairly relaxed, as no major decisions or conclusions are likely to be reached – it is more likely to be an interim meeting to report progress on a project. The alternative is a telephone call, which would save time but would be less personal.

2.2.3 Interview
An interview is a formal exchange between two people, or between one person and a small group. Interviews may take place for various reasons, as detailed in Unit 6, although the job interview is the type that most people are familiar with. Carefully prepared, interviews can be very effective, allowing those involved to exchange ideas and reach a conclusion. They do take up a lot of time, however, and, like all oral communication, they may not be recorded properly, so future reference to what was decided may be difficult. An exchange of letters or other written communication may be more effective in some situations, or may be necessary to confirm details and for future reference.

2.2.4 Telephone call

The advantage here is speed and directness, so if you needed an immediate answer you would use the phone. However, there are disadvantages: there is no written record of a phone call; you may time the call badly; the connection may be poor; and the other person may misunderstand what is said or what is meant. Local calls are cheap in comparison to letters, but other calls are costly. Conference calls, in which several people are linked by telephone, save travelling but need careful planning and firm control to prevent everyone from speaking at once.

The use of the telephone is considered in more detail in Unit 7.

2.2.5 Group meeting

Group meetings allow many people to come together to share their skills and to reach a conclusion agreeable to the majority. A company's annual sales conference would be such a meeting. However, group meetings need careful planning and direction, are time-consuming and can involve expensive travel. Poorly planned, they may also be more destructive than creative, damaging the relationships between individuals and groups. Alternatives include conference telephone calls and circular letters.

Meetings are discussed further in Unit 16.

2.2.6 Committee meeting

This is a special kind of group meeting, in that the committee meets at prescribed intervals and its meetings follow clearly defined lines. The advantages are that there will be a full discussion of items by a range of different people and the proceedings will be well recorded in formal 'minutes' or reports. The disadvantage is that too wide a range of views will cause uncertainty and delay agreement.

2.2.7 Full staff or employees' meeting

At such a meeting all the workers of an organization or a department are brought together to discuss, for example, the company's performance during the year. Such meetings are hard to organize as they take up working time, and they are difficult to run as it is important to make sure that everyone has a say without the meeting being unduly long. On the other hand, if they improve relationships between employers and workers they are very worthwhile, and they can be the best way of getting the views of all those involved, in comparison with letters or forms which might produce replies from only a small proportion of people. Even people who are usually too shy to speak out may be encouraged to air their views at a meeting where they are surrounded by their colleagues.

2.2.8 Formal presentation

A lecture – also referred to as a presentation or demonstration – allows one person to present a detailed account of a subject, often with the help of slides and other audio-visual aids. Presentations are often used in staff training and to launch new products. They are more immediate than a written report and can convey ideas to a large number of people at one time. Unless well planned and carefully delivered, such occasions can be very dull, however, and there is always the risk that some or all of the listeners will not grasp the main points being made or will not take them seriously. Alternatives are different company training methods (on-the-job training, written instructions, or interactive video) or a more imaginative form of printed presentation if the lecture is not for training purposes.

Presentations are covered in greater detail in section 6.5.

2.3 Forms of written communication

2.3.1 Informal note

This is the simplest kind of writing, rather like a letter written to a friend. A note would be sent to a colleague at work to convey a message about something which happened while he or she was out, such as a client calling during the lunch hour, or for some similar purpose. Notes are used only for small, simple matters. They have the advantage of immediacy and speed, but the disadvantage that, as no copy is kept by the sender and the message is usually written quickly, errors may be made and some essential part of the message may be omitted, such as where the caller may be contacted.

Informal notes are discussed in section 10.2.

2.3.2 Memo

A memo is a much more formal note sent between members of the same organization for a range of purposes. It is typed and a copy is kept by the sender, but it is usually short, allowing room for only the barest details. It may, for example, remind a colleague that an important client is visiting that day, or request from him or her details of a forthcoming conference. Longer memos allow more detail to be included, but they may put the reader off by their length. Alternatives would be a personal meeting, a telephone call or a letter, although the last would be sent only when information was confidential or of legal significance.

Whatever their length, memos are sent only within an organization, by internal mail or messenger service. If they are sent open, they may be read by unauthorized people and so are not suitable for confidential messages. In some organizations they may be sent in sealed envelopes and marked 'Confidential', allowing their use for private messages. Overall, they are a very useful form of internal communication.

Notes on writing memos are included in section 10.3.

2.3.3 Letter

This is an effective way of getting across a number of points clearly and in detail, with the advantage that the sender and receiver both have a copy of what is said. Letters are sent for a wide range of purposes. They may make enquiries about goods or services, for example, or confirm arrangements made during a meeting or telephone call. Although the real cost of a letter, including typing and stationery, is more than the price of its stamp – so that a local telephone call may often be cheaper – the permanence of a letter will often justify its expense. A letter may be marked 'Confidential' if the sender wishes, and letters also allow the reader to consider what to say before replying.

One disadvantage is that letters take at least one or two days to be delivered and so are unsuitable for urgent messages. Some matters are better handled by personal discussion, too: this is especially the case if something has to be discussed before a decision is taken, which would necessitate the exchange of a series of letters. Often, though, a personal discussion will be followed by a letter to confirm the decision reached.

Letters are not generally used within an organization, although sometimes – when there is a need for a formal record to be kept, or if the communication has a legal significance – they will be sent in place of a memo.

Units 11 and 12 discuss the principles of letter-writing, and outline some of the main types of letters used in business communication.

2.3.4 Circular letter

This is a letter sent to a large number of people at the same time, perhaps to tell them about goods or services or to request information of various kinds. The advantage of circulars is that they are simple and inexpensive to produce and reasonably effective in communicating a message which applies to a number of people – especially if they are made more personal by the use of a word-processor linked to a database (see section 17.3). The disadvantages are that they can often appear impersonal, thus discouraging the receiver from reading them, and that they allow information to flow in one direction only. For an exchange of views, a meeting, a series of meetings or several telephone calls will be needed.

Circular letters are considered in more detail in section 12.9.

2.3.5 Press release

When a company wishes to publicize an event – the opening of a new factory or branch, say, or the launch of a new product or competition – it will often issue a press release. This is a short statement, usually no more than a page or two in length, which gives details of the event, and a name and telephone number to contact for further information. The release is then sent to local and national newspapers and broadcasting stations, who will use it as the basis of a news item if they decide to report the story.

Guidelines on persuasive writing of all kinds appear in section 10.7.

2.3.6 Forms

Forms enable a great deal of information to be collected quickly, in a manner which is easy to read and to interpret. Common forms include those used to claim sickness or unemployment benefits and application forms for jobs. They have many disadvantages, however. Many people dislike completing forms, or complete them inaccurately; forms also allow the reader little chance to express his or her individual opinion. Questionnaires – forms designed to canvas opinions or ideas – have the same basic disadvantages: they are not always popular, and there is no way of ensuring that they are returned.

Alternatives are personal interviews or telephone calls, but these too have disadvantages. The former are more time-consuming than issuing a form or questionnaire, and the latter may achieve very little if people quite understandably refuse to give confidential information over the telephone.

Unit 13 looks at the nature of forms and questionnaires and gives hints on how to compile and how to complete them.

2.3.7 Notices

These are a simple and direct way of conveying a public message – about a training conference, for example, or an office party. Assuming that they are properly designed, the main advantage of notices is their visual impact, along with the fact that they can convey information to many people at once. There is no guarantee, however, that they will be seen by those for whom they are intended, nor that they will be acted upon.

Notices are discussed in more detail in section 10.5.

2.3.8 Reports

There are many kinds of report, ranging from single-page documents recording a department's weekly output to volumes the size of a telephone directory discussing the future development of a new town. While they are a valuable means of providing detailed and specific information in a permanent form, their sheer bulk may be a disadvantage, coupled with the time they take to research and compile. As a method of communication, reports are very specialized, and are often read only by a small number of people. Staff meetings and formal lectures may be more effective ways of conveying the same information.

Guidelines for report-writing appear in Unit 15.

2.3.9 Electronic means

The advent of information technology has made available some new means of written communication, and improved others which were already in use. All of the following can be used to send messages on paper much more quickly than is possible by post or even by messenger service.

Telex   This is a means of sending a written message across a telephone line and is particularly useful, for example, when a business wishes to send an urgent message to a client in another country. The sender types the text to be sent on a special keyboard, and it is then sent by telephone lines to the receiver's machine, which prints the message out. Telex is considered in greater detail in section 17.4, and notes on writing telexes and international telemessages are given in section 11.7.

Electronic mail   This is a more recent version of telex, which uses a telephone line to convey a message which appears on the screen of the receiver's computer terminal (see section 17.4).

Fax   This is an abbreviation of 'facsimile', meaning 'a copy'. Fax machines work rather like two photocopiers joined by a telephone line. The message to be communicated is placed on the sender's machine, transmitted to the receiver's machine, and a copy produced. In this way, confidential plans and designs, for example, can be sent long distances safely and rapidly. Fax services are discussed in section 17.5.

While these three forms of communication have the great advantage of speed, they also have important disadvantages. Not all businesses have facilities for fax or electronic mail – although a large number have the older telex service – and they are all costly, both in terms of capital outlay for the equipment and in their day-to-day running.

Telemessage   This is the most recent form of the telegram. A message is dictated by the sender at a post office or over the telephone, is transmitted to the post office nearest to the receiver, printed out on a computer printer, and delivered to the receiver. This method, too, combines the speed of a telephone call with the permanence of a letter, but is very expensive.

2.3.10 Other forms of written communication
These include company newsletters, training and health-and-safety handbooks, committee documents, and advertisements of various kinds. All of these are highly specialized and each is generally the only form of communication which fully meets the requirements of the task in hand. Thus the communicator's main concern lies not in making sure that it is the most suitable form of communication for the task, but that it is properly and appropriately constructed for its intended readers.

Newsletters and advertisements are discussed in greater detail in Unit 10, and committee documents in Unit 16.

2.4. Visual communication

As well as communicating using words, it is often possible to communicate by means of visual images – photographs, pictures and drawings, for example. In many cases these will be more effective than any number of words. A picture of a road accident, for example, will convey suffering far more immediately than a written description, and thus be far more effective in a campaign against drinking and driving. Similarly, cartoons can provide a very powerful form of political commentary. Visual messages can be used alone, but are often most effective when they are accompanied by a brief, punchy caption.

Moving images   Television and video are assuming an increasingly important role in business communication. The value of television as an educational medium has long been recognized by bodies such as the Open University, and there are now many specialist companies producing video programmes about aspects of business and industrial training. A group of trainees may well be more likely to accept information from a short video than from a memo or notice, while the use of visual aids of this kind in formal business presentations is discussed in greater detail in section 6.5.

The advantage of such media – as of all visual forms of communication – is their immediacy: an idea or situation can be conveyed instantly with the minimum of words. The disadvantage with these particular forms is that, because many people regard them as a form of recreation rather than of instruction, their message may not be appreciated unless the receiver is prepared to concentrate and take them seriously.

Graphic communication is a form of visual communication which relies on the use of charts, tables, diagrams and graphs to convey statistical information. These may be used on their own or in conjunction with verbal communication – either with written communication of various kinds (reports and other documents, for example) or as part of an oral presentation. Again, they often have far more impact than written forms: a railway timetable conveys information much more clearly and concisely than an explanation in prose, as does a graph of the changes in temperature of a patient in hospital.

Unit 14 offers guidelines on constructing tables, graphs and other forms of graphic material.

2.5 Oral and written communication: a comparison

Although the particular situation will often dictate the form that a communication should take, in some cases either a written or an oral form of communication might be appropriate. It is therefore worthwhile considering the general advantages and disadvantages of both.

2.5.1 Advantages of oral communication

Oral communication has the great advantage of allowing personal contact. When carried on face to face, rather than by telephone, it enables each person to see the way the others are responding and to interpret their expressions, tone of voice and general bearing (elements referred to as 'non-verbal communication' – see Unit 6) to gain a fuller idea of the message being conveyed. Often the mere existence of this human touch will be very valuable – the fact that a manager has taken the trouble to leave his or her office to talk to workers will count for a good deal, for example.

Oral communication also allows the exchange of points, so that some movement towards agreement can be made which would be impossible or very time-consuming in writing. Speed and spontaneity – even allowing for the fact that many meetings are carefully prepared – are further advantages.

2.5.2 *Disadvantages of oral communication*

As oral communication allows the good side of the personal touch to make itself felt, so it allows the bad side to appear. There is no doubt that the danger of personality clashes is greater in oral communication than in written exchanges, especially if those involved in disagreements do not make every effort to subdue personal sentiments and try to work with each other for the sake of the organization.

Oral communication can suffer from being poorly planned, too. There is often no record of what has happened, except in the more formal meetings which are 'minuted', and there is also no guarantee of success in solving problems or reaching conclusions.

Yet all of these disadvantages are the result of failure to approach the communication task sensibly and efficiently, rather than being faults inherent in the medium itself. A more serious disadvantage, perhaps, is that oral communication is time-consuming. Here again, however, the responsibility for planning and conducting meetings properly lies with those who hold them, and the amount of time which is wasted can be minimal if a meeting is well run. Careful preparation and the use of proper documents (see Unit 16) will also help ensure that meetings are effective.

2.5.3 *Advantages of written communication*

A written communication can be carefully planned and revised before it is committed to paper in its final form. In theory, this means that there is less chance for errors to be made than in the more spontaneous form of oral communication. It also allows the reader time to pause and consider, and perhaps carry out research of his or her own, before responding, whether by letter, memo, report, or some other means. All parties involved have a formal record of what has been communicated – a major advantage in long-term projects and business relationships of some complexity.

Finally, written communication may often be quicker than oral – especially in situations where a circular letter may be sent in preference to holding a full meeting. In this way, it is also possible to avoid the unwieldiness of some meetings, where many people may wish to talk at once or some refuse to talk at all. These last, though, are not disadvantages which should arise at properly conducted meetings.

2.5.4 *Disadvantages of written communication*

As the written word provides a permanent record, it cannot be altered or modified to take account of the reaction it receives from others, except by means of a subsequent communication. It takes a highly skilled communicator to change the opinions or ideas of others by written response: give-and-take of this kind is much easier in an oral exchange.

Written communication can seem formal and distant, lacking the personal touch which is often so positive a feature in oral communication. It may also seem discourteous – particularly if a letter is written to take the place of a personal visit – and it can put people off by its very permanence. Much written communication can be hard to keep confidential, as it passes through many hands – typists, secretaries and others at all levels may see a document and thus diminish its confidentiality.

All of these drawbacks, however, are more the result of the way we use written communication than of the medium itself. Letters will only be discourteous, for example, if a personal visit would be more appropriate; confidentiality will be breached only if a letter is not sent as 'Private and confidential'.

Perhaps the greatest difficulty with the written word is that it can mean two wholly different things to two different people, and they do not have the opportunity to query it immediately. Benjamin Disraeli, the Victorian Prime Minister and novelist, used to reply in these words to admirers who sent him large manuscripts of their own in the hope of gaining his advice: 'Many thanks: I shall lose no time in reading it.' The gulf between what he meant and what they thought he meant was, we may guess, considerable. Everyone who works with words should be aware of how they can take on new, different and disturbing meanings in the minds of others, and should guard against this by checking even the most apparently straightforward expressions before using them.

2.6 Conclusion

You will have noticed that each form of written and spoken communication has both strong and weak points, which become apparent according to the situation in which it is used. Often there is no perfect form of communication for a particular situation, but this need not be a problem if, before you do select a method, you have thought carefully about what you want to communicate, to whom you want to communicate it and what you want the outcome to be. Common sense and normal tact and consideration will usually be the best guides in selecting the best way to get your message across.

2.7 Quick questions

1 List the factors which help to decide which kind of communication to use.

2 What is meant by the following terms:

    (a) oral communication;
    (b) written communication;
    (c) visual communication?

3 Give two advantages and two disadvantages of:

    (a) interviews;
    (b) telephone calls;
    (c) full staff meetings;
    (d) short memos;
    (e) notices.

2.8 Longer exercises

1 Explain what sort of communication you would use in each of the following situations:

   (a) getting the reactions of the office staff – six people in all – to a new computerized information system;
   (b) congratulating an employee on passing an important professional examination;
   (c) reminding staff of the procedure for making and paying for personal telephone calls at work;
   (d) telling working colleagues about a Christmas party;
   (e) explaining the location of a hotel where your company is holding a conference;
   (f) displaying the past four years' sales figures;
   (g) reminding a colleague that you are meeting for lunch tomorrow to discuss a new product;
   (h) putting a nervous visitor at ease.

2 You are the health and safety officer of a small electronics company. What kinds of communication would you use to make sure that your staff are fully aware of the need for safety at work? Give full reasons for your answer.

Principles and practice of communication

3.1 Introduction

The two preceding units have looked at some of the reasons why communication is so important and have considered some of the forms it can take. These are practical issues which will be the main concern of the rest of this book. As well as the practical side, however, there is also a theoretical aspect of communication which we will outline in this unit. This is a topic which is rather specialized and which therefore figures in only a few of the major examination syllabuses. You may well find that it is not a part of your syllabus, but, even if it is not, you should still read this unit – though perhaps rather more quickly than those which are at the heart of your studies. What it has to say is related to all kinds of communication. The processes it describes are at the root of every act of communicating we perform. The difficulties it discusses beset even the most experienced communicators. Even if you do not have to answer an exam question on this aspect of the subject, a knowledge of the principles of communication will help you to improve your communication at every level and so translate theory into hard, practical reality.

3.2 The communication cycle

As we said on page 1, communication may be defined as

> the giving, receiving or exchange of information, opinions or ideas by writing, speech or visual means – or any combination of the three – so that the material communicated is completely understood by everyone concerned.

Communication specialists have developed a 'model' to explain how the communication process works. This is shown in fig. 3.1 and is usually referred to as the *communication cycle*. Before we look in detail at the various stages shown in fig. 3.1, however, let us first discuss some of the different terms associated with the communication process.

Motivation   This is the basic urge beneath the communication – the wider reason why communication takes place. In a company, it may be the urge to ensure that this year's profits are higher than last year's. In a charity, it may be to make sure that more donations are received. For most working people, it is probably the desire to do a job properly and get paid for it at the end of the month or week.

Aim   This is the more particular reason why the communication has been undertaken. There are three main aims:

(a) *Informing*   Here, the intention is simply to tell someone about something, as in a 'no smoking' notice, for example, or a letter giving news of recent events.

(b) *Influencing*   Here, the intention is to persuade someone to adopt a particular course of action or attitude towards something. The obvious example is advertising, but others include appeals to staff for extra productivity or requests for staff not to drive home after drinking too much at the office party.

(c) *Initiating action*   The aim of this kind of communication is to get the reader to *do* something – it might be to send in an expenses claim form on time, or to attend a meeting on safety in the office, for instance.

Sometimes all three aims are present within the same item of communication. You might, for example, write a letter to someone giving information about your company's decision to purchase products from him, attempting to influence him to deliver the goods very quickly and asking him to begin production straightaway.

Information   This is the material from which the communication will be constructed – the actual content to be put across to the listener or reader. It does not have to be factual information – it could be an idea or opinion, or a combination of fact and opinion.

The sender   The person or body responsible for sending the communication is called the sender. It can be an individual or a group such as a company, a department, or even a government ministry or a political party.

The message   Having defined the information to be conveyed, the sender puts it into the best form in a process called *encoding*. When the information has been encoded, it is known as the message. This simply refers to the form the communication takes: a letter, memo, telephone call, or even something as simple as a smile, a shrug of the shoulders or some other gesture.

The medium   This is the larger group of ways of communicating within which the particular communication can be classed. There are three main media:

● *Written communication* – letters, memos, books and articles, notices and posters, for example.

- *Oral communication* – that is, any method using the spoken word, such as meetings, telephone calls, interviews, lectures and informal discussions.
- *Visual communication* – a drawing, photograph or other means of putting over a message by pictorial means.

As well as these three, there is non-verbal communication – the combinations of gesture, expression, tone of voice and other elements discussed in Units 2 and 6.

The channel This is the physical means by which the message is conveyed.

- For written communication it might be a notice-board, an internal mail service or the public postal service.
- For oral communication it might be a personal interview, a committee meeting or a public telephone system.
- For visual communication it might be a computer printer, a printing press or a fax system.

Sometimes the relationship between message, medium and channel can seem a little confusing. It need not be, though, if you think of them as three separate but overlapping ideas, as they are shown in fig. 3.1. For example, the message might be an actual letter – the medium is then written communication and the channel is the Post Office.

The receiver This is the person or body which receives the message. It can be an individual or an organization – a company or some other large group of people.

Noise This is the name given to any factors which prevent the proper exchange of information apart from those caused by the sender and receiver.

Noise can be physical – such as the sounds of traffic, typewriters or telephone bells which interrupt a meeting – or it can be some other form of interference: a bad telephone connection, poor handwriting in a letter, a computer failure which causes the loss of documents on a fax line, or even a conflicting message – if the speaker's facial expression conveys a different message from that being given orally, for example.

Distortion may happen at the encoding stage, if the sender encodes a message in such a way that its meaning is changed or 'distorted'. It can also happen at the decoding stage, when the receiver interprets a message in a different way from that intended by the sender (see section 3.5.1).

Feedback This is the name given to information which the sender receives from the way in which the receiver accepts the message. If you are talking to someone and he or she laughs or smiles, it suggests a positive response: if he or she frowns or scowls, it suggests a negative one. Feedback only refers to immediate reactions of this sort. It does not refer to a more considered response – a letter in reply to an initial enquiry, for instance, or a verbal reply in a meeting.

To make sure that the sender is aware of feedback, he or she should constantly 'scan' for it. This means being aware of the initial reaction of the receiver, by looking for frowns, smiles or other signs. A skilled communicator will constantly do this and change his or her manner of speech accordingly.

Now that we have outlined the terms used in the cycle of communication, we can consider how the cycle operates. There are seven basic stages (fig. 3.1).

Stage 1 Here, the sender defines the information to be sent, by thinking about the aim of the communication and the content to be conveyed.

Stage 2 This is the *encoding* process of putting the information into the form which is most suitable both to the receiver and to the aim. In most cases, encoding involves putting an idea into words. Sometimes, however, it will be best to encode an idea in a picture, or even in a gesture. Non-verbal communication needs just as much care as verbal, though – how an idea is conveyed is vital to its effect on the receiver and so always merits a great deal of thought.

Stage 3 This is the actual transfer of information, by means of the message, medium and channel.

Stage 4 At this point the receiver takes in the message – by reading a letter, listening to a speech, or looking at an educational television programme, for example.

Stage 5 The next stage is that of *decoding*: the receiver interprets the message he or she has been given in order to obtain his or her own idea of the information it conveys. This may or may not be the same as the information which the sender wanted to convey. If the sender encodes the idea wrongly, ambiguously, or in terms which the receiver interprets according to his or her own experience rather than the sender's, then *distortion* is likely to occur and the receiver will gain a different message from that intended.

Stage 6 The receiver's first reaction to the message is the next stage, and is known as *feedback*. Mention has already been made of how a skilled communicator will scan for feedback when talking to an individual or group. Similarly, when listening to someone he or she should take part in the process by conveying feedback signals to the speaker – nodding and smiling to show understanding and agreement, for example, or adopting a posture which suggests concentration and eagerness.

Response This final stage is not so much a separate part of the cycle as a complete repetition of it. Someone who receives and reads a letter will then write a reply. Someone in a meeting will listen to one person's view and then give his or her own. A worker reading a notice will talk to the person who put it up about what it says. All of these are new cycles of communication, although they began in response to the first one – the letter, speech, notice or whatever.

We have thus traced the process of communication from its initiation at the definition of information and aim to the response from the receiver which starts

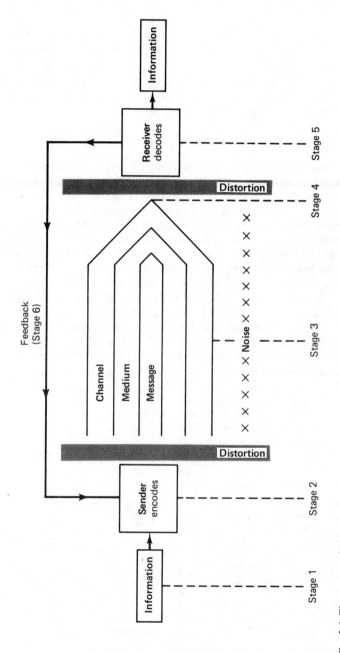

Fig. 3.1 The communication cycle

the whole process over again. It is a cycle in which we are all engaged at almost every moment of the day, and one which is integral to every part of this book.

Communication does not always take place without problems, however, as we have already seen in the discussion of encoding. There are many difficulties which may arise when we try to put the principles into practice. These will be considered in detail in section 3.5. Before that, though, we must consider the main ways in which communication functions in business organizations. Not only will this help in relating theory to practice, but it will also serve to identify some of the problems which are discussed later.

3.3 Communication in organizations

In small organizations which employ only two or three people, there is probably no difficulty in knowing who should communicate with whom – although that does not mean that there will be no problems in the actual communication. In larger organizations, though, the process is more complicated. If all employees in a company of a hundred or more workers were allowed to communicate directly with each other, chaos might result. Messages would be given to the wrong people, since it would be unclear who was responsible for what and to whom; time would be wasted; and efficiency would be reduced. On the other hand, if a very rigid policy were put into use by which people were severely restricted in communicating with each other, the organization would become divided, and individuals might well feel cut off from what was going on.

Finding a balance between these extremes is an important task for people who decide how a company is organized. A popular solution is to produce an organization chart, which makes clear the main lines of communication. Two examples are given in figs 3.2 and 3.3.

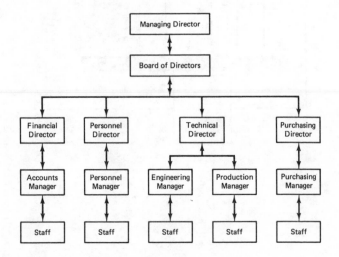

Fig. 3.2 Organization chart for a small company

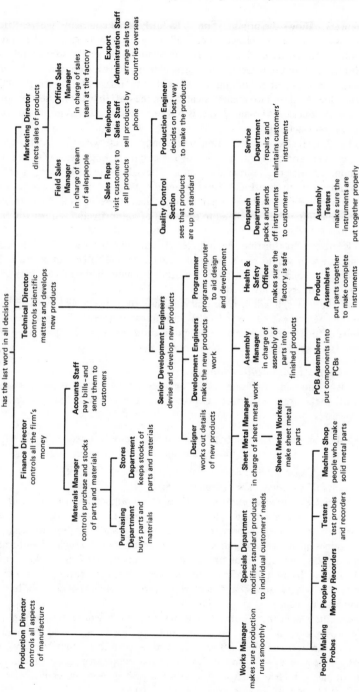

Fig. 3.3 Organization chart for a large company

Figure 3.2 shows the organization for a fairly small company, whereas fig. 3.3 shows that for a much larger one. While they differ in complexity they have in common clearly defined lines of communication. In fig. 3.2, for example, it is clear that the Engineering Manager communicates with the Technical Director, who in turn communicates with the Board of Directors. The Engineering Manager also communicates with the staff in his or her section and with the Production Manager, who is responsible for a different area of the organization's activities.

In fig. 3.3, the Development Engineers communicate with the Programmer and Designer, and also with the Senior Development Engineers, who in turn communicate with the Technical Director. The Sales Representatives (or reps) communicate with the Field Sales Manager, who in turn reports to the Marketing Director. In both organizations, then, there is a clear communication structure, which is related to the levels of authority and seniority in the company.

This process has distinct advantages. It cuts out the waste of time and resources which would result from allowing everyone to communicate with everyone else, and it ensures that a message is channelled to those who will understand the issues involved.

From the charts, it will be clear that communication takes place both up and down the structure (between levels) and across it (between departments). Because of the way these kinds of communication appear on the chart, they are known as *vertical* and *horizontal* (or *lateral*) communication.

3.3.1 Vertical communication
Vertical communication takes place between people of different levels of seniority in the organization. It can take place in two directions: upwards and downwards.

Upward communication   People involved at the most immediate level of the organization's activities communicate upwards to those at supervisory or managerial level. Communication may take the following forms:

- *Reports of various kinds*   (See Unit 15.)
- *Informal discussions and suggestions*   Communication of this sort is probably the most frequent, and can be the most important. It will involve workers talking to supervisors about events such as breakdowns in machines, ideas for new approaches, or any other matter which arises during the working activity of the organization. Company efficiency will increase through such communication both because the ideas will be put into practice if they are sound, and because each worker will feel that what he or she has to say is being heard.
- *Suggestion schemes*   Formal schemes by which workers may suggest improvements in work processes and conditions are used by many companies to make the staff feel involved. Special forms may be provided which the worker will complete, and a team or committee may be assembled to discuss the ideas put forward. Often a cash prize or other incentive is offered to encourage workers to use the schemes.

● *Polls and ballots* Issues of policy or procedure may be referred to the workforce by means of a ballot or opinion poll. Employees will be asked to vote for or against a proposal, and the results used in deciding whether or not to implement the proposed change. Upward communication of this kind is not common: if a company is going to consult its employees, it will usually organize a meeting or issue a questionnaire to canvass opinions.

● *Grievance procedures* If an employee feels that he or she has been badly treated – perhaps by failure to gain promotion, or unfair disciplinary action – he or she may follow a procedure laid down by the organization to make known the grievance. This might consist of completing a form, arranging an interview with a superior or contacting a trade-union representative.

Downward communication Communication vertically downwards is by far the most frequent form of communication within an organization. It may take any of the following forms, all of which are discussed in other units:

● memos;
● letters;
● notices;
● newsletters;
● training and induction documents;
● company handbooks;
● health-and-safety policy documents;
● joint consultative and other committees;
● full meetings;
● appraisal interviews;
● selection interviews;
● disciplinary interviews.

The most appropriate form of communication must be selected carefully, according to the principles laid out in Unit 2, so that the information is conveyed as clearly and accurately as possible.

3.3.2 Horizontal communication
Horizontal communication occurs between people of the same status in an organization – departmental heads, supervisors, directors and others whose work is similar but takes place within different sections of the organization.

As well as memos, letters and reports, horizontal communication can take the following forms:

● *Co-ordinating committees* Sometimes it is valuable to bring together representatives of separate departments to discuss new developments, so that people in each part of the company know what is going on in other sections. After such meetings, representatives may well report back to their own sections – another form of downward communication.

- *Group conferences or departmental heads' meetings* These are rather similar to co-ordinating committee meetings, except that they take place between heads of department.
- *Informal communication* At the simplest level, this consists of encounters in staff recreation rooms and canteens, but there are some other, more formal channels, including sports and social clubs, social gatherings such as annual parties or dinners, and committees concerned with recreational and charitable activities.

3.3.3 The grapevine

As well as the formal kinds of communication mentioned above, there is the informal kind known as 'the grapevine'. This term refers to the way in which unofficial information is spread by people talking to each other in the works canteen, on the way to work and at tea-breaks. The grapevine is not generally a form of communication to be trusted or encouraged by those in senior positions, as the ideas which it circulates are generally ill-informed and often untrue.

This does not mean that all informal communication is bad, though. If workers at all levels can chat informally when they meet, either about their work or about other matters, much will be done to improve the working atmosphere and sense of belonging. Only when it becomes a network of rumour and gossip is the grapevine a destructive force in a company. Skilled managers and communicators can make sure that this does not happen by informing all employees promptly and fully of any important news, so that negative rumours do not have time to take root.

3.4 Groups and networks

Although there are times when all employees should be kept informed of developments, there are also occasions when it is only necessary, or possible, for a small group to be involved or consulted. This small group forms part of the organization's *networks* of communication. These are formed where a special need arises for individuals to communicate directly – for the development of a new product, say, or to discuss a proposed change in the company's location. Networks of communication can do much to simplify and speed up communication since they bypass many of the usual restrictions and allow direct contact between those seeking information. Networks exist in various forms, some of which are outlined below.

3.4.1 All channels open

In this system, every member of a group may communicate with every other member, so that all channels of communication are open. Generally, this works best for a fairly small group, where the members know each other and can work well together. Sometimes, one member is appointed to act as a chair or facilitator. His or her role is to lead the discussion and help each member to contribute, much in the manner of a committee chair (see section 16.3). This is shown in fig. 3.4.

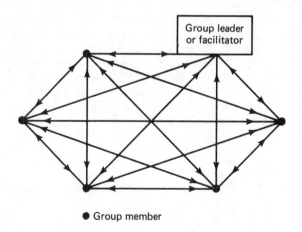

Group leader or facilitator

● Group member

Fig. 3.4 'All channels open'

3.4.2 The 'Y' system

This system is also suitable for a small number of people, but differs from an open system in that it directs communication along very clear channels. It is rather like a small section of a larger organization chart, but it can be very useful in a company where one person – at the centre of the 'Y' – brings together ideas from other employees at all levels. Figure 3.5 shows a typical 'Y' system.

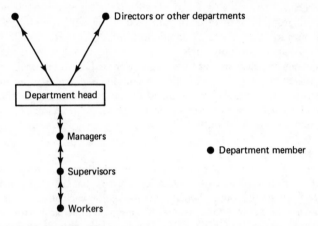

Fig. 3.5 'Y' system of communication

3.4.3 The fan system

Fan systems are used in large organizations to ensure that communication takes place only through very clearly defined channels. They are similar to the larger organization charts shown in fig. 3.3, but they do not allow any lateral communication. Instead, all communication is channelled through supervisors and managers. The advantage of this system is that a clear pattern of communication is created, which saves time: the disadvantage, that the group becomes very rigid, with divisions arising between levels of employees and with none of the benefits of horizontal communication at intermediate levels. For an example of the fan system see fig. 3.6.

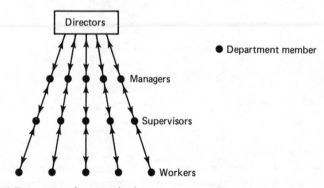

Fig. 3.6 Fan system of communication

3.4.4 The 'daisy' system

This system is used when a number of individuals report to a central group – usually the directors of a company. It has the advantage of being direct and simple, but the disadvantage of removing lower levels of employee from the system, which may cause feelings of isolation and resentment. A daisy system is shown in fig. 3.7.

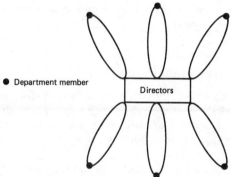

Fig. 3.7 Daisy system of communication

3.4.5 Networks within larger communication structures

All of the above systems allow a more direct exchange of information than would be possible in a conventional company structure. Sometimes, to ensure maximum flexibility and efficiency, a network system is used in conjunction with the conventional company communication system, in which case an arrangement such as that shown in fig. 3.8 will result.

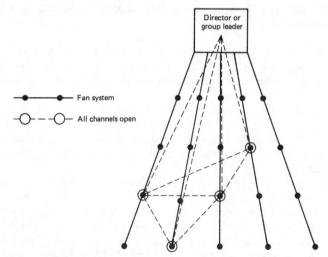

Fig. 3.8 Combination network

3.4.6 Conclusion

As we have seen, networks can speed up communication about one particular facet of an organization's activities, which is certainly a great advantage. Networks do have disadvantages, however, as they suggest that some workers are more important than others, having the right to consult others directly instead of going through the normal company channels. This may cause resentment, and networks therefore need to be implemented and monitored with care to avoid this kind of effect.

3.5 Barriers to communication

However carefully an organization or an individual plans acts of communication, it is inevitable that breakdowns will sometimes occur. These are best classified in two groups: those caused by the people or organizations concerned with communicating, and those which are due to external factors.

3.5.1 Barriers caused by the sender or the receiver

Most breakdowns in communication are caused by barriers created by the communicators. Often they are the result of the sender's lack of awareness of the receiver's needs or of the exact aim of the communication, or the receiver's misunderstanding of the message or failure to listen properly. Being familiar with potential causes of breakdown is the first step towards avoiding them.

Poorly defined aim or information   The sender must have a clear idea of what the communication aims to achieve before encoding the message. Similarly, the information which is to form the basis of the message must be clear and accurate. If either or both are unclear, the message will be inaccurate and a breakdown will result.

Distortion   This is the name given to barriers which arise at the encoding and decoding stages (see fig. 3.1). If the sender uses language or other signs which do not convey the intended message to the receiver, distortion will result. For example, people from different countries, or different parts of the same country, will use the same word to mean different things. In Britain 'a billion' usually means 'one million million'; in America, it means 'one thousand million'. Thus any communication between British and American companies which involves this term must rest on the certainty that it is being used by both in the same way.

Breakdowns are not caused only by what is said. Facial expressions, gestures and the way in which a message is conveyed can all result in the receiver gaining a false impression. Some receivers might interpret a friendly smile as a patronizing gesture; others might feel put off by language which is too formal. While some people will be flattered that the sender has tried to use language which he or she will understand, others will be angry and feel that they are being talked down to.

This problem can be overcome by considering who will be receiving the message and making sure that you use appropriate language (see section 4.10.1). This is not as easy as it sounds: striking the right note and interpreting other people's messages exactly are skilled procedures, and demand practice and care.

Use of the wrong medium Choosing the wrong medium of communication can be as disastrous as conveying inaccurate information. For example, if you had to tell a group of employees about their new salaries, each of which was different, it would be tactless to type a notice and display it on a notice-board. Personal letters should be sent. Such misunderstandings can be avoided by careful selection of the medium, as suggested in Unit 2.

Communicating at the wrong time Knowing when to communicate can be as important as knowing what medium to use. Trying to discuss a sensitive issue with someone when he or she is about to leave for an important meeting will almost certainly end in failure. Telephoning someone at the end of the working day when he or she is anxious to sign letters and complete the day's business will be similarly ill-fated.

3.5.2 Barriers caused by external factors

Noise Interruptions of this kind can be very disruptive. A poor telephone connection or physical noise in a room can be easily remedied by redialling or closing a window. Other forms of noise (see section 3.2) are less easily dealt with.

Organizational barriers These occur when the communication structure within an organization, or that between organizations, fails to allow communication to take place fully and accurately. All kinds of factors may cause this: employees may be allowed only to communicate with one individual supervisor, who works in a separate office at the end of a long workshop; the personnel director may be unable to talk directly to the workers and may thus remain unaware of complaints about conditions of employment.

Such barriers can be overcome by constantly reviewing the structure of an organization's system of communication, to ensure that the right pattern of exchange is used.

Human relations barriers You may think that this kind of barrier should have appeared in the previous section, as it is caused by people failing to work with each other. But while you should always attempt to put personal feelings to the back of your mind when working in a business environment, there are occasions when human relations problems go beyond the level of a simple personality clash, and it becomes clear that two individuals are unable to work together. Realizing that such a barrier is outside the responsibility of the people concerned is an important stage in solving the problem. If both parties become aware that a barrier exists, they can work harder at removing it. If this works, then the two will be able to function far more effectively and communicate well: if it does not, then some other solution – such as the transfer of one of the people to another section – may be possible, and will be arrived at without attributing blame to either person.

3.6 Conclusion

Knowing about the theory of communication and the communication structures within an organization is an important step towards more effective communication. At the same time, being aware of the sources of breakdown in communication can help us to avoid them.

Whether or not such topics form part of the syllabus for your examination, knowing about them will help you to achieve effective communication in any practical context. Using language which is suitable to the receiver and the aim of the communication is probably the most important skill of all, and one that you should strive to develop while working through each unit of this book and its associated exercises.

3.7 Quick questions

1 What is meant by:

(a) encoding;
(b) decoding;
(c) noise;
(d) channel?

2 Give a brief definition of:

(a) horizontal communication;
(b) vertical communication (upwards);
(c) vertical communication (downwards).

3.8 Longer exercises

1 Prepare an organization chart for the organization for which you work. If you are not at work, prepare a chart for your college or a social organization to which you belong.

2 What is a network? Draw diagrams of *two* kinds of network. Now list the advantages and disadvantages of communicating in networks. Finally, describe how communication in networks functions in an organization you know well.

3 Demonstrate the normal stages of the communication cycle with the aid of a diagram and outline the possible causes of breakdown which may occur at each stage.

(IPS, First certificate in purchasing and stores)

Language

4.1 The need for accuracy

Many people feel that, since communication is about conveying messages, the accuracy of the language used does not matter as long as the message gets across. 'Well, you knew what I *meant*' is a common retort from such people, who see grammar as something to be endured at school but otherwise important only to academics who have no contact with the real world.

Communication – and, indeed, life in general – would be a great deal easier if this were true and we all *did* know what other people meant regardless of how they expressed themselves. There are some occasions, admittedly, when the meaning is clear even though the expression is technically wrong. But you cannot be certain that everyone with whom you will communicate will understand the same expressions – remember the story about the music professor in Unit 1 – and so following the basic rules of grammar, vocabulary and word order is essential. After all, such rules are hardly arbitrary – they have been arrived at by mutual consent between people who use language. In addition, the process of expressing oneself accurately, in a manner which is both elegant and correct, can be satisfying in itself.

In the business world, accuracy of language is important for three principal reasons:

(a) To convey ideas precisely. Incorrect expression will mean that the ideas that are to be conveyed are not immediately apparent to the reader. Poor grammar will lead to ambiguity – the simultaneous existence of two, often contradictory, meanings – which will at best be irritating and at worst cause a costly misunderstanding.

(b) To establish a suitable relationship. Business communication is an important part of the larger relationship between people who work with each other. Using inaccurate language will endanger this relationship and the trust on which it rests.

(c)   To convey a favourable impression of the organization. Clear, accurate and concise writing will suggest efficiency and confidence to a reader, whereas careless, inaccurate expression will suggest inefficiency and a lack of attention to detail which may well extend to other areas of business.

This unit will help you to achieve such accuracy by discussing some of the fundamental features of language, looking at some common errors and showing how they may be avoided, and giving some advice about style in written communication.

4.2 How language works

The best way to avoid mistakes or inaccuracies is to know how language works. This means knowing about its various components and the way they fit together, rather like building a sailing dinghy or a piece of furniture from a set of parts. Fashion designers often buy garments made by their competitors and take them apart to examine each section in detail. We may usefully adopt the same approach with language, by starting with a complete unit of expression – a *sentence* – and seeing how it is built up.

4.2.1 The sentence
A sentence is a group of words containing a complete, self-contained idea or a group of related ideas. Here, for example, is a simple sentence:

George gave the money to his grandfather.

This sentence is built up of three main parts: the subject, the verb and the object.

The subject   This is usually the person or thing doing the action or existing in the way described in the sentence. In the example, the subject is *George*.

George gave the money to his grandfather.

Other examples are as follows:

The book was about astronomy.
I thought he would never go.
A team of reporters had gathered around the house.

The verb   This indicates an action or a state of being, usually telling us what the subject of a sentence is doing. For example:

George *gave* the money to his grandfather.
They *went* home slowly in the rain.
She *was* very angry at their decision.

The form of the verb depends on the person or thing to which it refers and on the *tense* – the time at which the action or state took place. For example:

George *is* pleased with the gift.
I *am* pleased with the gift.

The car *will skid* unless you slow down.
The car *skidded* on the wet road.

Every sentence, then, must include a verb in a form which makes clear who performed the action or was in the state referred to and when. This is known as the *finite form* of the verb.

Sometimes a verb is used in its *infinitive form* – preceded by the word 'to'. The infinitive does not relate to any single person or tense.

I will undertake *to complete* the review within three weeks.
It is not easy *to make* a decision.

Another common form of the verb is the *imperative*. This is the form which gives a direct order, as in these examples:

Come here.
Shut the door.
Be quiet.

In written communication the imperative is used mainly in direct speech – that is, when you are recording the exact words someone has spoken. It is also used when giving orders. In business communication, this will be done only when writing to a subordinate. For example:

Make sure that the room is available on Monday.
Be there in good time.

This is rather a terse style of writing, however, and in general it is more polite to use expressions like these:

Would you please make sure that the room is available on Monday.
Please would you make sure that you are there in good time.

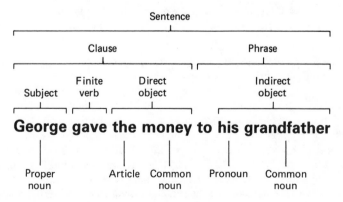

Fig. 4.1 A sentence divided into its component parts

You may also see a verb used with an -*ing* ending. This is neither the finite nor the infinitive form of the verb, although it has several important functions to perform, as section 4.3.4 will show.

Both the infinitive and the -*ing* form of a verb can only be used in a sentence with a verb in finite form. Look at these statements:

> Where to go next?
> Walking through the park in the snow.

Neither of these is a proper sentence. In order to be grammatically correct, they must be rewritten to include a verb in finite form, for example:

> Where *shall* we go next?
> He *liked* walking throught the park in the snow.

The object   Not all sentences have an object, but many do. It is the part of the sentence which tells you what the subject's action was done to or directed towards. For example:

> I opened *the parcel*.
> She took away *my cheque book*.
> They abandoned *the stricken ship*.

Some sentences have two kinds of object: a *direct* and an *indirect* object. The original example has two:

> George gave *the money* to *his grandfather*.
>
>   *Direct*   *Indirect*

The indirect object names the person or thing which is affected by what the subject does with the direct object. Here are some more examples:

> They offered *the post of executive director* to *Mrs Stilwell*.
>
>   *Direct*   Indirect

> The company presented *Mr Singh* with *a clock*.
>
>   Indirect   Direct

Not all sentences have an object, since some verbs describe actions which are complete in themselves. 'He opened' makes no sense unless we know *what* he opened; to complete the sentence, we would have to add an object and say 'He opened the can of beans.' 'He slept', by contrast, needs no object to complete it; it is a sentence in itself, because sleeping is not something done to other things or people. Verbs which take an object are known as *transitive* verbs and those not taking an object are known as as *intransitive* verbs.

Transitive verbs include 'to take', 'to pursue', 'to demolish' and 'to create', as used in these sentences:

She took the envelope from the secretary.
They pursued the car down the maze of narrow streets.
The planning committee voted to demolish the tower blocks.
She had created one of her finest sculptures.

Intransitive verbs include 'to go', 'to live' and 'to think', as used in these sentences:

I will go to the sea tomorrow.
He lives alone in Swaffham Prior.
Think carefully before making your decision.

Some verbs may be transitive or intransitive, according to the way in which they are used. 'To eat', 'to sing' and 'to write' are examples:

Transitive	*Intransitive*
He ate his lunch alone.	He ate alone.
They sang football songs on the way home.	They sang on the way home.
He wrote novels for a living.	He wrote for a living.

The three main components of a sentence are the subject, the verb and the object. Putting them together demands special care, as the later sections in this unit will show. First, though, we must look at the kinds of words which make up these and other components of a sentence - usually called *parts of speech*.

4.2.2 Nouns and pronouns

The subject and the object - both direct and indirect - of a sentence are composed of nouns and pronouns. These are simply names for things, people or ideas.

Common nouns These are names of everyday things - 'bird', 'letter', 'man', 'woman', 'committee', 'desk' and 'chair', for example. In sentences they are used like this:

The *bird* flew across the *garden*.
A *woman* walked slowly out of the *building*.
A *committee* has been set up to solve the *problem*.
They were *members* of several *sports clubs*.

Notice that common nouns refer to things in general, not one particular thing, and that they do not begin with a capital letter. If only one is referred to, it is usually preceded by an *article*: 'the', 'a' or 'an'.

Proper nouns These are names for one particular thing or person. George, Liverpool, Monday, Zimbabwe, The Stock Exchange - all these are proper nouns. The following sentences show how they work:

> *George* left early to catch up on his work.
> The train left *Liverpool* at 8.45 a.m.
> It was late on *Monday* when I received the letter.
> The marketing director was visiting *Zimbabwe*.
> *The Stock Exchange* was reorganized in 1986.

Note that proper nouns do not require an article, unless the article is part of the title – as in the last example above. Note, too, that proper nouns begin with a capital letter. More advice on when to use capitals is given in section 5.3.11.

Pronouns Useful though nouns are, it would be very irritating if they were used for every reference to a thing or person in a short piece of writing. Consider this passage:

> When Jane had eaten Jane's breakfast Jane put on Jane's coat and drove off in Jane's car.

To avoid such repetition, which is irritating and sounds ugly, we would normally replace most of the nouns by pronouns:

> When she had eaten her breakfast, Jane put on her coat and drove off in her car.

Pronouns may be used in direct, indirect or possessive forms, according to the nature of the noun they are replacing (see section 4.4).

4.2.3 Adjectives
Words which describe nouns are called adjectives. 'Pale', 'large', 'unclear', 'limited', 'pretentious', 'careful' – all are adjectives. As well as their basic or *positive* forms, many adjectives have two further forms: *comparative* and *superlative*.

As the word implies, the comparative form is used when a comparison is suggested, to show that one thing has more of the quality described than another. Comparatives are mostly formed by adding *-er* or *-r* to the adjective – to give 'larger', 'cooler', 'quieter' and 'later', for example – or by adding the word 'more' – to give 'more considerate', 'more basic' and 'more mature'. In general, words with one syllable in the basic form take *-er* in the comparative, whereas those with two or more syllables take 'more'.

The superlative form is used to describe the highest degree of the quality in question. Superlatives are mainly formed by adding *-est* or *-st* to the adjective – to give 'shortest', 'quietest' and 'remotest', for example – or by adding the word 'most' – to give 'most considerate', 'most unlikely' and 'most desirable'. As with comparatives, most adjectives with one syllable take *-est* or *-st* and those with two syllables or more take 'most'.

Superlatives can also be used to denote a very high degree of a particular quality, with no suggestion of comparison. For example, we can say that someone is being 'most helpful', to mean 'very helpful', as well as saying 'she is

Basic form	Comparative	Superlative
He looked *pale* as he read the letter.	He turned *paler* still when he saw the signature.	He was *palest* of all when he realized what this meant.
The notice was written in *clear* handwriting.	The notice in capital letters was *clearer* than the written one.	The printed notice was *clearest* of all.
The car was *large* and powerful.	It was a *larger* car than his own.	Gerald's car was the *largest* in the garage.
He spoke in a *pretentious* way.	Of the two books, that published in England is the *more pretentious*.	It was the *most pretentious* book he had read. The whole event was *most pretentious*.
I was *careful* to avoid being rude.	George is *more careful* than I am.	He is the *most careful* man I know. The process was carried out in a *most careful* way.

Fig. 4.2 The use of adjectives

the most helpful person I know', which makes a clear statement of relative value.

Figure 4.2 shows how adjectives may be used in sentences. Remember that a superlative should only be used if three or more items are being compared.

4.2.4 Adverbs

In the same way as adjectives are used to describe nouns, so adverbs may be used to describe verbs: they give more information about how or when an action was done. Many adverbs end in -*ly*: 'carefully', 'slowly', 'hesitantly' and 'gently', for example. In sentences, adverbs are used like this:

> They walked *carefully* over the broken glass.
> She drove *fast*.
> 'Can I help?' he asked *hesitantly*.
> He stroked her hair *gently*.
> 'She will arrive *soon*,' he assured them.

Adverbs can also tell us more about an adjective, as in these sentences:

> He was carrying a *very* large suitcase.
> Her face was *strangely* familiar.
> The tone of his letter was *openly* hostile.

Like adjectives, adverbs have comparative and superlative forms – for example, 'more carefully' and 'most carefully'. The superlative usually suggests not that the action has been performed with the greatest amount of a certain quality, but that it has been done with the highest degree possible under the circumstances. 'Most carefully' does not, for example, refer to the highest point on a imaginary scale of care, but means 'with the utmost care'. Consider the following examples:

> He treated the whole matter *most professionally*.
> She had approached the meeting *most hesitantly*, unwilling to become involved.
> He opened the package *most hurriedly*.

4.2.5 Conjunctions

These words join together two statements to make one larger unit. Their main use is to suggest a relationship of a particular kind between the individual elements of the sentence. The most common conjunctions are listed below.

And   simply links two statements. For example:

> I got up *and* [I] went for a walk.

But   can be used to make clear a contrast between two statements, as in:

> The first attempt was a failure *but* the second [attempt] succeeded.

It can also show that the second statement limits the meaning of the first, for example:

> The sky looked bright, *but* there was still a strong wind.

Because is used to join two statements, the second giving the cause of the first.

> He was late for work *because* he had missed the bus.

Or links two alternative statements.

> Send it by first-class post *or* deliver it by hand.

Whereas suggests a difference between two ideas being compared.

> Using the telephone is convenient, *whereas* a personal meeting involves travel and disturbance.

4.2.6 Phrases and clauses
The functions of many of the parts of speech described above can also be performed by groups of words instead of single words. These fall into two categories: *phrases* and *clauses*.

Phrases A phrase is a group of words without a finite verb. 'An early history of tapestry', 'the man in the bank' and 'as soon as possible' are examples of phrases. A phrase is not a sentence and so should not be presented as one. Some advertisements and other forms of popular writing break this rule, largely to add impact to an idea, or to slow down the pace at which words are read. For example:

> The new RX37 GTi will go from 0–60. In 5.8 seconds. Not to be sneezed at.

In formal writing, however, such a practice is out of place: it simply looks wrong, because it goes against the accepted standards of expression, and it will affect the ease with which the reader takes in the meaning. For accuracy and ease of reading, then, the example above should be reworded as follows:

> The new RX37 GTi will go from 0 to 60 in 5.8 seconds, which is not to be sneezed at.

To help you avoid using phrases as sentences, remember that a phrase works exactly as a noun, an adjective or an adverb, according to its nature and purpose.

- *Noun phrases* name people, things or ideas, such as 'a cookery demonstration', 'the man in the picture' or 'what he thought about cricket'.
- *Adjectival phrases* work like an adjective to describe something, such as 'with a large balcony' or 'for business users'.

● *Adverbial phrases* describe how or where something is done, how often it occurs, or some other detail of its performance. 'As quickly as possible', 'with painstaking accuracy' and 'several times during the last three weeks' are examples.

All of these should be formed into proper sentences, each with a main finite verb, if they are to have proper meaning.

> He attended *a cookery demonstration.*
> *The man in the picture* is wanted by the police.
> I do not know *what he thought about cricket.*

> It was a house *with a large balcony.*
> It is a computer *for business users.*

> I drove out of the garage *as quickly as possible.*
> She completed the form *with painstaking accuracy.*
> *Several times during the last three weeks* I have been late.

Clauses   A clause is a group of words containing a finite verb. The simplest sentences consist of one clause, but more complicated sentences contain two or more. Here, for example, is a one-clause sentence:

> Trains from Manchester leave from Platform Three.

Here is one with three clauses:

> She told them she would be there if she could.

1	2	3

Clauses in a sentence may be of equal importance, or one clause may be more important than the others, in which case they are known as the *main clause* and the *subordinate clauses* respectively. For example:

> I did the shopping when I had visited the hospital.

Main clause	Subordinate clause

Like a phrase, a subordinate clause may fulfil the functions of other parts of speech – it may be a *noun clause*, an *adjectival clause* or an *adverbial clause*.

> I was happy to accept *what he had said about my work.*

In this example, the subordinate clause (in italics) is acting as a noun, serving as the object of the sentence. You could replace it by 'his conclusions', or any other noun or noun phrase.

An *adverbial clause* functions as an adverb, to provide details of time or manner:

> The report was completed *when the researchers had collected all the necessary material.*

Again, the clause could be replaced by a single word such as 'satisfactorily'.

In the next example, the subordinate clause acts as an adjective, describing the noun:

He bought the microcomputer *which his colleague had recommended.*

Instead of the subordinate clause, you could put a suitable adjective – such as 'recommended' – before the noun.

Particular care is needed with this type of clause, since it may serve one of two functions which can be distinguished only by the punctuation used. Consider the following sentence:

The nurse *who had worked in a large casualty ward* was not distressed by what she saw at the accident.

The subordinate clause (in italics) defines one particular nurse, as distinguished from the others. It is thus known as a *defining clause* and should not be separated from the rest of the sentence by any form of punctuation. In this example, the next sentence might well be:

The nurses with her, however, had no experience of serious injuries and were quite upset.

The same words can be used to very different effect in a *non-defining* or *commenting* clause such as this:

The nurse, *who had worked in a large casualty ward*, was not distressed by what she saw at the accident.

Here, the commas mark off the subordinate clause as purely descriptive. The nurse in this example will have been mentioned previously and the clause is simply giving additional information about her. There is no implied comparison with any other nurse.

When using a clause as an adjective, therefore, you should consider carefully whether it is a defining or a non-defining clause, and use commas accordingly.

Knowing how language is used will help you to understand and judge the writing of others, and will lay a valuable foundation for the writing and speaking you do yourself. As well as this, however, you need to know how to use the components effectively and in the correct combinations. The following sections look at some points to remember when writing, and suggest ways of avoiding some common errors.

4.3 Using verbs

4.3.1 Agreement with subject
Verbs have different finite forms according to whether the subject they refer to is singular or plural. For example:

One man *was* there in the morning, but four women *were* there in the afternoon.

Here, it is clear that 'was' refers to 'one man' and 'were' to 'four women'. In other circumstances, however, the writer may be misled into using the incorrect form of the verb by the close presence of another noun. An example will make this clear.

A decision to install desk-top computers were taken.

This is clearly wrong: the subject of the verb is 'a decision', which is singular, and so the verb should be 'was taken'. Yet the writer has seen the noun 'computers', realized that it is plural and decided as a result to use a plural form of the verb. This process is known as *attraction*, because the verb is 'attracted' to the incorrect form by the nearby noun.

Particular care is necessary where two or more singular nouns are separated by the word 'or'. The verb in this case refers to only one of the alternatives and should therefore be singular:

A fine or a prison sentence is to be imposed.

You can avoid errors such as these by making sure that you know which noun is the subject of the verb and checking that the two agree – that both are singular or both are plural. This is not always as simple as it sounds, as section 4.4.1 will show.

4.3.2 Separation of verb and subject

One reason why the wrong form of the verb is often used by mistake is the distance between the verb and the subject to which it refers. Look at this example:

Business management, after being neglected for a long time in English schools and colleges, *is now beginning* to make up lost ground.

As well as increasing the risk of attraction – the use of the verb 'are' under the influence of 'schools and colleges' – this kind of construction is confusing for the reader. He or she may well lose track of the subject while waiting for the verb to appear. Such confusion is easily avoided by placing the verb next to the subject, like this:

After being neglected for a long time in English schools and colleges, *business management is now beginning* to make up lost ground.

Some might object to this on the grounds that the subject is not made clear at the outset whereas, for all its faults, the original version does state the subject at the very start of the sentence. One way of countering this criticism is to change the order of the sentence:

Business management is now beginning to make up lost ground after being neglected for a long time in English schools and colleges.

However, this alters the emphasis slightly: we are now struck by the fact that business management is beginning to recover its lost ground, whereas the earlier versions stressed its neglect.

Changing the order of the clauses in a sentence can therefore not only help in avoiding the error of attraction and the possible confusion for the reader in separating subject from verb; it can also alter the relative importance of the ideas expressed. This is a useful point to bear in mind when writing documents which rely on careful presentation of the relation between several ideas.

4.3.3 Active and passive forms

Most actions can be expressed in two ways:

> I wrote the letter.   (Active)
> The letter was written by me.   (Passive)

In business writing it is better to use the active form, since it suggests a positive, open and honest approach. The repeated use of the passive suggests the operation of an impersonal machine and does little to build a relationship with the reader. The active mood is also far more immediate than the passive.

Even when it is not possible to be precise in saying who was responsible for an action, it is still preferable to use the active form. Rather than writing:

> I regret that an error has been made.

it would be better to write:

> I regret that the company has made an error.

The latter is honest and open, and is far more likely to achieve a constructive response from the reader than the rather furtive-sounding passive, which manages to suggest that the error was nothing to do with the company or anyone who works for it. Sometimes it may be more discreet to say 'an error was made' as it avoids naming the person involved, but in general it is more open and more vigorous to use the active form.

4.3.4 Verbs with -ing

Verbs which end in -*ing* often cause difficulties. They are of three main types:

(a) the present participle;
(b) the gerund;
(c) the gerundive.

The present participle   This is the form of the verb which denotes that something is in the process of happening.

> All members of the office staff are *working* together as a team.
> There are several events *taking place* this afternoon.
> All of us are *hoping* that you will recover soon.

To be used correctly, participles with -*ing* must be used with a finite verb, to make clear who or what is doing the action to which they refer. Many people, when replying to a letter, might introduce a new paragraph like this:

Turning now to your second point.

This is not a sentence, as there is no finite verb. The reader expects there to be one: he or she wants to know who is turning, and the absence of this information is disconcerting. The expression should be recast as:

Turning now to the second point you have raised, I feel that your comments are quite unjustified.

or perhaps changed into two sentences.

I must now turn to the second point which you have raised. I feel that your comments are quite unjustified.

The second version has the advantage of greater clarity, allowing the main theme of the message – the writer's response to 'the second point' – to emerge much more strongly.

Present participles are often used incorrectly at the end of letters:

Looking forward to hearing from you soon.
Thanking you for your help.

Phrases such as these should be recast with the verb in finite form:

I look forward to hearing from you soon.
Thank you for your help.

Another common error when using the present participle is the failure to make clear who is doing the action it describes. This can result in nonsensical statements such as:

Eating our lunch, the bus set off for the seaside.

In this statement, there is no indication of who is eating lunch; the only possible subject of the participle is the bus. Errors of this kind are not always so easily detected, however. Consider the following:

Standing on the low wall, a man could be seen.

Does this mean that a man could be seen standing on the wall, or that when the writer was standing on the wall, he or she could see a man? The context will sometimes make clear the intended meaning, but it is this kind of ambiguity which causes difficulties for your reader and does little to inspire confidence in your abilities. Here, the sentence would be better reworded to read:

When I stood on the low wall, I could see a man.

Changing from the active to the passive form after a present participle is another frequent error which is equally disconcerting for the reader. Notice how the following sentence changes approach half-way through:

Having researched the subject, no truth is to be found in the rumour.

This should be:

> Having researched the subject, I have found that there is no truth in the rumour.

Participles can be a useful way of adding contrast to a sentence and of suggesting action, because they tend to indicate that something is taking place at the very moment of reading. They must be approached with care, however. The main points to avoid can be summarized as follows:

● Do not use a participle in a sentence without a finite verb.
● Make clear who is doing the action to which the participle refers.
● Do not change from active to passive after using a participle.

The gerund   This is a form of a verb ending in *-ing* which works as a noun to name an activity. The gerund is also known as a *verbal noun*. 'Thinking', 'eating', 'accepting' and 'welding' are examples, and their function as gerunds is shown in these sentences:

> We must do some serious *thinking*.
> *Eating* high-fibre foods is good for you.
> *Accepting* the umpire's decision is essential.
> The mechanic was not good at *welding*.

Because the gerund is used as a noun, any reference to the person or thing to whom the activity relates should be in the possessive form. For example:

> I was pleased by *his* writing to apologize.
> They were distressed by *my* leaving the company.
> The fact of *John's* being absent made me feel uneasy.

The gerundive   This is the *-ing* ending which works as an adjective. The gerundive is often used with a hyphen to link it to the noun to which it refers, as in 'a racing-yacht', 'the drying-room' and 'an engraving-tool'.

Although the context will usually make the nature of the gerundive clear, it is worth being aware of possible confusion with the present participle. The gerundive implies purpose and the present participle describes an action or state. For example, without the hyphen, 'a racing yacht' would mean a yacht that is *in the process of* racing, whereas 'a racing-yacht' is one designed specially *for the purpose of* racing, but not necessarily racing at the time of writing. Such ambiguities may not arise very often, but you should be aware of them. If it seems likely that a gerundive may be confused with a participle, make sure that you use a hyphen to make the meaning quite clear.

The following may help to clarify the three types of *-ing* words:

> He was swimming.   (Present participle)
> Swimming is fun.   (Gerund)
> They owned a swimming-pool.   (Gerundive)

4.4 Using nouns and pronouns

4.4.1 Agreement

Just as a verb must agree with its subject, so a pronoun must agree with the noun to which it refers. It must do this both in number (singular or plural) and in gender (masculine, feminine or neuter). It is easy, when writing quickly, to make errors such as:

> If any employee wishes to apply for promotion, will they please contact the personnel manager.

Here, the noun 'employee' is singular but the pronoun 'they' is plural; 'he or she' should have been used instead. Similar care is needed when using 'everyone', 'nobody', 'each' and 'either', all of which are singular nouns and take a singular form of the pronoun and verb. Occasionally, the pronoun 'they' is used as a non-sexist alternative to 'he', but it is usually preferable to use 'he or she' instead.

A special problem is caused by nouns such as 'company', 'firm', 'committee', 'management' and 'department'. In theory, all are singular nouns – one word for a single body composed of several people. In practice, however, they are often referred to as plurals. The best policy is to find out the common usage or house style in your organization and follow that. If there is no common usage, decide for yourself – but above all be consistent in your expression.

Similar issues arise when talking about a company by name. Which of the following is correct?

> Philips has launched a new CD player.
> Philips have launched a new CD player.

Once again, you should be guided by house style.

A related problem is the use of plural nouns as singular ones. 'Media', 'strata' and 'phenomena' are all plurals and thus take plural pronouns and plural forms of the verb. 'Data' is an exception: a plural noun, it is increasingly treated as a singular.

Relative pronouns – those which make clear the relation between an action and a doer – also need care. In particular, you should make sure that you use 'who' and 'which' correctly, for people and things respectively. For example, you should not write:

> the men *which* were working on the roof.

The correct form is:

> the men *who* were working on the roof.

4.4.2 Relating pronouns to the correct nouns

It is important to make clear exactly which noun a pronoun refers to, as the old example illustrates:

> I'll hold the nail and when I nod my head, you hit it.

The intended meaning of the final clause is 'you hit the nail' but, because 'my head' appears immediately before the final clause, the pronoun 'it' properly refers to 'my head'. Careful checking should ensure that your writing is free from errors and ambiguities of this kind.

4.4.3 Subject and object

Some pronouns have different forms for use as subject and object: 'I' changes to 'me', 'they' to 'them' and 'we' to 'us', for example. The most common error here is to use 'I' instead of 'me'. It would therefore be wrong to write:

Between you and I, it should never have happened.
All employees should see Mr Jones or I about overtime pay.

Instead, you should say:

Between you and me, it should never have happened.
All employees should see Mr Jones or me about overtime pay.

'I' should be used for the subject of the clause, 'me' for the object. In the following sentence, for example, it would be *wrong* to use 'me':

You know him better than I.

'I' in this instance stands for 'I do' and is the subject of the subordinate clause.

A similar distinction is made between forms of the relative pronoun: 'who' is used for the subject of a sentence, 'whom' for the object.

Who told you that?
To whom is the letter addressed?

4.5 Using adjectives

4.5.1 Over-use

Adjectives are often used too freely, especially by inexperienced writers, who somehow feel that no noun is clear unless it has two adjectives in front of it. It is far better to use a few adjectives properly than to cover your writing with unnecessary ones. This is particularly true of adjectives denoting quantity. 'Great', 'excessive', 'enormous', 'huge' and other words suggesting size are overworked, and your writing will be stronger without them.

4.5.2 Comparative and superlative

Remember that, where two items are being compared, you should use the comparative and not the superlative form, as the superlative refers to one of many. For example:

They chose the larger of the two designs and put it on the biggest display board they could find.

4.5.3 *Adjectives of quantity*

Confusion often arises over the use of adjectives of quantity, especially the adjectival phrases 'a number of' and 'an amount of'. The former should be used whenever the item referred to can be separated into units – 'a number of books' or 'a number of people', for example. The latter is used of materials not separable into units – 'an amount of petrol' or 'an amount of concrete'. In particular, the use of 'an amount of people' should be avoided, since it suggests a refusal to treat people as individuals.

Another two words which are often confused are 'fewer' and 'less'. The former is used of people and individual units, the latter of materials. For example:

There were fewer people there in the afternoon than in the morning.

We have used less timber than aluminium in the construction of the shed.

4.6 Using conjunctions

Conjunctions are very valuable words, since they make clear the relationship between parts of a sentence as well as joining them together (see section 4.2.5). Some conjunctions may also be used at the start of a sentence, to help signpost the direction of an argument, thus helping the reader to grasp the writer's meaning more quickly. For example:

Although the company has improved its sales this year, we still need to work hard to overcome competition.

Whereas our earlier models sold in areas where there was no competition, our new range sells in the most competitive market: central Europe.

Some conjunctions, however, should never be used at the start of a sentence. 'Or' and 'and' in particular should not be used in this way, even though advertising copy and popular journalism often break this rule. For example:

The new 467 won't make the tea. Or iron the clothes. And it won't walk the dog. But it will give you the best wash you've had for years.

This is part of the continuous process of change in any language; perhaps in some years' time this usage will be widespread and acceptable – as the use of 'but' to begin a sentence is now, when stressing a strong contrast with the preceding point. At the moment, however, using 'or' or 'and' in this way will only confuse the reader and is best avoided.

4.7 Using sentences

4.7.1 *Sentences without verbs*

In some circumstances it is acceptable to use a sentence without a finite verb for emphasis or effect. The novelist Charles Dickens – often cited for his long, complex sentences – used this technique, for example at the opening of *Bleak*

BLEAK HOUSE

---❖---

CHAPTER I

IN CHANCERY

LONDON. Michaelmas Term lately over, and the Lord Chancellor sitting in Lincoln's Inn Hall. Implacable November weather. As much mud in the streets, as if the waters had but newly retired from the face of the earth, and it would not be wonderful to meet a Megalosaurus, forty feet long or so, waddling like an elephantine lizard up Holborn Hill. Smoke lowering down from chimney-pots, making a soft black drizzle, with flakes of soot in it as big as fullgrown snow-flakes—gone into mourning, one might imagine, for the death of the sun. Dogs, undistinguishable in mire. Horses, scarcely better; splashed to their very blinkers. Foot passengers, jostling one another's umbrellas, in a general infection of ill-temper, and losing their foot-hold at street-corners, where tens of thousands of other foot passengers have been slipping and sliding since the day broke (if this day ever broke), adding new deposits to the crust upon crust of mud, sticking at those points tenaciously to the pavement, and accumulating at compound interest.

Fog everywhere. Fog up the river, where it flows among green aits and meadows; fog down the river, where it rolls defiled among the tiers of shipping, and the waterside pollutions of a great (and dirty) city. Fog on the Essex marshes, fog on the Kentish heights. Fog creeping into the cabooses of collier-brigs; fog lying out on the yards, and hovering in the rigging of great ships; fog drooping on the gunwales of barges and small boats. Fog in the eyes and throats of ancient Greenwich pensioners, wheezing by the firesides of their wards; fog in the stem and bowl of the afternoon pipe of the wrathful skipper, down in his close cabin; fog cruelly pinching the toes and fingers of his shivering little 'prentice boy on deck. Chance people on the bridges peeping over the parapets into a

B

Fig. 4.3 From an early edition of *Bleak House* by Charles Dickens. Notice the use of sentences in the opening paragraph (see section 4.7.1).

House, where there is a paragraph of eight sentences only one of which has a main verb – and that only in the second of two equal clauses (see fig. 4.3).

In business writing, however, the use of a finite verb is still essential, since without one your expression will lack precision and clarity. Instead of writing

With reference to your letter of 21 May.

you should write

I refer to your letter of 21 May.

As section 4.3.4 has made clear, too, a present participle cannot do the job of a finite verb, and such constructions should also be avoided.

4.7.2 Length

Many people feel that only long sentences can convey an impression of dignity and seriousness, not to mention authority. This is not so. Often a short sentence is equally effective in conveying decisiveness or control. But often a complex idea which depends on bringing together several strands of thought can be given full and clear expression only in a sentence which uses several phrases and clauses. There is, however, no point in linking unrelated ideas to produce long, straggling sentences, as this will only make it harder for the reader to grasp your meaning.

Look, for example, at the following sentence:

> If the current abuse of the right to make personal telephone calls from work continues (that is, if people continue to neglect to inform the switchboard operator that the calls are private and ask to be billed for them), I am sure you will understand that I shall have no alternative but to take appropriate action which may include removing the right to make private calls, at first for a trial period but ultimately, though regretfully, on a permanent basis so that the company's time and money are not used for matters which have no relation to its business.

Such a message is long and indigestible. Consequently it is unlikely that anyone will read further than the third or fourth line, let alone take heed of the warning given. The message would be far better conveyed like this:

> The right to make private telephone calls is currently being abused. Some employees are not telling the switchboard that their calls are private and asking to be billed for them. This means that the company's time and money are being used for matters which have no relation to its business. I am sure you will understand that, if this abuse continues, I shall have no alternative but to take steps to prevent it. These will begin with a temporary removal of the right to make private calls. If this has no effect, I will regretfully have to place a permanent ban on private calls from the company's offices.

Notice how separate sentences are used to establish the facts and to clarify the proper procedure for making personal calls, before other sentences say what preventive action will be taken. Thus the whole message is presented with greater logic as well as greater clarity. As a result, the passage is far more likely to be read and the warning heeded.

4.8   Using paragraphs

Just as long sentences will make a document difficult for the reader to understand, so writing which is not broken up into paragraphs will cause problems for anyone trying to follow the larger development of an argument. Whatever you are writing, you should try to break up your points into paragraphs, so that each paragraph covers a single point or group of related points. A 'topic sentence' at the start may establish the main point of the paragraph, and the sentences which follow it will add more detail or make subsidiary points. The final sentence may either repeat the main point or draw together the main ideas of the paragraph by touching on them again briefly. The use of paragraphs not only helps your reader to follow your argument; it also makes sure that you yourself have planned what you are going to write, by making you group your ideas under related topics and ensuring that points follow on in a logical order. The technique helps both writer and reader communicate with greater efficiency and precision.

4.9 Changes in language

The errors mentioned in this unit are only a small number of the more common mistakes. All should be avoided not only because they go against the accepted principles of grammar, but also because they will reduce the precision and clarity of your writing. In addition, you should try to be aware of changes in fashions of expression, which are inevitable as society changes and language develops. A few years ago, for example, no one would have said that he or she was 'really into biking'; instead, they would have said they were 'very keen on motor-cycling'. Similarly, the word 'green' – originally used of the colour, and then as an adjective meaning 'inexperienced' – has only recently started being used in a political context to refer to those concerned with environmental issues. 'Buyout', 'advertorial' and 'golden handshake' are other examples of words and phrases which have been added to the language in recent years. The widespread use of computer technology has introduced still more – such as 'user-friendly', which has subsequently given rise to related terms such as 'environment-friendly'.

Many new words, phrases and forms of expression add vigour and strength to the language, and can be very effective when used in the right context – most often a friendly, informal one. 'Zonked', for example, conveys its meaning of being absolutely exhausted with a force which no other word could equal. Other changes in language, however, may weaken its expressive powers and will be confusing to those who have not yet caught up with the social changes which have produced them. Those with no knowledge of computers, for example, will not understand the word 'interface' meaning 'meeting', nor the term 'K' from 'kilobyte' – meaning 'thousand'.

Language needs to be used with caution if you do not want to be ambiguous, inaccurate or totally incomprehensible in what you say. Even if a new word or mode of expression becomes common, and is heard in every television and radio news broadcast, try not to adopt it immediately and uncritically. Pause for a moment and consider whether it helps to clarify the idea it puts forward, or whether it simply obscures it. Only when you have made sure that the point concerned really 'works' as a tool of communication should you make use of it in your own writing.

4.10 Reader, purpose and style

Anyone who wishes to become a good writer should endeavour, before he allows himself to be tempted by more showy qualities, to be direct, simple, brief, vigorous and lucid.

This is an excerpt from H.W. Fowler's *A Dictionary of Modern English Usage*, a book which is required reading in many offices and government departments. If this section had to be summarized in a single sentence, it could not be done better than this. Simple, direct writing which is concerned with expressing ideas as accurately as possible rather than with impressing the reader is the most effective kind of writing for any business situation.

This, then, is the first commandment of verbal communication, and one which you should always bear in mind when writing or speaking. Later in this section we will look at some of the ways it may be put into practice, and some of the stylized forms of expression which it demands that you avoid.

4.10.1 Your reader

Whatever you are writing, you should always be aware of the person who will read the finished document. Think about the following aspects in particular.

Vocabulary　Think carefully about the kind of language used by your reader. If you are writing a letter in reply to a member of the public whom you have not met, you can make few assumptions about the range of his or her vocabulary, and should write simply and clearly, without being patronizing. If you are writing to a colleague in your own department, you will have a better idea of the kind of words he or she uses, and can choose your forms of expression accordingly.

As well as the general vocabulary of your reader, you should consider his or her specific vocabulary – the technical terms or jargon which he or she will understand which you could not use with someone not professionally involved in the relevant activity. Jargon is discussed in section 4.10.3.

Age　This may not always be of any relevance, but it is reasonable to assume that older people will be less aware of the changes in language and its use resulting from pop music, say. As a result, the usual need to avoid slang, clichés and fashionable expressions is even more marked. Be careful to avoid being patronizing, though: once again, simple clarity and directness are the best aims.

Relationship　When deciding on what language to use, you must also consider how well you know the reader. You can address a colleague of the same status at work with greater familiarity than your head of department, for example.

Attitudes　Ask yourself about the general outlook of the person or people to whom you are writing. Political attitudes will have little relevance to much business correspondence, so you should avoid including asides which are merely personal opinions and may be controversial. In some documents – such as reports which relate future sales projections to government policy on taxation, for example – political comments may be necessary, but you should try to make them as factual and impartial as possible. For example, you should say that 'fewer council houses are being built by the present government' rather than talking of 'the inhumane housing policy of the Tories'; and you should refer to 'the uncertain relationship between the financial institutions and a Labour government', rather than 'the refusal of big business to deal with socialists'.

It is also important to avoid sexist language – always using 'he' and 'him' instead of 'he or she' and 'him or her', for example. Often language can suggest a sexist attitude where none exists, causing resentment and anger in the reader which could be avoided with a little thought. For example:

I want to produce a play that people can take their wives and families to.

This suggests that only men are people. Similarly, an advertisement which reads:

We are looking for someone who has been outstandingly successful in everything he has done so far.

will imply that the person appointed will be a man, which may not be the intention.

Fig. 4.4 A poster from early in World War Two. It was criticized as being divisive – *you* do the work and *we* will have the victory.

Always check that your writing contains no potentially offensive or misleading material of this kind, and that it is generally suited to the outlook of the person for whom you are writing.

Range of readers The elements which have been considered so far have largely applied to individual readers. Many business documents, however, are addressed to a large number of people. Reports, circular letters and committee documents all have a readership of more than one person. As a result, you should make sure that the form of expression you use is appropriate to a range of readers. This will mean using a style which everyone can fully understand – in short, writing in the simple, clear and direct manner which is outlined in this unit.

4.10.2 Your purpose
As well as the reader of the document, you must also consider what the document is meant to achieve. Your purpose might be any of the following:

● to convey information;
● to request information from the reader;
● to begin action of some kind;
● to order goods;
● to give instructions;
● to obtain money (as a donation or in payment of an overdue bill);
● to achieve better service in future.

Whenever you write a document, letter or report, consider the desired outcome of what you are writing. For example, a letter of complaint is unlikely to achieve the desired result of improved service if it is downright abusive. A notice giving instructions will not achieve its purpose if it is pompous and long-winded, since readers either will give up reading it before the end or will not be motivated to co-operate.

4.10.3 Style
Until fairly recently, there was a separate language known as 'Business English'. Instead of thanking each other for their letters, writers would 'beg leave to acknowledge your esteemed favour of the 4th ult. which is to hand'. Rather than use the names of the months, they referred to *ult.*, *inst.*, and *prox.*, short for *ultimo*, *instant* and *proximo*, which in turn meant 'last month', 'this month' and 'next month'. They would ask that something be done 'at your earliest convenience' instead of 'as soon as you can', and ask to be 'apprised' of the result of an action, rather than simply 'told' about it. In theory, this was to give an air of proper seriousness and professionalism to their writing: in practice, it made it pompous and incomprehensible to anyone not familiar with its special code. An example of this kind of writing, together with its modern equivalent, is shown in fig. 4.5.

Certainly there is a need for seriousness and professionalism in business writing. Most business writing today, however, achieves this by simplicity and

Honoured Sir,

Your esteemed favour of the fourteenth inst. is to hand. We respectfully beg to advise you that the documents to which you refer have now been completed. We should be most grateful if you would be so kind as to honour us with your presence in this office so that you may sign the same at your earliest convenience.
Assuring you of our best intention at all times,
We beg the honour to remain, Sir,
Your most obedient humble servants,

Obediah Cringe and Partners

```
Mr B Johnson
15 High St
Carlingford
Staffs


Dear Mr Johnson

Thank you for your letter of 14 May.

The contract is now complete, and I should be glad if you would call
in and sign it as soon as possible.

I look forward to seeing you in the near future.

With kind regards

Yours sincerely

D. Cringe

D Cringe
Director
Marlborough Investments plc
```

Fig. 4.5 An example of a letter in formal 'Business English' of the nineteenth century and its modern equivalent

precision rather than elaborate obscurities. The business style which results from putting Fowler's principles into practice is clear, convenient and easy to imitate, lacking ostentation but nonetheless allowing the writer some scope for individuality.

An important feature of style is the writer's choice of words. The number and kinds of words used in written or spoken communication are usually referred to by the single word 'vocabulary'. Choosing the right vocabulary for each situation is quite a complex process and is influenced by many factors – as the earlier parts of this unit have made clear. There are, however, some basic principles which should be applied in every situation.

Avoid spoken terms in writing   When we speak, we all use expressions which are relaxed and informal. Pausing for breath, we might say 'D'you know what I mean?'; when we are unsure of the right word, we might say 'kind of'; and when we start a new part of a story we might begin 'Well, anyway . . .'.

Although such expressions can be useful when talking with friends, in business communication they are out of place. They suggest that the writing has not been properly prepared, and make the expression unnecessarily long and clumsy. There is no need to go to the opposite extreme and be very formal in everything you write, but you should certainly avoid the kind of language you would use in an informal conversation. For example, to a colleague you might say:

Get me an order form, could you?

In a letter you would write:

Please send me an order form.

Avoid slang   Groups of people often develop an informal style of language which they use amongst themselves. While you might say to a friend that you will 'give him a bell to see if his wheels are fixed', in a business letter you would write to a colleague that you will 'telephone him to see if his car has been repaired'. Slang is often vigorous, forceful and inventive but it has significant drawbacks: it is usually understood by only a small group of people, and it may not be particularly precise in meaning. For these reasons, it should not be used in more formal communication.

Avoid impressive language   Although slang is unsuitable for written communication, so too is language which deliberately sets out to impress. Do not use complicated words or phrases for simple things: avoid writing about 'acquiring a property' when you mean 'buying a flat'; say that something has occurred 'unexpectedly' instead of 'due to unforeseen circumstances'.

Avoid emotive language   This is language which seeks to direct the reader's emotional response to the matter under discussion. If a rise in taxation is described as 'scandalous', for example, we are directed towards a single response, regardless of our own feelings or the logical arguments and factual circumstances involved. Such expression is generally acceptable in conversation or popular journalism, but in serious business writing it is clearly out of place. As well as guiding the reader's response, it blurs the distinction between what is fact and what is opinion, by presenting the author's opinion as an established reality (see section 8.2.3).

Avoid inflated language Inflation can affect language as well as currency. Words tend to lose their effect through constant use, and more extreme words take their place. 'Incredible', for example, means 'beyond belief'; it is now used to describe anything slightly above average. Many people talk of 'over-exaggerating' when 'exaggerating' in fact means 'over-stating'.

There is little point in using adjectives which add no further detail to the noun they describe: talking of 'huge differences', 'vast investments' or a 'good improvement' not only makes it hard for the reader to grasp the exact significance of what is being said, but also suggests how he or she should respond to it – in bewildered wonder and admiration. It is far better to be specific and clear than to risk irritating and confusing the reader by expressions of this kind.

Take care with jargon People who work in particular trades or professions inevitably develop terms to describe specialized activities. In the newspaper industry, 'putting the paper to bed' refers to the final preparations for printing; proofreaders talk of 'checking for literals' when they mean reading through a text to check for any misprints; builders talk of 'topping off' a building to mean completing the roof surface and therefore the whole structure. All these are valid expressions used by people familiar with the processes they describe, and are quite justifiable uses of jargon.

Other kinds of jargon arise from a desire to avoid giving offence. 'Senior citizens' is a more respectful way of referring to older members of the community than 'old-age pensioners', which emphasizes their dependence. Similarly, 'ethnic minorities' is a term introduced in an attempt to be factual and to avoid the racially offensive language common for many years in official English.

Some expressions, however, are less valid. Some are simply pretentious, such as 'printed resource module' for 'book or periodical' and 'scoring parameters' for 'mark range'. Others are more sinister, such as 'collateral damage', a phrase used by military commanders to refer to the death or injury of innocent people.

Jargon of the kinds described in the first two paragraphs above is valid and useful, although you should make sure that you use it only when you are certain that your reader will understand its meaning. Expressions of the other kinds – the pretentious or sinister – should be avoided. Think carefully before using jargon and, if you are in doubt as to its validity, be ruthless and strike it out.

Avoid clichés   As well as individual terms, there are groups of words which are used so frequently that they tend to lose all their meaning and freshness. In the past, printers used to keep such groups of words made up together in a stick – known in France as a *cliché* – ready to be used in printing. There are plenty of current examples. 'At this moment in time' is a pompous way of saying 'now'; 'full and frank discussion' usually just means 'talk'; 'we apologize for any inconvenience' has become so common a statement that it has ceased to sound sincere.

If you find yourself using an expression which has been used so often that it falls into this category, you should think again and find a simpler, less hackneyed way of saying the same thing.

Avoid imprecision   Always give specific names to people and objects rather than referring to abstract ideas. Instead of writing 'a higher authority', say 'the managing director'; instead of saying that a delivery will be delayed 'for a considerable time', give a specific period – 'for six weeks', for example. In the same way, remember that there is no standard definition for terms like 'very soon' or 'a substantial amount'. Avoid imprecise terms like these and use a clear, exact expression in their place.

These principles are important in communication of every kind, not only because they ensure accuracy and improve the reader's impression of the writer, but also because they ensure that what is expressed is expressed honestly. They therefore enable people to trust each other more fully. Honesty and integrity are essential aspects of communication. George Orwell, in an essay on 'Politics and the English Language', makes this very clear:

The great enemy of clear language is insincerity. Where there is a gap between one's real and one's declared aims, one turns as it were instinctively to long words and exhausted idioms, like a cuttlefish squirting out ink.

In this essay, Orwell also sums up the principles of accurate communication with great succinctness in a series of rules which all writers should always bear in mind:

1 Never use a metaphor, simile or other figure of speech which you are used to seeing in print.
2 Never use a long word where a short one will do.
3 If it is possible to cut a word out, always cut it out.
4 Never use a foreign phrase, a scientific word or a jargon word if you can think of an everyday English equivalent.
5 Never use the passive where you can use the active.
6 Break any of these rules sooner than say anything outright barbarous.

4.11 Conclusion

The English language is a communication device of immense richness and variety and, used properly, it can convey ideas and information of every kind with vigour, clarity and elegance. The principles set out in this unit are only the most basic which should guide your writing, but you should try to apply them to the various kinds of writing you will need to produce in subsequent units. This will be useful practice for the time when your communication skills are needed for real-life situations.

Whatever the situation, remember to write as precisely, concisely and courteously as possible, using direct, unhackneyed language which suits both your purpose and your reader. This may not win any awards for literary merit, but it will ensure that your writing can meet any demand placed upon it.

Spelling and punctuation

5.1 The importance of accuracy

Unit 4 stressed the importance of accuracy in your use of grammar if you want to express yourself precisely and concisely. Spelling and punctuation are of equal significance in business communication. You may feel that a few mistakes will not stop you from getting your message across. But in business communication it is not only what you say that matters; it is also how you say it.

Spelling mistakes show a lack of concern for accuracy, which will suggest inefficiency to your reader – a 'couldn't-care-less' attitude which may well apply to your business dealings as well as your spelling. Poorly spelt letters and other documents suggest poor standards and, in the highly competitive world of business, may well prevent the reader from having confidence in you as an individual or in the organization you represent.

In addition, mistakes in punctuation can often alter the meaning of what you write. Look closely at these two sentences.

Some of the stock, which was damaged, can be sold at a cheaper rate.
Some of the stock which was damaged can be sold at a cheaper rate.

There is a clear difference in meaning here. The first sentence suggests that only a part of the stock was damaged, and that all of the damaged stock can be sold at a cheaper price. In the second, the suggestion is that all the stock was damaged, but that only some of it may be sold at a cheaper price – implying that the remainder must be disposed of in some other way. In a letter complaining about a consignment of stock that had just been delivered, the writer would have to be quite sure about which version to use, so that the reader – the supplier of the goods – knew exactly what the extent of the damage was. In a case like this, careless use of a comma could also alter the legal significance of a sentence and perhaps have very serious and expensive consequences. Overall, it would be better to reword the sentence to read 'The damaged stock . . .' or 'Some of the damaged stock . . .', and so make the meaning clear.

Incorrect punctuation, then, can alter the meaning of a sentence. This can have serious consequences in business relationships because of the delay, inconvenience and cost which will be involved in rectifying mistakes. These, too, will not give a good impression of your organization.

Try to learn the principles and examples in this unit, and put them into practice in whatever you write. Get into the habit of checking your writing for mistakes and correcting them before your work is passed on to anyone else. For documents related to your work, make a rough draft first; then check that your spelling is correct and that your punctuation has not affected the clarity of your message or its intended meaning; and finally write or type the actual document. Cultivate the habit of checking and double-checking. It may not be easy at first, but it will become simpler with practice. It will also make a great difference to your writing, whether in your studies or in your business career.

5.2 Some spelling principles

Perhaps because it has drawn its words from so many different sources, the English language has very few absolute rules about spelling. Words such as 'cough', 'bough', 'though', 'thought' and 'through' all have the same basic grouping of letters, but all are pronounced very differently. There are, however, some principles which are valid for a large number of words. Many of these principles depend on the nature of the vowels in the words concerned.

5.2.1 Vowels and consonants

All English words are made up of two kinds of letters: *vowels* and *consonants*. Almost every word includes a vowel – *a, e, i, o* or *u*. The other letters are known as consonants, except *y*, which is often called a 'semi-vowel'. In the word 'problem', for example, the vowels are *o* and *e*, the consonants *p, r, b, l* and *m*. Being able to distinguish between vowels and consonants is an important skill in spelling, since many of the rules depend on how the vowels are pronounced.

Short and long vowels and the final *e*   Short vowel sounds are the *a* in 'bat'; the *e* in 'fed'; the *i* in 'bid'; the *o* in 'pot'; and the *u* in 'run'. Examples of long vowel sounds are the *a* in 'mate'; the *e* in 'cede'; the *i* in 'wide'; the *o* in 'vote'; and the *u* in 'prune'. The rule here is that words with a short vowel sound do not have a final *e*, whereas words with a long vowel sound do. The above examples all show this in practice: those with long vowels – 'mate', 'cede', 'wide', 'vote' and 'prune' – all end with an *e*.

There are, however, some exceptions. The long *a* sound produces words which end in *e* spellings such as 'able', 'fable', 'cable' and 'table', but 'label' is the odd one out. Another exception occurs wherever a double vowel spelt *ea* or *ee* results in a long *e* sound. Words such as 'lead', 'read' and 'plead' do not have a final *e*, and neither do 'reed', 'feed' and 'seed'.

Doubling consonants   When you add letters to the end of a word to change its form – from 'step' (present participle) to 'stepped' (past participle), for example – you sometimes double the last consonant. The rule here is simple: if the vowel sound is short, double the consonant: if it is long, leave the consonant single. Here again there are exceptions: for example, 'focus' changes to 'focused', 'benefit' to 'benefited', and 'rivet' to 'riveted' – although they may be spelt with double consonants, depending on house style.

The lost *e* When you alter the form of those words with long vowels which end in *e*, you normally take off the *e* and leave the consonant before it single. 'Write' therefore changes to 'writing' (not 'writting') and 'dine' to 'dining' (not 'dinning').

The exception here is words with a soft-sounding *c* or *g*, as in 'notice' and 'charge' as opposed to 'car' and 'grape' where the *c* and *g* are hard-sounding. Such words lose the *e* as usual when you add -*ing*, to give 'noticing' and 'changing', but they keep the *e* when you add -*able*, to give 'noticeable' and 'changeable'.

Words with a vowel before the last *e* are much simpler. 'See' changes to 'seeing', for example. Even here, though, there are exceptions: 'die' changes to 'dying', and 'vie' to 'vying'.

5.2.2 Adding -able *or* -ible

Many words change their form by the addition of a *suffix*, which is a group of letters at the end of a word. Common suffices are -*able* and -*ible*, both of which change a verb into an adjective. For example, 'break' becomes 'breakable', 'laugh' becomes 'laughable', and 'read' becomes 'readable'. However, if the word ends in an *e*, the *e* is usually taken off before the suffix is added – for example, 'love' and 'adore' become 'lovable' and 'adorable'. The exceptions are the word 'like', which changes to 'likeable', and words with soft *c* or *g* sounds, as we saw above, where the final *e* stays in 'noticeable' and 'changeable'.

Words which end in *y* change form in a different way. The *y* is removed and replaced with an *i*, so that 'vary' becomes 'variable' and 'pity' becomes 'pitiable'. Some words change to slightly different forms: 'credit' to 'credible', 'horror' to 'horrible', and 'reduce' to 'reducible'.

5.2.3 Adding -ly

Most adverbs are formed by adding -*ly* to an adjective (see section 4.2.4). 'Honest' becomes 'honestly', 'rough' becomes 'roughly', and 'chief' becomes 'chiefly', for example. If there is an *e* at the end of the word, it usually stays – for example, 'free', 'strange' and 'large' become 'freely', 'strangely' and 'largely'. If there is a *u* before the *e*, however, then the *e* is lost: 'true' and 'due' therefore become 'truly' and 'duly'.

Those adjectives which end in *y* are treated differently. The *y* is replaced with an *i*, and -*ly* is then added. 'Happy', 'dreary' and 'airy' become 'happily', 'drearily' and 'airily'. Words which end in *l* take -*ly*, and those which end in -*ic* take -*ally*: 'thoughtful' becomes 'thoughtfully', for example, and 'automatic' becomes 'automatically'. There is one oddity, however: 'public' becomes 'publicly'.

5.2.4 Opposites

Many opposites are formed by adding a *prefix* (a small group of letters at the start of the word). The most common prefix is *un-*: in this way 'familiar' changes to 'unfamiliar', 'prepared' to 'unprepared' and 'pleasant' to 'unpleasant'. Another important group, though, takes *in-*. It includes 'formal' ('informal'), 'adequate' ('inadequate') and 'decisive' ('indecisive'). Some words take *im-*, as in 'immoral' and 'imperfect'. Many words which begin with the letter *r* take *ir-*: 'replaceable' becomes 'irreplaceable' and 'rational' becomes 'irrational', for example.

Yet another group takes *dis-*, and so we get 'disagreeable', 'disloyal' and 'dislike'. Only if the original word starts with an *s* will the opposite have a double *s* – for example, 'satisfy' becomes 'dissatisfy'. A word to watch for here is 'disappoint', which does follow this rule, but which many people want to spell with a double *s*.

An unusual opposite form is that of 'normal', which is 'abnormal' – from the Latin word *ab* meaning 'away from', suggesting that it departs from usual practice. Another unusual opposite form is made by adding *non-*, as in 'non-hazardous' and 'non-returnable'.

5.2.5 Plurals

Plural nouns are words which name more than one of something. Most are formed simply by adding an *s* to the end of the word, so that 'book' becomes 'books', 'desk' becomes 'desks', 'computer' becomes 'computers' and 'word-processor' becomes 'wordprocessors'. Notice that you do not add an apostrophe before the *s* – this is done only where ownership or belonging is indicated, as in 'the man's dog' (see section 5.2.7).

Words which end in *-ch* take *-es* in the plural, to give 'matches', 'sandwiches' and 'pitches', for example. Words ending in *o* need more care: some form their plurals by adding *s* – like 'dynamos' and 'videos' – but others take *-es* – like 'potatoes' and 'cargoes'.

Those which end in *y* fall into two groups. If there is a vowel before the *y* – as in 'survey', 'play', 'guy' or 'key' – then you simply add an *s* – to give 'surveys', 'plays', 'guys' and 'keys'. If, however, there is a consonant before the *y*, the *y* is taken off and *-ies* added in its place. Thus 'cry', 'factory', 'lorry', 'ferry' and 'laboratory' become 'cries', 'factories', 'lorries', 'ferries' and 'laboratories'.

Many words form their plurals without using an *s* at all. For some of these, there are basic rules which may be followed; others must be learnt as exceptions. Here are some of the more common ones:

Singular	Plural	
bureau	bureaux	These come from the French,
plateau	plateaux	so take *x* in the plural.
formula	formulae	A Latin construction; *-ae* is correct, but *-as* is increasingly used.

Singular	*Plural*	
medium	media	Latin again. Make sure you
memorandum	memoranda	use the correct form, as
		many people confuse the
		singular and plural.
phenomenon	phenomena	Greek this time. Again, be
		sure to use the right form.
stimulus	stimuli	Latin roots. These can often
cactus	cacti	be either -*uses* or -*i* in
syllabus	syllabuses/syllabi	the plural – check for
prospectus	prospectuses	house style.
crisis	crises	Latin once more. Take
		particular care over this
		one, as only one letter
		distinguishes singular
		and plural.
man	men	These are Old English –
woman	women	again, it's important to
child	children	get them right.
workman	workmen	
foot	feet	
sheep	sheep	
head of department	heads of department	For compound nouns – ones
spoonful of sugar	spoonsful of sugar	formed from two or more
head of state	heads of state	nouns – the *s* is usually
		added to the first word

Plurals of words with *f* at or near the end need special care. 'Knife', 'leaf' and 'thief' all take a *v*, to give 'knives', 'leaves' and 'thieves'. But 'roof' and 'hoof' keep the *f* to give 'roofs' and 'hoofs'.

5.2.6 ie *and* ei

You will probably know the first line of the old rhyme:

> *I* before *e* except after *c*

but the second line is less well-known:

> But only when the sound is *ee*.

This is one of the few rules which are almost unbroken in English spelling. 'Believe', 'reprieve', 'relief', 'grief' and 'thief' all follow it, as do 'receive', 'receipt', 'deceive' and 'perceive'. If the sound of the word is not *ee*, the spelling is usually *ei*. Examples include 'weight', 'height' and 'their'. The rule in the rhyme is almost unbroken, but not quite – words which go against it include 'weir', 'seize', 'science' and 'counterfeit'.

5.2.7 Apostrophes

Apostrophes of ownership Hundreds of years ago, if you wanted to indicate in writing that something belonged to someone, you added *-es* to the person's name. This produced expressions like 'the Kinges peace' and 'the mannes dog'. As the language grew and changed, people began to leave out the *e*. At a later date, to show that it had been left out, they put in an apostrophe, to give 'the King's peace' and 'the man's dog'. Today we still use the same procedure to show that something belongs, or is related to, something else: we add an apostrophe and an *s* ('*s*) to the noun naming the owner. The four main rules governing the use of the possessive apostrophe are given below.

(a) To show that one thing is related to another, you add '*s*, as in the following sentence:

Mr Brown was shown into the manager's office and told that one month's delay was inevitable as a result of the company's annual holiday.

(b) For words ending in *s* (often people's names) you still add '*s*. Look at this sentence:

Ms Williams's assistant will show you to Mr Jones's office.

Until recently, it used to be the practice simply to add an apostrophe after the *s* – 'Mr Jones'', 'Ms Williams'' – but, as written expression has moved closer to spoken language, and as it is impossible in speech to tell the difference between the normal and possessive forms of such words without an extra *s*, the usage has changed to that given above. At times, this can produce a rather ugly sound. Try saying 'Vaughan Williams's *Symphony in F minor*', for example. This may be avoided by changing the order of the sentence, to give 'the *Symphony in F minor* by Vaughan Williams'.

(c) For possessive forms of plurals, you add the apostrophe and no *s*, as in the following:

The managers' suite was empty because they had all gone to the executives' dining-room.

For the possessive of a plural form which does not end in *s* – such as 'women', 'men' and 'children' – you just add '*s*. For example:

Men's shirts, women's dresses and children's toys are all for sale on the first floor.

(d) If you need to show that something belongs to two people, add *'s* to the second name only, as in:

> We are all going to Mike and Jane's house, which is very near Johnson and Bailey's factory.

These four occasions are the only ones when when you should put an apostrophe before the final *s*. Many people will put one in before almost any *s*, where there is no need to do so. Errors of this sort will show a lack of accuracy in your work and give a very poor impression.

Apostrophes of omission   Apostrophes are also used where letters have been left out of a word, or where two words have been *contracted* – run together – in forms like 'I'm', 'you're' and 'we're' for 'I am', 'you are' and 'we are'. This also applies to negative forms such as 'couldn't', 'wouldn't', 'shouldn't and 'can't' for 'could not', 'would not', 'should not' and 'cannot'. Notice that 'cannot' is written as one word.

In business writing, there is a simple solution to problems with apostrophes of omission: write the expressions in full. This is appropriate because business correspondence is generally formal, whereas the use of such expressions suggests a more relaxed and informal relationship with a reader.

Some business writing does allow the use of contractions like 'I'm' and 'we're', as they can make the writing seem more friendly. So if you are writing to someone you have had dealings with for some time and you know each other well, it would be acceptable to write: 'I'm delighted to hear that all's well with our order.' This is largely a matter of 'house style'. If you are unsure about the use of contractions in your organization, it is best not to use them but to write the expression in full.

Common errors   The groups of words listed below demand special attention, as they are often used incorrectly.

its	'belonging to it'. Note that, although the word indicates ownership, it does not have an apsotrophe.
it's	contraction of 'it is'. The *i* has been left out, hence the apostrophe of omission.

An example will help to clarify these two usages: the first is the contraction, the second the possessive pronoun:

> The chairman said, 'It's hard to persuade the Ministry to change its policy.'

whose	the possessive form of 'who', used in phrases like 'the man whose car had been stolen'.
who's	contraction of 'who is' or 'who has', as in 'Who's stolen my car?'

your	'belonging to you', as in 'Thank you for your letter.'
you're	contraction of 'you are', as in 'You're an asset to the team.'
yours	a possessive pronoun, used about something belonging to you: 'this office is yours', for example.
their	'belonging to them', as in 'their offices'.
there	a place or direction, as in 'over there'.
they're	contraction of 'they are', as in 'They're friends of mine.'
theirs	a possessive pronoun, used about something belonging to them: 'The decision was theirs.'
there's	contraction of 'there is': 'There's a draught in this room.'

These are only some of the pairs or groups of words which sound the same but are spelt differently and about which you need to be careful when writing. It will help if you remember these two points.

● Words showing possession end in *'s*, except possessive pronouns like 'yours', 'theirs' and 'its' meaning 'something belonging to it', which have no apostrophe.
● Contractions are often too informal for business writing.

5.2.8 *Words easily confused*
These pairs or small groups of words sound the same but have different meanings. Make sure that you know which is which.

accept	'to receive' or 'to agree with'
except	'apart from'

I am prepared to accept all the items you have sent, except the large box of envelopes, which I did not order.

advice	a suggestion about future action or conduct
advise	the verb meaning 'to give advice'

I advise you most strongly not to accept advice from any unqualified people.

Note: this pair follows a general rule for words that can be spelt with a *c* or an *s*. The *-ce* ending denotes a noun and the *-se* ending a verb. 'Practice' and 'practise' are another example.

affect	the verb meaning 'to produce a change or result on something or someone'
effect	a noun naming the result or change
effect	a verb meaning 'to put into practice'

The move to the new offices will not affect our accounts staff, though the effects on secretarial staff will be considerable. I propose to effect the change as soon as possible.

bought   the past participle of the verb 'to buy'
brought   the past participle of the verb 'to bring'

The company has bought many new computers, which will be brought into service very soon.

chose   the past participle of the verb 'to choose'
choose   the verb meaning 'to select'

The employees were asked to choose between staying at the Manchester office and moving to Norwich, and almost all chose to stay.

dependant   a noun naming someone who depends on someone else for support
dependent   an adjective describing someone who or something which depends on something else

I have one child who is still a dependant and two dependent aunts.

device   a mechanism or a machine
devise   the verb meaning 'to work out or invent'

After much thought, the research staff managed to devise a solution, in the form of a device which produced the goods electronically. (See note on 'advice' and 'advise' above.)

here   'at this place'
hear   the verb meaning 'to be aware of aurally'

Although the machine was in operation here all the time, it was so quiet that no one could hear it.

knot   a fastening tied in string or rope
not   a denial or negative

Parcels should not be posted unless they are tied in string with a secure knot.

know   the verb meaning 'to be certain of something'
no   the opposite of 'yes'
now   at this moment

Even if a better offer were made, I know that the directors would say 'no' to it because of the economy measures now in force.

lead   the verb meaning 'to go first' (pronounced 'leed')
led   the past participle of the verb 'to lead'
lead   a dense metal (pronounced 'led')

Mr Jones will lead the sales team previously led by Ms King to market our new lead roofing material.

lose   the verb meaning 'to mislay, or fail to win'
loose   the opposite of 'tight' or 'secure'

It would be unfortunate if we were to lose the contract because vital components on the device became loose.

of   belonging to
off   the opposite of 'on'

The accident was caused by a box of paper falling off a filing cabinet.

Note: in writing, you should never use the expression 'off of'.

quiet   silent or peaceful
quite   fairly or moderately

I am quite sure that most people work better in conditions of quiet.

stationary   not moving
stationery   paper, envelopes and writing materials

All paper should be collected from the stationery cupboard in the basement, so use the lift but make sure it is stationary before attempting to open the doors.

there   the opposite of 'here'. Also used in 'there is' and 'there are'.
their   belonging to them

Employees working in the outer office should make sure that their belongings are not left there overnight.

to   towards or in the direction of. Also used to form the infinitive form of a verb (see section 4.2.1)
too   either 'as well' or 'excessively'
two   the number which comes after one

No more than two people are to go to Ireland. If anyone else would like to go too, special arrangements will have to be made, but it may be too late to find a hotel.

wear   the verb meaning 'to put on clothes', or 'to decay with time and use'
where   an indication of place

Visitors must report to the security office where they will be given protective clothing to wear.

weather   the climate
whether   which of two; used in sentences to introduce indirect questions or provide an alternative

Whether or not the building is completed on time depends on the weather.

5.2.9 *Some awkward spellings*

There are some words which are not covered by the rules or categories discussed so far, and which call for special care. The following list points out the ways in which their spelling is not what you would expect.

absent	no *c* after the *s*
accommodation	a double *c* and a double *m*, but only one *d*
acquaint	note the *c* before the *q*
all right	two words, with a double *l* in the first
argument	no *e* after the *u*
arrangement	a double *r*, and an *e* after the *g*
because	*au* not *ua*
business	the *i* comes after the first *s*, not before it
college	*-ege* not-*age*, and no *d*
correspondence	a double *r*, and *-ence* at the end, not-*ance*
definite	*-ite* not *-ate* at the end
disappoint	one *s* and a double *p*
dying	not 'dieing' (Note: changing the colour of cloth is spelt 'dyeing'.)
eighth	an *h* before and after the *t*
environment	an *n* before the *m*
essential	a double *s*
exaggerate	a double *g*
excellent	a *c* after the *x*, and *-ent* not *-ant* at the end
exercise	no *c* after the *x*
extremely	one *e* before the *m* and one after it
faithfully	remember the *i*
February	remember the *r* after the *b*
fourth	remember the *u*
fulfil	one *l* after each vowel (Note: all words ending in *-ful* and *-fil* have only one *l* – 'careful', 'doleful' and so on – except 'full' and 'fill' themselves)
height	*-ght* not *-ghth*
independent	*-ent* not *-ant* at the end
immediately	a double *m*, and the *e* is before the *l* not after it
instalment	one *l*
maintenance	*en* in the middle not *ain*
necessary	one *c* and a double *s*
noticeable	remember the *e* after the *c*
occasional	a double *c* and one *s*
occur	a double *c* and one *r*

occurrence	a double *c* and a double *r*, and *-ence* at the end
omit	one *m* and one *t*
omitted	one *m* and a double *t*
possession	two groups of double *s*
preceding	one *e* after the *c*, no *e* after the *d*
procedure	one *e* after the *c*
professional	one *f* and a double *s*
receipt	*ei* not *ie*
recommend	one *c* and a double *m*
representative	one *p*
safety	the *e* comes after the *f*, not after the *t*
secretary	remember the first *r*
separate	an *a* after the *p*, not an *e*
similar	an *a* not an *e* before the *r*
sincerely	remember the second *e*
strength	*-gth* not *-ght*
studying	remember the *y*
successfully	double *c*, double *s* and double *l*
twelfth	remember the *f*
writing	one *t* only
valuable	remember the *a*

5.3 Some points about punctuation

As we saw at the beginning of this unit, incorrect punctuation can completely change the meaning of a sentence. For this reason, and because poor punctuation presents a bad image to your reader, accurate punctuation is essential in business communication. Even if you think that you have a sound knowledge of all the main marks of punctuation and their uses, you should read the next few pages as they include some of the more common errors and give advice on how they can be avoided.

5.3.1 The full stop

Everyone knows that a full stop marks the end of a sentence. Yet, since many people have only a vague idea of what a sentence is, the full stop is often not used where it should be. Section 4.2.1 has established that a sentence is a self-contained idea with a finite verb and a subject. At the end of each such group of words, a full stop should appear. A very common error is to use a comma in its place, to produce long, rambling and loose constructions which the reader has to look at several times before the meaning becomes clear. The following is an example of the incorrect use of the comma:

> I am very grateful to you for working late on Tuesday night, this has helped to clear the backlog of typing.

In this example, the comma could be replaced by a semi-colon (see section 5.3.3). Alternatively, the conjunctions 'as' or 'because' could be inserted (see section 4.2.5). Far simpler than either of these, however, would be the use of a full stop. Both parts of the expression are complete sentences, each with a finite verb – 'I am' in the first and 'this has' in the second. Consequently, a full stop would be a perfectly acceptable form of punctuation between the two.

The tendency towards avoiding the full stop has perhaps been encouraged by the feeling that longer sentences sound more impressive than shorter ones. This is not true. Variation of sentence length is an important way of preventing monotony in writing and, even were the use of longer sentences always preferable, there would be no sense in creating them simply through incorrect punctuation.

If you are unsure whether to use a comma or a full stop, ask yourself whether or not there is a finite verb in both of the sections to be joined. If there is, you should use a full stop, as there are two sentences involved. Sometimes, however, a colon may be used (see section 5.3.4).

We have seen that the main use of the full stop is to mark a pause at the end of a complete sentence. Other uses are as follows:

- after a single initial as in P.J. Smith.
- after each initial in the abbreviated form of a name or title of an organization, such as the B.B.C. (the British Broadcasting Corporation) or the R.S.A. (the Royal Society of Arts). There is, however, a move away from this convention towards 'open' punctuation in which the initials are presented unspaced – for example, BBC and RSA. Which style you use will depend very much on the practice followed by the company you work for.
- after the more common abbreviations such as i.e., e.g. and etc. – standing respectively for 'that is', 'for example' and 'and others'. Be careful not to over-use these terms in business writing as they may suggest laziness, especially when etc. is used instead of a more complete list of points or examples.

There are two occasions when you may feel tempted to use a full stop but should not. These are:

- after contractions – shortened versions of words, formed from the first and last letter of the word and sometimes other letters as well. Examples include Mr (mister), Dr (doctor) and Ltd (limited).
- after ordinal numbers such as 4th and 12th.

5.3.2 The comma

Commas are used to mark pauses, but only when a pause is needed to clarify the grammatical structure or the meaning of a sentence.

The four main occasions when you are likely to use a comma are listed below. Uses other than these are unnecessary, and will only confuse and irritate your reader.

To separate items in a list   If a list of items is given, it is usual to separate each one from its neighbour by a comma, like this:

The library contained books, periodicals, newspapers, maps and some important historical documents.

Notice that the last item is introduced by the conjunction 'and', and for this reason it need not be preceded by a comma. Remember, too, that where longer items or groups of items are listed you should use a semi-colon, not a comma (see section 5.3.3).

Around words or phrases in apposition   These are words which describe the subject of the sentence, or which act as an alternative subject, and are added after the main subject. They can also be used in the same way with the object of a sentence. Although they add to the meaning of a sentence, they could be left out without damaging its sense, and so are placed between commas. Here is an example:

The training college, a Victorian Gothic building, stood opposite the railway station.

Around expressions in parenthesis   These are words and phrases which show the relationship between a sentence and the one before it – adverbs such as 'however' and 'meanwhile' and phrases such as 'on the other hand', for example. They are used as follows:

This is not always the case, however.
Meanwhile, I suggest that you contact the suppliers.
Staff holidays, on the other hand, are agreed by management and unions working together.

Notice that, where the phrase in apposition appears in the middle of the sentence, a comma is required both before and after it. A common error is to use only one comma.

The term 'in parenthesis' should not be confused with 'in parentheses', which means 'in brackets' (see section 5.3.10).

To separate adverbial phrases or clauses from a main clause   In this situation, the comma is inserted to make the meaning clear to the reader. The previous sentence illustrates this principle, 'in this situation' being an adverbial phrase and the remainder of the sentence forming the main clause (see section 4.2.6). The same practice is followed for an adverbial clause, as this example illustrates:

When the chairman had declared the meeting open, the secretary read the minutes of the last meeting.

In a sentence containing an adjectival clause, commas are necessary only if the clause is *non-defining* (see section 4.2.6).

Some organizations, notably those in the legal profession, have their own rules about the use of commas and other forms of punctuation, and you should find out if there are any you need to know when you start work. If you think of the comma as a short pause that separates different parts of a sentence and helps to clarify your expression, you should avoid the more obvious, irritating and ambiguous abuses of this overworked punctuation mark.

5.3.3 The semi-colon
This mark is used to join two clauses which might otherwise be joined by a conjunction – usually 'because'. This example illustrates its usefulness:

> Further protest was pointless; the decision had already been taken.

The semi-colon can also be used to separate long and complex items in a list, particularly where each item is described by a clause which includes its own commas to clarify its meaning. For example:

> The material contained several volumes of manuscript diaries, some of which had many pages missing; a set of notebooks which, despite being bound in paper, seemed to be complete; and a collection of sketches, some mounted but mostly on separate sheets torn from an artist's watercolour pad.

The use of semi-colons in this context makes clearer to the reader the break between each item, and they are thus an important tool for the writer.

5.3.4 The colon
Like the semi-colon, this is used to link two clauses, each of which has a subject and a main verb. The difference between the colon and the semi-colon lies in the relationship between the clauses which they join: the semi-colon joins one clause to another of similar meaning or two clauses in the relation of cause to effect, whereas the colon joins two clauses of opposite meaning. It may help to think that a semi-colon usually equals 'because', whereas a colon equals 'but'. Unfortunately this is not a hard and fast rule, but it is a useful rule-of-thumb.

> Yesterday's office depended on people: today's depends on electronics.

The other principle use of the colon is to introduce a quotation or list of items. This usage is demonstrated throughout Units 4 and 5, where a colon precedes the quoting of an example.

5.3.5 Inverted commas
Inverted commas have two main uses:

● to indicate speech;
● to indicate a quotation.

In business writing, you will rarely have occasion to use them for the former, but there will be many occasions when you will wish to quote material in a report or other document. You might, for example, wish to quote the exact words of a motion or an amendment in the minutes of a committee meeting (see section 16.4); to give the exact words of a contract of agreement in a letter; or to make a brief quotation from an article or speech in an abstract (see section 9.4). Inverted commas can be either single – ' – or double – '' –. Whichever you use, you should be consistent, always closing your quotation with the same kind of inverted commas with which you opened it. Most publishers and business users today use single inverted commas, reverting to double ones for quotations within quotations, but you should check with your employer to see if there is a particular house style.

When you quote a short phrase in inverted commas, remember that the punctuation of the sentence in which the quotation appears should come outside the inverted commas and not within them.

Here are some examples of the use of inverted commas in business writing:

The 1987 report said that the orbital road was 'exceptionally congested' during the rush hour.

Dr Jones thanked the committee for 'the outstanding generosity' with which it had welcomed her to Stockholm.

Although the statement referred to 'outrageous inaccuracies in reporting', it did not give evidence of specific instances.

There is another use of inverted commas which, while it has no official basis in the grammar of the language, is nevertheless quite common. This is the use of the marks to suggest that something is not quite what it seems. Look at this sentence, for example:

Mr Seddon, an 'expert' on road safety, said that there was no danger at the junction of High Street and Elizabeth Terrace; yet only three weeks later there was a fatal accident there.

Here, the use of inverted commas around 'expert' suggests that Mr Seddon is very far from being an expert, as the rest of the sentence confirms. This use of inverted commas can be very effective in business writing, but only if used sparingly. If it is used too often, it will lose its effectiveness.

5.3.6 *The question mark*
This is used to denote a direct question – one in which the usual order of verb and subject is reversed: 'have they' instead of 'they have', for example. The distinction is shown in these examples:

When will you finish the report? (Direct)
I should like to know when you will finish the report. (Indirect)

The most important point to remember is that a question mark fulfils the same role as a full stop. It finishes a sentence; it cannot be used in the middle of a sentence; it should not have any other punctuation after it; and where it is followed by another sentence this should begin with a capital letter.

Direct questions do not appear often in business writing. When they are used, however, they can be most effective. Their effect depends very much on their being followed by a new sentence, as this sets them apart and gives them greater emphasis. For example, compare these two ways of closing a business letter:

Please let me know when I can expect the final manuscript, as I need to confirm arrangements with the printer very soon.

When can I expect the final manuscript? I need to confirm arrangements with the printer very soon.

The second version is likely to have more impact, because the break after the direct question makes it seem more forceful.

5.3.7 The exclamation mark
This is a useful way of adding force to something in an informal or personal letter. Exclamation marks play a less prominent role in business writing, however, since the aim here is to be clear and factual and to avoid dramatic effects. For example, you might write enthusiastically to a friend: 'What a party!', but writing to a business associate about a party to launch a new product, you would probably say: 'The party was a great success.'

Exclamation marks are also used to emphasize a joke, or to suggest the writer's response to the idea under discussion, like this:

I do not think we will have much trouble in getting the union to agree to extra paid holiday!

You should never use more than one exclamation mark after a word, as this looks ridiculous and can lessen the impact. Remember: if you are in any doubt as to whether or not you should use an exclamation mark, it is better to omit it.

5.3.8 The hyphen
A hyphen is a short dash which joins two words. It is most commonly used in compound words such as 'sewing-machine', 'racing-yacht' and so on (see section 4.3.4), where it is a fixed part of the spelling of the word. A hyphen is also required when two words form a compound adjective before a noun; if the compound comes after the noun, it does not need a hyphen. Compare these two sentences.

Her performance was first class.
She gave a first-class performance.

The other main use of a hyphen is in word-breaks – when a word is broken at the end of a line through shortage of space and the remainder is written on the next line. Be careful that the word is broken between syllables – the separate units of sound which make up longer words ('manager', for example, has three syllables: *man, a* and *ger*). You should try to get enough of the word on the first line to allow the reader to see what is intended, but you should never take over only one or two letters. Look at the following examples:

(Wrong)   I am hoping to pass all my examinatio-
           ns next June.
(Right)   I am hoping to pass all my exam-
           inations next June.
(Wrong)   We must not miss our impo-
           rtant deadline.
(Right)   We must not miss our import-
           ant deadline.

In some words there will be an obvious dividing point – for example in words that end in -*ing* or -*ment* – but for others always try to go by what makes the best sense and will be of most help to the reader. Note that only one hyphen should be used, and that it should appear at the end of a line, not at the start of the following line.

5.3.9 The dash

The dash is used to show the addition of further information or detail in the middle or at the end of a sentence. This is an informal way of writing, which suggests that someone is speaking and has broken off from a point to illustrate it or to add further clarification. In this way, the dash can be very useful in making a piece of writing sound spontaneous. Its use will depend very much on your relationship with the reader but can be very effective. For example:

> Another major point – as far as I could see the only one worth taking seriously – was that staff were beginning to have doubts in the company's management.

This suggests that the reader is being taken into the writer's confidence, the statement of opinion between the dashes giving the idea of a confidential aside in a conversation. This is another useful tool of communication as valuable for the impression it makes as for the information it helps to convey.

5.3.10 Brackets

Brackets or parentheses are used to mark off an item of information which is of secondary importance to the remainder of the text. In business writing, brackets should be used rarely, since the reader will almost automatically assume that the material contained within the brackets is of little value. If you have to add information to a sentence, it is generally preferable to use dashes or commas to mark it off (see sections 5.3.9 and 5.3.2).

Compare the impact of these three sentences:

> I then returned the tyres, which were now unsafe, to the garage where I had bought them.

> I then returned the tyres – which were now unsafe – to the garage where I had bought them.

> I then returned the tyres (which were now unsafe) to the garage where I had bought them.

The first version makes the fact that the tyres were unsafe appear just as important as the rest of the sentence; the second makes it appear if anything more important, by the added emphasis provided by the use of dashes. The third, however, passes over the information about the lack of safety as if it were of little importance.

Brackets are best used in business communication only when making cross-references to other parts of a document, or including information which is genuinely of a secondary or supplementary nature.

5.3.11   Capital letters

Capital letters are used to begin the first word of a sentence and also within a sentence to identify proper nouns such as the names of people, places, rivers, days and months (see section 4.2.2). Titles of books, plays and other works of art also take capital letters. The seasons of the year are an exception, and always take the lower case.

Capital letters should be used sparingly and only to name the particular, never the general.

> Peter Smith is Managing Director of Brownco Ltd.
> Ms Patel is a manager for a paint manufacturing company.
> You should contact the Department of Education and Science on Monday.
> I will approach the appropriate government department in the autumn.

5.4   Conclusion

While the points made in this section attempt to reflect accurate usage of the English language, they should be read with certain important limitations firmly in mind. Remember that individual organizations have their own rules and procedures about the use of language. A clear example is the absence of most forms of punctuation – except some full stops – in many legal documents. When you start work or change jobs, always make a point of finding out about the accepted practice of that organization, asking for a 'style sheet' or house-style manual if one exists.

Remember, too, that language is constantly changing: punctuation, spelling, and even the meaning of words may alter with time. For example, scholars who edit Shakespeare have to update the punctuation of earlier editions so that the contemporary reader can gain a proper grasp of the meaning and movement of the speeches and their significance to the action. Words change their spelling, too. Well into the present century, 'today' was spelt with a hyphen – 'to-day'. Other words are still changing: 'week-end' can exist as two words linked by a hyphen or as a single word, 'weekend'; the past participle of 'benefit' may be spelt with one or two *t*s, the plural of 'syllabus' with *-es* or *i*.

Lexicographers – dictionary compilers – say that there is no such thing as 'correct' language, but only language which properly expresses the ideas of its users. This is a long-term view, of course, which cannot be used to justify poor spelling and inaccurate punctuation. It does, however, serve to warn us all against being too rigid in resisting change in language.

Try not to persist, then, in using 'correct' expressions and meanings when they have become outdated: you risk being misunderstood or, at best, sounding comically ridiculous. Instead, be aware that language is changing all the time, and make sure that your forms of expression are up to date without following the vagaries of linguistic fashion so closely that only the privileged few are able to understand you. Be clear, be accurate, and be concise, always choosing the words which make your point in the most direct way, and you will be able to communicate effectively in whatever situation confronts you.

Oral communication

6.1 Oral communication in business

Oral communication is the exchange of ideas or information by spoken word. In a business setting, it can take place between two people, or within groups of any size, at every level of every kind of organization. So common is it that there is a serious danger that it will be taken for granted and not seen as an integral part of the functioning of the organization, demanding a number of fairly complicated skills. Formal meetings of committees and boards of directors are planned with much care and forethought, but the spoken exchanges which take place throughout the working day, and which have just as much to do with the proper running of an organization, are often carried out with no planning and little concern for their overall effectiveness.

If a trainee gives a message to a manager, for example, an exchange of information takes place orally. Similarly, a worker requesting an item from the stores section is communicating orally. If a supervisor or manager tells a group of employees what their main task will be for the next week, oral communication is once again being used, and again if a departmental manager talks to his or her assistant about a new order or a new procedure.

There are other, more formal kinds of oral communication. Formal interviews of various types have an important role in most organizations; so, too, do lectures and presentations. Meetings are also of central importance, whether they be formal committee meetings or less rigidly structured encounters – between people working together on a new project, say. The telephone is another valuable communication tool in business, though special care is needed when using it as there are none of the usual non-verbal signs to rely on. The use of the telephone and the nature of meetings are discussed later, in Units 7 and 16 respectively, but many of the fundamental points about oral communication are the same in these settings as in the exchanges between smaller groups which are dealt with later in this unit.

6.2 Oral communication in practice

Because we communicate orally with each other almost all the time, often in a relaxed, social context with friends and relatives, we perhaps fail to realize just how complicated the process is. We may summarize it as follows.

Idea First, we have to work out exactly what we have to communicate – or indeed whether we need to communicate anything at all. When we talk to friends on the way to a football match or at a tea-break, for example, we often say things which are not really necessary, but which show that we are keeping up a friendly contact. Communication for a purpose is rather different. The first rule of oral communication in business is therefore to know what information you have to communicate, or what questions you wish to ask.

Outcome You should always have a clear idea of what you want an exchange to achieve. It may be simply to tell a person not to use a particular room because the roof leaks; it may be something more complicated like gaining the support of supervisors for a new production method. Every oral exchange in business should rest on a firm concept of its intended outcome.

Expression Once you have an idea of what to say and what you want to achieve by it, you have to find the best words to express it. This is much more easily said than done, especially in a difficult or sensitive situation. Planning and forethought are essential. Think about all the factors mentioned in section 4.10 with regard to matching your language to your reader. Try to apply these points here. Put yourself in the listener's place: how would *you* react to different kinds of expression? This simple exercise will greatly improve the way you express yourself orally.

Feedback Whenever you talk to someone or to a group of people, observe their reactions. These are known as *feedback* (see section 3.2). A change of expression, a sudden gesture, a sharp intake of breath or some other element of non-verbal communication (see section 6.3) will tell you just as much about someone's feelings as anything he or she might say. It might even tell you more, as people generally try to control their feelings when they speak, but have less control over their facial expressions or body movements.

Reply After you have made a point, your listener will usually respond to it. In doing so, he or she will repeat all the stages listed above, defining the idea to be conveyed, thinking about the desired outcome, putting the idea into the most suitable form of expression and watching your reaction.

From this, it will be clear that the process of oral communication needs care, both in planning before it takes place and in keeping alert during the exchange. As well as being aware of the stages of the process, there are two further points to consider: the personalities of those involved, and the role of the listener.

6.2.1 Personality

One of the great advantages of oral communication is that it brings people together on a personal level. If the boss chats with an employee about gardening or
decorating the spare room when the two meet by chance, a relationship of
genuine trust is more likely to develop. Yet the human aspect also has its drawbacks. Try as we might, there are some people with whom we just cannot get
along. Occasionally there will be people at work who seem to do the reverse of
what we think is right, and with whom it is impossible to see eye to eye.

That such relationships exist is inevitable, but this does not mean that we can
do nothing to improve them. A vital rule of oral communication is to reject
feelings of personal dislike while you are talking to someone on a business
matter. Try to see things from the other person's point of view, and to understand why he or she acts in a way you find difficult to accept. If this fails, try seeing the encounter as a sort of formal role-play, almost as if the two of you are
playing parts on stage. This will prevent your becoming personally involved,
and stop feelings of anger and frustration breaking through. It will not be easy,
but it may be essential if you are to continue a satisfactory working relationship
which, after all, will help both of you as people as well as the organization which
employs you.

6.2.2 Listening skills

With so much attention being given to saying things in the right language, it is
easy to forget that listening is an equally important skill. Do not fall into the
trap of thinking only about what you have to say. When the other person is talking, listen: do not think about what you will say in reply, but really concentrate
on the ideas being put forward.

There are various ways in which you can do this. Look at the person who is
speaking, as this will show that you are concentrating on what is being said.
Gazing out of the window, flicking through your diary, looking at your watch
or reading a letter will suggest that you are not listening. Give your full attention
to the speaker, as anything less will be discourteous and reduce the efficiency of
the communication. It is also important to encourage the speaker. Nod, smile,
and say 'Yes' or 'I see' at suitable points, to show that you are following what he
or she is saying. Try, too, to draw out ideas: asking 'What do you think?' will
make the speaker feel that you value the contribution he or she can make, and
encourage a fuller exchange.

The importance of listening is discussed again in Unit 16, where the value of
listening to others in meetings and helping them to express their ideas is made
clear. This is something which cannot be stressed too much. People with ideas
are far more eager to talk than to listen, and you must always strive to give your
full attention to what other people say, to make the most of any exchange.

6.3 Non-verbal communication

In the preceding sections, we have referred to the way in which people's
behaviour – such as looking at the speaker or nodding and smiling – can convey

messages just as effectively as anything they might say. Actions of this sort – which may be made consciously or subconsciously – are known as 'non-verbal communication' or 'body language' and are an important part of the communication process.

The main kinds of non-verbal communication are described below.

6.3.1 Circumstances

The situation in which an exchange takes place has a lot to do with the impression you convey, and thus the overall message which the other person receives. Circumstances include factors such as the amount of preparation you have done for the discussion; whether you arrive punctually; and whether the meeting proceeds without distractions. If you arrive late for an interview, have not read the relevant letters or papers, and have three telephone calls in the first ten minutes, then the person you are talking to will receive a very clear message: that you have little interest in what you are meant to be discussing.

Whenever you arrange an interview or a meeting, then, make sure that the circumstances are such that there will be no interruptions; that you arrive on time; and that you have done the necessary preparation.

6.3.2 Arrangement of the room

The physical layout of a room can have a great influence on the communication which takes place there. If, for example, a manager sits behind her desk throughout a talk with an employee, the difference in rank between them will be emphasized. If, on the other hand, the two sit at a table, or in easy chairs in a different part of the office, an air of equality will be immediately created.

This is also true of larger meetings. One person standing in front of others who sit in neat rows will suggest a very formal lecture: a group sitting around a circular table, with no clear 'head' or centre of authority, will suggest people getting together to share their ideas in an atmosphere of equality.

Another essential point is that all participants should be able to see one another. Someone hidden behind a pillar or in a dark corner will feel cut off, and will contribute little to the meeting. Eye contact should be possible for everyone who takes part – that is, everyone should be able to see one another's eyes. You will have noticed that good teachers and lecturers make sure that they can see everyone and that everyone can see them. Otherwise, communication will be very limited and ineffective.

6.3.3 Dress and appearance

How you dress makes an important statement, not only about what you think of yourself but also about how you regard the person or people you are talking to. Smart, clean clothes will convey efficiency and suggest that you have taken the trouble to dress formally, demonstrating courtesy and consideration. Personal considerations are clearly important here, and many people wear clothes which reflect their personality. But it is up to you to decide whether having your hair dyed purple, green and orange can compensate for the knowledge that other people will probably pay more attention to your appearance than to what you have to say.

6.3.4 Body direction

The best-known aspect of non-verbal communication, this concerns the ways in which the body may convey signals about a person's feelings. Body direction can be divided into four areas: orientation, posture, proximity and contact.

Orientation   This is simply the direction in which the body is facing. Facing the person you are speaking to suggests involvement; speaking with your body turned away suggests restlessness or a lack of commitment.

Changes in orientation can convey significant changes of mood during a discussion. If someone turns and walks away from you it may suggest boredom, or the desire to conceal deep feeling. Conversely, if he or she turns and walks towards you it implies a greater involvement, or perhaps the need to make a direct appeal of some kind.

Posture   This refers to the position of the body. Someone sitting forward, looking intently at the speaker, is probably very interested in what is being said. Conversely, a person sitting well back in her chair, looking at the carpet, probably lacks interest or concentration. Other signs convey different messages. 'Closed' body postures – arms folded across the chest and shoulders hunched, for example – suggest a defensive or threatened attitude. 'Open' postures – such as leaning back with the hands crossed behind the head – suggest extreme confidence.

Once again, changes in posture suggest changes in mood. If someone pushes his chair back from a table it suggests disengagement – the idea that the discussion has broken up without success, or is simply at an end. A change from a closed to an open posture – in which someone removes her glasses, for instance, and leans forward over a table – will imply that something personal or confidential is about to be revealed.

Proximity Much can be understood from how close a person stands to another person. In business, a friendly relationship of mutual trust can be shown, for example, by walking round from behind your desk to meet a visitor on equal terms. When you deal with people at work, you should try to become familiar with their feelings about proximity. Some welcome close, informal seating arrangements: others feel threatened by people who approach them too closely, and will respond nervously when they are treated in this way.

Contact Physical contact will be minimal during a business encounter, but it plays an important part nonetheless. A firm, welcoming handshake can establish goodwill most effectively at the start of an interview, and can also be used to signal its formal conclusion. Some people will respond to a friendly pat on the arm or slap on the back: others will find it intrusive or offensive, even if it is intended to establish trust and friendship. People of different races will respond differently – some will use touch as a sign of goodwill, whereas other will feel threatened or offended by any such contact. Once more, you should get to know your colleagues as individuals and treat each in an appropriate manner.

6.3.5 Movement and gesture

People's body movements can convey a great deal about their mood. If they fidget with their hands, frequently cross and uncross their legs, tap their feet or drum on the table with their fingers, it is a sure sign that they are nervous or anxious about something. Try to recognize such signs and deal with the person sympathetically in what you say and in the non-verbal signals you yourself give out.

Some movements can be very distracting. Scratching your head, stroking your beard (real or imaginary) or cleaning your spectacles can interrupt the speaker's flow, so try very hard to avoid such movements.

Gestures which reinforce points made in a speech or statement are much more constructive. They must be clear and unambiguous, however, and not too forceful. Waving arms and banging fists are fine on a political platform, but out of place in an office.

6.3.6 Head movements

If movements of the body can convey signs about someone's feelings, movements of the head can make those feelings even clearer. Nodding and shaking are perhaps the most basic forms of human communication, nodding suggesting agreement or understanding, and shaking conveying disagreement or disapproval. Shaking the head can also convey puzzlement or disbelief, especially if accompanied by a frown.

Both are important ways of conveying reactions quickly, and are especially useful as a means of encouraging a speaker. Smiling and nodding when someone is explaining something will let him or her know that you understand what is being said. These are therefore valuable signals when communicating.

6.3.7 Facial expressions

Like nodding and shaking the head, facial expressions are clear indicators of feeling. A smile suggests amusement, agreement, or at least good humour; a frown, concentration or displeasure; a vacant, distant expression, boredom or frustration. Visual signals are often much stronger than verbal ones, so you should always try to match your own facial expression to what you are trying to say, as the listener will otherwise be faced with conflicting messages. Similarly, take account of your listener's expression when he or she is replying to you, as well as what is being said verbally. Only in this way will you read others' messages with any degree of accuracy.

6.3.8 Eye contact

The importance of eye contact has been discussed in section 6.3.2. Looking someone directly in the eye suggests openness, whereas looking away gives an impression of dishonesty or shiftiness. If you have to give a formal lecture, however, you should make sure that you let your eyes roam regularly and rapidly around the room rather than fixing your gaze on one or two people. This will ensure that everyone feels involved in the proceedings (see section 6.5).

6.3.9 Voice

Tone and volume   The tone of someone's voice can convey a great deal about how he or she feels. Someone who speaks calmly and distinctly at a reasonable pace and volume will convey an impression of control and assurance. Someone who speaks very quickly, however, with variations in pitch and volume, will appear nervous and lacking in self-control.

One situation in which your tone of voice and general manner are particularly important is in dealing with complaints. A customer or client may have a strong grievance against your company and, in order to deal with the matter swiftly and to everyone's satisfaction, you will need to be tactful and understanding. Here, the first few moments of the encounter are of crucial importance. Listen carefully and show interest and concern. If you can, apologize to the customer at an early stage – even by simply saying 'I'm so sorry that you've been given all this trouble.' An essential principle is to avoid treating the complaint as a personal matter. Establish calmly what the facts of the complaint are, and then make clear what you will do to give redress. Anger and abuse will achieve little in such a situation. Even if the customer or client begins by being angry, try to remain calm and steer him or her towards a calmer frame of mind so that something positive can be done to counter the problem.

In a formal meeting, you should always try to speak calmly and with assurance, making sure that your voice can be heard easily by everyone involved. Use variations of pitch and tone positively, to stress important words and to avoid speaking in a drone. At the same time, pay attention to others' speech. If someone gives the impression of being nervous, try to help by speaking calmly and reassuringly. Above all, try not to become angry or excited, as this will achieve very little other than making other people angry too. The intended outcome of the meeting is then unlikely to be achieved.

Paralinguistics This is a rather formal term used to describe the noises of agreement and encouragement which people make when listening to others – 'uh huh', 'hmm' and so on. Like nodding and smiling, these encourage a speaker by showing that you are listening and concentrating.

6.4 Oral communication checklist

Before going on to look at some of the business situations in which oral communication takes place, it will be useful to list the factors which must be considered when conducting an oral exchange.

1. Define the idea or information to be conveyed.
2 Define the desired outcome of the exchange.
3 Put the idea into language suitable to the listener.
4 Observe the listener's reaction.
5 Put aside personal considerations if they are likely to damage the exchange.
6 Listen carefully to the other person.
7 Use and watch for elements of non-verbal communication.

Following this list is not easy, but it is essential if the oral exchange is to be courteous and above all effective.

A word of reassurance: if the whole process seems complicated at the moment, remember that we all conduct oral exchanges all the time. After a while, you will find that the processes listed above become almost instinctive, and that you can carry out effective oral communication without having to run through the checklist every time you open your mouth.

6.5 Presentations

A presentation is the modern, business equivalent of the formal lecture, in which one person talks to a group of others about a topic of business interest – a new product, a change in company policy or an aspect of training, for example. Because it is formal, a presentation must be prepared and delivered with considerable care.

6.5.1 Preparing a presentation

First, you should prepare your subject very thoroughly. Consult reference books, specialist colleagues and other sources for information, and think about how you will treat it. Make rough notes to develop your ideas and, as the time approaches, prepare more complete notes which you can use when you speak. These should take the form of a set of headings rather than a full, written text – otherwise your presentation will turn into a reading and you will lose personal contact with the audience.

Another stage of preparation involves finding out about your audience. How many people will be there? What specialist knowledge will they have? How experienced are they in business in general, and in the area about which you will be speaking in particular? Some of these questions can be answered relatively easily by talking to the organizers of the function or conference at which you will be speaking. Others will need more investigation, or even some intelligent guesswork. Once you have a good idea of your audience, you will be better able to 'pitch' the presentation – set it at the right level so that you neither confuse nor patronize your audience.

You should also prepare any documents which you will need to circulate at the presentation. What these 'handouts' will consist of is a matter of personal preference. You might like to give a list of your main points in note form, provide references for further reading, or perhaps give a brief prose summary of what you are saying. Whatever their content, handouts must be well presented, typed, and copied legibly in good time for the presentation.

6.5.2 Audio-visual aids

A good presentation will often make use of audio-visual aids. Great care should be taken when preparing these: little is more frustrating than to sit in a darkened room while someone changes a series of slides so that they are projected the right way round on the screen. You might use any of the following:

Chalkboards   These are the oldest teaching aid. They are good in that they allow you to write down key words or demonstrate concepts quickly; poor in that they are often hard to see. If you use them, remember to write in large, legible handwriting and avoid talking to the board – turn round and face the audience when you have something to say.

Marker boards   These are like chalkboards but use felt marker pens on a plastic board. They are usually smaller than chalkboards, and are best used for presentations to small groups.

Flipcharts   A flipchart is like a very large notepad placed on an easel. A felt marker is used to write on one of the sheets, and when the sheet is full it can be flipped over to reveal a new one beneath. Flipcharts have the advantage that they can be prepared in advance and then revealed to the audience, but they can only be used successfully with groups no larger than 15 or 20.

Overhead projectors   These project an image from a transparent sheet on to a screen or wall. They have several advantages. Transparencies can be prepared in advance, often with overlays – sheets which can be added on top of a basic sheet to give further information or subsequent parts of a diagram. You can curtain off part of a list and reveal new points as you go through the presentation, to help people concentrate on what you are saying rather than on what you mean by the next point on your transparency. A pen laid on top of the transparency can act as a useful pointer to aid concentration on one topic or one part of a diagram.

Overhead projectors do have disadvantages, though. Small writing will be illegible; the motor for the cooling fan may be noisy; and unless the screen is properly aligned, the image may well be distorted. If there is a suitable blank wall in the room, it will often be better to project on to that than on to an insecure screen.

Slide projectors These are very good for high-definition reproduction of images – photographs of a new product, say, or of situations relevant to safety training. Do make sure, though, that the projector works properly and that you know how to insert the slides correctly.

Video recorders These are used increasingly in business training, to present specially made training or briefing programmes. They can be used as part of a longer presentation, but careful preparation is needed to ensure that the video recording and your presentation run smoothly together and that the former successfully illustrates the latter. Care must also be taken to ensure that the audience really concentrates, instead of regarding the programme as a television comedy show.

Audio equipment Sound systems are less likely to be used in a presentation as people find it harder to concentrate on sound than on images. A popular device, however, is a tape/slide presentation, where a recorded commentary accompanies a series of slides. Such presentations can be carefully prepared, which is an important advantage, but they often lack the immediacy and intimacy of a personally delivered lecture.

6.5.3 Giving a presentation

Talking to a large number of people is something that many of us find difficult, and so you need to do all you can to avoid or control nervousness. The best way to do this is by careful preparation. Make sure that you know exactly what you are going to say, and arrive early to check that the audio-visual equipment is working and that the handouts are available.

Starting There are various ways to start. You could begin with a joke; with a story that seems irrelevant but which turns out to be closely related to your topic; by asking a question which you will answer during the presentation; or by saying what you would like to cover in the time available. Whichever method you choose, make sure that you know exactly what to say. People's concentration will be high at the start, and you can win the audience over by beginning well – or lose them completely by starting badly.

Speaking If you are not used to speaking in public, try to get some practice beforehand. Speak loudly and firmly and take plenty of deep breaths. This will help you to overcome your nerves. If you know that you will be a little nervous, prepare an opening sentence and memorize it exactly, so that you get off to a firm, confident start.

Building Develop your ideas clearly and logically, following your notes carefully. At the same time, build a relationship with your audience. Look carefully around the room while you are speaking, making eye contact with people without staring at them. This makes them feel personally involved, and helps maintain their interest.

Scan all the time for feedback and be aware of people's concentration. If it lapses quickly, perhaps you are not speaking loud enough. Be aware, too, of variations in concentration. Most people can concentrate only for seven or eight minutes at a time – so try to vary the intensity of your delivery by introducing a summary of a main point before going on to the next one, or by making a joke or comic aside every so often.

When you have given several presentations, you will find that you can relax and respond to your audience freely, allowing yourself to modify your ideas and approach according to the situation. Experienced speakers usually find that a speech adapted to the audience in this way gets a better reception than something scrupulously planned. But when you are giving a presentation for the first time, it is best to prepare a plan and stick rigidly to it.

6.6 Interviews

An interview is generally regarded as the kind of meeting which occurs when someone applies for a job. This is certainly an important kind of interview which many people encounter during their working lives. There are, however, a large number of other kinds of exchange which can be categorized as interviews.

At the least formal end of the scale, there are the simple, short exchanges of information or ideas of the kind which are referred to in sections 2.2.1 and 2.2.2. If you follow the oral communication checklist in section 6.4, such encounters should present few problems. In general, you will need simply to decide whether such a brief exchange is the most effective way of conveying the information; to consider the disadvantages of having no written record; and to set aside a little time for its completion.

A more formal kind of interview is the meeting between two people or a small group to discuss routine matters or affairs of particular concern within their organization. Such meetings may take place between section heads and their deputies, or between employees at any level of the organization. Routine meetings of this kind may also take place between members of different organizations. A call from a representative with samples of new stock to show to chief buyers; a visit by contractors for printing work or for the manufacture of components; and a meeting between a wholesaler and a retailer – all may be described as interviews in the widest sense of the term.

Some of the more common forms of interview which occur within an organization are discussed in more detail below.

6.6.1 Selection interviews

These are the encounters most people associate with the term 'interview' – the kind which take place to decide whether or not somebody will be given a job. The selection process may include tours of the factory or premises and informal discussions with other members of staff, but the most important part will be the interview itself. Here, one or more senior staff, or in some cases a personnel officer, will ask questions about the candidate's background and experience, ambitions and general interests, and any other subjects which will help in assessing his or her suitability for the post in question. More information about how to conduct these interviews is given in section 6.7, and section 6.8 offers some advice on how to behave when you yourself are being interviewed for a job.

6.6.2 Promotion interviews

Promotion interviews take place when an employee has applied for a job of a higher grade within the organization. They are conducted in a manner similar to selection interviews, and aim to discover whether the applicant has the necessary qualifications and abilities to perform the job in question. They are generally conducted by a person or people in positions of some seniority within the organization, perhaps in a group so that the applicant's suitability can be assessed from a number of different viewpoints.

6.6.3 Appraisal interviews

Appraisal interviews are a way of assessing the work done, and progress made, by an individual employee. Sometimes called 'update interviews', they generally take place at yearly intervals, and are conducted by a department or section head. The interviewer reviews the worker's progress during the past year, and then moves on to future prospects such as the likelihood of promotion, staff training, and possible transfer to other work or to a different department. Appraisal interviews may also give an employee the chance to make suggestions about the organization's procedures.

Effectively conducted, appraisal interviews are a way in which an employee can be made to feel an active part of the organization. As such, they are a very important part of business communication.

6.6.4 Instructional interviews

Interviews can also be used to issue instructions about new procedures to key individuals within an organization. These meetings resemble other interviews in terms of their general conduct, but must be prepared with greater care to ensure that the procedures concerned are demonstrated and explained with perfect clarity. If this is not done, the interview will achieve very little, and may even be harmful by giving the employee a limited or incorrect notion of the new procedure.

6.6.5 Disciplinary interviews

Disciplinary interviews are the least pleasant kind of interview, as they are carried out by a senior employee when a worker has been accused of committing a breach of company regulations. Preparation must include a complete study of the facts, and the conduct of the interview must be based solely on these, to avoid considerations of personality clouding the judgement of the interviewer. Often the interviewee will be permitted to bring a friend or colleague to speak in his or her support and to witness the proceedings. Above all, it is important that the interview is conducted with complete impartiality, and that the decision reached is a just one.

6.6.6 Grievance interviews

Interviews of this kind take place when an employee feels that he or she has been wrongly treated by another member of the organization. Like disciplinary interviews, they should be conducted on a basis of sound, factual knowledge, the objective being to arrive at the truth so that the appropriate action may be taken. Most larger organizations have a clearly defined grievance procedure, which dictates how and with whom complaints should be registered. Again, the presence of a friend or colleague at the interview is often permitted. Such interviews demand considerable tact and understanding, and for this reason are usually undertaken by senior employees.

6.6.7 Decision-making interviews

Unlike the interviews considered so far, decision-making interviews are essentially small meetings between company members of equal status. The arrangement of furniture and general conduct of the encounter should reflect this equality (see section 6.3), ensuring that the views of all parties are expressed fully and considered in detail before a decision is reached. Preparation for such interviews will include gathering all the information necessary to gain a full picture of the facts, which will then form the basis of any decision.

6.7 Planning and conducting an interview

An interview of any kind – from a friendly encounter between equals to a formal grievance interview – should be organized according to certain principles if it is to be successful. An interview will be more effective if the organizer gives careful consideration to the following six areas:

(a) preparation;
(b) activation;
(c) attention;
(d) structure;
(e) summary;
(f) action.

6.7.1 Preparation

All interviews need careful preparation, which should cover four areas: considering the purpose of the interview; gathering the necessary information; planning a suitable setting for the interview; and thinking about the people who will be involved.

Purpose   The reason why the interview is being held must be clearly defined. The most concrete way of doing this is in terms of the intended outcome. Ask yourself what you wish to have achieved by the end of the meeting. This may be a detailed knowledge of the progress of a particular employee in the past year, or a firm decision about the development of a new product. The nature of the desired outcome will depend very much on the nature of the interview, but you should always have an idea of what you want to achieve, bearing in mind what is realistic within the time available.

Information   Before an interview you should obtain all the relevant information and familiarize yourself with it. Read any relevant correspondence, look at job application forms, consider files of documents or study reports. You may find that you wish to take notes from some of these sources (see Unit 9) to make sure that you have a brief yet complete outline of the data.

Once you have assimilated the information, you should note the main topics which you wish to discuss, or particular questions which you would like to ask during the meeting. You should keep all of this information with you so that, if necessary, you can consult it during the interview. It is best not to rely too heavily on your notes, though, as you will then be able to concentrate on discussing the ideas in hand and on listening to the other person's responses.

Setting   You should set a time and place for the meeting which are convenient for all concerned. A room of a suitable size, well lit and properly ventilated, should be made available, with the furniture arranged appropriately – either a desk and chairs or a table and chairs depending on the nature of the interview and the relationship you wish to establish with the interviewee (see section 6.3.2). Finally, make sure that you will not be interrupted during the meeting, by arranging for telephone calls to be taken elsewhere, putting an 'engaged' sign on the door or using other means to ensure that everyone can concentrate fully without distractions.

People   One part of your research before the interview may well concern the other person or people involved. This will be particularly true in the case of selection, appraisal, disciplinary or grievance interviews, but will also be of importance in other, less formal exchanges. It is always worthwhile thinking briefly about the person or people with whom you are meeting, and about their attitudes. You may find the suggestions in section 4.10 helpful in deciding on the right language to use. If you are meeting someone for the first time, finding out a little about him or her will also be a sign of courtesy, as it shows that you have taken the time and trouble to consider his or her feelings.

6.7.2 Activation

This is possibly the most important priority in conducting an interview. Remember that your task is to get your interviewee to talk freely and expansively, so that you can have a full exchange of ideas. Try to put the interviewee at ease, by adopting a friendly and reassuring manner from the start, so that he or she can relax, forget any feelings of unease and concentrate fully on the meeting. This is particularly important in selection and promotion interviews, but is also valid for meetings of other kinds.

One important technique is the use of 'open' questions. These are questions which give the respondent an opportunity to express his or her views and ideas in full, unlike their opposite – 'closed' questions – which suggest that 'yes' or 'no' are the only possible answers. For example, instead of saying 'Did you like my suggestions for a new centralized computer system?', you might say 'You've read my ideas about the centralized computer system: tell me what you think of them.' Open questions suggest a genuine interest in the other person's point of view, and so encourage full responses, especially when they are supported by careful and attentive listening.

6.7.3 Attention

As an interviewer, you should always give the other person your undivided attention. All the techniques of listening – such as smiling, nodding, looking at the speaker and using paralinguistics (see sections 6.2.2 and 6.3.9) – should be employed to make clear that you have a genuine interest in what is being said.

6.7.4 Structure

One aspect of your preparation will have been the drawing up of a list of points for discussion, rather like the formal agenda of a committee meeting (see section 16.4). Many meetings fail because of the lack of such planning, and drawing up an informal list of points – perhaps in consultation with the other person involved – will ensure that the interview comes close to achieving its desired outcome.

Once you have listed the points to be covered, you should make sure that the time available is used properly, so that minor points are dealt with quickly and there is time for a full discussion of more complicated matters. Making sure that a clock is clearly visible to both parties will help in this. So, too, will controlling the discussion so that irrelevant ideas are not introduced or – if introduced – that they are not discussed in depth.

6.7.5 Summary

It is important that both people involved have a clear idea of what has been decided during an interview. For this reason, it is good practice to stop after you have discussed each point on your list to summarize what you have decided. At the end of the interview, a summary of all these points will be useful.

It is also a good idea to write up these points while they are fresh in your mind, and then incorporate them in a letter or memo to the interviewee so that you both have a record of what was said and agreed. In more formal interviews, a secretary may be present just to take notes, but in most cases those who take part will do this themselves at suitable points in the discussion.

6.7.6 Action

An important part of your summary will concern the action which is to be taken as a result of the discussion and who is to take it. These points can then be incorporated into the letter or memo sent just after the meeting, to make clear who is to do what. This ensures that the decisions made are put into practice, and that the outcome desired is actually achieved.

6.7.7 Conclusion

Interviews or meetings between individuals, whatever their purpose, will be much more efficient if they follow these principles. Although they may appear most relevant to more formal interviews, they are also valuable for any encounter which is more than a casual exchange of ideas as a result of a chance meeting.

From a broader perspective, these principles form the basis for organizing clear and effective meetings of larger groups of people, and underlie the formal procedures used by committees as detailed in Unit 16. Used in conjunction with the principles of oral communication outlined earlier in this unit, they will meet their intended aim, and also ensure that oral exchanges of ideas are an efficient and enjoyable way of increasing mutual trust and respect between all concerned.

6.8 Responding in an interview

The preceding section has discussed the ways in which you should organize and conduct an interview with another individual. In the early stages of your career, however, you are more likely to take part in interviews as the partner who responds – be it to a senior employee within your own organization or to someone interviewing you for a new job. Responding in an interview of this kind is something which needs careful consideration, and once again there are a number of basic principles to be followed.

Follow the checklist   All the principles in the checklist in section 6.4 are just as appropriate for someone being interviewed as they are for the person directing the interview. In particular, you should note the following points:

● *Use the right forms of expression.*   As interviews – especially those for jobs – tend to be quite formal occasions, you should always try to use language suitable to the questioner. This will usually be rather more formal than the kind of language you would use with your own friends or relatives.
● *Listen carefully.*   As your fitness for a job will be evaluated on the basis of your answers, you need to listen very carefully to the questions. Think carefully, too, before answering. No one will mind if you pause briefly before speaking.

● *Send the right non-verbal signals.*   Dressing smartly will show that you take the interview seriously and that you respect those who are conducting it. An alert posture, showing interest without anxiety, will convey a sense of involvement and commitment. Try to speak clearly and calmly so that you can be heard by everyone in the room. Be pleasant and polite when answering questions and, although you should look mainly at the person who asked the question, glance quickly at any other people present to show that you are including them in what you are saying.

Prepare for the interview   If you are attending a job interview, find out something about the company before the interview by looking at its products or sales brochures. Try to work out what kind of questions you will be asked, and how you might answer them. You may well be asked why you want to work for that particular company, and it will be of little value to answer that you 'hadn't really thought about it' or that it was 'one job out of several' you have applied for. Watch the news the night before the interview in case you are asked about current events; think about your hobbies, recreational interests and other pursuits which might form the basis of questions. All this will help you to answer readily, which will give you confidence and convey a better impression of your general character and your suitability for the job.

Think before speaking   Try not to rush in with your ideas. Work out whether they are really valid, and try to think of a complete sentence which expresses them clearly and in language appropriate to the interviewer. This will create a far better impression than saying the first thing that comes into your head in careless, inappropriate language.

Be honest Although you should match your form of expression to the interviewer, you should not simply say what you think he or she expects or wants to hear. There is no point in being offensive, but remember that the aim of an interview is for the interviewer to get an idea of your views and personality. There is nothing to be gained by giving bland, non-committal answers to questions.

Try not to fidget Nervousness is often betrayed by body and head movements of various kinds (see section 6.3). Try to control your anxiety by sitting in a comfortable but fairly formal position, with your hands by your sides, not near your mouth where they may cause you to be misheard.

Remember that an interview is an exchange Above all, remember that the purpose of the interview is to get your views on a topic, or to gain a general idea of your suitability for a job. Giving a false impression will probably only create problems at a later stage and, while you should not stubbornly refuse to compromise your views, there is no point in presenting a false picture of yourself. The interviewer will want you to be relaxed and natural, so that the meeting is, as far as possible, one between equals. Do your best to behave naturally so that a full exchange of ideas can take place.

6.9 Conclusion

We spend a lot of time talking and it is easy to overlook the fact that oral communication is a complex undertaking and that even experienced communicators sometimes have difficulty in making themselves understood. You need to be tactful, patient and prepared to work at getting your message across. If you can make use of the principles outlined in this unit, which are fundamental to all oral exchanges, you will see that the effort involved pays off. Successful oral communication not only makes an organization more efficient but also makes it a more pleasant place in which to work. If people feel that they are part of an organization, they will have more interest, confidence and trust in it. But communication cannot come from one direction only: everyone needs to be aware of the principles involved.

6.10 Exercises

1 Explain the importance of listening in oral communication. What other points should you remember when communicating with someone orally?

2 What does the expression 'non-verbal communication' mean? What kind of NVC signals would you associate with:

   (a) confidence;
   (b) nervousness;
   (c) attentive listening;
   (d) making someone feel welcome?

3   In what circumstances would you expect to encounter the following:

    (a) an appraisal interview;
    (b) a selection interview;
    (c) an instructional interview;
    (d) a disciplinary interview;
    (e) a promotion interview;
    (f) a decision-making interview;
    (g) a grievance interview?

Choose *one* of these and explain how you would conduct such a meeting.

4   Explain, with examples, how non-verbal communication can influence one's view of another person, at first meeting.

(Southern Examining Group, GCSE specimen question)

5   Write an article to be published in a college magazine on how to behave when being interviewed for a job. It should be about 250 words long.

Using the telephone

7.1 Introduction

Using the telephone at home to talk with friends or to make social arrangements is usually straightforward. There is little need to prepare the call, or to think carefully while you are making it. Using the telephone for business purposes is rather different, for several reasons.

- You cannot use the same tone to talk to a business associate as you would to a friend. You need to talk in a business-like manner to show the listener – who may be an important client or customer – that your firm is efficient and properly run.
- Unlike a social call, a business call must be precise, since mistakes can be costly and damaging to your company's reputation.
- You need to be concise, since day-time calls are costly, especially when made over a long distance.

Nonetheless, the telephone is a vital method of communication for the modern business. This unit describes how to make the best use of it by conveying a good impression to your listener, avoiding misunderstandings and achieving the most effective exchange of information for the lowest cost.

7.2 Knowing the technology

Until recently, office telephone systems were controlled by a switchboard operator and all the individual telephone unit could do was make and receive calls. But recent developments in micro-electronics and increased commercial competition mean that complex and sophisticated equipment is now available. Instead of having to ask the switchboard operator to connect you or to provide an outside line, you will probably have on your desk a machine with a wide range of facilities. It may be able to:

- 'stack' incoming calls and answer them in rotation;
- be used as an intercom or public address system;

- answer calls from any instrument in the building (thus making a switchboard unnecessary for smaller users);
- connect several extensions for a conference by telephone;
- transfer incoming calls from your usual number to another one if you are working in a different office or building.

The telephone may have more to offer now than it did a few years ago, but in order to get the most from your system, you need to spend some time familiarising yourself with its operation. Many modern systems offer so many facilities that they come complete with instruction booklets or even a short training course.

The first principle for using the modern business telephone is therefore to make sure that you are thoroughly familiar with your telephone system, its capabilities, and how to operate it.

7.3 When to call

Knowing when to use the telephone is the next step towards using the instrument effectively. Like any other tool, the telephone is only effective when it is used in the right situation. Used in the appropriate context, it can achieve quick and efficient results; used in the wrong situation, it will achieve very little, and may even serve to add confusion to an already uncertain state of affairs.

The main situations in which a telephone is invaluable are:

(a) when speed is important – that is, when you need to give information or exchange views more quickly than is possible by first-class post;
(b) when you need to discuss something with someone and cannot do so in person;
(c) when you need to discuss documents in detail but a meeting is impossible.

There are also situations when a telephone call will not be suitable, such as:

(a) when the subject is highly confidential;
(b) when a full written record of an exchange is needed;
(c) when the subject is complicated and needs to be considered carefully and at some length by the other person.

Some situations demand a combination of telephone call and letter. The most usual practice is to send a letter of confirmation following the call, to provide a record of what has been said or agreed on.

All these points may be reduced to a single principle: the telephone should be used when a letter or an exchange of letters would be too slow and when a personal meeting is not necessary or possible, assuming that the subject is not too complex for full discussion without written explanation.

7.4 Using the telephone

Whether making or receiving a call, your use of the telephone will be far more effective if you follow these principles.

Be courteous This is a vital rule. You may deal with people whose only contact with your business is by phone, so that their whole impression of it will rest on your telephone manner. It will be easier to reach agreement and will generally smooth the process of communication if you are polite and considerate.

Be brief Time wasted on the telephone costs money and holds up other work. To save time:

- avoid irrelevant topics and idle chat;
- avoid jargon or slang which the other person might not understand;
- plan your call carefully (see section 7.6.2);
- if you do not have the information you need, say so. Call back later when you have found it, or pass the call over to someone who can deal with it.

Establish identity Make clear who you are by giving your name, position and department within the company at the start of a call – whether you make or receive it. Similarly, make sure that you know the name of the person to whom you are speaking.

Keep your writing hand free Always hold the receiver in the hand you do not use for writing, so that you can make notes if necessary.

Use a notepad Always keep a pad and pencil next to your telephone. Whether you are making or receiving a call, you may well need to record details of some kind, and hunting around for a pencil while a caller hangs on wastes time and suggests inefficiency.

Speak distinctly A telephone works by transmitting only a part of the full range of sound frequencies detectable by the human ear. You therefore need to follow some basic rules when speaking on the phone to prevent your voice sounding indistinct. This is not only extremely annoying to the listener, but can also lead to misunderstandings. Try to remember the following points.

- Use your normal voice – don't put on a special 'telephone voice' in the hope of sounding impressive.
- Speak at a reasonable pace.
- Spell out unusual names or technical terms.
- Take particular care over numbers. It is easy to confuse numbers such as 'forty' and 'fourteen'. Avoid this by saying 'forty – that is, four; zero' and 'fourteen – that is, one; four'. It is better to say 'zero' than 'O' on the telephone, as the former is clearer and easier for the listener to grasp.
- Always repeat numbers or difficult names.
- Hold the receiver close to your mouth throughout the call.
- As far as possible use clear, everyday language.
- Speak in simple, brief sentences.
- If you are listening to an explanation or other long statement, show that you can hear and that you understand by saying 'yes' or 'I see' at suitable points.

7.5 Answering a call

When you answer a call, always make sure that you give the following essential information.

(a) If it is an external call, give the name of your organization.

(b) If it is an internal call, or one received through a switchboard, give the number of your extension, the name of your department and your own name. This is important so that if the caller is cut off or wishes to repeat the call at a later date, he or she will know exactly whom to contact.

Listen carefully to the caller, who will usually begin by stating the reason for the call. At the same time, make it clear that you are following what is being said in the way described in section 6.2.2.

When you have established the reason for the call, you should respond in the appropriate way. If you can supply the information that the caller requires, do so quickly, clearly and courteously. If you cannot do so, then say so – calls are expensive, and there is no point in wasting time. Either suggest someone else who may be able to help, or say that you will find out the necessary information and call back, or suggest some other way in which you will deal with the problem. This will avoid the impression of inefficiency which a blank denial would provide. Be careful, however, that you do call back: often, the expressions 'I'll call you back' or 'I'll come back to you on that' are used as an excuse to forget all about the enquiry – not the best way of impressing the caller!

If the caller has information to give you, make a note of it immediately, checking numbers or unusual spellings by repeating them back to him or her. If you need to discuss matters, do so, making sure that you give the caller time to express his or her views before you give yours.

When you have concluded the main business of the call, briefly confirm any action which is to be taken and who is to take it. This may be done by a simple statement such as 'I shall put the details in the post to you this afternoon' or, for a more complex matter, 'I shall see you at 12.30 in Hounslow on the fifteenth.' This may seem unnecessary, but it does make certain that nothing is omitted or misunderstood.

Before you end the call, you should make sure that you have the caller's name and company, and any other information which you need, writing it on your notepad so that you do not have a chance to forget it. When you have finished the exchange, say goodbye courteously but briefly, and make sure that you replace the receiver properly. If you do not, it will lead to wasted time and frayed tempers for others who are trying to call you.

While the call is still fresh in your mind, make a brief note of what has been discussed if it is anything other than a very brief, routine enquiry. Your note should include these items:

(a) date of call;
(b) time of call;
(c) caller's name and company address;

(d) caller's number and extension;
(e) main points of discussion;
(f) action to be taken, and who is to take it;
(g) your own signature or initials.

This will act as an aid to memory and help anyone else who has to deal with the matters raised in the call at a later date. It will also help you if you have to write a letter or produce other documents as a result of the call. Finally, see that the note is placed in the correct file as soon as possible after the call. An example of a note recording a telephone call is shown in fig. 7.1.

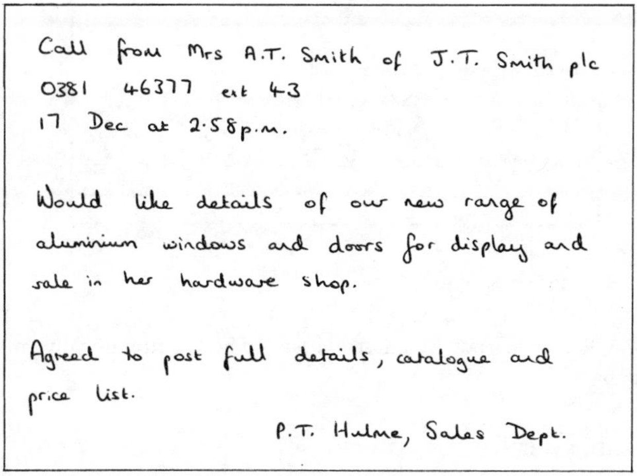

Call from Mrs A.T. Smith of J.T. Smith plc
0381 46377 ext 43
17 Dec at 2·58 p.m.

Would like details of our new range of aluminium windows and doors for display and sale in her hardware shop.

Agreed to post full details, catalogue and price list.

P.T. Hulme, Sales Dept.

Fig. 7.1 A note recording a telephone call

7.5.1 Taking a message

If you take a call for someone who is not available, you should record the details carefully and transfer them to a proper telephone message form as soon as possible. You should then make sure that the form is passed on immediately to the person involved.

A message form should include space for all the necessary details about the call and the caller – as fig. 7.2 illustrates. It is important that the form is completed and passed on at once, since otherwise contact will be broken and the caller will have to call again.

It is good practice to place a copy of the message in the relevant file, as well as passing one to the person concerned, as this will make sure that there is a permanent record of the call. For this reason, some organizations use specially

```
                    TELEPHONE MESSAGE
    For _____
    From _____ of _____
    Tel _____ Ext'n _____
    Message:




    Action required:    Please call back
                        Caller will call back later
                        No action required
    Message taken by _____
    Date _____ Time _____
```

Fig. 7.2 Telephone message form

printed NCR ('no carbon required') forms which automatically produce a
carbon copy.

7.6 Making a call

7.6.1 Choosing the right time to call
Some times of day are better than others for making calls. Two factors are
important here.

Cost Calls are cheaper in the afternoon and evening than in the morning. This
should not, however, stop you from making a very important call at the morning 'peak rate'.

Convenience It will usually not be convenient to make a call first thing in the
morning, when most business people are dealing with incoming mail, or last
thing in the afternoon, when they are completing the day's business or signing
letters.
   Try to think about the business of the person you are calling and judge the
time of your call accordingly. Most shopkeepers, for example, will be less busy
first thing than during the mid-morning rush of shoppers. If you call some
people regularly, ask them when is the best time to call. Similarly, let other
people know what is the best time for you to receive calls.

Although some firms are best reached at certain times, others must be called whenever you can contact them. Getting through to a government department or a railway station is always difficult, and the same is true of solicitors, airports and hospitals. Just keep trying until you get through. Many small businesses are also difficult to contact: plumbers, carpenters and builders, for example, may well be out on a job for most of the day, and calling very early may be the best solution.

Thinking about matters like this will help increase the chances of actually speaking to the person you want. It also shows consideration for others, which will improve relations between your business and its clients.

7.6.2 *Before the call*
If you are not used to calling strangers, or have a difficult call to make, it is a good idea to make a full plan like the one shown in fig. 7.3. If you are used to making calls, you will only need to write down the main points you wish to make.

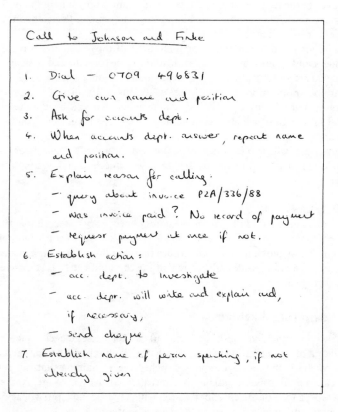

Fig. 7.3 Plan for an important telephone call

Before the call you should also make sure you have all the information you need in front of you. Collect all the documents you may need to refer to, and make sure that you have a pencil and paper at hand.

7.6.3 Dialling the call

First find out whether you can dial the number yourself or whether you have to use a company switchboard. If you need to go through the switchboard, give your name and extension number first, and then the code and number you want. Some switchboard operators will expect you to wait while they dial the number, others will ring you back. Find out the procedure followed in your organization and stick to it, as this will make the process simpler and avoid any misunderstandings.

7.6.4 During the call

Once the call is answered, give your name and company and ask for the person you wish to speak to. Getting to know the extension numbers of people you call regularly will save time here. Once you have been connected, make sure that you have got the right person, and repeat your name and your company. Then you can go ahead and conduct the call, putting into practice the telephone technique outlined in section 7.4.

It is important to be aware of the limitations of the telephone. It is easy to misunderstand or mishear what is said, so try to be tolerant and patient if the person you are speaking to has difficulty in understanding what you are saying. Repeat your point more clearly if necessary: this will achieve far more than becoming angry, abusive or sarcastic. Remember that you have none of the non-verbal signals of personal communication to depend on when you use the telephone. You should consequently avoid interrupting the other person, and indicate clearly when you yourself have finished speaking, by pausing or lowering the pitch of your voice, or by asking a clear question and waiting for the answer.

7.6.5 After the call

When you have finished the call, make notes as necessary to record the details, and place them in the correct file. If you are sending a letter of confirmation, do so as quickly as possible. This will ensure that you do not have the chance to forget what you have said, and ensure that the communication is completed or the next stage clarified.

7.7 Answering machines

An answering machine consists of two linked tape-cassette decks. One has a tape with a pre-recorded message, the other a blank tape. When an incoming call is received, the message tape is switched on, explaining that the person being called is unavailable and inviting the caller to leave a message. At the end of this tape, a tone or 'bleep' sounds, after which the second tape switches itself on and records whatever message the caller chooses to leave.

7.7.1 Recording a message

If you own an answering machine, you will need to record a message to be played to callers. This will normally consist of the following elements:

(a) a statement of your number and your name;
(b) an apology that no one is available to answer the call in person;
(c) an invitation to record a message after the tone;
(d) a statement to the effect that the caller will be contacted as soon as possible.

Your message may also contain details of where you can be contacted in an emergency, or a reminder that there is only a short space of time available on the tape for a message to be left.

If you need to record a message, speak clearly and at your usual speed. Remember that the message will be heard by complete strangers as well as people you know, so avoid any personal references and use everyday, direct language. Keep the message short, and try to sound encouraging – many people ring off when they hear an answering machine, so urge them not to!

7.7.2 Leaving a message

It can be rather off-putting to find yourself talking to a machine. The best way to deal with this is to imagine that you are talking to the person you are calling, and to use his or her name before you give the message – 'Hello George, this is Sue', for example. You cannot do this if you are calling a company, of course, but you can still imagine that you are talking to a real person and not a machine.

Your message should include these elements:

(a) your name;
(b) your telephone number and extension;
(c) the nature of your call (very briefly);
(d) times when you can be called back.

Your message might run something like this:

Hello, this is Sue Bright of International Copiers. I'm calling to arrange a service visit for your photocopying machine. Could you call me back on Northwick 456688, some time tomorrow afternoon? Thank you. Goodbye.

Answering machines can be annoying to the caller, but they can also be very convenient. If you are faced with one when making a call, try not to hang up. Instead, leave your message and carry on with your other work while waiting to be called back.

7.8 Calls with documents

Situations will often arise where you need to discuss a business document. A meeting may not always be practical, and on such occasions the telephone can be very useful. Calls of this kind need to be planned and carried out carefully, however, and to communicate effectively you need to follow these rules:

(a) Make sure that both people have identical documents, otherwise misunderstandings will arise.

(b) Allow plenty of time for the call. Unless you do this, discussion will be hurried, and there will not be enough time for you to study and discuss the documents and reach a decision.

(c) If you have access to a telephone with a loudspeaker, use this so that you can have both hands free to make any notes or alterations to the documents.

(d) Refer to page or section numbers wherever possible. This will save time for the other person, and reduce the risk of misunderstanding.

7.9 Conference calls

Calls which involve three or more participants, which are known as 'conference calls', must be booked in advance with the telephone company, so that the relevant lines can be connected. They are useful where considerations of time or distance mean that a full-scale meeting is not possible, and can be a very effective way of exchanging views and making decisions.

For a conference call to work effectively, however, it must be planned very carefully. Draw up and circulate an agenda shortly before the call. This will list all the matters to be discussed in the call, and will allow the other participants time to think about them. It should also list any documents which the speakers should have before them during the call.

One person should act as the 'chair' for the call, in the manner described in Unit 16. His or her role will be:

● to ensure that the matters listed on the agenda are discussed fully, in the right order;
● to ensure that no one dominates the conversation;

- to allow equal time to all participants;
- to allot time to each item and make sure that proper progress is made by preventing the discussion of irrelevant matters.

Everyone involved should help by saying only what is absolutely necessary as briefly as possible, and then listening to the contributions of others.

7.10 Conclusion

If you know what you want to say and are careful to be polite, precise and brief, the telephone can be an extremely useful means of communication. If you do not prepare important calls or if you forget the limitations of the telephone, it can cause confusion, anger and delay.

Always be aware of the disadvantages of communicating by phone. You cannot use many of the non-verbal signals we usually rely on when talking face to face, nor do you have the time to think carefully about what to say in reply as with a letter. This means that you need to prepare your information, listen particularly carefully and be very patient when using the telephone. Having an argument in person is not pleasant: having one on the telephone is frustrating and upsetting. Always keep calm, think about what you want to say and about the person you are saying it to, and be courteous. Then, using the telephone should be a pleasant and effective way of communicating with colleagues and clients.

7.11 Quick questions

1 What items should be included in a telephone message?

2 What should you say when you lift the receiver to answer a call?

3 How can you minimize the cost of a non-urgent phone call, apart from keeping it short?

4 At what times should you try *not* to call people?

5 How would you organize a conference call?

6 What should you say when asked to leave a message by an answering machine?

7.12 Longer exercises

1 Using the telephone demands a variety of communication skills. List as many as you can and explain why they are important to effective business communication.

2   Design a telephone message form which can be produced in large numbers for use in all business situations.

3   You work as a receptionist for a busy general practitioners' surgery. Work out the text of a message you have to record to be played on an answering machine when the surgery is closed. It should include details of normal surgery hours and an emergency contact number.

4   Draft some notes for a short talk you have been asked to give to new company employees on using the telephone. Use these headings:

   (a)   Before calling;
   (b)   During calls;
   (c)   After calls.

Reading and understanding

8.1 Introduction

People who are involved in communication spend so much time writing that it is easy for them to forget the importance of the skill on which writing depends: reading. You may think that, once you have learned to recognize words, puzzle out those which are new to you and work out how they are related to each other on the page, you have mastered the process of reading and have nothing more to learn. In some ways, this is true: you will be able to understand what is being said in most of the books that you read, and if you use a dictionary properly you should be able to cope with material such as legal documents and government reports which use less familiar terms.

Yet there is much more to reading than this. The process is a highly complex one, involving careful co-ordination of eye and mind to achieve the required result – the complete understanding of the ideas to which the signs printed on the page refer. We read for different purposes, too. If we read a poem, we are concerned to appreciate the sounds, rhythms and associations of the words as much as their literal meaning; if we read a newspaper report of a football game, we want primarily to find out the facts – what the score was and who scored the goals; and if we read a business report, we want to know what information it contains, what ideas it puts forward, and what action it suggests.

In a business setting, you will need to read all kinds of written material for different purposes, and each will demand a different kind of reading. It is quite likely that you already do this to a certain extent without thinking about it – as mentioned above, the way in which you approach a poem differs considerably from the way you approach a football report. But it is important to be able to recognize the different techniques of reading, and to know which to adopt according to the nature, difficulty and length of the writing involved. Unless you can master this major communication skill, you will find it hard to grasp exactly what the writer means to convey, or it will take far longer than necessary to do so. This may result in all kinds of misunderstandings.

You may think that your job does not involve a lot of reading, but most written communication depends on the ability of the sender to read the information necessary to compile it, and on the receiver's ability to read and understand it. Writing skills are covered in other units, so here we will concentrate on approaches to reading, which are fundamental to a sound grasp of the printed word and hence of much importance to business communication.

8.2 Reading techniques

The three main techniques used in reading are scanning, skimming and a more detailed approach – used for studying documents, textbooks and business reports, for example.

8.2.1 Scanning

The process of looking quickly through a text to find one particular piece of information is known as *scanning*. To scan a piece of writing, move your eyes quickly down the text, looking for key words related to the topic in question – rather as you would look around a car park for your own car, or around a crowd of people for a close relative.

Scanning is used most often for reading street or telephone directories to find a particular name. For example, if you were trying to find a manufacturer of plastic mouldings in your area, to get a quotation for some boxes in which to sell take-away sandwiches in your snack-bar, you would use a classified directory and scan the addresses of firms in the category 'Plastics', until you found one in the right location. Scanning is not only used for directories, though. It is also valuable when you need to go through a piece of continuous writing to find a specific piece of information. You might, for instance, need to go through the *Annual Abstract of Statistics* to find data about trends in take-away food shops.

Scanning is useful for many kinds of printed material encountered in business. Annual reports of companies provide a great deal of data about their activities, and scanning them can be a quick way of getting to know what your competitors are doing. Catalogues from sales representatives and major suppliers can also be scanned, to gain a general idea of what goods are available. The regular economic reports and digests issued by government departments can also be scanned to gain an overall view of movements in trade and the economy in general. Anyone in a position of seniority in a company will also have to read reports, abstracts and other documents produced by employees. Here, scanning is esssential, since it allows the reader to grasp the main drift of the report, select aspects for specific attention and perhaps pass on certain sections to other staff for more detailed analysis, thus saving valuable management time.

8.2.2 Skimming

Skimming involves quickly looking through a passage of writing to gain an idea of its overall meaning. You might do this when reading a report or letter quickly before going to a meeting, or before deciding whether you need to read the whole of a book or article in detail.

You can increase the speed of your skimming by two methods. The first involves drawing a finger down the centre of the page, moving your eyes rapidly from side to side as you follow it down. The second method is the 'curtain' technique. Move an envelope or piece of paper down the page, curtaining off the lines you have read. Both methods stop you from going back and rereading material you have already covered, and also make sure that you concentrate on reading quickly.

8.2.3 Detailed reading

There will be occasions when you will need to read something in detail – when you are studying a report or reading a textbook, for example. To do this you must read more slowly than when skimming, but still concentrate on whole sentences rather than individual words so that you take in complete ideas. Ask yourself questions while you are reading. How does this sentence develop the point made in the last paragraph? What is the main point of the whole section? Doing this will increase your concentration, and help you to develop a clear idea of what the author is saying.

After reading a chapter or section, stop and think about what has been said. Work out whether or not you agree with it, and think about how it fits into the argument of the book as a whole. This will further aid your concentration and understanding and will help in any later note-making.

Reading of this kind is necessary for the crucial documents in business life. These include contracts and other legal documents, the 'small print' of which is easily overlooked. Your organization may well have a legal department to offer specialist advice, but if you are in a position of responsibility in the organization, it is important that you realize the full implications of such documents for yourself. This demands very close, analytical reading.

Other documents which demand detailed reading include:

● research and development reports chronicling the growth of new products;
● market research reports from specialist agencies;
● relevant sections of annual reports from rival companies;
● financial projections in publications such as the clearing banks' reviews or specially commissioned reports on economic trends.

While reading, you should take care to distinguish between fact and opinion. This can generally be done by checking whether evidence is provided in support of a particular point. The source of any statistics should always be acknowledged, either in the text or in a note at the foot of the page or at the end of the text. Points about historical events should also be supported by evidence, either quoted or referred to in the text. In general, events which are described can be regarded as facts: causes, interpretation or conclusions will be opinions. (Section 15.3 discusses fact and opinion in reports in greater detail.)

In particular, you should look out for sentences which begin with expressions such as: 'It has long been established that . . .', 'Everyone knows that . . .', and

'Few would deny that . . .'. All of these suggest that there is no possible doubt about the idea which follows, while offering no evidence to support such a suggestion. In this way, fact and opinion may well be confused.

The writer's choice of vocabulary may also reveal that what is being stated is a matter of opinion only. The use of emotive words or phrases – those which are likely to create an emotional rather than a rational response in the reader – will lead the reader towards a particular view which might not be borne out by the facts of the case. You should look out for language like this in your detailed reading. For example:

The company has made impressive growth this year.

Here, the word 'impressive' is emotive, since it tells us we should be impressed by company growth without giving any evidence of the growth.

The surprisingly easy acquisition of the major rival brought new opportunities for expansion.

Who is surprised by the ease of the acquisition, and why? Again we are told how we should react, without any reasons being given.

Sales have mushroomed in the first quarter.

In this example, not only is the word 'mushroomed' vague, it also suggests that we should respond to the increase with pleasure, if not amazement.

In business, it is essential to develop a questioning approach to what you read, in which you are unwilling to accept the author's view without direct evidence. Detailed reading will make you aware of the many ways in which a writer can seek to influence the reader's opinion and you will soon be able to detect misleading uses of language, such as the use of emotive language to blur fact and opinion.

8.2.4 Conclusion

Skimming, scanning and detailed reading all help to improve the way in which you take in information. Deciding which method to use will depend on the length, difficulty and nature of the material involved, as well as your reason for reading it. Having a quick look through some material which is only slightly related to your business will call for skimming, for instance, whereas a technical account of the latest changes in procedures closely related to your work will call for detailed reading, especially if it is a complex and demanding piece of writing.

For many business purposes, a combination of these and other techniques will be most appropriate. This process of reading a text fully so as to gain all the necessary information is known as *critical reading*.

8.3 Critical reading

There may be occasions in business when you need to carry out research into a subject. Unit 18 discusses how to find books, reports and other documents you need by means of a literature search. Once you have found the material you require, you will need to read it critically, making sure that you obtain from it all the relevant information. This may be done by taking notes – a process discussed in detail in Unit 9 – or, in the case of shorter items, by close reading and careful thought. The stages involved in critical reading are outlined below.

8.3.1 Appraisal

Reading a book, report or other document from cover to cover is not always the most effective method of assimilating the information it contains, nor the most economic use of your time. Instead, you should start by getting to know exactly what the piece of writing has to offer – a process we can call the *initial appraisal*. This consists of reading certain elements in a particular way and recording information about them.

Details of the publication You should always keep a record of the material that you consult, for two reasons: you will be able to find it again should you need to and, should you decide to quote from it or to summarize its main points in a report, abstract or other document, you will be able to acknowledge your source. You will need to record the following details:

(a) author's full name;
(b) title of piece;
(c) title of periodical (if an article);
(d) date of publication;
(e) edition;
(f) publisher;
(g) place of publication;
(h) issuing company (if a report or similar document);
(i) library classification number.

Here are examples of what this information should look like:

> Lobley, Derek, *Success in Commerce*, 1988, 3rd edition, John Murray, London, 380.1

> Rhodes, John, 'Communication – Use of English', *Comlon*, Winter 1988, London Chamber of Commerce and Industry, Sidcup.

General appraisal This is what you do when you pick up a book in a bookshop and want to find out something about it before deciding whether or not to buy it. Look at the author's name. Is he or she described in any way, as a teacher or lecturer perhaps? Has he or she written any other books? This might indicate the status of the book, although the fact that the writer is the principal of a major college and has written several other books is no guarantee that this is the book you are looking for.

Most books contain a short statement of what they are about, usually on the inside flap of the dust-jacket if it is a hardback, or on the back cover if it is a paperback. There may also be excerpts from reviews of the book or comments by experts in the field who have read it.

Appraisal is just as important for other printed material. If you are considering a company report, for example, you need to find out the nature of the company's work, products or services, in order to decide how relevant the report is to your own operations. You would do this by looking at a subtitle, an introductory section or another relevant passage to glean the necessary information.

The contents page   This is a list of chapters which appears at the front of every book. Sometimes it does no more than give the title of each chapter; sometimes it gives the title of the chapter followed by a list of subheadings. The contents page of this book, for example, comes into the second category. Glancing quickly through the contents page can be a valuable way of gauging what the book has to say, and thus whether or not it is relevant to your research.

Many business documents and reports list their contents in this way. Careful appraisal of such pages will help you decide whether or not the material is relevant, and which parts you need to read in greater depth.

The index   Contrary to popular belief, this is not an alternative term for the contents page. The index is an alphabetical listing of all the major topics covered by the book, together with the numbers of the pages on which they appear. An index can save you a considerable amount of time when researching, since it enables you to find specific references to a topic without having to read through the whole work.

When appraising a book, it is a good idea to check whether an item in which you have a particular interest appears in the index, and how often it appears. If there is a series of page numbers for it, or one reference to a longer section ('124–37', for example), then it is clear that the book covers that topic in some depth.

Business documents may well not have a full index, but they may reveal their contents in other ways. Annual reports, for example, often use subject headings, like headlines in newspapers, to emphasize the main topics. They may also have running headings – captions at the top of each page which tell you what topic the page covers. Routine reports will also use clear headings, very often cross-referring you to other sections of the report (see section 15.5). Others may contain short quotations from the body of the report in larger type, or encased in a box, in the centre of a page. This technique is often used to highlight major points, and so help the reader to find his or her way quickly around the document. Flicking through a document or report and noting what the author has chosen to highlight will reveal more about the probable contents.

The introduction   Many books and reports begin with a short introduction which outlines what they are about. Reading this can often be very useful. It may make clear that the book is concerned with an aspect of a topic which is of no immediate interest to you, in which case you can return it to the shelves and move on to the next stage of your research. On the other hand, it may make clear that it is exactly the material you have been looking for.

Some publications may have an introduction under another name, or their first chapter may fulfil the same function. Be on the look-out for this, and glance quickly through the first chapter in case it gives information of this kind.

First and last paragraphs   Very often the writer will establish the main concerns of a chapter in the first paragraph. In a similar way, the last paragraph of a chapter may well summarize the main points or draw conclusions. Skimming through these paragraphs quickly – using the techniques discussed earlier – can often give you a basic grasp of what the chapter covers, so that you can decide whether or not to work through it in detail.

Summaries and conclusions   Some publications contain sections which summarize the main points made in a chapter or other sections. This is often the case with texts used for unaided study, or books specially designed to form part of a study course. Such summaries provide a valuable way of assessing the main content, and should be skimmed through as part of the appraisal process.

Other books may contain sections which give the conclusions reached in more extensive chapters or sections. These should be read with care since, like the recommendations sections of reports, they will only make their point clearly when read in conjunction with the arguments which precede them. They do, nevertheless, represent a further way of finding out about the book and should be skimmed through at the appraisal stage.

Business publications of any real value are produced by people who know that time is precious to business readers. As a result, they often include summaries or abstracts, or concentrated outlines in the first or last paragraphs. They may also have short summaries in boxes, or quotations from the text which express a main point briefly and succinctly. All these can help greatly at the initial appraisal stage.

8.3.2 Skimming
Once you have completed the appraisal stage you will have a clear idea of the nature of the book, whether it is relevant to the topic you are researching and which passages you need to read. Next, skim through the material – using the technique outlined in section 8.2.2 – to gain a general idea of what it says, in preparation for the more detailed reading which will follow.

Once you have completed a rapid reading of the passage, you should pause for a moment to consider the main theme of the chapter or section. Make sure that you can define it clearly in your mind before continuing.

8.3.3 Detailed reading
Go through the passage slowly – as outlined in section 8.2.3 – thinking carefully about its ideas and any examples or details it contains which make the main points clearer. Ask yourself questions as you read through it, to make sure that you understand exactly what is being said.

8.3.4 Review

On completing your detailed reading, pause again and review what you have read. Try to give the passage a brief descriptive title which conveys its main ideas: if you can do this without too much trouble, then you probably have a clear understanding of the subjects covered.

When you have completed the four stages of appraisal, skimming, detailed reading and review, you should have a clear idea of the main points raised in the chapter or passage and should genuinely understand what the writer is attempting to convey. It is a process rather different from that normally described as reading, but it will ensure that you have a far stronger grasp of what you have read and that you are able to put it to whatever use is necessary – your studies, an examination or a business report, for example.

8.4 Conclusion

From this unit it can be seen that reading as a means of taking in information is a complex skill which demands care, practice and concentration. Reading is an essential part of success in study, however, and it is worth persevering with the techniques described here. Not only will they help you to understand complex ideas in the subjects you may need to study for business and professional examinations, but they also form the basis of a successful research method which will be invaluable throughout your professional career. In addition, they provide a firm foundation upon which to develop note-making and summarizing skills – as the next unit illustrates.

8.5 Quick questions

1 Write down the information you would need when keeping a record of the book from which the page shown in fig. 8.1 is taken.

2 What are the following, and when would they be used:

   (a) scanning;
   (b) skimming;
   (c) detailed reading?

3 In a sentence, explain the difference between a contents page and an index.

8.6 Longer exercises

1 Explain the nature of abstracts and their importance within a business company.

2 Write an article on the importance of reading, for inclusion in your company's staff journal or your college magazine. It should be about 300 words in length and show, in a vivid and readable style, how reading is an essential part of business communication.

© David Cox 1988

First published 1979
Reprinted 1981
Second edition 1983
Reprinted 1984, 1985
Third edition 1986
Fourth edition 1988

All rights reserved. No part of this publication may be reproduced, copied or transmitted save with the written permission of John Murray (Publishers) Ltd, 50 Albemarle Street, London W1X 4BD, or in accordance with the provisions of the Copyright Act 1956 (as amended), or under the terms of any licence permitting limited copying issued by The Copyright Licensing Agency, 33–34 Alfred Place, London WC1E 7DP.

Any person who does any unauthorised act in relation to this publication may be liable to criminal prosecution and civil claims for damages.

Printed and bound in Great Britain by
Richard Clay Ltd, Bungay, Suffolk.

British Library Cataloguing in Publication Data

Cox, David, *1946–*
Success in elements of banking.—4th ed.
—(Success study books).
1. Banks and banking—Great Britain
I. Title
332.1'0941 HG2988

ISBN 0-7195-4528-5

Fig. 8.1 Information about a book (usually printed on the back of the title page).

Notes and abstracts

9.1 The need for note-making

In the last unit, we looked at ways of reading material to make sure that you fully understand its meaning. In this unit, we take the process a stage further, by looking at a method of taking notes to record what you have read. A similar method can be used for taking notes from lectures or presentations.

First, it may be useful to consider some of the reasons why you may need to take notes.

For study purposes If you have studied subjects with a high factual content, such as economics and law, you will know that it is easier to absorb a large amount of information from your own notes – provided that they are thorough – than from a textbook or other source. If your notes are good it means that you have understood what you have read and will be able to learn it.

For your business career Every job demands some communication skills and you will no doubt find that there are many situations where note-making skills are important. For example:

- You may be given a long, complex report to read, and need to make a shorter version of it for your own use or perhaps for circulation among members of your department.
- You may have to compile *abstracts* for your company's archives – short summaries of articles in the national press or in trade or professional journals related to your company's activities, which are kept for employees to refer to when they are conducting research of various kinds.
- You may be asked to compare the products or services offered by your company's competitors, which will require you to skim through catalogues and reports and extract and summarize the relevant information.
- You may have to carry out research into possible areas of development for your company – selling to a new export market, say, or the launch of a completely new product. Note-making is an integral part of the research process (see section 18.5).

It is clear, then, that note-making is an important skill for the communicator to possess. It is not a difficult skill to develop, however: all you need is the willingness to take it seriously; the ability to follow a set procedure, working methodically through each stage; and – perhaps most important of all – plenty of practice.

9.2 The note-making procedure

Figure 9.1 outlines the note-making procedure. Although it is mainly self-explanatory, there are some points which need to be expanded.

9.2.1 Passage and purpose
In some business contexts the passage for summary will be given to you – if you are asked to prepare a short report from a longer one, for example. At other times – when you are writing an original report, say – you will need to find relevant material for summary yourself. When doing so, make sure that you know exactly what topic you are interested in so that you can select just the right passage. Otherwise you may waste time taking notes which are not needed.

9.2.2 Reading
Unit 8 has outlined how to read a passage so that you understand it – quickly at first, and then in detail. Follow this process when making notes, making sure that you understand the meaning of the whole passage before you write anything down.

Giving the passage a title is a good way of checking that you have grasped the subject matter. Instead of a one-word heading, though, invent a title which covers the approach or particular angle of the article. Imagine, for example, that you have to make notes from an article on the way expensive advertising affects children. Rather than calling your notes simply 'Advertising', you could write 'Advertising: its cost, benefits and effects on children'. Time spent here will be valuable in later stages of note-making, since you will only be able to summarize a passage if you fully understand it.

9.2.3 First draft
It is unlikely that you will be able to keep in your head the contents of the whole passage to be summarized, and so it makes sense to break it into shorter sections and deal with each in turn. Most writers make sure that each paragraph contains a major point, with supporting arguments or evidence, so these may be useful divisions to follow. The main idea of the paragraph is often contained in the first or 'topic' sentence, from which you may take the heading for this section of your notes. The main point is often repeated at the end of the paragraph, too, so that the start and end of each paragraph need careful attention.

Beneath the heading you should list each point on a separate line, to make sure that each one is presented as clearly as possible. Use your own words – except for technical terms – as this will show that you have understood the ideas of the passage and not just copied out words which seem important.

Note-making procedure

A *Passage and purpose*
1 Select exactly which parts of book, article etc you need to take notes from.
2 Define your reason for needing the notes.

B *Reading*
1 Quickly read or skim the whole passage.
2 Read the whole again carefully, asking yourself questions about it to make sure you understand it.
3 Give it a brief title covering:
   (a) subject
   (b) way subject is treated.

C *First draft*
1 Divide passage into short sections, usually paragraphs.
2 Give first section a heading. Number and underline it.
3 Note down points under this heading, taking care that you:
   (a) use your own words except for technical terms
   (b) put each point on separate line with own number
   (c) keep notes short by omitting verbs and unnecessary words
   (d) look for general points, not details or examples
   (e) examine start and finish of section with special care
   (f) keep points separate.

D *Checking*
1 Check draft against passage for:
   (a) inclusion of all necessary points
   (b) accuracy of all points
   (c) exclusion of irrelevant points
   (d) accuracy and clarity of expression.

E *Final version*
1 Rearrange order of points if necessary.
2 Change presentation to increase clarity if necessary.
3 Make sure abbreviations are understandable.

F *Concluding details*
1 Record source (author, title of book, periodical or article, date and volume of publication).
2 Give notes a title, revising your first one if necessary.

Fig. 9.1 Note-making procedure

Make sure that each point is expressed as concisely as possible. You can do this by following these rules:

(a) Avoid phrases where single words will do. For example, 'due to the fact that' can be replaced by 'as'; 'little by little' by 'gradually'.
(b) Use abbreviations, but make sure you do so correctly – e.g. as 'for example', i.e. as 'that is'. Notes are the only form of writing where such terms are really acceptable.
(c) Omit articles – 'the', 'a' and 'an'.
(d) Omit verbs, as long as the meaning is still clear.
(e) Use punctuation exactly. Semi-colons and colons can often replace conjunctions or make verbs unnecessary when they are used to link two clauses.

9.2.4 Checking

After writing the first draft, you should check your notes carefully to make sure that they are an appropriate length. If the notes are too short:

(a) Make sure that you have not left out an important point, by reading the original passage carefully and comparing it with your notes.
(b) Check that your expression is not too brief. If any point is too concise to be clear, rephrase it.
(c) If both of these fail to help, check to see if you have joined together two points which are really separate ones. This achieves brevity but causes confusion and can be remedied by rewriting the two as independent ideas.

If the notes are too long:

(a) Check that all the points that you have included are made in the original.
(b) Check that you have not included points from the original which are not needed for the purpose of the notes.
(c) Check for long-winded expression.
(d) If all of these fail, make sure that you have not included the same point twice, perhaps in different sections.

9.2.5 Final version

With a little practice, you will find that your first draft will need very few changes to make it an acceptable final version. You might, however, wish to change the order of your points, or to combine two or three sections. If so, you should do it at this stage.

9.2.6 Concluding details

Remember to record the source of the passage in case you need to refer to it again. You should also check the title at the head of your notes, revising your original version if necessary, to make sure that it fully and accurately describes the passage.

9.3 Note-making in practice

The passage reproduced as fig. 9.2(a) is part of an article from a business journal, which appeared in an examination paper for summary in note form. This section looks at the stages which you might work through in producing notes from the article, and shows how the process described in section 9.2 works in practice. A set of notes from the passage is given in its final form as fig. 9.2(b), but please do not look at it yet. Instead, read the passage carefully in the manner described earlier, and try to think of a title which will describe it.

In the widest sense, public relations is a means of using any form of mass communication to create a favourable image of the company and its products, without actually buying space or time in the media. Hence it differs from advertising, where the company buys the right to say, within reason, what it wishes, subject only to the restraints placed on advertising by the law.

Public relations is concerned with several 'publics', whereas advertising is mainly concerned with the company's customers. Public relations is also concerned with the company's customers, but only to the extent that the more favourable an image of the company and its products, the more likely are people to buy the product. Product publicity in this case is a sales weapon, and a means of backing up the work of the salesman. You can appreciate the value of product publicity achieved by means of an appearance in a television play or documentary, or in articles in the press. Hence product publicity is an important part in any public relations campaign, but it is by no means the whole concern of public relations.

A favourable impression of a company and its products may also with advantage be created among the shareholders of the company, with the object of keeping up share prices and encouraging new investors. In these days investment is also made by people from other countries, and hence the value of the company image among investors on a worldwide scale. In addition to the shareholders, the company's suppliers may be influenced to think well of the company with advantage, because in times of short supplies, for example, suppliers will naturally tend to favour those customers with whom they are on the best terms, and of whom they think the most highly.

A fourth public of major importance today is the company's employees because companies are no better than the people in them; thus good industrial relations are imperative. Regrettably, many companies treat their employees, both senior and junior, badly and many still deny those who work in the company any say in the running of its affairs. You cannot run a successful exporting company, or one which works on a truly international basis, without paying great attention to the needs and wants of all your staff, and the wider the company's interests the more necessary this becomes.

Fig. 9.2(a) Passage for note-making

It is clear that the passage is concerned with public relations, and that these words must figure in the title. They will not, however, be sufficient on their own: a phrase is needed to make clear precisely what aspects of public relations are being discussed. From the first paragraph, it is clear that the passage distinguishes between public relations and advertising; however, a reading of the whole passage reveals that the main topic is the range of different 'publics' to which public relations is addressed. A suitable title, then, might be:

Public relations and its targets

To include the material of the first paragraph, this might be expanded to:

Public relations: its nature and targets

Having arrived at a draft title – which can, after all, be changed after working through the passage in detail – you should move on and divide the passage into sections. The first paragraph seems to be a self-contained unit, as it establishes the meaning of public relations as distinct from advertising. A suitable heading for this might be 'Public relations and advertising: a comparison'; and beneath the heading you could list the two main points which establish the difference between the two.

Public relations: its nature and targets

A *Public relations and advertising: a comparison*
1 PR uses mass communication to create 'favourable image' of company and products without paying directly.
2 Advertising buys space to promote company.
3 Advertising aimed solely at customers: PR aimed at other groups too: investors, suppliers and employees.

B *Product publicity*
1 Product publicity is getting products shown on TV or in press.
2 Valuable support for sales drive.
3 Important part, but not whole, of PR.

C *Investors and suppliers*
1 Good PR maintains share prices.
2 Also encourages new investors.
3 As investment is international, PR must be worldwide.
4 Good PR with suppliers important, to help maintain supplies.

D *Employees*
1 Good industrial relations are important to success.
2 Staff needs must be considered, especially in large or international company.

Fig. 9.2(b) Notes from passage in fig. 9.2(a)

The remainder of the passage would be dealt with in the same way, first by reading a section carefully, then by giving it a general heading, and finally by listing beneath the heading the main points made in that section. The second paragraph, then, continues the distinction between advertising and public relations, and goes on to discuss the importance of a company's public image and product publicity. The third paragraph deals with the task of publicity among shareholders, international investors and suppliers; and the last mentions the company's relations with its staff.

On the face of it, each paragraph deals with a different aspect of the subject, and your reaction in the first draft would probably be to make each one a separate section. However, you might choose to incorporate into the first section the point about the difference between advertising and public relations which is raised in the second paragraph. This would bring together at the start of the notes all the points about the differences between the two kinds of communication, leaving the other sections to detail other topics.

Notice that, although the bulk of the notes in fig. 9.2(b) is expressed in words different from those of the passage, there are some terms which have been retained. 'Public relations' cannot be expressed more clearly in other terms, nor can 'industrial relations'. The initial definition, too, is hard to express more precisely – and so the term 'favourable image' has been retained to describe what public relations aims to promote.

The notes in figs 9.2(b) and 9.3 show how the procedures described in this unit can be employed to produce lucid, well-presented notes which can be filed as part of a company's resource archive. Figure 9.3 provides – in note form – a guide to taking notes from spoken sources, which you will doubtless be required to do as part of your study, work or professional training. Read both sets of notes carefully before you go on to the next part of this unit, as this will help you when you come to produce notes of your own.

9.4 Abstracts

Abstracts are a special form of summary. Like notes, they give the ideas of a passage in shortened form but, unlike notes, they use continuous prose, without headings and numbered points. They usually concern an aspect of news, government policy or technical development which is of interest to the organization concerned, and they are often kept in its library or archives.

9.4.1 Writing an abstract

The writing of abstracts depends on the combined skills of note-making and prose writing. To make sure that you include all the necessary information in your abstract, you should first produce a set of notes and then expand them into continuous prose. This is a simple process if you follow some basic principles.

(a) Add verbs, articles and other words omitted from notes. This will make sure that the writing is grammatically correct and fluent to read.

Making notes from spoken sources

A *Before the session*
1 Make sure you have enough paper and an extra pen.
2 Know the context of the meeting – seminar or presentation, for example.

B *During the session*
1 Don't write all the time: listen for complete point before writing.
2 Listen very carefully and question what you hear.
3 Try to distinguish between new points and repetitions/enlargements of old ones.
4 Be selective with examples – go for main points first.
5 Use digressions/questions/anecdotes to get points down.

C *The speaker*
1 Get to know how the speaker works. Does he/she:
   – list main points of presentation at start
   – allow points to emerge during course of presentation
   – pause regularly to sum up or draw points together
   – give final summaries
   – give references for points made?
2 Vary your note-making technique according to the speaker's approach.

D *Layout*
1 Note time, date, speaker and subject.
2 Leave plenty of space when writing – alternate lines if possible. This allows later additions.
3 Use any abbreviations and codes you can.
4 Try to use main headings, sub-headings and numbered points as far as possible.
5 Note questions, uncertainties and points for checking as you go.
6 Put names and unfamiliar terms in capitals.
7 If speaker permits, ask about unfamiliar terms.

E *After the session*
1 Rewrite using clear layout at first opportunity.
2 Check names, dates, spellings and other uncertainties.
3 Ask speaker if unsure of anything.
4 Relate what's written to your other notes.
5 Add points and comments of your own, making sure they're separated from speaker's points.
6 Share/compare notes if subject is difficult.

Fig. 9.3 Making notes from spoken sources

(b) Subject headings can often be turned into a topic sentence by the addition of a verb. They may also be combined with one or more of the points which appear beneath them in the notes.

(c) Avoid slang or jargon, and also any very ornate language. Instead, use a simple, direct style which anyone likely to read the abstract will understand.

(d) Use abbreviations only when you know that the reader will understand them. For example, bankers will not need to be told what 'IMF' stands for, but general readers will need the full explanation – 'International Monetary Fund'.

At this stage an example may help to clarify the theory and practice of writing abstracts. Figure 9.4(a) shows an article about new methods of test marketing – a preliminary investigation of how well a particular product might sell. Figure 9.4(b) shows an abstract which has been produced from the article for company use – perhaps by someone working in a market research company who has been requested to produce abstracts about new methods being used by the company's competitors. In practice you would not write an abstract of such a short article, but this passage serves well to illustrate the technique you would use. Read the article and the abstract carefully before going on to the next section.

9.4.2 Format

As well as the summary itself, an abstract will usually include the following elements:

A reference number   This usually consists of a code number, the abstract writer's initials, and the date the abstract was made. It thus establishes some basic information about the abstract and makes it possible for it to be filed accurately according to the system the company uses.

A title   This will be formed in the same way as a title for notes: a statement of the abstract's subject and an indication of the way it is treated.

Source   Like notes, all abstracts should include a clear indication of the article or passage they summarize. It should contain these elements:

(a) author's name;
(b) title of book or article;
(c) volume number and date (if article);
(d) date of publication (if book).

This information is included so that anyone who is interested in the data that the abstract contains may check it with the original passage.

9.4.3 Length

Abstracts vary in length, according to the length and nature of the material being summarized and the practice of the company. You will usually be given

New tests for new products

BOSTON

Many American companies are fed up with the standard procedure for test marketing their products. The usual try-out in three or four cities can cost around $1.5m, take nine months to assess and more often than not tell them the product is a dud. So Management Decision Systems, a Massachusetts market-research company, has developed another way. Called "Mall Intercept", it is catching on. After some 400 trials, it is now standard practice for about 100 companies, including Procter & Gamble, L'Oréal and Unilever.

Shoppers are enticed by a $2 gift to walk into a van in a shopping mall. In this simulated supermarket, they see a range of soaps or cereals on shelves (including the new product) and choose a brand. There are telephone follow-ups three weeks later to see if consumers who bought a product in the van would do so again. It costs around $50,000 to bag 300 consumers in three different malls over three days. The results are produced in less than three months, with a rate of errors that companies find acceptable.

An even newer method of product testing has been developed by a Chicago market-research company called Information Resources (which now owns

Management Decision Systems). It is called "Behaviour Scan" and has aroused fears of Big Brother. Its test patches are six areas where the population does almost all its supermarket shopping locally. Pittsfield, Massachusetts, is one of them. In return for a gift (a toaster, for example), 25,000 consumers in each area, all of whom have cable television at home, agree to allow the details of their grocery bills to be filed in a computer.

With the aid of a widget linked to the consumers' televisions, the advertisements that they watch are monitored. This behaviour is then compared with their supermarket shopping. Companies can tailor their advertisements according to what they learn from the scans—for old products as well as for new ones.

Fig. 9.4(a) Passage for summary as a company abstract

Index number (subject classification, writer's initials and date)

Descriptive title

436/SJS/9.86

TEST MARKETING: NEW SYSTEMS (MALL INTERCEPT AND BEHAVIOUR SCAN)

To avoid high costs and long delays, Management Decision Systems has introduced its 'Mall Intercept' test marketing method. Shoppers are given $2 and asked to choose a product from a range including the test product, and telephoned to later to see if they would choose it again. It costs $50 000 to test 300 people's reactions and results are ready in 3 months.

Information Resources has developed 'Behaviour Scan' which records consumers' grocery bills, with their permission and in return for free gift. Their cable television sets are monitored to record what advertisements they watch, to see if this influences their shopping.

'New tests for new products', The Economist, 14 June 1986

Body of abstract in simple, clear style

Details of source

Fig. 9.4(b) Abstract from passage in fig. 9.4(a)

information about the length required and any other details of format, which all form part of a company's house style. Some companies prepare abstracts on a card-index system, in which case they cannot be longer than about half a side of A4 paper. With the increasing use of computer databases, many companies are preparing abstracts which are 'one screen' in length – that is, the number of words which can be presented at one time on a visual display unit (see section 17.2.1).

9.5 Conclusion

Abstracts and notes are an important part of an organization's information network. They demand specific skills which will be important throughout your business career and which you will need to keep sharp with frequent practice. The time and effort that you invest in developing your note-making and abstracting skills will be amply repaid, as they will help you to improve your understanding of written material and your ability to express the ideas you read clearly and confidently in your own words.

9.6 Quick questions

1   When writing a set of notes from a passage, what two aspects of the contents of the passage should you include in the title?

2   Give three ways in which notes which are too long may be shortened.

3   Give three ways in which notes which are too short may be lengthened.

9.7 Longer exercises

1   Describe the situations when note-making is important in business communication, using examples from your own experience to illustrate your discussion where possible.

2   In your own words, make a summary of the following passage. Your summary should be no more than 180 words.

> ### Inflation
> Inflation may be defined as a sustained upward pressure on prices resulting in a general rise in the level of prices and thus in the cost of living. The rate of inflation is the percentage increase in the general price level for a given period (year, month etc.). It is usual to differentiate between demand–pull (or 'demand') inflation and cost-push ('cost') inflation.
>
> Demand inflation is the upward pressure on prices that results when aggregate demand is in excess of aggregate supply of goods and services and supply is inelastic. Suppliers in a free economy will then

charge the highest prices they can for goods in short supply. This type of inflation can be caused by a consumption boom with a decreased willingness to save by consumers and a corresponding fall in investment demand. Or it can be due to increased government expenditure without restriction of consumer demand or by an export boom without curtailment of home demand.

Cost inflation occurs when pressure on prices is caused by increases in costs without corresponding growth in output. This can be due to lack of productive resources (capital, plant and labour), excessive wage increases or unwillingness of the productive workers to work harder or longer hours. Increased wages are not the major culprit, however. Rises in prices of imported raw materials (as at the end of the 1970s with oil), increased cost of capital due to high interest rates, and excessive drive for higher profits are other substantial contributory factors.

In fact in all cases of inflation both demand and cost elements are present. Like unemployment, inflation tends to feed on itself. If the community expects inflation to continue they will make allowances for it in their economic bargains. Individuals will strive for higher earnings. Firms will seek higher profit margins. This can be aggravated by incautious government actions ranging from increases in direct and indirect taxes to maintenance of artificially high exchange rates to bolster the currency. Hyperinflation is said to exist when inflation rates reach very high figures.

The bad effects of inflation are insidious. Even when the rate is low and is not expected it leads to a redistribution of wealth and income with no regard to social justice. High rates disrupt economic life leading to more bankruptcies and higher unemployment. If it gets out of hand (hyperinflation) there can be a breakdown of the whole economic system and it can undermine a country's political system.

Marketing executives have a very real interest in what happens to inflation. The end result for them can be intensified competition as firms fight to maintain their sales volume from a smaller cake of total demand. Inflation can also put up their operating costs until it becomes doubtful if the firm can continue with some or all of their operations. Customers' willingness to buy can decline rapidly. Marketing executives, with their colleagues in other departments, must study the whole complex problem and deduce the implications for their firm's business.

(LCCI, English for commerce (higher))

3　Write an article of about 200 words on 'How to make notes in lectures', for publication in a college handbook.

4　Make a note-form summary of the advice given in Unit 8 on how to read a business reference source.

5   In your own words, make a summary of the main points of the following
     passage. Your summary should be no more than 180 words.

Coping with Change

The anxiety caused by a process of change is a normal and inevitable
reaction to taking a step into the unknown, to re-evaluating habitual
behaviour and to learning to behave differently especially if it is combined with meeting normal job responsibilities. Such anxiety is not
confined to a particular age or grade. It occurs in young and old alike,
in senior and junior grades, in the office and on the shop floor and
amongst trade union representatives as well as managers. Some people
are by temperament more inclined to accept such challenges than
others, and their enthusiasm is useful in getting the process going, but
enthusiasm can bring its own problems. It can tempt people to move
ahead without proper, but time-consuming, consideration of options
and consultation with interested parties. It can mask a desire to right
real or imagined wrongs of the past. It can threaten those who are
naturally inclined to move more slowly.

People need help if they are to find their way through, making constructive use of enthusiasm and paying sympathetic attention to
genuine fears, irrational as well as rational. In their different ways all
the organizations we have examined found it necessary to offer this
kind of help. All of them provided training in special skills like suppor-
tive management and effective group-working. Some, in addition,
used advisers to provide more specialized help. Such advisers might
come from within the organization and from outside; both have a
particular role to play. They should all be skilled in helping people
through a process of change. Those from within can provide inside
knowledge of how their organization works and of some of the key
personalities involved. However, because they are themselves part of
the structure, the progress of their own career is inevitably affected by
how they work as advisers. This can limit their impact at crucial times.
For instance, it takes a brave, some would say foolhardy, person to
press an authoritarian personnel director to examine the way he treats
his subordinates, when it is the personnel director who decides whether
or not the adviser is promoted.

In supporting and advising senior managers, an outsider can be
vital. The external consultant is not governed by considerations like
promotion within the organization, although he or she faces other
pressures – the need to earn fees, for instance. But there are times when
the view of the outsider with his experience of going through similar
processes in other organizations is very helpful indeed. The outsider
can also be an asset in helping trade union representatives work
through their own problems – a situation in which internal advisers can
find their effectiveness reduced because their independence is, rightly
or wrongly, suspect.   (LCCI, English for commerce (higher))

6   Using your own words as far as possible, write a summary of the following passage in not more than 120 words. Give the summary a title and state the actual number of words that you use.

He argues that most people judge the efficiency of a computer system in the same way as they would judge that of a factory flowline; by how many invoices are churned out per hour, like cans of soup. He says that, instead, you should measure whether an information system makes management more effective. By effective, he means; Does it give the customer a better service and increase the 'value added' to the company as a whole?

He came to this conclusion after measuring the profitability of several groups of companies against the amount they spent on computers, and finding that there was no correlation between the two. In one study of 138 American wholesalers, he unearthed a healthy 11.3 per cent return on assets in firms with no computer, but only 8.8 per cent in those with a heavy usage of computers.

In some of the less profitable companies, he found that the more computers they installed, the more money they lost. This does not mean that all money spent on computers is thrown down the drain: Strassman found that the profitable, well-managed companies increased their profits by investing in computers.

The difference is that good managers insist on sensible and effective use of computers and make them work for the company profits. Unfortunately, the bad ones just throw money at their computer departments, hoping that tomorrow will show the 'pay off'.

Usually their mistake is to mechanize existing systems around archaic company structures without reorganizing. This does not take advantage of what Strassman sees as the real benefit of computers, which is to simplify organization by cutting out links in the cumbersome communication chains. Computers can now pass the messages and instructions which hierarchies of managers used to.

Meanwhile, professional staff, accountants, planners, designers and marketeers (who Strassman calls information workers), sitting at their workstations, with access to all the information they need to do their job, will become more effective. They will also become less specialized, and able to give a wider range of services to their customers. *The Times*

(ABE, Business communication)

Writing for colleagues and the public

10.1 Introduction

Although oral communication plays an important role in business, there are situations in which you will need to communicate in writing. When you are agreeing terms with a supplier, for example, you will need to send a formal letter setting out proposals and outlining any special provisions; if you receive a letter of complaint, you will need to acknowledge it. There are a number of formal principles for writing business letters and these are covered in Units 11 and 12. Often, though, situations will arise for which some other, less formal means of communication will be appropriate: a note to a close colleague, an open memo to all members of your department, an entry in the staff newsletter, an attractive and colourful notice in the works canteen, or a small ad in the local newspaper.

This unit looks at the most common kinds of written communication used to communicate internally within an organization and externally with the general public. It also includes a section on persuasive writing, which is important for devising sales leaflets and press releases, as well as for notices and advertisements.

10.2 Informal notes

There may be occasions when you need to contact a working colleague quickly, but find that she is not available because she is visiting a client or has some other appointment. In these circumstances, the best thing to do is to write a short note and leave it on her desk or in her in-tray, to make sure that she will see it on her return. Informal notes are written by hand, to save time in having them typed, and are ideal for making contact quickly. They should not, however, be used to communicate with anyone except a colleague whom you know quite well; they are much too informal for use with a client or someone working for another firm. Similarly, they should not be used for routine communication, for which memos are much more efficient (see section 10.3).

10.2.1 Layout of notes
Look carefully at the example of a note shown in fig. 10.1. You will see that it includes the following components:

Date and time These are essential to show exactly when you communicated the information. You might need to refer to this later, so make sure that all your informal notes include these details.

Salutation This can be fairly relaxed in tone. You can begin 'Dear Nick' or just 'Nick' – either will do, so long as it is clear whom you are addressing.

Information This will probably be in two parts. First comes the reason or background for the communication: second, the action you would like the reader to take, or the information or message you need to convey.

Signature You should always sign a note, to make clear exactly who wrote it. Unless you know the reader very well and are sure that he or she can read your signature, print your name at the end of the note. If necessary, put your own

Thursday 15 August
4.15 p.m.

Dear Nick,

A Mrs Owen rang this afternoon to speak to you: she said you were arranging insurance cover for her son to drive her car — a 1968 Morris Minor, registration PDQ 436C.
Could you ring her back as soon as possible to let her know if the insurance has been arranged? Her son wants to start using the car.

Thanks

Gordon

Fig. 10.1 Informal note to a colleague

position or department, or the telephone extension number on which you can be contacted.

10.2.2 Writing a note

The important point to remember when writing a note is that its purpose is to convey essential data quickly and clearly. You can do this by following six basic rules.

(a) Have a clear idea of the *essential* points you wish to communicate.
(b) Use simple, clear language.
(c) Keep the note short.
(d) Give all the necessary details – times, dates, telephone numbers and other data such as invoice or account numbers where appropriate.
(e) Make clear where you can be reached for further details if necessary.
(f) Always write legibly. There is no point in writing a note if no one can read it.

10.3 Memos

If you want to pass on information or instructions to someone within your own organization and more than a quick note is needed, then you will normally use a memo. 'Memo' is short for *memorandum*, a Latin word meaning 'something to be remembered'. This suggests the purpose of a memo – it is a note reminding someone of some fact or detail. Memos should never be used for communicating outside your organization.

Unlike notes, memos are typed on forms which are specially designed to make them easier and quicker to produce. There are two main kinds of memo, named after the size of paper on which they are printed: A4 and A5. Apart from their length, there is no real difference between them.

10.3.1 A5 memos

An A5 memo should be used to convey a single, brief message. It can be used between people at different levels within an organization – subject, of course, to any restrictions in the organization about who may communicate with whom (see section 3.3). Memos may thus be sent from a superior to a subordinate; from a subordinate to a supervisor; from a superior to all members of his or her section or department; or between employees of equal status. Specific uses of A5 memos include:

- giving brief instructions about a new procedure;
- conveying a single item of information;
- reminding people about existing arrangements or regulations;
- requesting information or suggestions;
- serving as a covering note to send with a report, a file of documents or other material.

Since memos are usually distributed by office messengers or through internal mail systems, they may easily be read by any member of an organization.

Consequently, they should not be used to convey confidential information; this is best dealt with in a letter sent in a sealed envelope marked 'confidential', or discussed in a private meeting with the person or people concerned.

When memos are typed, a copy is usually taken so that the sender has a record of what has been said. This makes a memo far more effective as a means of communication than an informal note, of which there is often no record. The efficiency of memos is also increased by the way in which they are presented, as section 10.3.3 will show.

10.3.2 A4 memos

Sometimes you may need to send a rather longer memo, and for this you will need an A4 memo form. A4 memos follow the same format as A5 memos, but are printed on larger paper. Some of their more common uses are:

- giving details about a major change in company policy, such as a merger with another company or a move to a new building;
- giving instructions for new procedures – on the computerization of a department, say, or expansion into a new area of activity;
- giving instructions about a new piece of equipment and how it should be used – as a supplement to training or instruction sessions.

From these examples, it may appear that longer memos are usually sent from those in positions of authority to those working under them. This is often the case. Sometimes, however, a longer memo will be sent from a subordinate to a superior – giving a reaction to suggested changes in operating procedures, for example, or a response to a report or discussion document. Memos may also be used to put forward suggestions as part of a suggestion scheme when separate forms are not available.

10.3.3 Presentation of memos

Sample layouts of A5 and A4 memos are given in figs 10.2 and 10.3. They consist of the following elements:

1 Main heading The heading 'Memo' or 'Memorandum' makes clear the purpose of the printed form, and ensures that it stands out in a pile of other papers or letters. An organization's name and address do not usually appear in the heading, as they do on other letter-heads, since a memo is used only for correspondence within an organization.

2 'To' and 'From' headings These make clear who sent the memo, and to whom, and can be completed easily and quickly by the sender. Always give both the name and the position of the sender and the receiver, except when sending identical memos to several people, when a general term such as 'To all sales staff' will be adequate.

3 Date and reference A date is essential on a memo, to indicate when the communication was sent. It may be part of a sequence of memos and letters, in which case the date will allow it to be filed correctly. The reference, if included, will usually give the initials of the writer followed by an oblique stroke and the initials of the typist. It may also have another set of letters or figures, which refer to an account or file number.

4 Subject heading   This should be brief and exact, making clear immediately what the memo is about.

5 First paragraph   This provides a background, context or reason for the information or instructions contained in the second paragraph. Again, it should be kept short.

6 Second paragraph   This is the actual message – information, instructions or reminder – and should follow on logically from the first paragraph.

7 Initials of sender   In some organizations, the writer will add his or her initials at the foot of the memo. These are by no means essential, and their inclusion depends largely on company practice.

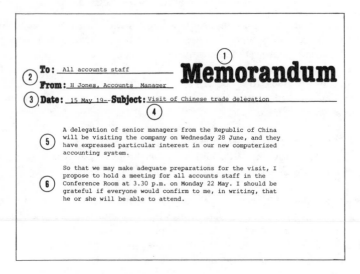

To: All accounts staff   **Memorandum**
From: H Jones, Accounts Manager
Date: 15 May 19-- **Subject:** Visit of Chinese trade delegation

A delegation of senior managers from the Republic of China will be visiting the company on Wednesday 28 June, and they have expressed particular interest in our new computerized accounting system.

So that we may make adequate preparations for the visit, I propose to hold a meeting for all accounts staff in the Conference Room at 3.30 p.m. on Monday 22 May. I should be grateful if everyone would confirm to me, in writing, that he or she will be able to attend.

Fig. 10.2 A5 memo

Both A4 and A5 memos, then, are effective and rapid ways of conveying information. Care should be taken, however, to make sure that no more than a single idea or a group of closely related ideas is conveyed in a memo, whatever its length. Memos can easily become complex and unwieldy, and thus lose their effectiveness.

To: All office staff

From: Pat Green

Memorandum

Date: 1 June 19-- **Subject:** Redecoration of general office

As some of you may already know, the general office is to be redecorated. At the same time, the layout will be changed to allow for the installation of new workstations linked to the central computer. This work will begin on Monday 10 July, and should be completed by the end of the following week.

During this period, I am hoping to ensure that the office's work will continue without interruption, and for this reason I should be grateful for your co-operation with the following temporary arrangements.

Over the weekend of 8-9 July, staff from Maintenance will move the existing desk-top computers into the old staff canteen, which will be used as a general office for the period of the redecoration. At the same time, essential files and other material will be moved to the canteen, so that work should continue without interruption.

Staff should report to the old canteen for work at the normal time on Monday 10 July, and on the following days until the redecoration is completed. Under no circumstances will anyone be allowed into the general office while work is in progress, as the contractors' insurance does not cover liability for our staff members. As a result, you should make sure that all personal belongings or material needed for work are removed on Friday 7 July for use in the next two weeks.

If for any reason essential documents or materials are left in the office and need to be retrieved, those who need them should contact me or my secretary, Ms Mukerjee, so that they can be retrieved when the decorators have finished work for the day.

I realise that the redecoration will cause much disturbance, and that working in the much smaller space of the old canteen will not be easy. However, once the office is completed we shall have excellent, modern working conditions and I am sure you will agree that the sacrifice will be worthwhile. I know that I can count on your help and tolerance during this brief period of inconvenience.

P. G./

Fig. 10.3 A4 memo

10.3.4 *Other kinds of memo*

NCR memos or 'ping-pongs' Some organizations use memo forms which consist of three copies of the same form attached at the top or side (see fig. 10.4). These are printed on special paper and whatever is written on the top copy is transferred to all lower copies, hence the term 'no carbon required' or NCR. The sender types or writes the memo in the usual way, detaches the bottom copy for his or her own files and sends the top two copies to the receiver.

The receiver then writes his or her reply in a special space left blank at the foot of the form, detaches the second copy for the file, and sends back the top copy to the original sender. This shuttling backwards and forwards has led to the name 'ping-pong memo'.

This system has two main advantages over the conventional memo, both of which improve its efficiency as a means of communication. First, the receiver is given a space for a reply, making it much easier for him or her to respond to the memo. Secondly, both sender and receiver have a copy of both the original message and the reply. Ping-pong memos are expensive to produce, however, and may encourage unnecessary paperwork if they are used without good reason.

TEAR OFF AND KEEP BACK COPY, BUT PLEASE DO NOT TEAR OFF THIS STUB. SEND TOP TWO COPIES INTACT TO REGIONAL OFFICE

PT2

THE OPEN UNIVERSITY

ACTION/REPORT FORM TO REGIONAL OFFICE

REGIONAL OFFICE TO RETAIN

From .... To ....

No. ☐☐☐☐☐☐ Region Code ☐☐

Study Centre .... Date ....

ISSUE RAISED AND ACTION TAKEN TO DATE (If any). If it relates to a student state name and serial number. Please use ONE form for EACH student problem.

Student .... Undergraduate No. ☐☐☐☐☐☐☐☐
and/or
Course(s) .... Associate Student No. ☐☐☐☐☐☐☐☐

COMMENTS BY REGIONAL STAFF

Signed .... Date ....
(for Regional Office)

Fig. 10.4 'Ping-pong' or NCR memo. In this example, the space for the message is headed 'Issue raised', and that for the reply is headed 'Comments by regional staff'.

Longer memos Some organizations use the term 'memo' to refer to longer documents. These might include a special kind of report; some personal thoughts or opinions on an item of company policy; detailed instructions about events; or even annual reports on the work of a department or suggestions for possible changes, to be read and discussed by all members of a department.

Memoranda of agreement A memorandum of agreement is a form of legal contract, drawn up to describe an agreement between two or more parties about the sale of goods, the production of a book, or co-operation in trade, for example. Drafting such memoranda is a highly specialized task, usually undertaken by accountants, solicitors or senior staff of an organization.

10.4 Staff newsletters

Many large organizations produce regular newspapers or magazines which are issued to all employees, directors and retired members of staff. Their purpose is to make sure that everyone knows what is going on in other departments, offices and works and thus feels a part of the organization. Newsletters will also contain other important information of the kind which might be included in memos sent to all members of a department – about changes in company policy, a move to new premises or the launch of a new product, for example. In some cases, these publications have a full-time editor and secretarial or production staff, and are produced on a lavish scale, using the latest technology and colour printing. This is usually only the case in the largest organizations, however; it is far more usual for a company to produce its own staff newsletter. This will be typed and duplicated, or sometimes printed, the length and size varying from organization to organization.

Newsletters commonly contain articles on the following topics:

● news about developments within the company, such as new products or new export markets;
● details of important new orders or similar matters which might affect employment;
● information about recently recruited staff at management or board level;
● 'human interest' stories such as details of the retirement of long-serving employees or results of sports matches played by the organization's teams;
● results of competitions, suggestion schemes and interdepartmental productivity contests.

10.4.1 Producing a newsletter

Newsletters should be clear, short and well presented. If they are not, people will not read them. The basic principles below provide a useful guide.

(a) Make sure that the content is interesting and that it is necessary – either because it conveys essential working information, or because it concerns matters of genuine interest about members of staff.

(b) Separate essential information – anything concerning changes in holiday dates, new premises and similar matters – from items of 'human interest'.

(c) Make sure the layout is simple but attractive. Highlight essential items with lines, boxes or large typefaces, so that the reader's attention is drawn to them.

(d) Keep all items short. There is little point in writing a whole page about a football match in which the works' team lost by fourteen goals to nil: a single paragraph will be enough.

(e) Write in a direct but interesting style. Nobody will read articles which are dull and poorly written: keep them punchy and appealing.

(f) Use language which you know everyone will understand, without appearing to 'talk down' to your readers. Think of the style used in a local newspaper or magazine that most of the staff members read, and try to model your writing on that.

In many organizations, the staff newsletter is compiled or edited by a senior secretary or someone with considerable experience of writing and editing. Nevertheless, it is possible that you may at some time be asked to write an article or suggest material for inclusion in one. Follow the principles listed above, and you should find that this will present few problems. Look closely at the excerpt from a newsletter in fig. 10.5, which shows the kind of material that may be included, and the style in which it should be written.

NEWSLETTER No. 46   **WEEK ENDING 14 FEB. 19--**

General arrangements

Building work has begun on the extension to the staff dining room. We hope that this will be completed within four months, but much depends on the state of the weather. While the work is in progress, we ask for your co-operation with the building workers. Regular progress reports will be given in the Newsletter and on noticeboards.

New order for France

An order for twenty specially-equipped medical supplies delivery vehicles has been received from France. This means that staff in the Special Products Division will have their work cut out over the next few months - but it also means that dividends in the profit-sharing scheme will be increased, and the order may lead to further orders in the all-important export market.

Staff

We are pleased to welcome Mr N Chadha as General Assistant in Personnel. He joins us from a distinguished career in educational administration, and will have special responsibility for seeing that our programme of in-service training and personal development is expanded. We wish him every success and happiness in his new post.

Good wishes are also extended to Mrs James, who retired from the company this week after thirty-one years' loyal service. At a ceremony in the Directors' Dining Room on Tuesday, Mrs James was presented with a grandfather clock as a token of esteem and gratitude for her 'constant and generous contribution to the company's growth in its formative years'.

Fig. 10.5 Excerpt from a staff newsletter

10.5 Notices

Memos are a valuable way of communicating with an individual or a small group of people within an organization. On some occasions, however, they are not appropriate. You might, for example, wish to make sure that what you have to say is seen and read by people frequently, to remind them of an important rule or practice, perhaps to do with safety or a routine procedure. You might wish to publicize an event to a wide range of people, in which case sending memos would be impossible, not only because of the number of people involved, but also because you would not know who your audience might be.

For situations like these, notices provide a fast, attractive and simple means of communication. To be effective, however, they must be carefully thought out in three key areas:

(a) content;
(b) expression;
(c) design.

In other words, you must know what to say, how to say it, and how to make the message stand out. A fourth and equally important consideration is where the notice will be displayed.

10.5.1 Contents of a notice

Knowing what to put in and what to leave out is very important when you are planning a notice. Put too little in and the reader will receive an incomplete message, and be confused or annoyed: put too much in and the reader may well lose interest before he or she has received the message.

Whenever you are asked to write a notice, your first step should be to define exactly what information you wish to convey. Some notices will be fairly simple in this respect: those which give simple directions or instructions, or a single piece of information, for example.

INSURANCE CLAIMS OFFICE ON THIRD FLOOR

PLEASE RING FOR SERVICE

STORES OPEN 9.30 a.m. TO 5.00 p.m. DAILY

Most notices, however, will be more complicated than these. You may wish to use them to convey complex information about a procedure, publicize a forthcoming event, or advertise a service of some kind. To produce effective notices of this kind, you need to list the points which you think are important before beginning to think about wording or design. This can be done quite quickly as a rough set of notes, like those in fig. 10.6.

When you have completed the rough list, check it through carefully. Ask yourself whether you have left out any vital information – the date or venue of the meeting, for example. Check, too, that you have not included anything which is not strictly necessary. Do you really need to list all the performers in the staff Christmas pantomime, or give a full timetable for the stores department's

```
┌─────────────────────────────────────────────────────────────────────────┐
│  SUBJECT: ·  Training  weekend  on  computer  sales  techniques          │
│                                                                           │
│  DATE :      24 - 26  April                                               │
│                                                                           │
│  TIME :      Starts  Friday  evening  at  7·30                            │
│              Finishes  Sunday  at  2·30                                    │
│                                                                           │
│  PLACE :     White  Horse  Hotel,  Little  Wenlock                        │
│                                                                           │
│  DETAILS :   Seminars                                                      │
│              Address  by  Pres.  of  Institute  of  Computer  Management  │
│              Free  accommodation  in  4-star  hotel :  good  food         │
│                 and  bar                                                   │
│              Recreational  facilities  include  squash  court  &  sauna   │
│              2  days'  paid  leave  for  those  who  attend               │
│                                                                           │
│  CONTACT :   George  Watkins,  Personnel  (ext  376)                      │
└─────────────────────────────────────────────────────────────────────────┘
```

Fig. 10.6 Notes for a notice

annual training weekend? Questions of this kind are essential before you start work on the final notice.

10.5.2 Choosing the right expression

Once you have decided what you need to say, you have to decide how you are going to say it. In many ways this means thinking about the same points that you would consider for any other form of written communication: matching your expression to the vocabulary and attitude of your readers, and using language which is clear, concise and courteous. In particular, you should bear the following things in mind.

Consider the range of readers　Is your notice intended to be read by a few people in one department of the organization, who are used to reading documents about their work which use specialized language? If so, you can use specialized terms. On the other hand, if your notice is to be read by a larger group or by the general public, it must use far simpler language so that non-specialists can understand it.

Avoid offending your readers　If you are writing a notice which gives instructions, you should make every effort not to arouse resentment or even anger in your readers. A notice which reads

　　SHOP-FLOOR WORKERS KEEP OUT

will make readers feel resentful, and emphasize a division among employees.

Instead, try to include a reason for your statement, like this:

SECURITY STORES: AUTHORIZED PERSONNEL ONLY

This does not apply to very brief notices which are concerned with safety, or which apply to all readers, such as:

NO SMOKING

HAZARDOUS CHEMICALS – KEEP OUT

EMERGENCY ACCESS ONLY

Be brief A notice in a busy corridor will be useless unless it is short enough to be read by people as they walk past: an advertisement for a company open day outside a company's offices will not be effective unless someone going past on the top of a bus can take in what it says.

10.5.3 Designing a notice

Clear design is just as important as clear expression in a notice. The following are important principles.

Have a clear heading Many notices begin with the word 'NOTICE' in large letters. This serves very little purpose. Instead, you should work out a simple heading which conveys the essence of your message, and display it prominently. 'ANNUAL SPORTS DAY', 'FULL STAFF MEETING', 'OVERTIME PAY CLAIMS'; used as headings, these would all establish quickly and clearly what the notice beneath was about.

Keep the message brief Cut out everything that is not essential. You can always give a name, address or telephone number for people to contact for further information: do not clutter up a notice with unnecessary details.

Use lots of space Graphic artists and advertisers talk about 'white space', by which they mean blank paper around the main message of a notice or advertisement. Use plenty of white space when designing notices.

● Leave space between lines – the equivalent of writing on every other line of lined paper.
● Leave wide margins at top and bottom and on both sides.
● Make one or two rough sketches of the layout before you complete the final version, to make sure that you get the best and clearest layout.

Make important words stand out This can be done by using different colours, underlining, using larger sizes of lettering, placing lines around key words or putting individual words on separate lines with lots of space around them. Dates and times of meetings, telephone numbers, places to assemble in case of fire, and other essential information can all be treated in this way.

Using a different typeface can help, too – though you should be careful to avoid using too many styles, as this can look fussy and confusing. Remember, too, that small letters are easier to read from a distance than capitals.

Use illustrations A simple cartoon or illustration can often help to get a message across. It can be humorous or serious and, even if it is not up to professional standards, it can convey the idea of your message well. Keep illustrations simple, though: a small notice crowded with pictures so that the words are crushed into a small space in the centre will only succeed in confusing the reader.

The notice shown in fig. 10.7 attempts to put these points into practice, taking the essential information from the list in fig. 10.6. Look at it carefully, and ask yourself how well it conveys its message, and how you might attempt to convey the same points in a more striking way.

COMPUTER SELLING

IN THE

TWENTY-FIRST CENTURY

A company training weekend

FRIDAY 24 - SUNDAY 26 APRIL

* Free accommodation
* Four-star luxury hotel in the country
* Free transport
* Recreational facilities include squash courts and sauna

TWO DAYS' PAID LEAVE FOR ALL WHO ATTEND

Contact George Watkins (ext'n 376) to reserve your place

Fig. 10.7 A notice

10.5.4 Displaying notices

No matter how well a notice has been designed, it will not be effective unless it is displayed in the right place. Notice-boards should be carefully placed so that they can be seen by all staff; they should not be put behind doors, or in small rooms used only by certain groups of employees. They should also be put at a suitable height, so that everyone can read them.

Notice-boards should be kept in good order. They should be cleared regularly, to prevent notices being posted on top of each other. Some organizations date-stamp notices for display, and remove them after a set period – a month or six weeks, perhaps.

It is also useful to divide notice-boards into separate parts for notices on different topics – health and safety, union and staff announcements, for example. A space should be left for 'urgent annoucements', and should be used only for such notices, so that people will see and act upon them. If urgent notices are put up among the general clutter of a disorganized board, they may well be ignored.

10.6 Press advertisements

The drafting and design of advertisements for large-scale press or broadcasting campaigns, or for advertisement hoardings, is a highly sophisticated skill. It is very unlikely that you will have to produce anything on such a lavish scale. However, there are two kinds of advertisement which you may well be asked to produce: the *small ad* or *lineage* advertisement, and the *display ad*.

10.6.1 The small ad

Small ads are those advertisements which appear – classified under subject – in most local and some national newspapers. Examples are shown in fig. 10.8.

PAINTING, decorating, interior or exterior. Artexing, all building work undertaken. Very reasonable prices. Free estimates. – Westport 7642

PAINTING & DECORATING. All work undertaken, free estimates. – Ring Tony. Westport 5123

VIDEO IMAGES. Weddings, christenings, birthday parties, functions. Westport 1999

ROLLS ROYCE car hire at discount prices when you book our wedding photography. – Telephone Brian at Westport 5243

SECRETARY book-keeper with knowledge of PAYE required for Wednesday afternoons, 12.30pm to 6pm at Westport Nursing Home, 3 Park Road, Westport. Tel. Westport 4701

Fig. 10.8 Small ads

Small ads serve various purposes, but the most common is to advertise goods or services for sale. Generally, they are paid for at a set rate per word, and so brevity is important. However, it is no use being so brief that no one knows what you are trying to sell or whom they should contact in response.

Small ads should contain:

(a) a description of the item or service;
(b) the price;
(c) an address or telephone number to contact.

Some small ads have a different function: they may advertise a vacancy for a member of staff. Here again, there are three basic elements:

(a) a description of the job, either just by its title – 'shop assistant'; 'trainee accounts clerk' – or by a short phrase – 'person wanted to assist generally in busy garage'.
(b) some indication of the pay that is offered. This can be a simple statement – '£5 per hour' – or a suggestion – 'top rates paid'.
(c) an address or telephone number to contact. Here a name or position – 'Ms Pradesh, Personnel Manager' – will help to make sure that applicants speak to the right person.

10.6.2 The display ad

The display ad is a combination of a notice and a small ad, with the layout of the former and the contents of the latter. Display advertisements present much the same information as small ads, but use more space and different sizes and styles of type to make them more eye-catching.

Advertisements of this kind appear in various sizes, usually referred to by the fraction of the whole page which they occupy. In a magazine, a quarter-page advertisement would be quite large and used to advertise a major product. An eighth or sixteenth-page might be used to advertise a vacancy in a small company. Newspaper advertisements are sometimes referred to in the same way, although, because advertising rates are much more expensive in national newspapers – and in some local ones – space is often sold by the 'single column centimetre'. This is the space convered by a column-width of type extending a centimetre down the page. Figure 10.9 shows double- and single-column-width advertisements.

PERSON REQUIRED
FOR
PLUMBING AND HEATING STORE
FOR LOCAL BUILDERS' MERCHANTS

Knowledge of heating and plumbing trade essential and must be prepared to attend Aga fitting course.

Apply in writing to:

COMPANY SECRETARY
JOHN BENNETT & CO
ELM ROAD, WESTPORT

ACCOUNTANT/ OFFICE MANAGER

A person of proven ability with computer and manual accounting systems is required by

DAVIS & SON LTD
BENNET STREET
WESTPORT
SUFFOLK

If you feel you have the accounting ability to meet the demand of this position, which requires a shirt-sleeve approach and the ability to work to tight time schedules, then apply in writing to the Company Secretary at the above address.

WESTPORT
GOLF CLUB
ASSISTANT
GREENKEEPER
required. Previous experience essential. Knowledge of course machinery an advantage. Salary negotiable.

Apply to: The Secretary/Manager
Westport Golf Club, Bury Road,
Westport. Tel W'port 7558

WANTED
OUTDOOR
MACHINISTS
for ladies' and children's coats and jackets. Work collected and delivered.

Tel. 0123 45678

Fig. 10.9 Display ads – double- and single-column width

When drafting a display advertisement, you should remember all the principles for designing a notice. Have a clear idea of what you need to say; use a clear layout that attracts attention; and use language appropriate to the post on offer. Remember, too, that you should not use language which could be interpreted as implying that the job is open only to men or only to women. A properly-worded advertisement will avoid any possibility of prosecution under the equal opportunities legislation, which would not only be costly but would certainly be bad for the organization's public image as well. Specific terms such as 'storeman' should be replaced by the more general 'storekeeper', and you should make a point of saying 'he or she' or 'the successful applicant' rather than just 'he'. Every company should have an equal opportunities policy, but if you actually state in the advertisement that your company operates such a policy, you will imply that your company does more than pay lip-service to the law.

10.7 Persuasive writing

Many communication tasks in business call for a persuasive approach. Press releases, sales circulars, promotional leaflets, catalogues, factsheets and posters all attempt to influence the reader in some way – to accept the image of the company or organization if not to purchase its products.

How should you go about writing persuasive documents? It is an exact and demanding science, which depends as much on marketing skills as on literary ability, but there are some basic principles which will make the task easier.

Define your aim   Unless you know exactly what you want people to do, you will stand a poor chance of persuading them to do it. The first stage, then, is to plan exactly what you want to achieve from your writing. Do you want people to buy a particular product or do you simply want to increase their awareness of your whole range of products – in what is called a 'consciousness-raising campaign'?

Your aim must be realistic. It is no good expecting people to switch allegiance to an out-of-town hypermarket on the strength of a single leaflet put through their letterbox. Instead, you might hope to get them to visit the store and see what it is like. Once they are there, you can use other kinds of persuasion to get them to come back. Similarly, when planning a promotional letter, think about what you can realistically achieve. If you are trying to sell an expensive encyclopaedia, it would be unwise to include a reply form saying 'I enclose a cheque for £1645. Please rush me my new encyclopaedia.' Instead, a request for a representative to call, or for a more detailed brochure to be sent, would be more likely to encourage potential customers to respond.

Know your facts   It is often said that the first rule of selling is to know your product. This is certainly true for persuasive literature. You must spend time studying the item you wish to promote – whether it is a new encyclopaedia, the service of your garage or the proposed route of a by-pass. Without this knowledge, you will be unaware of the strongest points in favour of the goods, services or course of action you are promoting, and will be unable to communicate them to your reader. Initial research of this kind is therefore essential.

Define your market   You must also research your market. Are you writing for the public in general – in a newspaper advertisement or sales leaflet, say – or for a particular kind of reader – in a press release to the editor of a newspaper or a reporter at a local radio station?

When you have decided on the kind of market you are aiming at, you must consider all the factors relevant to choice of language which are outlined in section 4.10.1. Every aspect of your language must be carefully judged to match the expectations of the intended reader, to make him or her feel that your product or idea is exactly suited to his or her way of life. Writing a prospectus for a new share issue in the language of a popular music paper, for example, will achieve very little; instead, the emphasis should lie on the fact that the investment offers a chance for 'high growth' or 'rapid return' – phrases which will be understood by the readers you are hoping to attract.

Direct your appeal   Once you have identified the kind of person to whom you are writing, you can think about how you are going to direct your appeal. Modern persuasive writing tends to analyse the reader's nature and appeal to certain facets within it. One of these is the reader's self-image or sense of status. A recent advertising campaign had much success in selling a *vin ordinaire* as something beloved by the French and therefore rather special and by no means ordinary. Similarly, a car may be advertised as intended 'for individualists only'. Both of these approaches appeal to the potential customer's sense that he or she is different or special.

Other examples of persuasive writing might appeal to the reader's sense of duty – 'Don't you owe it to your family to fit security locks?' – or to his or her physical well-being – a sales letter for weatherproof footwear, for example. A leaflet about holidays in Paris might call on the reader's desire to recapture a lost youth. Persuasive writing often takes account of current preoccupations, such as the rash of products described as 'natural' or 'from the country' and accompanied by a picture of a field, a cow, a thatched cottage or some other rural image to suggest that they are untainted by artificial additives or industrial processes.

Have a clear message   We are accustomed to highly sophisticated methods of persuasion in television and magazine advertising, in which the products themselves often do not appear but are replaced by evocations of a particular way of life, symbolizing the excitement and glamour surrounding the product. There are signs, however, that such techniques do not always achieve their desired end: people certainly remember the stylish advertisements, but have no idea of the products they are promoting.

This reinforces a simple rule of persuasion: always make clear what it is that you want people to buy or to do. This is particularly important if the medium you are using is the printed word, since there is no guarantee that your reader will understand oblique references which attempt to sell the product by association. Be direct in stating your aim, otherwise – however stylish your approach – your results will be limited.

Don't oversell   The foot-in-the-door salesman who will not go away and the telesales person who rings up about double glazing and just will not accept that you are not interested are familiar images of the sales function. These are both examples of what is called 'the hard sell'. Nowadays, however, the opposite approach – 'the soft sell' – is much more common.

The reason for this is simple. If you adopt a hectoring approach, insisting that the customer buys your goods, it is far easier for the customer to tell you in forceful terms that he or she is not interested. But if you adopt the manner of an old friend or personal adviser, it is far harder for the customer to ask awkward questions. The morality of this may be rather dubious – but its success is undeniable.

The same is true of persuasive writing. Always make your points in a forthright manner but do not be too emphatic. A strong product and a forceful argument which points out the product's advantages over its competition will be much more effective than repetitive messages which attempt to bully the reader into agreement.

Keep it short   Much 'junk mail' – unsolicited advertising sent by post – fails because it is too long. Letters written on wordprocessors which pretend to be personal communications from the director of a bank, building society or other company and which take up two or more pages are very unlikely to be read: concise, single-page statements of what the company has to offer will be far more effective. Many kinds of persuasive literature – not only junk mail but also leaflets and press releases – are read by people who have little time to spare. The more concisely you can get your point across, the more likely you are to persuade the reader to buy your product or accept your idea.

10.8 Conclusion

All the kinds of communication discussed in this unit meet important needs within an organization's communication system. They are effective, easy-to-produce and – generally – cheap methods of conveying information in a range of different contexts. Each has a specific use, and being able to identify when to use each one is a key skill which you should develop. Although they may seem straightforward – and they should always be worded with simplicity in mind – you should think about them and plan them carefully before you start writing. In particular, you should make sure that you are familiar with the basic principles of layout and content for each, as outlined in the preceding pages, so that you can produce memos and other documents quickly and efficiently under pressure.

10.9 Quick questions

1 List the four headings which should appear at the head of a memo.

2 List five key principles for designing a notice.

3 Give three examples of the kinds of items which might appear in a company newsletter.

4 What is the purpose of the first paragraph of a memo?

5 When should you use an informal note?

10.10 Longer exercises

1 Write a notice reminding office employees of the dangers of being careless in the use of electrical equipment. Use every technique possible to make the notice stand out and convey its message strikingly.

2 You are assistant to the financial manager of Farm Supplies, a wholesale distributor of agricultural supplies and cattle feed, with head offices in Wrexham. Your superior tells you to draft a memo asking all travelling salespeople to submit their claim forms for travelling expenses for the last three months before 7 March. He goes on: 'After then, the finance staff will be doing the annual audit and won't want to be bothered. Get them to do it on the PT7 forms as usual, with subsistence on a PT9, and remind them that these aren't swindle sheets they're completing – genuine expenses only, please.' Prepare the memo.

3 Read these notes carefully. Select from them the necessary information to complete the task which follows.

You have been elected Secretary of the Manningham branch of ICM students, which has 200 members. The Annual Dinner of the branch is to be held (by kind permission of the Principal, Dr R Goodfellow) in the training restaurant of Manningham Polytechnic, Downs Road, Manningham. The date chosen is Saturday 26 July 1986. The meal will be cooked and served by second-year students on the HCIMA course at the college, who have earned an excellent reputation locally. The time arranged is 19.00 for 19.30. The restaurant closes at 22.30. Lounge suits should be worn, and the cost of the tickets will be £10 per head, the price to include sherry before the meal and a glass of wine with dinner. There is a licensed bar at the restaurant. The guest speaker will be Mr John March, senior partner in the firm of March and May, financial consultants in the City. Only 60 guests can be accommodated in the restaurant, and in the past there has been a heavy demand for tickets for this annual function.

Compose a brief notice (small enough to fit on a postcard) to publicize the date and time of the event, with all enquiries to you in your office. The notice is for your own firm's noticeboard.

(ICM, Business communications (part))

4   Read the following job description then, using approximately 60–70 words, draft an advertisement for the post.

The Personnel and Management Services Department at the Town Hall, Bridgeford, provides a comprehensive personnel service for the council. There is at present a vacancy for a secretarial assistant. The person to be appointed will be responsible to the Principal Assistant Personnel Officer and will be a member of a small team which provides a shorthand/typing/clerical service to officers of the department. Duties will include collating and distributing internal and external post at regular daily times, the regular clearance of personal trays, photocopying, and general filing, including council minutes. He/she will also be required to undertake general secretarial duties for the officers of the Personnel and Management Services Department. There will be some audio typing of correspondence. The post would be suitable for a young person wishing to gain experience in local government general office practices. The successful applicant will preferably have a minimum of 3 GCSEs, including English language, together with Intermediate Stage Typewriting and 80 words per minute Shorthand (or the equivalent level LCCI Group Secretarial Studies Certificate). He/she will, ideally, have successfully completed a course of secretarial training. Previous work experience would be an advantage but is not essential.

Business letters: content and layout

11.1 Introduction

Despite the recent growth in electronic communications, and the ease and convenience of the telephone, letters are still a very widely used medium of communication in business. They are cheap to produce, and postal delivery is quick and generally very reliable. Additional material relevant to the contents of the letter can be sent with it in the form of an enclosure. Letters also provide both the receiver and the sender with a permanent record of what has been discussed or agreed for later reference. Letters may lack the personal touch of a meeting or the immediacy of a telephone call, but when matters are relatively straightforward and there is no great urgency for a decision – as is the case with most routine business – they are an effective and valuable form of communication.

Every letter communicates two messages: the information it is intended to deliver to the receiver, and all kinds of signals about the writer. The clarity of the layout, the accuracy of the expression, and the inclusion of all the necessary details are all important in helping the reader to formulate an impression of the writer. In business, this can have considerable impact on your success, especially if you are writing a letter aimed at selling goods or services.

Layout and expression are discussed later in this unit; first, we will look at the details essential to a successful business letter, and where they should be placed.

11.2 Parts of a letter

As well as the information to be communicated, a business letter must include the following details:

(a) who it is from, and how the sender can be contacted;
(b) who it is for;
(c) when it was written;
(d) how it relates to earlier correspondence.

This information is contained in a number of separate parts of the letter, all of which must be included for it to be fully effective.

Some of these would also appear on a personal letter to a friend: your own address and the date, for example. A business letter, however, is intended to convey these and other details as quickly and efficiently as possible, and certain conventions have therefore evolved to ensure that this is done.

In the list which follows, the numbers refer to the sample letter shown in fig. 11.1.

1 Letter-head
Most organizations use specially printed stationery for letter-writing, known as 'letter-heads' after the printed information at the top – and sometimes also the foot – of the page. This always includes the company's name, address and post-code, and may include other items, such as the company's *logo* – an emblem which usually consists of initials or a small drawing of some kind – or a brief description of the nature of its work – 'educational publishers' or 'manufacturers of fine chocolates', for example. Often, too, the headings 'Reference' and 'Date' will be included in the letter-head, with a space next to them for the details to be inserted (see 5–7 below).

Finally, under company law the names of company directors, the company's registration number and the address of its registered office – if this is different from that already given – must be included. Often these appear at the foot of the sheet, to avoid cluttering the top with information.

2 Telephone number
The telephone number should appear just below the address. If the name of the exchange is to be included, this should appear first, followed by the dialling code in brackets, and then the number itself, like this:

Tel: Madingley (0954) 77777

Without the exchange, the telephone number would appear like this:

Tel: 0954 77777

3 Telex number
If the company has a telex facility – as most do nowadays – the number should be given just after the telephone number, usually in this form:

Telex: 43856 Jonson S

4 Fax number
Most companies now have a fax machine (see section 17.5) as well as a telex, and the number for the fax should be given beneath that for the telex. It will look something like this:

Fax: 0954 77771

Thurays Sports Ltd (1)

10 High Street
Greybury
Essex WV21 3AB
(registered office)

(5) Our ref: TS/WJ

(6) Your ref:

(2) Tel: Greybury (1980) 12345
(3) Telex: 54321 Grey G
(4) Fax: 1980 54421

(8)
(9) Jane Fenton
Sales Manager
Sports Supplies Ltd
Willow Road
(10) Haston
Cambridgeshire
CB31 3RR

(7) 5 November 19--

(11) Dear Ms Fenton

(12) Stock for 19-- season

We are anxious to increase our range of tennis and cricket
equipment for the forthcoming season.

I would be grateful if you would advise us of the prices at
which you could supply us with the following:

(13)
20 junior tennis racquets
25 size six cricket bats
20 boxes of leather cricket balls
50 boxes of tennis balls.

I would be grateful for an early reply.

(14) Yours sincerely

(15) *Tim Smith*

T Smith (16)
Director (17)

Directors T. Smith, J. Thuray
Registered in England: No. 987654

Fig. 11.1 Parts of a letter (see section 11.2)

5 *Our ref*

This is short for 'Our reference' and will be followed by a number, or a group of numbers and letters, assigned by the writer as a way of linking the letter to other records or files of correspondence with the company involved.

Often, the reference is simply the initials of the person who wrote the letter, followed by those of the person who typed it, like this:

Our ref: SJS/TK

6 *Your ref*

This usually appears below or beside 'Our ref' at the top of a letter. A reference is only given if you are replying to a letter you have received – in which case you will quote the reference given to you under 'Our ref' in the initial letter. It is most important that this is done accurately, since otherwise your letter may end up in the wrong department, leading to delay and misunderstanding.

If you are not replying to a letter, you should still write 'Your ref', but leave a blank space next to it.

7 *Date*

All letters should have a date, so that the correspondence can be filed in the correct order, and a check can be kept on how an exchange is proceeding. It is best to give the date in one of the following forms:

4th July 1990
4 July 1990

Of these, the second is the simpler and more common. You should never use the forms '4.7.90' or '4/7/90'. On the Continent and in America this will be read to mean '7 April 1990' rather than '4 July 1990', and confusion will result. You should also avoid abbreviating the month – to 'Jan.' or 'Jul.', for example – as this looks clumsy and untidy.

8 *Receiver's name*

Unless you are writing a general letter of enquiry to a company, your letter should give the name of the person to whom you are writing. You should use the correct title before the person's name: Dr, The Rev., or more usually Mr, Mrs, Miss or Ms. Sometimes a man's name will be followed by 'Esq.', short for 'Esquire'. This is, however, falling out of use, and 'Mr' is far more common.

The use of 'Ms' instead of 'Miss' or 'Mrs' is also quite common now. Many women prefer this form, since it does not indicate whether or not they are married – something which, after all, is not relevant to their working lives. If you are not sure which form to use, find out which the person in question uses and follow her example.

Some companies, especially the more modern ones with younger staff, do not use titles at all, and instead give the first name of the person – 'George Mason' or 'Valerie Cooke', for example. Unless you are sure that this is acceptable, you should use one of the more formal titles given above.

If you are writing a general letter of enquiry and do not know the name of the person who will receive your letter, this stage may be omitted.

9 Receiver's position

The rank of the receiver in his or her company should come on the line below the name. For example:

Laura Powers
Managing Director

This will help to make sure that it is delivered to the right department since, in a large organization, the mail-room staff may not know all the employees by name.

The inclusion of the receiver's position is also important because it shows that the letter is being written to him or her in a formal, business capacity. It can also be of particular importance if you later need to confirm that a letter was sent to a particular person within a company – for example, that a letter asking for payment of an overdue invoice was sent to a company's chief accountant.

10 Receiver's address

The receiver's address should be given in full, including the postcode. If you need to refer to a letter for legal purposes, this establishes beyond doubt that it was addressed to the particular person named. It also provides a record of the receiver's address, which ensures that your file copy is placed in the right file. Finally, it makes it possible for the letter to be forwarded should the envelope be damaged or become illegible in transit.

11 Salutation

This is the opening greeting of the letter. The form it takes is decided by how well you know the person to whom you are writing. The usual forms are given below.

Dear Sirs   This is used when you are writing a letter to a firm in general, and not to any individual person within it.

Dear Sir *or* **Dear Madam**   Either of these is used, as appropriate, when you have neither met nor previously written to the addressee, but when you know his or her name and sex.

Dear Sir or Madam   This used to be considered a form to avoid, since it was accepted that 'Dear Sir' was used whenever you did not know a person's name. However, with increasing awareness of sex bias in language, 'Dear Sir or Madam' is becoming more acceptable. You should use it when you know the position, but not the name or sex, of the person to whom you are writing. You should also use it when writing a circular letter – a letter sent to a large number of people (see section 12.9).

Dear Mr/Mrs/Miss/Ms Cooke These are used to begin letters to people whom you have met or written to before. When deciding whether to use Mrs, Miss or Ms, follow the example set by the writer herself.

Dear Valerie Cooke This is used when writing to someone you do not know (see 8 above).

Dear Jane *or* **Dear Jim** These should be used only when you know the person to whom you are writing very well, on a personal as well as a business level.

12 Subject heading

The aim of the subject heading is to state the letter's subject briefly and clearly, to save the reader time in establishing what it is about. Generally it will be five or six words at most. It may consist of a descriptive heading, such as:

Proposed residential training course

or it may give the number of a contract or document:

Fire Insurance Policy No. AY/73362/4

If you wish to quote a reference number in this way it is better to include it here, rather than in the 'Your ref' or 'Our ref' sections, which should only give references to do with the letter itself, not with documents which form its subject.

Remember that the heading comes after the salutation, not before. If you met someone, you would not immediately start talking about a business matter; you would at least say 'hello' or 'good morning' first. The same is true of a letter. First make the salutation, and then state the subject.

All business letters are much more efficient items of communication if they use subject headings.

13 The body of the letter

Most business letters fall into three sections:

(a) an opening paragraph which gives the reason for writing, some background information, or other material by way of introduction;
(b) one or more paragraphs which go into the subject in more detail;
(c) a final paragraph which suggests what action might be taken, either by the writer or by the reader.

These are discussed in more depth in section 11.6. As a general rule, though, you should remember that successful business letters are those which are short and clear, and use no more than three or four brief paragraphs. Anything longer runs the risk of becoming dull, with the result that the reader will not take in all that it contains. There will, of course, be times when you need to write at greater length, but it is often better to use the format of a report (see Unit 15) or a set of notes rather than a letter in these instances. You can then write a brief covering letter to introduce the document.

If a letter is longer than a single page, it is continued on a *continuation sheet* headed with the name of the receiver, the date and the page number. However, as mentioned above, letters of more than one page should be used only rarely.

14 Subscription or complimentary close
This is the formal conclusion of the letter. Its form is decided by the form of the salutation (see 11 above).

● Letters beginning 'Dear Sir', 'Dear Madam' or 'Dear Sir or Madam' should end 'Yours faithfully'.
● Letters beginning 'Dear Mr/Mrs/Miss/Ms Cooke' or similar should end 'Yours sincerely'.
● Letters beginning 'Dear Jane' or similar can end less formally – 'Yours, George', for example.

Sometimes, a writer may include a more personal greeting before the close – 'With best wishes', for example, or 'Kind regards'. This makes the letter end on a warmer, more personal note. It should, however, be done only when the writer and the addressee know each other well.

15 Signature
When a letter is typed, a space is left after the close for the writer to sign his or her name. The same procedure should be followed when you write a letter.

16 Writer's name
After the signature, you should print the writer's name. Most letters are signed in a hurry at the end of the day, just before the post goes, and as a result it is not always easy to read the signature. For the sake of clarity the name is placed beneath it. Many people will sign their names in full, so that it will usually be clear whether they are male or female. Some, however, simply give their initials. A woman who signs with initials only has, until recently, been expected to put '(Miss)' or '(Mrs)' after her name, but this is no longer essential.

Sometimes a letter may be signed 'pp J. Carter'. This means that it has been signed *'pro persona'* – on behalf of the person – by a secretary or deputy, because the writer was not available. Sometimes the following phrase is added.

Dictated by Mr Carter but signed in his absence.

This shows that the letter has indeed come from the writer, and was not written by an assistant, despite the signature. This is a courtesy to the receiver, to show that the writer is personally involved in the correspondence.

17 Position of the writer
The writer's position in the company should appear beneath the printed name. This makes clear exactly what role he or she plays in the company, and also ensures that any reply will reach the right person quickly.

18   Enclosures

If items are to be enclosed with the letter, the abbreviation 'Enc' is typed beneath the signature at the foot of the page. This is to remind the sender to enclose the item, and also make sure that the receiver does not discard it with the envelope.

19   PS

This stands for '*post scriptum*' – literally, 'after writing'. It is used when you wish to add something which has been left out from the body of the letter.

In a business letter, you should plan your writing so that nothing is left out. The only circumstance in which a PS is acceptable is when new information comes to light just before a letter is sent out, and there is no time to alter it.

20   Copies

The names of people to whom copies of a letter are sent may be printed at the foot of the letter, or perhaps at the top, beneath the letter-head. This is a mark of courtesy to the reader, to let him or her know who else is to see the letter, and is useful in letting recipients know whom they may contact for further discussion of the contents. It also serves to remind the secretary or typist to take the right number of copies and to make sure that they are sent to the people concerned.

Special instructions

In a large company, letters will be opened in the mail room and then sent by messenger to the people to whom they are addressed. For general correspondence this is quite in order, but some letters may contain confidential information. Such letters should include the heading 'Confidential' in the top left-hand corner of the envelope, just above the receiver's name and address. They will then be opened only by the receiver or his or her deputy. If a letter is to be read only by the person to whom it is addressed, it should be marked 'Personal' in the same place.

11.3 Layout of a letter

The elements discussed above should be presented in a clear, attractive manner. Although most companies have their own house style for presenting letters, they usually follow one of two standard layouts.

The use of a standard layout has much to recommend it. It allows people to write and to read letters more quickly, since they know where every separate part should appear. When you write a business letter, you should always use one or other of the two forms in common use, which are shown in figs 11.2 and 11.3. Look closely at them, and use them for reference when you start writing letters yourself, until you are quite sure that you can set out a letter correctly in whichever of the two styles you choose, or whichever one your company prefers.

14 Grove Avenue,
LIMEHURST,
Kent,
LT5 8HJ.

Tel: 06782 4367

14 May, 19--

Kent Omnibus Company Ltd.,
48 High St.,
MALDEN,
Kent,
MN6 4TQ.

Dear Sirs,

I should like to make a complaint about the unreliable service
which has been provided recently on your route no. 47, which travels
from Limehurst into Malden and back.

On three occasions in the last month, my wife and I have had to
wait over twenty minutes for the bus to arrive at The Green, Limehurst.
On complaining to the driver, I was told that delays were unavoidable
because of heavy traffic in the town centre.

I know that the town centre is always congested and that it must
be difficult to run the buses to time. However, I feel that a better
service than this could be provided, perhaps by adjusting the
timetable to take into account the heavy delays.

I should be interested to hear your views about this matter.

Yours faithfully,

Harry Green

H. T. Green

Fig. 11.2 Semi-blocked letter

Transglobe Tours

147 Oxford Street
Manchester M22 7BD
Tel: 061 768 3840

Our Ref: RF/TS   Your Ref: Date: 30 November 19--

Ms T C Cranleigh
14 Hawthorn Drive
Manchester
M5 4JG

Dear Ms Cranleigh

Summer cruises in the Caribbean 19--

Thank you for your letter of 9 January, in which you enquire
about the availability of places on our Caribbean cruises next
summer.

I am happy to say that there are currently several vacancies
for both the cruise departing on 17 July and that departing on
12 August. I would, however, advise you to book early, since
there is usually a heavy demand for these holidays.

I enclose a copy of our brochure which gives full details of the
cruises and their prices.

Should you have any further queries, please do not hesitate to
let me know.

Yours sincerely

Ronald Fraser
Manager

Enc

Fig. 11.3 Fully-blocked letter

11.3.1 Semi-blocked style

This style is generally used by individuals when writing to companies, but is also used by some commercial organizations. Note that:

(a) The sender's address appears at the top right-hand corner, with each successive line indented. It is followed by the telephone number and the date.

(b) The receiver's address appears at the left-hand side, and is not normally indented. Each paragraph begins about 1.5 cm from the left-hand margin.

(c) The complimentary close and the name typed beneath it are centred at the foot of the page.

If this layout is used by a company, the letter-head may be printed to appear at the right-hand side, in the centre, or across the full width of the sheet, and will include the telephone number, telex and two references in any suitable places.

11.3.2 Fully-blocked style

This style is becoming increasingly popular. It saves time for the typist, since everything begins at the left-hand margin and no calculations are necessary to ensure that the close is exactly central.

Notice that the punctuation is 'open'. This means that there is no punctuation in the address or other preliminary details, and there are no commas after the salutation or complimentary close. This creates a further saving in time, and also gives a smooth, uncluttered appearance. Punctuation in the body of the letter remains as usual, although the use of commas is kept to a minimum.

11.4 Planning a letter

Like any other piece of writing, a letter should be carefully planned before it is written, so before starting a letter you should always ask yourself the following questions.

What is your relationship with the reader? How well you know the reader will affect the choice of salutation and close, as noted in earlier sections. It will also affect the tone of the letter: if a letter is to a perfect stranger, it will be fairly formal; if it is to someone with whom you have done business before, it can be more relaxed.

What is the letter's purpose? Unless you know why you are writing a letter, you will be unable to write it effectively. Are you asking for information, giving instructions, suggesting action or confirming arrangements, for example? Make sure you know the main purpose before starting to write.

What do you wish the reader to do? This follows closely from the letter's purpose. When writing, you should always be aware of the response which you are trying to get from the reader. You can then select the most suitable expression to achieve this. Put yourself in the place of the reader, and ask yourself whether *you* would do what was being asked of you.

11.5 Principles of letter-writing

The way in which you compose a letter – choosing one word rather than another, and deciding how to join your words together – will depend on the person to whom you are writing, the reason for your letter, and the reaction you wish to prompt. In short, it will depend on the answers to the questions in the last section. A letter applying for a job and addressed to a stranger will be different in tone and vocabulary from one to an employee congratulating him or her on passing an exam, for example.

There are, however, some basic principles to keep in mind when writing letters of any kind. The art of good letter-writing could be said to lie in keeping a balance between three elements, all of which are essential, but which sometimes seem to conflict:

(a) courtesy;
(b) clarity;
(c) conciseness.

Courtesy is essential in business correspondence if you wish to remain on good terms with people in other companies. Even when you have something unpleasant to say, you should try to say it courteously. A thoroughly offensive letter of complaint might give you a sense of satisfaction, and help lower your blood-pressure, but it is unlikely to achieve any positive result in the form of helpful action from the receiver.

When you are communicating in more pleasant circumstances, too, it helps to be courteous, since a request will be far more welcome than an order, and more effective in achieving the desired result.

Clarity is even more important. Unless you make your language simple and direct, your meaning may not be understood. Your reader may simply lose interest in the letter, or may not reply because he or she does not realize an answer is required. Worse still, he or she may interpret the letter differently from the way you intended, and may act accordingly. Direct statement is therefore essential.

Conciseness is another basic aim. Unless you can express your ideas briefly, the reader will become bored and fail to respond.

How these principles may be balanced in practice is best shown by looking at a typical business letter. Imagine that, as the assistant to the chief buyer of the fabric department of a large department store, you have been asked to draft a letter for your boss to sign. It is to a textile manufacturer who has sent you some fabric samples and has recently telephoned to ask when you will be able to give him a decision on them. The chief buyer has decided against them, but wishes to remain on good terms with the supplier since she has done business with him for many years, and may wish to do so again. How do you write a letter which explains your decision clearly, without going into lengthy details about changes in market demand which have meant that you do not wish to buy his textiles, and without offending him or suggesting that you do not wish to do business with him in the future?

First, you need to decide on the content of the letter. There are three main points to be included:

(a) an apology for the delay in reaching a decision;
(b) a statement that you do not wish to buy the fabric;
(c) some indication that you want to keep on good terms with the supplier.

Next, you need to be sure that your message is quite clear and unambiguous. Courtesy might lead you to write something like:

> I am afraid that it is unlikely that we shall be able to purchase goods from you in the foreseeable future.

This has the advantage of being courteous – it expresses regret in the words 'I am afraid' and it shows a desire not to offend in suggesting, rather than openly stating, the position. However, it is not a direct statement of your decision and therefore succeeds only in sounding evasive.

Under these circumstances, it would be far better to say simply that you have decided not to purchase the goods, like this:

> I am afraid that we shall not be able to purchase the textiles which you sent us.

This is quite direct and unambiguous, yet it is also courteous as it expresses regret.

You might feel that you need to give an elaborate explanation of your decision, perhaps like this:

> I am sorry that we have not been able to reach a decision before, but there have been a large number of other matters to be dealt with, and I wanted to see all the alternative suppliers' cloth before making a final choice. The decision was reached as a result of a fall in demand for cloth of the type you supplied, and because other textiles were available more cheaply elsewhere. In the circumstances, I am sure that you will understand that we are unable to purchase your cloth on this occasion.

This contains a number of awkward and unsuitable expressions. The reference to a 'large number of other matters' suggests that you place the decision – and therefore the supplier – fairly low on your list of priorities. Wishing to see all the other cloths hints strongly that you think the samples supplied are of a poor quality, and the reference to other cloths being cheaper reinforces this. 'The decision was reached' is much weaker than 'I decided', suggesting that you are trying to avoid responsibility for your decision. Finally, the last sentence is patronizing and unconvincing. The reader is unlikely to understand or sympathize with the writer after the preceding paragraph!

This passage could be improved by making several changes. First, a simple, short apology for the delay would be adequate, with no complex explanation for its cause. Comparison to other cloths can also omitted, to avoid offending the reader. The use of the active rather than the passive throughout will make the whole letter far stronger. You will then have a passage which reads like this:

> I must first apologize for taking so long to reach a decision – especially since I am afraid that we shall not be able to purchase the textiles you sent us. This is largely the result of a fall in demand for cloth of this kind.

This gives a much stronger, more direct account of the situation which, at the same time, should not cause offence.

We now have the basis of the letter, which needs only the addition of an opening and a closing paragraph to be complete. The final version is shown in fig. 11.4. Notice how the first paragraph is very short, allowing the writer to go straight to the main point. Notice, too, that the last paragraph is courteous without being patronizing, making clear the writer's wish to do business with the reader again at some time in the future. In this way, the three demands of courtesy, clarity and conciseness have been met, in a letter which is firm yet friendly in tone. You should aim for this balance in all the letters you write.

11.6 Structuring a letter

As mentioned in section 11.2, most letters fall into three parts, each of which has a clear function in conveying the letter's message. Each part needs to be approached in a different way.

11.6.1 The opening

The main aim of the opening is to make a purposeful start to the letter. A subject heading will help greatly in this, as there is no need to repeat what the heading says in the first paragraph.

A common ways of opening a letter of reply is to thank the reader for his or her letter. When doing this, you should always state the date of the reader's letter and very briefly summarize its subject. This may well make up the whole of the first paragraph: there is no reason why an opening should not consist of a single sentence of this kind, as shown in fig. 11.4.

If you are not replying to a letter, you need to establish the purpose of your communication quickly and effectively. Avoid phrases like this:

> As personnel manager of Trulove Brothers, I am writing to . . .

All the information given here is conveyed in other ways by the letter. Your position and the name of the company are given in the close and in the letterhead respectively, and it is self-evident that you are writing. Such an opening simply wastes time, and does not encourage the reader to proceed.

EDWARD HUDSON & SONS LTD
57-62 High St
Newtown NW7 9JT

Tel 0568 77456-8
Telex 71734 Hudson G
Fax 0568 79900

Our Ref TP/JS
Your Ref CK/YM
Date 17 June 19--

Mr Charles King
Sales Manager
Arkwright Textiles Ltd
Apollo Mills
Saltville
SE5 8UJ

Dear Mr King

Textile samples for the winter season

Thank you for your letter of 4 May and the textile samples which
you kindly enclosed.

I must first apologise for taking so long to reach a decision -
especially since I am afraid that we shall not be able to
purchase the textiles you sent us. This is largely the result of
a fall in demand for cloth of this kind.

However, I am sure that this fall is only temporary, and that
demand will grow again next year. I do hope that you will send
further samples of your textiles then, and that we will be able
to resume our long and mutually beneficial business association.

Yours sincerely

T Perkins

Teresa Perkins
Chief Buyer, Fabric Department

Fig. 11.4 Final version of a business letter (see section 11.5)

The reason for your letter should be established more directly, perhaps like this:

> This company is currently planning its annual residential training course for maintenance personnel, and I am anxious to find a suitable location for it.

Such a letter – to the manager of a hotel or conference centre – would then go on to state the requirements of the training course and ask if they could be met by the reader's organization.

11.6.2 The middle paragraphs

These will carry the main weight of the letter, conveying the essence of the information, requesting the details required, or carrying out in some other way the letter's main aim. Here you should use simple, straightforward language, and avoid unnecessary length of the kind shown in the draft for fig. 11.4, on page 173.

The exact nature of this central passage will depend on the purpose of the letter. Letters of various kinds are discussed in greater depth in Unit 12.

11.6.3 The closing paragraph

At the end of a letter, you should prompt future action by suggesting what you or the reader will or should do to further the business under discussion. There is no need to do this at great length: one sentence will often suffice.

Never add a final paragraph simply to 'pad out' a letter. Often, a simple sentence like this will be all that is required:

> I look forward to hearing from you in the near future.

Alternatively, if you are answering a letter of enquiry, you might finish with:

> Please do not hesitate to let me know if I can help in any other way.

Simple statements like these are much more effective than lengthy offers of help or pompous constructions which begin:

> Let me in conclusion once again state . . .

You should also avoid closing a letter with phrases such as:

> Hoping to hear from you soon.
> Assuring you of our best intentions at all time.

Both of these are grammatically incorrect, since they do not contain a finite verb (see section 4.3.4). The second is also unsuitable because it is old-fashioned and rather pompous.

11.7 Telexes and international telemessages

A telex is a printed message which is sent as electronic impulses through a telephone line to the receiver's office, where it is converted into a printed copy.

macbryde holdings   21 E 52nd St - NY10537

K Patel
Senior Manager
Hunter and Stone
Goldlees Industrial Park
Leeds LS24 90A

20 June 19--

Dear Mr Patel

As you know, we are approaching the deadline for the completion of
the first phase of our company's new building in Dockside.

I feel that it is important for us to get together and discuss the
final details of the interior fittings and furnishings so that work
on these may begin as soon as the structure is completed.

I shall be in Leeds on Thursday 30 March and would be pleased to call
on you at your office to discuss the matter in detail. I should be
grateful if you would let me know if 10.30 a.m. on this day will be
convenient for you.

I hope that this will be the case and look forward to seeing you
then.

Yours sincerely

TS MacBryde

T S MacBryde
Managing Director

Fig. 11.5 Letter for rewriting as a telex

Telemessages are dictated over the phone by the sender and a printed copy is delivered to the receiver by the service company. These two forms of communication are discussed in greater detail in section 2.3.9 and Unit 17. Here, we are concerned solely with how to compose them.

Like the regular telephone service, telexes and telemessages are charged to the sender in units of time, so it is important to know exactly what you have to say before you dial the relevant number. It is also important to keep your message as short as possible – but not so short as to be unclear or ambiguous. For example, look at the letter in fig. 11.5. If this information were to be sent by telex, it would be better reworded as follows:

> URGENT WE DISCUSS FITTINGS AND FURNISHINGS OF DOCKSIDE BUILDING. AM IN LEEDS THURS 30 MARCH. SUGGEST VISIT YOU 10.30 AM. PLS CONFIRM. MACBRYDE.

All unnecessary information has been cut out, leaving only the essential parts of the message: the purpose of the meeting; a suggested date, place and time; a request for confirmation of the arrangements; and the sender's name. Grammatical elements which do not affect the meaning – such as pronouns, articles and some verbs – have also been omitted. 'Please' has been abbreviated to 'pls', 'Thursday' to 'Thurs', and the usual subscription has been deleted, leaving only the name of the sender.

It is important, however, not to omit too much information. If the third sentence had been:

> SUGGEST MEET 10.30

it would not have been clear where the meeting would take place, and another message would have been necessary. Similarly, if Macbryde had referred only to 'fittings' rather than 'furnishings and fittings', Patel would have come to the meeting unprepared to discuss the latter.

11.8 Conclusion

In addition to the points in this unit, you should also remember the more general advice given in Unit 4 about using language economically and effectively in all forms of business communication.

Unit 12 covers the main kinds of letter which you may need to write. While you are working through it, you will probably need to refer to this unit, especially the sections on the parts of a letter and on letter layout. By the time you have finished Unit 12, however, you should be able to produce business letters of all kinds quickly and accurately.

11.9 Quick questions

1 List the constituent parts of a letter in the order in which they would appear.

2 Which five questions do you need to answer before writing a letter?

3 When should you start a letter with:

   (a) Dear Sir;
   (b) Dear Mr ---;
   (c) Dear Sir or Madam?

4 Give the correct complementary close for use with the following salutations:

   (a) Dear Madam;
   (b) Dear Ms Jones.

5 Which of these is the correct form of writing a date on a letter? Why is one of them not acceptable?

   (a) 10 February 1991;
   (b) 10.2.91.

11.10 Longer exercises

1 Look carefully at the letter in fig. 11.3. Think about the letter to which it is replying. Put yourself in the place of the writer of that letter, and write the answers to the five questions in the writing checklist (see question 2 above).

2 Do the same for the letter in fig. 11.4

Business letters: some applications

12.1 Introduction

This unit examines the main kinds of letters which are produced in business correspondence. It also looks at situations in which letters are used within an organization in preference to other forms of communication. In addition, it covers the process of writing letters from notes, which is an important skill to develop for work, study and personal use. If you have not already read Unit 11, you should look through it before approaching this unit, since it discusses the layouts and the forms of expression most commonly used in letter-writing.

12.2 Letters of confirmation

Letters of this kind simply confirm arrangements made between the sender and the receiver in person or by telephone. Their main purpose is to provide a written record of the arrangements and so make sure that nothing is over-looked. Usually they are very short, often produced on A5 rather than the standard-size A4 paper, and consisting of one – or at most two – paragraphs. An example of this kind of letter is shown in fig. 12.1.

12.3 Letters of acknowledgement

These are sent to acknowledge the receipt of a letter, order or other important item, when there is no justification for a telephone call. They might also be sent to acknowledge the receipt of a document or another item which demands your subsequent attention. In these circumstances, they should make clear that you will reply in greater detail at a later date. Organizations which frequently receive such material often use printed cards for this purpose, which are filled in as appropriate and sent on receipt of an item. An example of a letter of acknowledgement is shown in fig. 12.2, and examples of acknowledgement cards in fig. 12.3.

EDWARD HUDSON & SONS LTD
57-62 High St
Newtown NW7 9JT

Tel 0568 77456-8
Telex 71734 Hudson G
Fax 0568 79900

Our Ref TP/JS
Your Ref CK/YM
Date 17 June 19--

Ms Danielle Salt
Sales Manager
Aztec Fabrics
Jupiter House
Newtown
NW14 5PS

Dear Ms Salt

Following my telephone call this morning, I am writing to confirm
our meeting at 11.00 a.m. on Monday 21 May in the Meetings Room
at our High Street offices, to discuss your fabrics for our
forthcoming winter range.

I look forward very much to meeting you then and seeing your
current fabric samples.

Yours sincerely

T Perkins

Teresa Perkins
Chief Buyer, Fabric Department

Fig. 12.1 Letter of confirmation

Gibson Photographic

17-21 Main Street
Dundee DD176BL
Tel: 0382 21118

15 March 19--

Stanley Perkins Esq
57 Lime Kiln Rd
LONDON E18 6JK

Dear Mr Perkins

Thank you for your letter of 12 March.

I was glad to receive the negatives of your most recent photographs,
and will begin work straight away on their processing and mounting
as requested.

I estimate that this will take about a week, and will telephone you
when the material is ready for collection.

Yours sincerely

Peter James

Peter James
Manager, Processing Department

Fig. 12.2 Letter of acknowledgment

Her Majesty's
Stationery Office

HMSO

Your reference

Dated

Our reference

Date

St Crispins
Duke Street
Norwich NR3 1PD

Telephone:
Direct Dialling (0603) 69
GTN Code   3014 "

Switchboard (0603) 622211

Fax-Gp3 0603-695582

Telex 97301

Subject ....

Thank you for your letter/memo/application which/is receiving
attention/has been forwarded to

....

....

....

Signed ....

Name (in Capitals) ....

R15/13   MCR 393428/1/G45719 3m 8/87 TL

JOHN MURRAY   50 Albemarle Street, London w1x 4bd

We acknowledge with thanks the receipt of

which will receive careful attention.

Although every reasonable care is taken of material while in our possession, we cannot
accept responsibility for any loss or damage.

Please send .... to cover the cost of postage now so that there is less delay if
your material has to be returned.

Fig. 12.3 Acknowledgment cards. Notice how each has been designed to convey a
range of different messages.

A further kind of acknowledgement is that sent on receipt of an enquiry about your company's goods or services. You might well enclose a brochure giving general details, and end with an offer of further help should it be needed. More specific enquiries should, of course, be answered in greater detail, by supplying the relevant information. If you are unable to do this, you should pass on the enquiry to the right person, who will write the reply, explaining that the letter has been passed to him or her. An acknowledgement of this kind is shown in fig. 12.4.

12.4 Letters of enquiry

Sometimes you may need to write to another organization enquiring about the goods or services which it offers. Such letters should be brief, but should also include detailed reference to the kind of information you require, so that the request may be satisfied fully. If you hold a position of some seniority in your organization, you may well include a suggestion that the receiver contact you directly to arrange a meeting, as outlined in fig. 12.5. If, however, you are writing from a position of lower authority, your final paragraph would be less forceful, and perhaps run like this:

> I should be very grateful if you would kindly let me have details of the range of products which you manufacture, together with price lists and delivery dates.

12.5 Letters of collection

This sort of letter is less pleasant, as it is related to the collection of unpaid bills. Letters of this kind should be courteous but firm – abuse is unlikely to obtain results. The nature of the debt should be stated simply and factually, with an assumption that the delay has been caused by an oversight or some other unintentional cause rather than deliberate unwillingness to pay (see fig. 12.6). Should a polite reminder of this kind fail to produce a reply, a firmer letter should be sent, making clear that legal proceedings will be begun if payment is not received within a specified period (see fig. 12.7). Such a letter should only be sent as a last resort and by someone in a senior position within the organization. Notice that again it is not impolite or abusive, but simply factual.

Before sending a letter of collection, many companies will issue a second copy of the original invoice, with a stamp or sticker attached to the effect that it is overdue. This gives three possible stages of communication, but in most circumstances the first will be effective. The most important point to remember about letters of collection, however, is that they should be sent only by a person of some seniority in the organization – usually a head of department – or by someone acting on his or her authority.

Transglobe Tours

147 Oxford Street
Manchester M22 7BD
Tel: 061 768 3840

Our Ref: RF/TS   Your Ref: Date: 30 November 19--

Mrs G Udeogalanya
47 Wood Street
Manchester M16

Dear Mrs Udeogalanya

Thank you for your letter of 27 November in which you enquire
about our current range of holidays to European and Caribbean
countries.

I have pleasure in enclosing a copy of our brochure which
gives full details of all our holidays for the summer 19--
season. You will find the information you require on pages
16-20 and page 47.

Should you require any further information about this or
any of our other services, my staff and I will be very happy
to assist you.

Yours sincerely

Ronald Fraser
Manager

Enc

Fig. 12.4 Letter of acknowledgment enclosing brochure

WIMBLEDON SERVICES PLC
43-57 High Street, London SW19 6GH
Telephone: 01 947 8844 Telex: WIMLES 76654 G

Our ref HY/GD
Your ref

13 July 19--

The Marketing Manager
Eastern Communications
96 King Street
Hammersmith
London W7 4KL

Dear Sir or Madam

Our company is currently renewing its provision of telephones for
both internal and external communication.

I wish to enquire about the possibility of one of your
representatives visiting the company to advise us about the number
and nature of telephone instruments we would need to provide us with
an up-to-date communication system.

Perhaps you would telephone my secretary to arrange an appointment
to call and discuss the matter with me in the near future.

Yours faithfully

Hector Young

Hector Young
Joint Managing Director

Fig. 12.5 Letter of enquiry

Johnson and Smith Ltd
Bank Chambers
Casterfield
CF6 4TH

Tel: Casterfield (0236) 5674
Telex: 76953 Josmith G

Our ref: IJ/RT

Your ref:

Date: 15 March 19--

P C Jenkins Esq
14 Lime Street
Casterbridge
CE9 1TG

Dear Mr Jenkins

Invoice No 63345/90

According to our records, the above invoice, dated 15 February
19--, has not as yet been settled.

If, by the time you receive this letter, payment has been made,
please accept my apologies for troubling you. If this is not
the case, however, and the payment has been accidentally
overlooked, I should be grateful if you would kindly settle
the account as soon as possible.

Yours sincerely

Ian Johnstone

Ian Johnstone
Senior Accountant

Fig. 12.6 Initial collection letter

Johnson and Smith Ltd
Bank Chambers
Casterfield
CF6 4TH

Tel: Casterfield (0236) 5674
Telex: 76953 Josmith G

Our ref: IJ/RT

Your ref:

Date: 15 April 19--

P C Jenkins Esq
14 Lime Street
Casterbridge
CE9 1TG

Dear Mr Jenkins

Invoice no 63345/90

I see from my records that, despite our earlier reminder, the above invoice for the sum of £764.43 in conjunction with our auditing services has not been paid.

I regret to say that, unless payment is received within the next seven days, I shall have no alternative but to place the matter in the hands of our solicitors who will begin legal proceedings for the recovery of the amount.

Yours sincerely

Ian Johnstone

Ian Johnstone
Senior Accountant

Fig. 12.7 Final collection letter

12.6 Letters of complaint

Not everyone in business will be as efficient as you hope to be yourself, and so there will be occasions when letters of complaint will be needed. Although the temptation to be sarcastic, offensive or downright rude may be strong, try to resist it: a letter which is abusive will not encourage the reader to put things right. Instead, state your facts simply and logically. You should write in the first instance to the person with whom the original complaint arose, only approaching a superior when a satisfactory outcome still has not been achieved.

Figure 12.8 gives an example of a letter of complaint which is firm but courteous.

12.7 Letters of apology

However efficient an organization, there will be occasions when errors are made, and as a result letters of apology will be needed. The best approach here is to accept responsibility for the mistake, to offer to rectify any losses and to apologize without reservation. The only exception to this is where legal matters may be involved. Accepting responsibility for an occurrence which has seriously inconvenienced a customer or other organization may constitute a legal admission of guilt, and so care should be taken with letters of this kind. Again, if the matter is serious it should be dealt with by someone in authority, perhaps after he or she has taken advice from legal consultants.

More straightforward letters of apology may be sent in the form shown in fig. 12.9.

12.8 Letters of introduction, recommendation and reference

There will be times in business when a new or potential employee will need to be introduced and recommended to clients or potential employers. For these purposes, a formal letter is often used.

12.8.1 Letter of introduction

This is usually written by a superior or an employer to introduce a representative or a new employee to a client or other person with whom he or she has to do business. It will usually be kept fairly brief, and will be given to the representative to be passed on to the recipient. An example of a letter of introduction is shown in fig. 12.10.

12.8.2 Letter of recommendation

A letter of recommendation is also written by an employer for a client to read, but deals in more detail with the person about whom it is written. Instead of the brief introduction it will say more about the person, covering his or her qualifications, experience and general suitability for the task in hand. Like a letter of introduction, the letter will be given to the client or employer by the person about whom it is written. An example is given in fig. 12.11.

14 *Lime Tree Avenue, Newport, Gwent NP7 6TG*

The Manager
Mason's Ltd
43-47 High Street
Newport
Gwent   27 January 19--

Dear Sir

Three weeks ago I purchased a Honshu video cassette
recorder, model no. PN 46638/2, with a twelve-month
warranty to cover both parts and labour.

In that time, the machine has failed to eject a
cassette proberly on three occasions, while
otherwise it has worked faultlessly. On telephoning
your shop I was told 'It will sort itself out soon',
and that it was probably not installed on a level
surface.

When I telephoned again to say that the fault was
persisting, I, was told that a service engineer
would call. This was ten days ago and no engineer
has called.

Since then, the machine has ceased to operate
entirely. I should be grateful if you would
arrange for the machine to be replaced with
another which is in proper working condition.

I look forward to hearing from you in the near
future.

Yours faithfully

T G Smart

T G Smart

Fig. 12.8 Letter of complaint

Johnson and Smith Ltd
Bank Chambers
Casterfield
CF6 4TH

Tel: Casterfield (0236) 5674
Telex: 76953 Josmith G

Our ref: IJ/RT

Your ref: PCJ

Date: 20 April 19--

P C Jenkins Esq
14 Lime Street
Casterbridge
CE9 1TG

Dear Mr Jenkins

Invoice no 63345/90

I was very sorry to learn, from your letter of 15 April, that although payment of the above invoice was made by cheque in mid-March, our company has failed to record this.

The mistake was the result of an error in our accounts department, which wrongly credited the sum to the account of a Mr P Jenkins, another of our customers. I assure you that such errors will not occur again, as we have taken special measures to ensure that customers with similar names are given separate reference numbers on our files which will be quoted on all invoices.

In the circumstances, I can only express the hope that you will accept my sincere apologies for the mistake. Should you wish to discuss the matter further, or require any advice about your auditing requirements in future, do please contact me personally by telephone.

Yours sincerely

Ian Johnstone

Ian Johnstone
Senior Accountant

Fig. 12.9 Letter of apology

GB Textiles Plc
Newfoundland House
76-84 Tadema Rd
Manchester
M7 6KL

Harry Battacharya
General Manager
Drayton Clothing
16-18 High St
Salford
SD5 6GN   14 March 19--

Dear Harry

This is to introduce my new Eastern Sales Representative, Sandra
Martell. Sandra joins us with impeccable references and I'm sure
you will be very pleased with the deals she can offer you.

While Sandra is with you, perhaps you would be kind enough to
show her around the warehouse and introduce her to the staff
members she will have to deal with.

Yours sincerely

G. Fenton

George Fenton
Sales Manager

Fig. 12.10 Letter of introduction

Marsh and Groundling (CHARTERED ACCOUNTANTS)
Excelsior Chambers, Fore St, Plymouth, Devon PL6 7DS

```
G D Stone Esq
Company Secretary
Windrush Holdings
Cathedral Close
Portsmouth
Hants PS6 1WD                                    17 January 19--
```

Dear Mr Stone

I write to recommend Mr Abdul Khan, a new partner in our firm, as an accountant who is admirably qualified to conduct your company's annual audit.

After full-time studies in accountancy at City University, Mr Khan joined the staff of a leading city analyst where he rapidly gained a reputation for quick and efficient action with standards of the highest probity.

Since 198-, Mr Khan has been one of the partners in our firm, and has specialised in undertaking audits and financial analysis and projection work for a range of clients which already includes such well-known names as Highlands Communications, GBH (Property Development) and the Langham estate agency chain.

I assure you that you can have every confidence in Mr Khan, and am delighted to be able to recommend him to you for your audit.

Yours sincerely

Robin Marsh.

Robin Marsh
Senior Partner
Marsh and Groundling

Fig. 12.11 Letter of recommendation

12.8.3 Letter of reference

Most job application forms ask the applicant to name two people who may act as *referees* – to make written statements about the candidate's qualifications, experience and suitability for the post in question. Unlike a letter of recommendation, however, a reference is posted directly to the potential employer. Because of its nature it should be marked 'Confidential', and in most cases the person about whom it is written will not be allowed to see it. An example of this kind of letter is given in fig. 12.12.

12.9 Circular letters

These are letters which are sent to a large number of people at the same time. Each copy is identical: instead of giving the full name and address of each recipient, the opening lines are often replaced by a statement such as 'To all subscribers' or 'To all customers'. The salutation will usually be 'Dear Sir or Madam', or a more specific greeting such as 'Dear Customer' or 'Dear Shareholder'.

Circulars are often sent out by organizations to publicize their goods or services. Where a new business has been set up, for example, circulars may be sent to all potential customers, or an established company may use them to announce new items for sale, new services or special offers. The advantage of this kind of communication is that it is simple and cheap to produce, yet it allows information to be sent to a wider range of people than would be possible with individual letters, and with greater personal impact than a newspaper advertisement.

Circulars can also be sent within a company, when employers or department heads wish to convey a particular piece of information to all their workers. Occasions for which they are used will vary with individual companies, but might include the following:

- giving details of a new wage offer;
- conveying information about health and safety procedures;
- announcing important new matters of policy;
- giving information about a new member of staff;
- announcing a departmental reorganization.

Circulars are often chosen in preference to memos or a company newsletter, posters or a staff meeting because they are more personal, and because they suggest that the company is concerned to let each individual know what is happening in the organization. They can also be kept for reference, whereas a notice is soon covered up or forgotten. The decision whether to use a circular or another kind of communication may be a matter of personal preference or of company procedure, but you should always weigh up the various considerations carefully.

Some circular letters may contain certain elements which make them more personal: the salutation may be handwritten separately for each recipient, or a postscript with brief personal comments may be added to supplement the

GB Textiles Plc
Newfoundland House
76-84 Tadema Rd
Manchester
M7 6KL

D P Waldstein
Personnel Manager
D G Design
47 Regent Street
Henley-on-Thames
HT6 8IL

26 June 19--

Dear Ms Waldstein

GERALD FRANCIS KELLY

Thank you for your letter of 22 June, concerning Mr Kelly's application for the post of textile designer with your firm.

I am very pleased to give my enthusiastic support to Mr Kelly's application, my only regret being that, for understandable reasons of career advancement, he has chosen to move away from his present employment with us.

Mr Kelly joined us in February 19--, having completed a course in textile design at the London College of Fashion and Design. From the outset, his considerable abilities were very clear. He has a very strong sense of colour and visual design, coupled with the ability to match designs with the purpose and nature of the fabric on which he is working.

This ability is matched by a capacity for hard work which enables him to meet tight deadlines and work reliably within production schedules. He is also a skilled communicator, having the ability to explain his ideas very clearly, even at early stages of development, and is very popular in the small design section within which he now works.

As far as I know he is in excellent health. I can see no reason why Mr Kelly should not make an excellent member of your fashion textile design team, and I recommend him to you warmly and wholeheartedly.

Yours sincerely

Zoe Goldhorn
Director (Fashion Textiles)

Fig. 12.12 Reference letter

contents of the letter. This is only possible, however, when a small number of letters is being produced, and will depend very much on the individual policy of your organization.

Examples of circular letters are shown in figs 12.13 and 12.14.

12.10 Standard letters

A standard letter is one which is used to convey the same information to different people in response to a situation which recurs frequently. An example is given in fig. 12.15. Standard letters can take several forms, including many of those we have looked at so far in this unit. The letters of collection in figs 12.6 and 12.7, for example, may be stored and used on many occasions, since they cover a typical business situation.

Most organizations keep a bank of standard letters. These may be stored in a variety of ways. A single reference copy may be kept, which is simply typed out again with the address of the recipient every time it is needed; or the letter may be reproduced by spirit duplicator or photocopier and only the new address typed in. In some cases – usually in large organizations which use many copies of the same letter – standard letters are specially printed. Some standard letters are produced with blank spaces, so that individual details such as invoice numbers, the sum payable or the names of products ordered may be inserted later, either by hand or on the typewriter.

With the advent of wordprocessing, by far the simplest and most effective way of storing standard letters is on computer disk. The letter required is simply called up from the computer files, the necessary details are entered into the spaces, and the letter is printed out. In this way a perfect copy of the letter can be produced every time it is needed. This procedure is discussed in more detail in section 17.3.

Many companies also keep a file of standard paragraphs from which letters may be constructed. This may also be done on computer, and in some cases letters will be answered wholly by selecting the right paragraphs from such a collection and printing out the letter, to give the impression that it has been answered personally.

Paragraphs which might be used in this way include the first paragraph of fig. 12.2, the second paragraph of fig. 12.12 and the last paragraph of fig. 12.4.

12.11 Internal letters

Although communication within an organization is usually done by means of memos, routine forms or meetings of various kinds, there are occasions when letters may be sent from one employee to another, or from an employer to a member of staff. Some such occasions have already been mentioned in section 12.9 but there are others which call for more personal letters.

Most often, such letters will be sent by a head of department or section to an individual employee – to congratulate him or her on passing an examination, for example, or on some other personal achievement such as marriage or

BATTERSBY FINANCIAL SERVICES

Invicta House
Basildon BL9 4KL

Tel 0268 473369
Telex Batters 679921 G

Dear Sir or Madam

A NEW FINANCIAL SERVICE

Battersby Financial Services is a new, energetic company which can offer you far more than just a traditional accountancy service.

We can offer a full tax accounting, management accounting and auditing service, true: but we can also discuss with you your needs for expansion and mezzanine finance and, through our unparalleled range of contacts, we can arrange investment in your plans by some of the country's leading venture capital funds.

If you have problems with slow payers - and what small business doesn't - we can put you in touch with factors who will take over your debts, ensuring that your cashflow is stable and reliable at times of crucial growth and development.

Interested? If you are, get in touch by phone or letter. Better still, drop in for a chat at our new offices. You'll find our offer is hard to refuse.

Yours faithfully

U Heep
Financial Director

Fig. 12.13 Advertising circular sent to local businesses by a newly established company

DG **EXTRUSIONS** PLC
SHAKESPEARE INDUSTRIAL ESTATE
GRIMTHORPE
LINCS GE4 9TS

TEL: GRIMTHORPE (0967) 566771-5   OUR REF: GK/WR
TELEX: GRIMEX 766554 G   YOUR REF:

To all supervisors

Dear Colleague

Safety precautions for public tours of the works

I have taken the step of writing a letter to everyone in person in
view of the serious accident which occurred in the works yesterday.

As some of you may know, a member of the public was injured when he
bent forward to examine the working of a machine from which the
safety guard had inadvertently been removed.

This accident is now the subject of a rigorous internal enquiry, but
it has made clear to me that the company's high standards of safety
have slipped somewhat in recent months.

May I urge upon you all the vital importance of ensuring that no
machine is operated without a safety guard, whether or not members
of the public are touring the works. I know that some workers feel
greater output - and hence higher earnings - are possible if guards
are removed, but we must all impress upon them that the risks to
life and limb are simply too great.

I shall shortly be beginning a campaign, using posters, meetings
and messages in pay slips, to stress the importance of this to all
workers. Meanwhile, I look to you for your help in making sure that
we stamp out this highly dangerous practice and restore our hitherto
very good safety record.

Yours sincerely

G. King

Geoff King
Safety Officer

Fig. 12.14 Internal circular letter

THAMES INSURANCE
56 UPPER THAMES STREET
LONDON EC2 4YH
TEL: 01 736 5689
TELEX: THAMES 89975 G

MOTOR INSURANCE

You will be aware that your policy for the insurance of your car,
registration number   , falls due for renewal on
                    19--.

You will shortly be receiving a renewal invitation from the company
about the policy.

I am writing to point out the advantages of increasing your cover
from Third Party, Fire and Theft to Full Comprehensive cover. Costs
of repair are increasing every month and, as you will know, car
prices - even for secondhand vehicles several years old - are also
on the increase. In the circumstances, you may well feel that a
fully comprehensive policy is the best course of action.

If you choose to increase your cover when renewing your policy, we
can offer you fully comprehensive cover for a first year's premium
of just £   . For an additional £   , this cover can be extended
to protect any member of your family driving with your consent.

Should you be willing to bear the first £25 of any claim, we can
reduce the premium to £   : if you agree to pay the first £50, we
can cut it still further to £

Please let me know if you would like to take advantage of this very
special offer. If you would like further details, please feel free
to telephone our enquiry service at the above number.

Yours sincerely

Yvonne Vidor
Customer Services Manager

Fig. 12.15 Standard letter – space has been left below the letterhead for the recipient's
address and the salutation to be inserted.

performance in a sporting or other competitive event. A personal letter may also be sent to convey good wishes to an employee who is unwell or in hospital, communicating personal concern on the part of the employer, as well as showing that the organization cares for its workers' welfare. On a more routine basis, letters may be sent to employees giving details of salary increases and promotion to new grades, or perhaps the results of internal appraisal interviews.

Letters may also be used on less happy occasions. Individuals may have to be informed that they have been unsuccessful in applying for promotion. It may be necessary to issue the results of a disciplinary hearing to the employee concerned, or to give formal notice that further failure to meet the company's conditions of service will result in dismissal. Letters of dismissal, too, will have to be written, and others giving notice of redundancy. However, letters of this kind are usually written by people in very senior positions within an organization, often in conjunction with its legal advisers.

Individual employees may have occasion to write a formal letter to a superior – in response to a congratulatory letter of the kind described above, for example, or when applying for promotion or tendering resignation. All such letters need to be planned and written very carefully, and are best kept short and sincere. The style will depend very much on the nature of the organization and on the relationship between employee and employer, but it is best to use simple, direct language.

Letters of the kind discussed in this section are not easy to write. The general principles suggested in Unit 11 are a useful guide, but no example of this kind of letter has been included here, since each one will be written in response to a different set of circumstances, with a different aim, and using a different tone and choice of vocabulary.

12.12 Letters with reply forms

If a standard or circular letter requires a reply giving some simple and straightforward information, it is common practice to attach a reply slip to the letter. This allows the recipient to reply simply and quickly without having the bother of writing a separate letter.

The inclusion of a reply slip can often make all the difference between receiving the information you require and hearing nothing further from your addressee, and for that reason it is important that you know something about how such letters and forms should be worded. A sample letter is shown in fig. 12.16. Notice that the letter itself is kept short, to allow as much space as possible for the form. The design of forms is dealt with in greater depth in Unit 13, but the key point to remember is that space and clarity are essential if a form is to be read, understood and completed. Remember, too, that the address to which the form is to be returned should be given on the form as well as on the letter-head. This is because the form will be detached from the letter, and the address might easily be lost or forgotten by the reader unless it appears on the form itself.

ICD Manufacturing   **Victoria Road**   **Derby**   **Notts**   **DY7 5GM**

Tel 0776 68995   **Telex 345679 Bolts G**   **Our Ref** J89**Your Ref**

To all employees   15 June 19--

Dear Colleague

Emergency contacts

I am currently revising the information held about our staff
for use in case of emergency. This consists of routine personal
information which can be used should the company need to make
contact with the employee or his/her relatives urgently, as the
result of accident or plant failures.

In consequence, I should be grateful if you would complete and
return the attached form. All information will of course be kept
confidential, but you are welcome to see the data held about
yourself on our emergency contact file simply by telephoning my
secretary on extension 327 to arrange an appointment.

Yours sincerely

J. Mason

Jackie Mason
Personnel Department

- -

Please complete and return to Jackie Mason, Personnel Dept.,
ICD Manufacturing, Victoria Road, Derby, Notts DY7 5GM

Surname _____   Forenames _____

Employee Number _____   Department _____

Home Address _____   Tel No _____
             _____
             _____

Emergency contact   Name _____

                     Address _____
                             _____
                             _____

                     Tel No _____

                     Relationship to employee (if any) _____

Fig. 12.16 Letter with reply form

Letters with reply forms are a valuable way of gaining simple data of a routine kind from a large number of people. They should not, however, be used where the information required is complex or lengthy, or where it is highly confidential. In such cases, personal meetings or longer, specially designed forms will be more effective (see Unit 13).

12.13 Formal invitations and replies

Letters of this kind differ from routine letters in that they have no salutation, no complimentary close and no signature. They are written in the third person, either on notepaper or on plain white cards.

12.13.1 A formal invitation

A formal invitation will state the name of the person making the invitation and that of the invited guest. It will give the time and date of the function, and perhaps suggest what the function is. Usually it will contain the letters RSVP – short for *Répondez s'il vous plaît*, French for 'Please reply' – and an address to which the reply should be sent. A formal invitation will look like this:

Mr George O'Hara
requests the pleasure of the company of
Ms Indira Mukerjee
on Sunday, 14 June at 8.00 p.m.
at 14 Gladstone Gardens, London SW1 6EK.

RSVP 4 Johnson Place, SW15 3KJ

12.13.2 Formal acceptance

This will follow the style of the invitation and look like this:

Ms Indira Mukerjee
is pleased to accept the kind invitation of
Mr George O'Hara
for Sunday, 14 June at 8.00 p.m.
at 14 Gladstone Gardens, London SW1 6EK.

12.13.3 Formal apology

If you are unable to attend the function to which you have been formally invited, you should reply like this:

Ms Indira Mukerjee
very much regrets that a prior engagement
prevents her from accepting the kind invitation of
Mr George O'Hara
for Sunday, 14 June at 8.00 p.m.
at 14 Gladstone Gardens, London SW1 6EK.

12.14 Routine letters

There will be occasions when you will need to write a letter which does not fall into any of the above categories. In these situations you should remember the general principles of letter-writing covered in Unit 11, making sure that you plan your letter carefully and that you choose the most appropriate expression for your reader and your purpose. The sample letters in this unit will help by showing the kind of language used in most routine correspondence.

12.15 Letters from notes

One of the tasks you will inevitably be faced with at some stage in your business career is to construct a letter from a set of notes. You may need to respond to a telephone message from a potential customer, passed on to you in note-form by a colleague, for example, or your superior may give you a letter of enquiry from a client and a set of points to be made, and ask you to draft a reply. Alternatively, you may be given notes from an informal meeting and asked to draw up a circular letter to company employees outlining the decisions taken. Whatever the situation, if you follow the procedure outlined below, you will ensure that nothing is left out.

(a) Bear in mind whom you are writing to as this will affect your choice of tone and vocabulary. If you are drafting a letter for someone else to sign, give some thought to his or her relationship with the recipient.

(b) Arrange the points you wish to make, or have been given to make, in the most logical order.

(c) Devise a suitable subject heading where possible.

(d) Select the most appropriate layout – semi-blocked or fully-blocked (see section 11.3). Company practice may dictate this for you.

(e) Insert your address and that of the recipient, any references and the date in the correct places.

(f) Decide on an appropriate salutation.

(g) Write in the subject heading.

(h) Write the body of the letter, following your rough draft and arranging separate points in paragraphs. If working from someone else's notes, use your own words as far as possible, but bear in mind the style of the person who will be signing the finished letter.

(i) Choose the most appropriate subscription.

(j) Check whether a copy of the letter is to be sent to anyone else and if so add 'cc' and his or her name.

(k) Check whether there are any enclosures to be sent with the letter, and if so add 'Enc' at the foot of the letter.

(l) Make a final check that:

● all points have been included;
● all points are accurately represented;

- the tone and vocabulary are suitable to both the sender and the recipient;
- spelling, grammar and punctuation are correct.

An example of this kind of letter, and the notes from which it is written, are given in figs 12.17 (a) and (b).

12.13 Conclusion

Letter-writing is one of the most important skills in business communication. It is one which is best acquired through practice – try to make sure that you take every opportunity to produce letters which will be sent to people for a specific, real purpose. If your job offers little chance of this, try writing letters to business organizations requesting information, or writing letters instead of making telephone calls about matters of importance outside work. Make sure, too, that you are thoroughly familiar with the elements of layout and presentation discussed in Unit 11, so that you can produce letters of all the kinds discussed in this unit easily and efficiently.

MEMORANDUM

To: Clerk - Training Section - Personnel Department
From: Training Officer

Ref: TO/6/3
Date: 12 June 19--

RESIDENTIAL TRAINING COURSE FOR SENIOR SALES ASSISTANTS

The company intends running the above course for senior sales assistants from all shops. The course will be from 2 p.m. on Tuesday 9 October to 4 p.m. on Thursday 11 October 19-- and will be repeated from 2 p.m. on Tuesday 13 November to 4 p.m. on Thursday 15 November 19--.

The aim of the course is to improve sales techniques generally, but in particular, to familiarise sales personnel with the new range of electronic cash registers the company will be introducing this November.

I need to find a suitable hotel for the course. Please draft a letter to send to hotels asking if they can provide at least 25 single rooms and a large room with blackout facilities and electric sockets suitable for lectures/seminars with film or video presentations. I also need to know what social amenities are available and whether the hotel will provide coffee/tea for morning/afternoon breaks. You must ask for the cost for full board per person per day and the charges for the large room and the coffee/tea breaks.

Please treat this request as urgent.

J. Lester

Fig. 12.17(a) Memo giving notes for a letter

Pattersons Confectioners plc

79-83 Applewood Road
Southport
Merseyside L34 0DF
Tel: 0704 22555

The Manager

Dear Sir or Madam

Residential training course

My company intends holding a residential training course for its senior
sales assistants from 2 p.m. on Tuesday 9 November to 4 p.m. on Thursday
11 November, and again from 2 p.m. on Tuesday 13 November to 4 p.m.
on Thursday 15 November 19--.

I am currently looking for a suitable venue for the course, and am
writing to enquire whether your hotel would be able to provide the
necessary accommodation.

We would need at least 25 single rooms with washbasins, and a large
room for use for lectures and seminars. This room should have blackout
facilities and electric sockets so that it can be used for film or
video presentations.

I should be grateful if you would kindly let me know if the hotel
would be able to provide morning coffee and afternoon tea during the
breaks in sessions, and also let me have details of the social amenities
you have available. Full details of the cost for full board for each
person, the use of the large room, and the provision of coffee and
tea should also be included.

As I am anxious to make the arrangements as soon as possible, I should
appreciate a reply in the very near future.

Yours faithfully

J Lester
Training Officer

Fig. 12.17(b) Letter from notes – space has been left beneath the recipient's title for
the insertion of the recipient's address.

12.17 Exercises

1   Write a letter of application for the post described in the advertisement below.

TYPIST/RECEPTIONIST

required full-time or part-time, for busy offices/showrooms in city centre. Lively personality an advantage.

Salary negotiable.

Contact Wendy Yorke on 0342 09090

---

2   Draft a letter for signature by the Company Secretary of Wittgenstein Industries plc, 101 Berkeley Square, London W1X 5DA, asking for a reference for Miss Marian Jennifer Jones who has applied for a job as receptionist. Ask whether her appearance, manner and attitude are considered suitable for such a post, and enquire about her health and punctuality. The company would also like to know whether she is considered trustworthy and honest, since she will have access to some confidential information and be responsible for dealing with incoming mail. The letter is to be addressed to the Personnel Officer of Standard Holdings plc, whose address is PO Box 181, Board Street, Reading, Berkshire RE4 6NG. The letter should be marked 'Private and Confidential'.

3   You work in the Domestic Installations Division of GDP Installations Ltd, 217 Western Boulevard, Southampton. You have received a letter from a customer in Portsmouth: Mr L. Denton of 380 Freeway Road.

He complains that your recent installation of a boiler and radiator system was completed six weeks later than promised (which is true) and that in some ways the installation differs from the layout originally discussed. He is asking for a reduction of ten per cent of the total charge.

You have mentioned this to your manager, who said: 'Yes, we were late, but only because we had to wait for parts during the national transport strike. As for the differences, there wouldn't have been any if he had measured the rooms properly in the first place! Sorry – no discount; but put it nicely!'

(LCCI, English for commerce (higher))

4 Read the following letter received by Mrs Jack:
  Using the notes below, write a reply for Mrs Jack's signature.
                  (LCCI, Secretarial studies certificate (part))

Primrose Cottage
Larkhill
Steepleford
SR1 2LK

1 June 1987

Dear Mrs Jack

I understand that you welcome visitors at your fish processing
factory at Sandthorp, near Grimsby.

Members of the Larkhill Women's Institute have expressed an
interest in an outing to your factory at some time -during the
next three or four months.

We meet weekly on Wednesday afternoons, and we are hoping that a
visit can be arranged during October.

I look forward to receiving your reply.

Yours sincerely

Jennifer Hughes

Jennifer Hughes (Mrs)
Secretary, Larkhill Women's Institute

Maximum group size - 30
Facilities for disabled, but regret no guide dogs (food factory)
Tour takes up to 3 hours
Visiting hours 10.00 - 16.00
Either Wednesday 21 October or 28 October suitable
Warm clothing advisable
No children please
Guided tour covers whole operation - fresh fish to
frozen product
Light refreshments provided (on arrival and departure)
Introductory talk by Production Director (Vernon Lambert)
on arrival
Visitors receive discount shopping vouchers and
recipe book
Quick reply please - many requests for visit
Estimated number of visitors (approx) and date
chosen - please inform.

5 You are the assistant to Melinda Davis, Marketing Director of William Davis & Co, a publishing house specializing in reference books. You have been asked to draft, for Ms Davis's signature, a circular letter, which will be sent unsolicited to members of the public selected at random. The purpose of the letter is to publicize *New World*, a new encyclopaedia your firm is launching. Notes for the circular are given below.

In addition, you are asked to draft a separate form, for inclusion with the letter, requesting a sales representative to call at a time to be fixed by the recipient, and asking for those specific details about the prospective purchase which you feel necessary.

```
-  Of value to everyone
-  Each volume has 850pp
-  Special easy payments plan - pay for one volume per month and
   receive all after initial payment (subject to credit worthiness)
-  Latest information from universities and experts
-  12 volumes
-  Fully illustrated in colour
-  Free prospectus with sample pages available on request
-  Durable binding in handsome cloth
-  Written in direct, readable style
-  Boon to schoolchildren and adults alike
-  Cost only £18.50 per volume
```

6 You are the Assistant Personnel Manager of Chemtran Ltd. This firm's manufacturing processes involve the use of highly inflammable chemicals and the production line requires staff to observe meticulous timekeeping, otherwise output is severely affected.

Today, your manager received an unpleasant letter from a former employee who was dismissed for persistent lateness. The dismissal was preceded by trade-union-approved procedures for verbal and written warnings. However, in his letter the employee has claimed that, on legal advice, he intends to sue your firm for unfair dismissal.

Your manager has passed the letter on to you for reply and added the note: 'Nonsense! He's got no case at all. The union wouldn't back him; our procedures were correct. Tell him to forget it – he's bluffing – but try to stop him giving us any bad local publicity if you can.'

Write a suitable reply to the letter.

(LCCI, English for commerce (higher))

7 Using 150–200 words, write a correctly laid out letter on behalf of your firm (R. Cullen & Co. Ltd, 2–12 Gilbert Street, Oak, Oakshire AB1 3BA), to the editor of *Dean Daily News*, 140 Sullivan Street, Dean, Oakshire PZ0 6LY, pointing out that your company will be opening a shop dealing in radio, television and hi-fi goods in Dean in the near future and asking for the paper's advertisement rates. State that you would like a two-page advertise-

ment to announce the shop's opening and then you plan to take a half-page advertisement each Friday. Add any other information you think may be necessary.

(LCCI, English for commerce (intermediate))

8 Write a correctly laid out reply, in 150–200 words, to the following letter which has just been received by your company.

(LCCI, English for commerce (intermediate))

J. Rowland & Co. Ltd
24-30 Clare Avenue
London XZ6 6KO

1 July 19--

R.L. Smith (Clocks) Ltd
Hook Street
Enkawaite
Lancashire
L10 2BB

Dear Sirs

Accura clocks - order no. L/3458

The above order was delivered to us on 3 June this year. We put these clocks on display in our shops and sold quite a number of them. We then began receiving complaints from our customers that the alarm on the clocks would not work at all. We tested the alarms on all the clocks and found that none of them worked.

We have been dealing with you for over ten years and, until now, have been very pleased with your clocks. However, this latest batch with faulty alarms has made us look rather ridiculous to our customers. I should like you to collect these clocks and replace them with some that function properly. Failing that, I can send them back to you providing you agree to pay what will be a heavy postal bill.

I hope that you can assure us that this kind of thing will never happen again because if it does, we shall, reluctantly, have to find another clock supplier.

Yours faithfully

J. Rowland

J. Rowland
Managing Director

Forms and questionnaires

13.1 The nature and purpose of forms

Forms are an everyday feature of communication. When we apply for a job, we usually do it on a form; if we hire a television or video, we give details on another form; if we're admitted to hospital, we have to fill in a form before we can be treated. If we want to licence a car, book a holiday, order clothes from a catalogue, have our post redirected to a new address or enter for an examination, there will inevitably be a form to be completed. Even the most important details of our existence – birth, marriage and death – are recorded on certificates which are specially designed forms.

Forms have become a major way of communicating information in every area of human activity. This is especially so in business and commercial activity, where almost every organization has its own range of forms for internal and external use, and specialist companies now exist to design and produce forms to meet these requirements. Any kind of communication which has achieved such widespread use must have a great deal to offer, and the advantages of forms are indeed considerable.

For the organization issuing the form, the advantages are perhaps greater than for those who have to complete it. For the issuers, forms offer a way of gaining essential information in a format which is very easy to read and to process in large numbers. In comparison with letters, forms present only the information required, with no irrelevant additional material.

For the person completing the form, there are two main advantages: first, the nature of the information required is clearly stated, and secondly there is no need to write a formal letter – a task which many people might find off-putting. The form tells the reader exactly what information is needed; it may well give a series of alternative answers to choose from; and the space provided for answers indicates how much detail is required. All of this makes it easy for the writer to provide all the data required simply and quickly.

For both parties, forms offer a quick and reliable way of transferring information. They have the permanence of a letter and something of the speed of a telephone call, and if they are properly designed and accurately completed they can simplify and improve communication in a great range of business circumstances.

There are, however, some disadvantages. Many people feel that forms are an intrusion, asking questions which the issuing organization has no right to ask. Forms also suggest bureaucracy – endless paper-work which serves no useful purpose. Many people also dislike completing forms because they give no idea of an individual's personality – everything is reduced to a series of questions and answers, and the individual's own nature is not expressed at all. A further disadvantage is the extent to which a form's success as a means of communication depends on its wording and layout.

For all these reasons, it is essential that forms are properly designed. Questions must be properly worded, and should ask only for information which is really necessary. They must avoid offending the reader, and should never be ambiguous or unclear in meaning. The layout of every form should be clear and attractive, so that the reader is encouraged to complete it. If these principles are followed, a form will prove an invaluable method of quick, efficient communication which will help both parties involved: if they are not, no one will wish to complete it, and both parties will suffer.

13.2 Completing a form

If a form has been properly designed, it should be fairly straightforward to complete. Nonetheless, you should follow some simple rules to make sure that you complete it accurately.

First, make sure that you read through the whole form carefully before attempting to fill it in. Have a look at the kind of questions asked, and get a general idea of the kind of information required. Only if you know why the form has to be completed will you be able to provide the data that it requires, and this can only be done by careful and thorough reading.

When you have a general idea of the purpose of the form, go through it in more detail. Work out whether you have to answer every question, or whether only some are appropriate to your needs or circumstances. Work out the exact meaning of the questions. Often, questions on related information are grouped together, and so it may help to read the group as a whole. This will stop you from entering data required by a later question in your answer to an earlier one. Make sure, too, that you have read the whole question: be careful that it does not continue over the page.

When you have read and understood the questions, you should pause and think carefully about your answers. Often they will be fairly straightforward, but sometimes you will need to consider your response before writing anything down. If a space has been left for your answer, work out a way of saying what you have to say within the room allowed; if necessary, write your answer out in rough first. Check that spelling, expression and content are accurate, before entering your answer in the space provided.

When completing forms, you should always take great care with your writing. Remember that the person who reads the form will probably not know your handwriting and will have very little time to puzzle it out. Wherever possible, use block letters and try to write slowly and clearly. Few people like filling in forms, and we all feel tempted to do it as quickly as possible. Try to resist this temptation. If possible, use black ink: the form may have to be photocopied, and black ink will produce a far clearer copy.

Remember that, if the form cannot be read, the communication process will be interrupted. At best, you will be asked to complete another form; at worst, the form will be thrown away – and if it is an application form, your application will be ignored. Anything you can do to make the reader's task easier will help you too. In particular, make sure that you respond to questions which are not relevant to your own circumstances, to make clear that you have read and understood them and not just passed over them in error. Indicate that they are not relevant by putting a line through the answer space and writing 'N/A' or 'Not applicable'.

Many questions offer a series of alternative answers or give other instructions about answering, rather than just leaving a space for your response. You should always read any directions with great care. If a question says 'Delete where *not* applicable', remember to cross out the *wrong* answer, not the right one – a common error in form-filling. If you are asked to put a tick next to the right answer, make sure that your tick is next to it, and not half-way between it and another answer. If you are asked to put a ring round the right answer, ring only one item, not several.

Often, you will be asked to complete information in a grid system, to simplify the processing of the form. You should be careful to complete the grid by inserting only one letter in each space. Some forms also give special instructions about dates. For example, you may be asked to use 02 04 88 for 2 April 1988. If so, make sure that you put the figures in the correct compartments, otherwise mistakes will occur when the form is read. Many forms are processed in part by computer so that, unless you complete the boxes in the manner requested, your form may well be rejected, causing delay and inconvenience.

Make sure that you know important dates about yourself before completing an important form – your date of birth, dates of schools attended, dates of exams and dates of any other important events. Remember, too, to get these dates right: according to one recent report, around 40 per cent of people completing forms for university places entered into the 'Date of birth' box not their date of birth, but the date on which they were filling in the form.

When you have finished the form, read it through carefully and check for errors. By working out what to say beforehand you should have avoided making any mistakes, but you should always check to make sure. When you are happy with the form, make sure that you have a copy of the information it contains. If you have written out your answers in rough first, keep this draft. If you are typing the form, take a carbon copy – but remember that you will only have a copy of the answers. The best way to keep a record is to photocopy the form, which can be done in many shops and offices at the cost of only a few pence. This will take a little more time and trouble, but it will ensure that you have an exact record of questions and answers. This is particularly useful in the case of job application forms which will be used as the basis of interviews.

13.3 Designing a form

For any form to be fully effective, it must be properly designed. The main considerations determining a form's design can be summarized as follows:

(a) purpose;
(b) information required;
(c) readers and wording;
(d) kinds of questions;
(e) order of questions;
(f) layout;
(g) processing.

While each of these can be considered separately, the test of a good form is that it fulfils all of these requirements equally.

13.3.1 The purpose of a form
This is perhaps the most important stage in planning a form – making sure that it is genuinely needed as the solution to a communication problem. Forms are most valuable where similar information is required from a wide range of sources. Their other main advantage is speed; unless a form can be completed quickly and accurately by many people, and processed easily by those who need the information, another kind of communication may well be more appropriate.

13.3.2 The information required
Your next task is to decide exactly what information you really need. People are often reluctant to fill in forms, so they should be kept short, only going beyond a single side of paper when really necessary. Resist the temptation to ask questions which *might* be useful at a later date or for some other purpose. Loading a form with unnecessary questions will increase the reader's unwillingness to complete it – so make sure that you request only essential data.

13.3.3 Readers and wording
Having defined the purpose of the form and the information required, you should next consider the people who will have to complete it, since this will determine how the form is worded. Think about the age, vocabulary, attitudes and general outlook of your readers. If you are writing a form for a specific group of people – members of staff in an office or factory, for example – think

RR4

Fill in this form if you are getting less Housing Benefit now, or no Housing Benefit, because of the changes introduced on 1 April 1988

Surname

Title   Mr/Mrs/Miss/Ms

Other names

Address

Postcode

Daytime phone number

Date of birth   /   /

Were you or your partner getting Housing Benefit on 21 March 1988?

No ☐
Yes ☐   What was the name and address of the Housing Benefit office which paid your Housing Benefit then?

What was your Housing Benefit reference number then? If you can tell us this number we will be able to deal with your application more quickly.

■ If your Housing Benefit is dealt with by a different Housing Benefit office now, what is the name and address of the office?

What is your Housing Benefit reference number now?

Are you or your partner getting Family Credit, or waiting to hear about a claim for Family Credit?

No ☐
Yes ☐   How much Family Credit are you or your partner getting a week?

£

What is your Family Credit reference number?

If you receive a transitional payment, do you agree that we can pay it direct to your local council to cover any rent or rates that you owe?

No ☐
Yes ☐

Please read the Declaration on the other side of this form and sign your name

Fig. 13.1 A clear, well designed form (*continued opposite*). Notice the wording of instructions, the division of the form into sections, and the carefully judged use of space.

Declaration

I declare that the information that I gave my local authority to do with my Housing Benefit for the time between 21 March 1988 and 4 April 1988 was correct and complete

that none of the information has changed, or, if any of it has changed, that I have told the local authority about the changes

I agree that I will tell DHSS Transitional Payments in Glasgow about any of the changes listed below

You should write straight away and tell us if any of these changes happen to you or your partner, or if they have already happened

- start to get Income Support, or stop getting Income Support
- stop being responsible for paying rent, or rates, or both
  This might be because of
  - starting to buy your own home
  - going to live permanently
    in a hospital
    in a nursing home
    in a residential home
    abroad.

I understand that if I get any transitional payments, they will be paid on the basis that all the information to do with my Housing Benefit is correct and complete

I agree that I will pay back any transitional payments that I am paid on the basis that the information to do with my Housing Benefit is correct and complete, if in fact this information is not correct and complete

that I will pay back any transitional payments that I am paid, if I fail to tell DHSS Transitional Payments in Glasgow about any of the changes I have agreed to tell them about

I understand that if I have to pay any money back my transitional payments may be stopped until I have paid the money back.

- This is my application and declaration for a transitional payment.
- I give permission for my local authority and Social Security office to exchange any information that affects my Housing Benefit or application for a transitional payment.

Signature

Date
/ /

Send this form to   DHSS (Transitional Payments)
FREEPOST
PO Box 462
GLASGOW
G40 1BR

You will not need a stamp.

▲ CUT HERE
**Send this form to
DHSS** (Transitional Payments)
FREEPOST
PO Box 462
GLASGOW
G40 1BR
You will not need a stamp

Remember
If you or your partner are working for 24 hours or more a week, and bringing up a child, you may be able to get Family Credit.

Get a claim form **FC1** *Help for working people with children* from a post office or local Social Security office.

Leaflet RR 4
Issued by the Department of Health and Social Security
Printed in the UK for HMSO
Dd 8940396 J0838NE (HSSS)
5000M July 88

carefully about them. If you are designing a form for members of the public, you will be unable to envisage them so precisely. Instead, try to think of two or three widely different people whom you know, and design a form which all of them would be able to complete. Many government forms are designed for people with a reading age of twelve: this is a good basis to work from when designing any form to be used by the public, since you can then be sure that most readers will understand it.

In practice, this means that all directions on the form must be very clear. Make sure that you establish clearly and at an early stage which sections should be completed by which groups of people, and that you explain fully what the reader must do to answer the questions. Remember, too, to give instructions about what to do with the completed form, including an address to which it should be posted, or the name of a person to whom it should be given.

Although directions must be clear, they should also be brief. Many forms simply have a picture of a pen writing a tick above a list of alternatives. This is simpler than 'Please tick where appropriate', uses less space, and gives an element of contrast to the appearance of the form.

You must take care not to offend readers by the wording of individual questions. Some readers may object to being asked if they are 'Married, single, widowed or divorced': if you really need this information, it may be better to put 'Marital status' with a space next to it for the reader to complete as he or she wishes. Avoid making assumptions about your reader. For example, writing 'Christian names' will be inappropriate to Jewish, Sikh and many other readers: 'Forenames' is a neutral word which has the same meaning. Similarly, 'Mr/Mrs/Miss/Ms/Dr/Rev/Other' provides titles which are appropriate for as wide a range of people as possible.

13.3.4 Kinds of questions

Choosing the right kind of question is an important part of designing a form, since it will have a strong bearing on the kinds of answers which are received. The main kinds of questions are outlined below.

Direct question with space for answer   This is the simplest type, which is useful for three kinds of information.

(a) It can be used for personal details such as the name, address or educational qualifications of the person completing the form. It is most effective if the available space is carefully organized, perhaps in columns with appropriate headings.

(b) It can be used to request information which is particularly complex and cannot be obtained in any other way. In some cases, the required answer may take the form of a piece of continuous writing – a kind of essay. Job application forms, for example, may well ask applicants to give details of their sporting and recreational interests; insurance claims forms will ask the claimant to describe the accident, perhaps with the aid of diagrams or sketch maps.

(c) It can be used to give the person completing the form a chance to convey any additional information or further details not covered elsewhere. This is important for two reasons: it ensures that nothing is overlooked because it is not related to the more specific questions; and it gives the writer an opportunity for self-expression, which is also useful to the person processing the form – especially in the case of job applications, where a certain amount of selection is done at application-form stage.

When using questions of this sort you should take care to give adequate space for the answer. Too little space will make the reader frustrated and angry, and result in cramped, incomplete answers; too much space will suggest that a great deal of information has to be provided, and also reduce the space available for other questions.

'Delete where not applicable'   This is used most often where there are two or three alternative answers. All are presented, and the reader is asked to cross out those which are wrong, as in this example:

I do/do not* wish to attend the meeting.

*Delete where not applicable.

This can be a very straightforward way of gaining information, but it can be used only for simple, direct alternatives like that shown above. Even so, there is always the danger that some readers will delete the right answer instead of the wrong one.

'Tick box'   This is useful where there is a small range of possible answers. It provides a simple and rapid way of gaining basic information, but needs to be carefully designed so that the boxes are directly beside the appropriate answers. Boxes may be arranged vertically or horizontally: the former method is much clearer, but the latter saves space, as the following examples show:

Would you accept a job which is (please tick box)	Full-time	
	Part-time	
	Shift work	
	Nights	
	Temporary	

Title (please tick box)	Mr	Mrs	Miss	Ms	Rev	Dr	Other

'**Ring or underline correct answer**'   This is an alternative to ticking boxes. It takes up less space, but in general is less satisfactory as it is often untidily completed, causing doubt as to the answer intended. Here is an example:

Please ring or underline the kind of driving licence you possess

| Motor | Motor cycle | Public service vehicle | HGV1 | HGV2 | HGV3 |

13.3.5 Order of questions

This must be carefully planned and follow a logical sequence. For most forms, personal details will need to come first, followed by the more specific details required. An accident claims form, for example, will begin by asking for the name, address and insurance policy details of the claimant, before requiring information about the accident; a job application form will start with the name, address and age of the applicant, and then go on to work experience and career aspirations.

The precise order of the questions will vary with each kind of form. In general, however, a logical sequence should be followed and related questions should be grouped together in sections. If each of these is carefully ruled off from the others and perhaps even given a heading, the form will be much easier to read and complete, helping both parties involved. The form in fig. 13.1 shows this principle in practice.

13.3.6 Layout of a form

The physical layout of a form is an important part of its success as an item of communication. The need for clearly defined sections has already been stressed, but other factors should also be borne in mind. For example, a form which uses plenty of space will make the reader feel relaxed and thus more likely to complete the form than if confronted by lots of questions crammed into a single sheet. On the other hand, a form several pages long will put off some readers. With experience, it is usually possible to strike a balance between these considerations and to produce a form which is attractive and accessible to readers, yet efficient in its use of space.

13.3.7 Processing a form

When designing a form, consideration should be given to those who will have to process or interpret the information it contains, as well as to those who have to complete it. The use of a clear layout, with easily read headings and plenty of space will certainly help the processor. Other aids might include locating the name of the applicant at the top right-hand corner, to make it easy for the processor to flick through a pile of forms and find the right one, and the use of blank spaces on the form for data to be added later, perhaps marked 'For office use only'.

Important though such considerations are, you should remember that unless the form is attractive to the reader he or she will not complete it. Consequently, ease of completion should always be put before ease of processing when a form is being designed.

13.4 Using forms

As mentioned earlier in this unit, there are many business situations where the use of a form will be helpful and appropriate. Some of the most common uses are discussed below.

13.4.1 Internal uses

Many companies use forms as a way of communicating information within and between departments, where the information is of a standard type and there is a frequent need to convey it. *Telephone message forms* are a simple but very reliable application, as they ensure that all the necessary details of a call are recorded and given to the person involved. Message forms are discussed in section 7.5. *Report forms* of various kinds are also common. They may record the output of a particular department or section in a given period, or record accidents involving employees at work. Both of these kinds of forms are dealt with in Unit 15.

Other forms which are important in a company's communications include those related to ordering and supplying goods. Most companies make use of *order* or *requisition* forms, which ensure that all the relevant points are specified: the item ordered; the quantity; the cost; any further description; the order number; the authorizing person; the date; and the name of the department to which the item is to be supplied. *Invoices*, too, are often designed as forms, with blanks to be completed showing the nature of the goods, the price and other details (see fig. 13.2).

There are also forms which are concerned with the individual's place within the organization, which differ slightly from those above. These include *claims forms* for travelling and other expenses; *returns* detailing orders processed or other work completed; and *application forms* for training conferences, courses and other company functions. Related to these are *assessment forms* which some companies use to monitor the progress of each employee. They are completed by supervisors or managers after an appraisal interview with the employee concerned, and are used to record the nature of the person's work, together with comments on his or her progress during the year and any other relevant information.

13.4.2 External uses

Most organizations have forms which are completed by customers, other businesses or individuals enquiring about some facet of their activities. Order forms are perhaps the simplest example, but others include forms requesting information about certain products; forms applying for the supply of services such as gas, electricity or the telephone; and forms requesting brochures or samples.

Similar to these are forms related to transactions between an organization

INVOICE

43011

Sports Supplies Ltd

Willow Road
Haston
Cambridgeshire XY31 3RR
(registered office)

Telephone Haston 31111
Telex 0011 2345

VAT reg. 831765123

To: Thurays Sports Ltd
　　10 High Street
　　Graybury
　　Essex　WV21 3AB

Date: 5.3.19..

Your order no: 7631

Quantity	Description	Unit Price	Total	VAT	Total
		£	£	£	£
30	T241 Racquets	15.00	450.00	67.50	517.50
25	C106 Bats	20.00	600.00	90.00	690.00
20	C193 Cricket balls	48.00	960.00	144.00	1104.00
50	T109 Tennis balls	6.00	300.00	45.00	345.00

Invoice total　2656.50

Terms of trading:	7 days settlement:	5%
	28 days settlement:	2½%

E. & O. E.

Directors F. Ball, C. Batt
Registered in England: No. 876543

Fig. 13.2 Invoice

and an individual. The withdrawal or deposit of money in a bank or building society, or a request for a particular book or periodical in a specialist library, will usually be carried out by the completion of a form, to make sure that certain necessary information is kept on record. Loan applications, credit agreements and other financial transactions between organizations and individuals are usually made on standard forms, which greatly simplify the work of large organizations. Another important form which links individual and organization is the job application form, which is increasingly taking over from the more formal letter of application, largely because forms are easier to process.

13.4.3 Public and official forms

In addition to forms issued by organizations for internal and external use, there are a very large number of forms produced by government departments and public services. Claim forms like that in fig. 13.1 enable people to claim various benefits from the State, for example. Special forms are available for the redirection of mail and the provision of other services by the Post Office. The licensing of road vehicles involves forms, as also do applications for driving licences and driving tests, while various medical forms are used to record a patient's medical history, the nature of a patient's condition after an operation, and the transfer of a patient from one doctor's practice to another.

13.4.4 Conclusion

All of these forms fulfil an important and clearly defined function, and make possible the transfer of large amounts of information quickly, accurately and to the convenience of all those involved. If forms are well designed, they can help people to carry out their jobs efficiently and rapidly: if they are poorly designed, they will only add confusion and resentment to the process. Make sure that any forms which you are asked to design fulfil the requirements detailed in this unit, and thus fall into the first category and not the second.

13.5 Questionnaires

Questionnaires are a special kind of form designed to record people's opinions. They are widely used by commercial organizations – for researching consumers' preferences for various goods or public attitudes to major issues, for example. They are also employed on a slightly smaller scale within organizations – to gain an indication of employees' feelings about proposed changes to working hours or canteen facilities, for example. A questionnaire may well form part of the research undertaken in the preparation of a formal report, as discussed in Unit 15.

13.5.1 Presentation and layout

All the points made about the design and layout of forms in section 13.3 apply to the presentation of questionnaires. If anything, they are even more important. Most questionnaires rely on the public's desire to help: the people who respond to them give freely of their time, and are under no compulsion to complete them. This means that a questionnaire must be made as straightforward as possible to avoid putting people off.

This can be achieved to a large measure by using a clear and attractive design, and language which is simple and direct and will not offend anyone who is likely to read it. Attempting to create a good relationship with the respondent will also help. All questionnaires should begin with a polite request to the reader to complete the form, along with a brief indication of the reason why the information is needed. This should be followed by an assurance that all information will be treated in confidence, to encourage people to answer fully and frankly.

At the end of the questionnaire, clear directions about where to send the form should be prefaced with a brief statement of thanks to the reader for having completed the form.

Elements such as these will help to make sure that the rate of return for your questionnaire is as high as possible. If you are distributing individual questionnaires by mail, you should, however, expect only a small proportion of returns. In some areas of marketing, a reply rate of between five and ten per cent is considered very high indeed. It is often more effective to approach people personally and ask them to complete the form on the spot. Many people find it hard to refuse such a request, and your success rate will be a lot higher.

Some questionnaires are designed to be read aloud by an interviewer – an approach popular among market research firms who conduct surveys in the street. For such questionnaires, an attractive layout is less important than ease of recording and processing, since it is the skill of the interviewer – not the presentation of the form – which will decide whether or not someone responds. If you have to design a form of this kind, however, don't be tempted to cram in as many questions as you can. The patience of the person answering will soon be exhausted, and the processing of the form will become very complex.

The most important factor in ensuring that people complete a questionnaire is the nature and wording of the questions. Be ruthless in excluding unnecessary questions: they make the form unduly long, and also give the impression of intruding on the reader's privacy. In almost all cases, requests for the respondent's name and address can be omitted, saving space on the questionnaire as well as confirming the confidentiality of the information.

13.5.2 Kinds of questions

Factual questions with alternative answers   Questions like this are used mainly to establish facts and circumstances about the reader before he or she is asked for statements of opinion. They can be answered simply and quickly, especially if presented in the 'tick box' style outlined in section 13.3. Clear directions should be included as to how they are to be completed, allowing the reader to answer them quickly and pass on to matters of opinion.

If such questions are to be effective, care must be taken to make the alternative answers specific. If the question is:

How often do you use your washing machine?

the possible answers should *not* be:

Often/Sometimes/Rarely/Never

since these are open to interpretation. Instead, you should offer the range:

Every day/Twice a week/Once a week/Less often

Although this type of question is very useful for establishing routine matters of this kind, it is less effective when used for opinions, as people may feel that they are unable to express their own feelings directly.

Reactions to statements   In this kind of question, a statement of opinion is made and the reader is asked to give his or her response. Usually this is done by ticking one of a number of boxes. For example:

Please tick the column which comes closest to your feeling about this statement:

	Agree strongly	Agree	No feeling	Disagree	Disagree strongly
Football hooligans are treated fairly by judges					

If the directions for answering are clear, and the statements themselves well worded, this can be a very effective way of canvassing opinions. A large number of statements can be put forward, with the alternative answers arranged in columns, again making it possible for the form to be completed quickly.

It is not an entirely reliable method, however, in that responses may easily be influenced by the way in which statements are worded. Care must be taken to avoid asking questions which can only be answered in one way, as this will produce inaccurate responses and so distort the overall meaning of the answers received.

Ringing numbers　This is another useful method for ensuring rapid response. For example:

Please circle the appropriate number – the 3 at the the left for a very strong NO, the 3 at the right for a very strong YES, with 0 as no feeling either way.

Should judges be firmer with football hooligans?	3	2	1	0	1	2	3

Like the previous kind of question, several of these may be presented as a table to save space and to cut down the amount of time needed to answer them. For example:

Think about each of the statements in the left-hand column. Then circle the appropriate number – the 3 at the left for a very strong NO, the 3 at the right for a very strong YES, and 0 for no strong feeling.

Should heavy lorries be banned from city centres?	3	2	1	0	1	2	3
Is enough being done to combat lead pollution?	3	2	1	0	1	2	3
Should more freight be sent by rail?	3	2	1	0	1	2	3
Are Britain's small airports being used enough?	3	2	1	0	1	2	3
Are there too many cars on the roads?	3	2	1	0	1	2	3
Is the local bus service good enough?	3	2	1	0	1	2	3
Is the national rail network large enough?	3	2	1	0	1	2	3
Should people use public transport and not cars in cities?	3	2	1	0	1	2	3

In general, however, this system is less reliable than others discussed above. Many people will find it hard to understand exactly what is required of them, and once again the way the question is worded will influence the way it is answered. Researchers who are aware of this problem will incorporate 'check' questions into their questionnaires which ask for the same information in different ways. Having set the hooligan question above, for example, they might include the following questions later in the column:

Are judges too lenient with football hooligans?
Do football hooligans get what they deserve from judges?

In this way it is possible to check that a reader's response is not swayed by the wording of the questions and that he or she has understood the working of the questionnaire. But there are significant disadvantages: check questions take up a great deal of space, and they may be seen by some readers as an affront to their intelligence.

Open questions Although open questions – simple requests for information – have a place in a questionnaire, they are usually outnumbered by questions about opinions and preferences of the kinds listed above. There are, however, two areas which necessitate the use of open questions which the reader is required to complete in his or her own words: first, where there is a need for factual data not easily provided by alternative methods of answering – for example, addresses (if they are strictly necessary) or other variable items of information; and secondly, where the reader is given space to add any individual opinions not covered by the questions elsewhere in the form. It is good practice always to conclude a questionnaire with such a question, allowing the reader to express feelings or opinions in his or her own words, rather than through the rather mechanical process of alternative answers. This is an important opportunity to make the reader feel that his or her opinions matter, and will further encourage people to complete and return the form.

Examples of two different kinds of questionnaire are given in figs 13.3 and 13.4. You will notice that they employ the kinds of questions discussed in this unit and that they are fairly brief, making the fullest use of the space available, yet stressing the value of the completed questionnaire to those requesting the information.

13.6 Conclusion

If they are used properly, forms and questionnaires can be an important communication tool. As well as those discussed in this unit, situations in which they are used include letter-writing (see section 12.12) and routine report-writing (see section 15.2).

For the person answering it, a form must be easy to understand, simple to complete, and should ask only questions which are essential to its purpose. It must avoid giving offence in the wording and content of questions, and – perhaps most important of all – it must be kept as short as possible. For the person who has to process it, a form must be clearly laid out, with the information required organized in a logical order. Gaps should be left for other data to be added at the processing stage.

Designed and used correctly, forms and questionnaires can make life easier for all concerned. Designed badly and used incorrectly, they can not only prevent an organization from getting the information it needs: in extreme cases they may also damage its public image, revealing it as an intrusive and discriminatory body with little consideration for its customers or employees.

Kwik-Fit ///

Help Us To Help You

DEAR CUSTOMER

Please help us to give you the best service by giving your frank opinion on this card. Your comments will assist us in maintaining and improving our standards. Thank you for your co-operation and your custom.

Tom Farmer, Managing Director

Depot visited _____

Receipt No.

Please ✔ as applicable

Which of the following did you buy on this visit?

Tyres ☐   Exhaust ☐

Battery ☐   Shock Absorbers ☐   Other ☐

What prompted you to visit us on this occasion? Please ✔ the main boxes that you feel apply.

Television ☐   Local Newspaper ☐   Recommended ☐

Passing by ☐

Radio ☐   Yellow pages ☐   Telephone enquiry ☐

National Newspaper ☐   Past experience ☐   Freefone ☐

Was this your first visit to Kwik-Fit   Yes ☐   No ☐

Now please would you give us your comments on the service you received. Please ✔ each statement if you agree.

My car was treated with respect and seat covers were used ☐

My car was examined in my presence and I was given a frank and honest appraisal of the work required ☐

I was told the cost of the job before the work started ☐

The finished work was examined in my presence ☐

The parts removed from my vehicle were offered for my retention ☐

The depot was clean and tidy ☐

Finally how would you rate the overall service you received?

Excellent ☐   Good ☐   Satisfactory ☐   Unsatisfactory ☐

Please make any further comments:

_____

_____

Name and Address _____

Fig. 13.3 Questionnaire asking for customers' comments

PARKER JOHNSON PLC

PROPOSED FREE BUS SERVICE

It has been suggested that a free bus service to transport employees to and from work would help people to get to work on time, and thus aid productivity and increase output - something which would benefit us all.

To find out the demand for this service, I would be grateful if you would complete this questionnaire and return it to me, Ian Johnson, Personnel Manager, by Friday 8th June. You are not asked to give your name, so please feel free to give your views frankly. Thank you for your help.

1   In which department do you work? _____

2   How often do you work night shifts?   Please tick box

                                    Once a fortnight
                                    Once a month
                                    Every other month
                                    No regular pattern
                                    Not at all

3   How far away from the works do you live?

                                    Less than a mile
                                    1-2 miles
                                    3-5 miles
                                    6-10 miles
                                    Further than 10 miles

4   Do you think that a free bus services would be:

                                    Very good
                                    Good
                                    No feeling
                                    Poor
                                    Waste of company money

5   In your opinion, would a free bus service help to improve productivity?

                                    Yes
                                    No

6   Have you any other views about the proposal? If so, please give them in the space below.

Fig. 13.4 Questionnaire for use within a company

13.7 Quick questions

1 What are the main points to be considered when designing a form?

2 On a form or questionnaire, what is the best way to ask people:
   (a) their date of birth?
   (b) how often they visit a supermarket?
   (c) if they have ever had any of several common diseases?
   (d) how far they agree with current government policy?

3 What should you remember when you are filling in a form?

13.8 Longer exercises

1 A new clinic for preventive medicine for senior citizens is being opened in Burton Road, Falworth, by the area Family Practitioners' Committee. A standard letter is to be sent to all patients giving them general details of the scheme and informing them that an appointment has been reserved for them at a specified date and time.

As a clerical officer in the Health Department, Queen's Drive, Falworth, you are asked to design a simple reply slip for inclusion with the letter. The recipient should be able to provide the following information:

● whether or not he or she wishes to be a patient of the new clinic;
● whether or not he or she can attend at the date and time specified;
● if he or she cannot attend then, a suitable alternative date and time;
● his or her name and National Insurance number;
● the name of his or her doctor;
● his or her signature;
● the date.

2 Complete the enrolment form in fig. 13.5.

3 As a member of your students' union executive, you have been asked to prepare a report on the facilities offered by your college canteen. Before you can write the report, however, you need to find out how those who use the canteen feel about what it has to offer. Design a questionnaire to gain people's feelings on the meals available (both full meals and snacks); arrangements for queueing; speed of service; cost; number and layout of tables; and general standards of decoration and cleanliness. Decide which of these aspects are the most important, and design your questionnaire so that people will be able and willing to complete it quickly and accurately.

Girobank

APPLICATION FOR A CURRENT ACCOUNT

Complete this application form for your Girobank account and send it to your nearest Girobank office (address overleaf)

I/We wish to apply for a Girobank Current Account

Please use block capitals

1

Surname .... Mr/Mrs/Miss/Ms ....

First name .... Date of birth ....

Surname .... Mr/Mrs/Miss/Ms ....

(joint account only)

First name .... Date of birth ....

Address ....

.... Postcode ....

Home Telephone Number ....

How long at this address .... years .... months

Previous address if less than 5 years ....

....

At which two post offices will you wish to cash cheques?

1. ....

2. ....

Please state your existing bank account number if you have one

Girobank ....

Other .... Sort Code ....

Do you have a cheque guarantee card? YES/NO

Occupation ....

How long in this employment? .... years .... months

Previous employer (if less than 1 year) ....

Address ....

How long did you work for this employer? .... years .... months

Please tick the box if you wish to open a Girobank Deposit Account ☐

2

Please sign here (In the case of a joint account both applicants should sign)

Signature .... Date ....

Signature .... Date ....

The operation of your current account is subject to the conditions held in the Girobank Handbook, copies of which are available on request.

3

In the case of a joint account the second applicant hereby authorises you to dispense with the statutory requirement to send separate statements of account to him/her.

Signature .... Date ....

Signature .... Date ....

(second applicant joint accounts only)

4

I/We wish to apply for a LINK card to enable me/us to make withdrawals at around 1000 cash dispensers nationwide. I/We accept the LINK conditions of service opposite.

Signature .... ☐

Signature .... ☐

Note for joint account holders: Both parties must sign the application, even if only one party requires a card. Please tick the box to the right of your signature if you require a card in your name.

5

If you wish to have your pay credited directly to your account please complete the authority below and as soon as your application is accepted Girobank will send the authority direct to your pay office, who will make the necessary arrangements

Employer's Name .... Address ....

....

.... Postcode ....

I (full name) ....

Pay number .... wish to have my weekly/monthly pay credited direct to my Girobank account:

Girobank account number ....

(to be completed by Girobank)

To be completed by Pay Office.

Mr/Mrs/Miss/Ms ....

You will wish to note that your wages/salary will be credited to your Girobank account with effect from (date) ....

Signature .... Pay group ref ....

6

For full written details of our range of services, please tick the relevant box(es) below:

☐ Deposit Accounts ☐ High Interest Savings ☐ Flexiplan*

☐ Personal Loans* ☐ Girobank Visa* ☐ Mortgages*

☐ Travel Services ☐ Sureplan General Insurance Services

*These services are available only to persons aged 18 or over (21 for Flexiplan). For mortgages a first charge over the property and life insurance cover are required.

Fig. 13.5 An application form to open a Girobank account

Graphic communication

14.1 Introduction

Graphic communication is communication through pictures, symbols and diagrams of different kinds. It is a means of putting across ideas and information instantly and forcefully. International road signs and safety symbols are a good example of how effectively graphic communication can work: drivers respond almost instinctively to signs for steep hills, slippery roads or uneven surfaces, while symbols for high voltage wires or radioactive materials are accessible even to those who are unable to decipher written warnings. Such symbols are also understood internationally as there is no written language involved.

Other forms of graphic communication do not have quite so much force, but are nonetheless highly effective. For instance, think how much easier it is to find a convenient train to catch by looking at a timetable than by reading a long essay which describes when trains leave and arrive at various stations. A graph can tell you how the number of journeys made by air has grown in the last ten years, whereas a newspaper article would take much longer to convey the same data.

Sometimes, graphs and diagrams are used in conjunction with passages of writing. This technique ensures that the reader receives both a verbal and a pictorial message, the two working together to ensure that the information is fully understood. Reports, notices, lectures and meetings can all benefit from the use of well-presented graphics.

There are many kinds of graphic communication. Some, like engineering drawings or architects' blueprints, are used only by specialists in a particular area. Others, such as graphs and pie charts, can be used in all areas of business, and are an essential feature of the skilled communicator's art. This unit discusses the main types of graphic communication used in business and the contexts in which they most frequently appear. It also provides guidelines on how to construct and interpret graphic material, and how to avoid distorting statistics in your use of graphics.

14.2 Tables

Tables are the most direct method of presenting large amounts of statistical information. They usually present a set of figures in columns, which can be read off against some form of scale or sub-categorization on the left-hand side. Each column has a brief explanatory heading, supplemented by details of the units that the figures represent (£ sterling, numbers of people, thousands of cars produced, for example).

Tables should be carefully planned, to ensure that they present the data in the clearest and simplest way. If two sets of figures are likely to be compared – output for two firms, related departments or time periods, say – they should be placed in adjacent columns. There should be clear gaps at regular intervals – both horizontally between rows and vertically between columns – to prevent people from accidentally looking at the wrong figure. Any information which canňot be presented as part of the table – reasons for gaps in the information, or special circumstances about one set of figures, for example – should appear as footnotes. An indication of the source of the data should also be included, either as part of the heading or as a footnote.

Although tables present data in an immediate and carefully ordered way, they do have disadvantages. They are not always easy to read and offer no clear interpretation of the figures they present. While this prevents the figures from being distorted, it also means that the full significance of the figures is not always transmitted to the reader.

To avoid these difficulties, tables are often presented in conjunction with some other form of communication. For example, a report will often give the salient points of a table in words, or by means of bar charts, pie charts or one of the other forms discussed in this unit, presenting the full table as an *appendix* to the text (see section 15.5.10). Occasionally, tables appear with instructions on how they should be used.

14.2.1 Constructing a table

If you are asked to construct a table of figures, there is a basic procedure you may find useful to follow.

(a) Decide on a suitable heading for the table.
(b) Decide on the categories you wish to include as column headings, and the scale or sub-categories which will dictate the order of the horizontal rows. There are no hard-and-fast rules to follow here, but – in general – tables contain more rows than columns. You may find it helpful to bear in mind the purpose of the table: in fig. 14.1(a), for example, the subject of the table is methods of transport; the categories to be considered are 'Users of public transport' and 'Users of other forms of transport', and these provide the column headings. The various age groups are a means of sub-dividing the main categories, and therefore appear on the left-hand side. The same figures can be presented differently – as in fig. 14.1(b) – but it is then far more difficult to compare the two categories.

Age group	Method of transport		
	Own means	Public transport	Totals
Under 18	12	6	18
18–25	15	10	25
25–40	25	18	43
40–55	13	32	45
Over 55	6	12	18
Totals	71	78	149

Fig. 14.1(a) Simple table: correct layout

Method of transport	Age group					
	Under 18	18–25	25–40	40–55	Over 55	Totals
Own means	12	15	25	13	6	71
Public transport	6	10	18	32	12	78
Totals	18	25	43	45	18	149

Fig. 14.1(b) Simple table: incorrect layout

(c) Make sure you have included an indication of the units you are working in.

(d) Arrange the headings on the left-hand side in the most appropriate order – according to age, dates, size or cost, for example.

(e) Decide whether any two columns need to be put next to each other for ease of reference.

(f) Decide on the best order for the columns.

(g) Draw guide rules in pencil to keep the columns straight and separate.

(h) Fill in the figures, checking carefully for accuracy.

(i) Ink in lines on the finished table as necessary, to make the divisions between columns and between rows as clear as possible. If the table is particularly complex, you may need a line between each column and each row, perhaps with a heavier line every second or third. In a simple table such as fig. 14.1(a) you will probably not require any vertical lines, and in some companies this style is followed for all tables, however complex.

14.2.2 Timetables

Timetables are a special form of table. Figure 14.2 shows a typical railway timetable: notice that the stations are listed clearly on the left-hand side, with each train service in a separate column to help the reader identify a suitable train quickly. Further information is provided by notes at the right-hand side which

Liverpool—Runcorn→Stafford—Nuneaton—Rugby—Milton Keynes—Watford Jn—London

MONDAYS TO FRIDAYS

	MO 🛏	MX 🛏	A☕	A⊠	AⓅ	⊠	☕	Ⓘ
Liverpool Lime Street	0015	0015	0603	0610	0710	0825	0940	1021
Runcorn	—	—	0620	0627	0727	0842	0957	1038
Stafford	0132	0132	0714	0707	0805	—	—	1130
Nuneaton	0243	0249	—	—	—	—	—	1231c
Rugby	0258	0304	0809c	—	—	—	—	—
Milton Keynes	0346	0352	—	—	—	1025	1139	—
Watford Jn	—	—	—	—	0920	—	—	—
London Euston	0441	0446	—	0847	0940	1106	1225	—

	Ⓟ	×	☕	Ⓘ	Ⓘ	Ⓟ	⊠	Ⓘ
Liverpool Lime Street	1140	1310	1325	1440	1530	1610	1710	1728
Runcorn	1157	1327	1342	1457	1548	1627	1727	1745
Stafford	—	1414	1435	—	1648	—	1827c	1835
Nuneaton	—	1445	—	—	—	1759c	—	—
Rugby	1342c	—	—	—	—	1813c	—	—
Milton Keynes	—	1524	—	1650	—	—	1928c	2049c
Watford Jn	—	—	—	—	—	1826	1928	—
London Euston	1423	1608	—	1731	—	1847	1950	—

	Ⓘ		Ⓘ	FO Ⓡ☕
Liverpool Lime Street	1840	1915	2010	2340
Runcorn	1857	1932	2027	2357
Stafford	1945	2024	2117	0052
Nuneaton	—	—	2144	—
Rugby	—	—	2158	—
Milton Keynes	—	—	2255b	—
Watford Jn	2104	—	2247	—
London Euston	2124	—	2307	—

SATURDAYS

	🛏	☕	Ⓘ	Ⓘ	Ⓘ	Ⓡ☕	Ⓡ☕	Ⓘ
Liverpool Lime Street	0015	0603	0610	0710	0825	0835	0840	0940
Runcorn	—	0620	0627	0727	0842	0852	0857	0957
Stafford	0132	0710	0713	0805	—	0940	0950	—
Nuneaton	0249	—	0750	—	—	—	—	1104
Rugby	0304	—	—	—	—	—	—	—
Milton Keynes	0352	—	—	—	1025	—	—	—
Watford Jn	—	—	—	0920	—	—	—	—
London Euston	0446	—	0905	0940	1106	—	—	1217

		Ⓘ		Ⓘ	Ⓘ	☕	☕	☕
Liverpool Lime Street	1040	1140	1240	1310	1510	1530	1610	1728
Runcorn	1057	1157	1257	1327	1527	1548	1627	1745
Stafford	1154	—	1354	1418	1607	1648	—	1835
Nuneaton	1231c	—	—	1445	—	—	1759c	—
Rugby	—	1338c	—	—	—	—	1813c	—
Milton Keynes	—	—	—	1524	1711	—	—	—
Watford Jn	—	—	—	1614e	—	—	1826	—
London Euston	—	1423	—	1608	1751	—	1847	—

	Ⓘ		Ⓘ
Liverpool Lime Street	1740	1915	1925
Runcorn	1757	1932	1942
Stafford	—	2024	2030
Nuneaton	1906	—	2057
Rugby	1938c	—	—
Milton Keynes	2049c	—	—
Watford Jn	2026c	—	2154
London Euston	2020	—	2214

Liverpool—Runcorn→Stafford—Nuneaton—Rugby—Milton Keynes—Watford Jn—London

SUNDAYS

	C🛏	B🛏	Ⓘ	B☕	Ⓘ	B☕	CⒾ	BⒾ
Liverpool Lime Street	0015	0015	0740	0858	0926	1037	1146	1146
Runcorn	—	—	0759	0917	0945	1056	1205	1205
Stafford	0243	0302	1004c	1057	1144c	1233	—	—
Nuneaton	—	—	—	—	—	—	—	—
Rugby	0421	0431	1044	—	1227	—	—	—
Milton Keynes	—	—	—	—	—	—	1509	1518
Watford Jn	0539	0549	—	—	—	—	—	—
London Euston	0608	0618	1218	—	1414	—	1614	1619

	B☕	Ⓘ	Ⓘ	Ⓘ	Ⓘ	☕	Ⓘ	
Liverpool Lime Street	1400	1429	1535	1605	1710	1718	1840	1940
Runcorn	1419	1448	1552	1622	1727	1735	1857	1957
Stafford	1607	—	1632	—	—	1829	1944	2045
Nuneaton	—	—	—	—	1901c	—	—	—
Rugby	—	—	1711	—	1914c	—	2051c	—
Milton Keynes	—	1729	—	1805	—	—	—	—
Watford Jn	—	—	—	—	1938	—	2117	—
London Euston	—	1814	1824	1850	1959	—	2138	—

	Ⓘ
Liverpool Lime Street	2010
Runcorn	2027
Stafford	—
Nuneaton	—
Rugby	2152
Milton Keynes	—
Watford Jn	2244
London Euston	2305

NOTES

Times in **bold** type indicate a direct service. Times in light type indicate a connecting service. Some connecting services shown are not InterCity and do not convey first class seating accommodation, please enquire for details.

- MO Mondays Only.
- MX Mondays Excepted.
- 🛏 InterCity Sleepers available.
- Ⓟ Liverpool Pullman (except Bank Holidays). Full meal service to First Class ticket holders in designated seats. Buffet service of hot food, sandwiches, hot and cold drinks available to all passengers.
- ⊠ Full meal service to First Class ticket holders in designated seats. Buffet service of hot food, sandwiches, hot and cold drinks to all passengers for all or part of journey.
- × Full meal service in designated seats. Buffet service of hot food, sandwiches, hot and cold drinks to all passengers for all or part of journey.
- Ⓘ Buffet service of hot food, sandwiches, hot and cold drinks for all or part of journey.
- ☕ Service of cold snacks, hot and cold drinks for all or part of journey.
- Ⓣ Trolley service of cold snacks, hot and cold drinks for all or part of journey.
- Ⓡ Seat reservations are strongly advised for whole or part of journey.
- A Outward Saver Tickets are not valid on this train to Milton Keynes, Watford or London.
- B Until 14 August.
- C From 21 August.
- D Outward Saver Tickets are not valid on this train from London, Watford or Milton Keynes.
- E Return Saver Tickets are not valid on this train from London, Watford or Milton Keynes.
- F Until 13 August.
- G From 20 August.
- b Change Rugby.
- c Change Crewe.
- e Change Milton Keynes.
- f Change Crewe. From 21 August depart 1336.
- g Change Crewe. From 21 August depart 1542.

The British Railways Board accept no liability for any inaccuracy in the information contained in this timetable — which is subject to alteration especially during Bank holiday periods.

Fig. 14.2 Railway timetable

are linked to the table by letter symbols. In this way, a large amount of complicated information is conveyed quickly and clearly, in the minimum of space.

Reading a railway timetable is simple provided that you follow these steps:

(a) Decide when you need to be at your destination.
(b) Find your destination in the left-hand column. Read across the timetable until you find a train which arrives at about the right time.
(c) Read up the column until level with your point of departure. This is the time the train leaves.
(d) If there is no time given in this space, read across towards the left, until a time is given. You will need to take this train and change at an intermediate station.
(e) Don't forget to check with the footnotes that this train runs on the day you want to travel.

14.3 Bar charts

These are one of the most popular ways of presenting statistics. A bar chart consists of a group of strips of different lengths, each representing a numerical figure (see fig. 14.3) – the longer the bar, the larger the figure it denotes. Bar

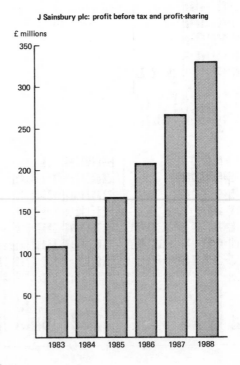

Fig. 14.3 Bar chart

charts can therefore present the comparative size of figures very clearly, and in this respect are often more effective than tables as a means of graphic communication.

14.3.1 Constructing a bar chart

(a) Decide on the scale in which the figures will be presented in the chart – for example, 1 cm might represent £500, or 2 cm might represent 1000 tons of imported raw materials. Make sure that this scale allows you to include the longest bar – and make sure, too, that the shortest bar will be large enough to understand. Working in units which can be easily divided will make the task of constructing the chart much easier.

(b) Draw the *axes* – the lines on which the scale is marked. Mark off the scale at regular intervals. In fig. 14.3, for example, the scale is marked off in intervals which each represent £50 million. Negative amounts – losses rather than profits in a company report, for example – may be indicated by running the scale down beneath the zero line (see fig. 14.4).

(c) Decide on the order of the bars. If they show statistics over a period of time, they should be arranged in chronological order, with the earliest first. In other cases, they should be arranged in ascending or descending order of size – with either the smallest or the largest first and the others following in sequence. Bars may be arranged vertically or horizontally, although the vertical form is usually more effective.

(d) Label the bars if necessary, making sure that all writing is horizontal, so that it can be read easily.

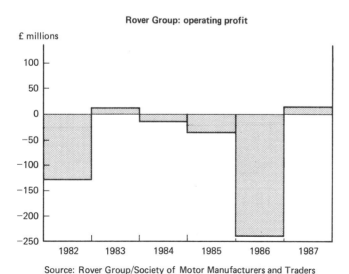

Fig. 14.4 Bar chart with positive and negative values

(e) Give the chart a clear heading, if possible at the top.
(f) Give the source of the data used, to reassure the reader that the figures are accurate.

14.3.2 Histograms

Bar charts are sometimes confused with histograms, which are more complex charts in which the frequency with which something occurs in a particular group is represented by the area of a bar of block, with other bars or blocks representing the frequency in other groups. For example, fig. 4.5 shows a histogram indicating the number of workers with wages in various ranges, not all of which are the same. Constructing such diagrams for unequal ranges will not be considered here, as it is a process usually carried out by trained statisticians or senior staff.

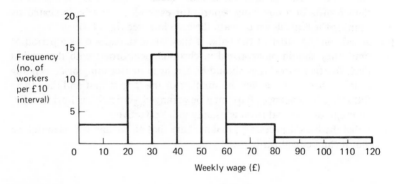

Fig. 14.5 Histogram

14.3.3 Percentage bar charts

These are like the basic bar chart, except that they consist of one bar only. The bar is divided into sections to show the portion of the whole made up by each component. Figure 14.6 gives an example of a percentage bar chart, showing how much oil is produced by each of the major companies.

To find the size of each section, read off on the vertical scale the points at which the section starts and finishes, and subtract the lower figure from the higher one. Mobil, for example, begins at 1.1 million barrels and ends at 2.4 million, giving an output of 1.3 million.

The advantage of such charts is that they give an instant impression of the relative size of each part of the whole – we can tell at a glance that Shell's share is much bigger than Chevron's. The disadvantage is that they are not easy to read in detail, depending as they do on the process of finding the 'start' and 'end' figures for each portion and subtracting one from the other. Consequently, it is a good idea to give the relevant figure and the percentage of the whole next to each section.

To construct a percentage bar chart:

(a) Assemble a table of the figures you need to display.
(b) Add all the figures to give a total.
(c) Decide on a scale. This must be such that the total will fit within the space available. Try to choose a simple scale, such as the 0.5 cm to one million barrels of oil per day in fig. 14.6.
(d) Starting with the smallest component, work out its corresponding size according to the chosen scale and mark this off in pencil on the vertical axis, starting from the base line. For example, Texaco produces 1.1 million barrels per day, so a point is marked off 0.55 cm from the base line.
(e) Work out the corresponding length of the next highest figure. Here, this is Mobil's 1.3 million barrels, which represent 0.6 cm on the vertical axis. Starting from your last pencil mark – the top of the previous component – measure off the distance of the second component.
(f) Continue with all the other figures. When you have finished, you should reach the top of the axis.
(g) Double check that you have calculated all the figures correctly to scale.
(h) Using a ruler and set square, draw in the divisions between the components.

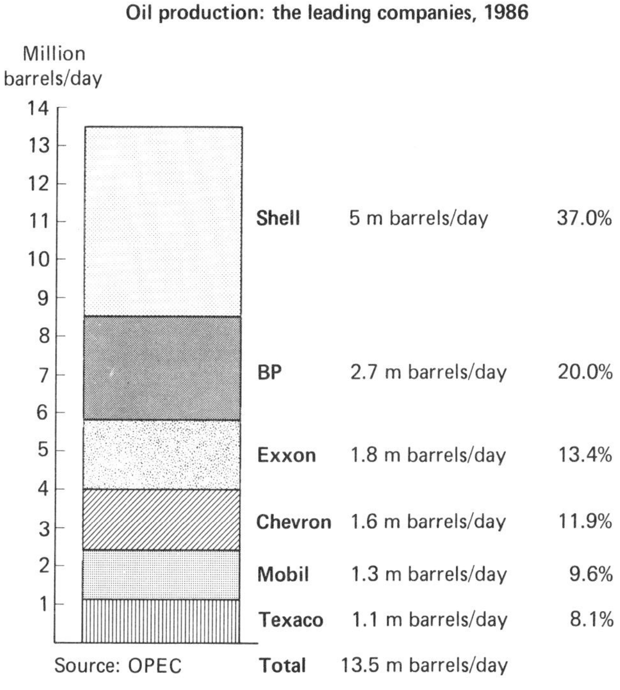

Oil production: the leading companies, 1986

Million
barrels/day

Shell	5 m barrels/day	37.0%
BP	2.7 m barrels/day	20.0%
Exxon	1.8 m barrels/day	13.4%
Chevron	1.6 m barrels/day	11.9%
Mobil	1.3 m barrels/day	9.6%
Texaco	1.1 m barrels/day	8.1%

Source: OPEC

Total 13.5 m barrels/day

Fig. 14.6 Percentage bar chart

(i)   Use different colours or shadings to distinguish the different components.
(j)   Label each component clearly, giving the name and the figure represented.
      If you wish, you can also calculate and include the percentage of the whole
      which each individual component represents.

14.4 Pie charts

Like percentage bar charts, pie charts are used to show the relative sizes of
separate components of a whole. They might be used to show how the income
of a country is spent, how a company's resources are employed, or similar
divisions of revenue or expenditure.

Constructing a pie chart is slightly more complex than constructing a percentage bar chart. Imagine that you have been handed a set of figures in the form of
a table (see fig. 14.7(a)) and asked to produce a pie chart from them. You will
need to go through the following stages.

(a)   First, you need to work out the size of each component as a percentage of
      the total. In fig. 14.7(a), for example, North America accounts for £12 993
      million out of the total exports of £79 852 million. As a percentage, this is
      16.3 per cent.
(b)   Next, you must calculate the corresponding sizes of the segments of the
      pie. In the example, North America as 16.3 per cent of the total 360° will
      take up a segment of 59°.
(c)   Using a set of compasses or a suitable template, draw a circle. Then draw a
      radius – a straight line from the centre to the edge of the circle.
(d)   With a protractor, measure off the number of degrees for one of the
      components, and draw another radius to mark off this segment.
(e)   Repeat for each of the remaining components.
(f)   When you have finished, you can make the divisions between segments
      clearer by colouring or shading each one differently.
(g)   Finally, label each segment, either by writing within it or by linking labels
      outside the circle to the appropriate segment with an arrow, as in fig.
      14.7(b). It may be helpful to your reader to include the percentages and the
      figures they represent, either within the chart or as a separate table.

Pie charts are an immediate and striking way of conveying data. Although at
first they may seem difficult to construct accurately, they become much easier
with practice. They are most appropriate where up to five or six components are
involved; if you attempt to draw in more than this number, the segments will
have to be rather thin, and the chart will be difficult both to construct and to
interpret.

14.5 Pictograms

A very simple way of showing the comparative size or quantity of an item is by
means of a pictogram. There are two main types: those using standard-size
symbols, and those with symbols of variable sizes.

United Kingdom exports: geographical distribution, 1987

	£ million
European Community	39 416
North America	12 993
Rest of world	10 053
Other Western European countries	7 621
Oil-exporting countries	5 222
Other developed countries	4 046
TOTAL	79 852

Fig. 14.7(a) Table of figures for presentation as a pie chart

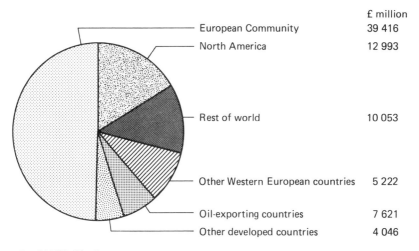

United Kingdom exports: geographical distribution, 1987

	£ million
European Community	39 416
North America	12 993
Rest of world	10 053
Other Western European countries	5 222
Oil-exporting countries	7 621
Other developed countries	4 046

Fig. 14.7(b) Pie chart

14.5.1 Pictograms with standard-size symbols
In this kind of pictogram, a symbol is designed to represent a certain number of units. A small drawing of a car, for example, might represent 50 cars produced by a factory. A chart is then constructed by using the corresponding number of these symbols for the figure quoted, as in fig. 14.8. Any numbers which constitute less than a complete symbol are shown by fractions of a symbol.

The advantage of this system is that it shows not only the size of the figure and the relative importance in comparison with other figures – in this case with other years – but it also shows instantly the nature of the item under discussion.

Henley Replicas Ltd: output of replica classic cars

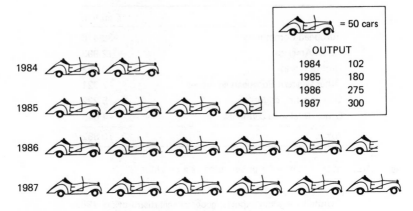

Fig. 14.8 Pictogram with standard-size symbols

The disadvantage is that such pictograms are less accurate than bar charts: whereas an accurate figure can be arrived at from the scale provided on a bar chart, parts of symbols in a pictogram give only a rough indication of size.

To construct a pictogram, first choose a symbol and experiment with drawing it clearly. It should be something simple and easily recognizable, and above all should represent the item in question – a diagrammatic man for population figures, or a loaf for output from a bakery, for instance.

Now choose a scale – 100 cars for each car symbol, or 5 tons of bread for each loaf, for example. Work out how many symbols you will need to represent the largest figure, and make sure that you can fit these into the space available. Make sure that the smallest figure can be shown graphically – if a figure requires less than a quarter of a whole symbol it will be hard for the reader to interpret it easily. Then draw the pictogram, not forgetting to add details of scale.

14.5.2 *Pictograms with variable-size symbols*

Pictograms of this kind also use symbols to represent the item under discussion. However, instead of using varying numbers of standard-size symbols to represent different figures, they simply use one symbol and vary its size. An example of this kind of pictogram is given in fig. 14.9.

In essence, such charts are really an elaborate version of bar diagrams, with the bars replaced by symbols. They have the same advantages as pictograms with standard-size symbols, in that they are immediately understandable, but they are perhaps less exact in conveying the comparative size of each component. Remember that it isn't just the length or height of the symbol which shows the statistic: it is the *area*. Most people find it much harder to judge relative areas than relative lengths, and so variable-size symbols are more difficult to construct and to interpret.

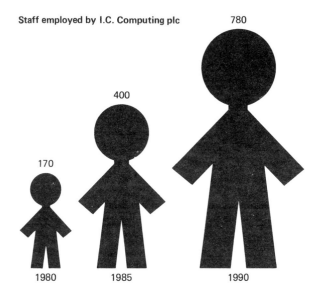

Staff employed by I.C. Computing plc

Fig. 14.9 Pictogram with variable-size symbols

Both forms of pictogram are valuable methods of conveying statistics. Simple and attractive in appearance, they overcome many of the difficulties which many people have in taking in figures. If the symbols are well designed, they may even introduce an element of humour into the presentation – which may be valuable in a long and complex report or other business document.

14.6 Graphs

Graphs are a particularly valuable form of visual communication. They are a means of presenting data on the relationship between two constantly changing elements in the form of a single line, the shape of which reveals the nature of the relationship at a glance.

Perhaps the most common form of graph is that which shows how something – a company's sales, the profit from an item of goods, or even the temperature of a patient in hospital – has changed over a period of time. Simply by glancing at the line of the graph, the onlooker can see whether the figure has risen or fallen, and to what extent.

14.6.1 Drawing a graph

Drawing a clear and accurate graph is something which takes practice. You should follow these steps, which were used to construct the graph in fig. 14.10.

(a) Use graph paper – paper with small squares printed on it – if available. This will help greatly in setting out the two scales and marking off the points which are to be joined by the line of the graph.

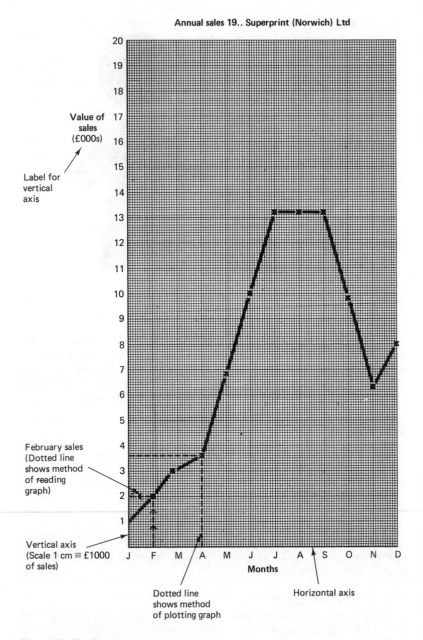

Fig. 14.10 Graph

(b) Every graph has a vertical axis and a horizontal axis – the lines on which the scales are marked. If your graph measures change over a period of time, you should always use the horizontal axis for time.

(c) Choose scales for the two axes which will fit the graph paper and which will cover the whole range of figures to be shown. Wherever possible, work in units of ten, as this will help in constructing and using the graph. Check that the highest figures to be included will fit within these scales.

(d) Mark off the axes at regular intervals. If the figures all fall within a limited range – £125 million to £150 million, for example – then the vertical axis should start at the lower of the two figures. If the figures cover a wide range, the axis should start at zero.

(e) When you have marked out the axes, you can start *plotting* the points. If sales were £2000 in February, for example, make a small cross where the vertical line upwards from 'February' meets the horizontal line across from '£2000'. Continue until you have plotted all the points.

(f) Draw the line of the graph. Whether this is done by connecting the crosses with straight lines, or by drawing a straight line or smooth curve which passes as close to as many of the plotted points as possible, will depend on the nature and purpose of the graph.

(g) Make sure that each axis is labelled to show what information it gives and the scale used.

(h) Give the graph a clear title.

14.6.2 Reading a graph

Look again at fig. 14.10. If you want to find the sales figures for April, for instance, begin by finding April on the horizontal axis. Then trace an imaginary line straight upwards until you reach the line of the graph. You can use a rule if necessary. From the point of meeting, trace another line across until you reach the vertical scale, and then read off the figure there. This gives you the sales in April: £3600. With practice, you will find that you can do this quickly and accurately without using a rule.

As well as finding individual figures, you may need to describe the general nature of the graph. To do this, you should record two aspects, the *range* of the movement and the *nature* of the movement.

The range of movement is simply the difference between the lowest and the highest figures on the vertical axis. In fig. 14.10, for example, the highest figure is £13 200 (in July and August), the lowest is £1000 (in January). This gives a range of £1000 to £13 200 in the whole period covered by the graph, or a difference of £12 200 between the highest and lowest figures.

The nature of movement Some graphs record a change that is simple and consistent. These are usually called 'straight-line' graphs, because the line moves regularly up or down in one direction. Other graphs are less simple. The line may begin by rising sharply, reach a peak at some intermediate point, fall gently for a short period, and then level out for a while before rising again gently. If you are asked to describe the nature of the change shown in a graph, you should use terms like these, quoting figures at relevant points. For example, the nature of the graph in fig. 14.10 may be described as follows:

> Income from printing at the beginning of the year was £1000. It then rose sharply, reaching a peak at £13 200 in July, and then levelled off until it fell sharply in September, reaching a low point of £6300 in November. Thereafter it recovered steadily, reaching £8000 in December.

14.7 Cartograms

A cartogram is a special kind of map used to convey information about the distribution of people, things or phenomena within a country or region. The density of population in China, the number of car owners in Britain, or the number of visits to the doctor per year in each of the London boroughs might all be depicted very clearly in a cartogram. Cartograms use variations in colour or shading to represent variations in distribution, and they have the important advantage over other forms of graphic communication that any concentration in a particular geographical area is immediately obvious. In fig. 14.11 for example, it is apparent at a glance that house prices in Great London rose far more than elsewhere in the British Isles in 1981–6.

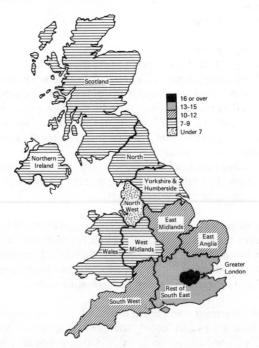

Fig. 14.11 Cartogram showing average annual percentage increase in house prices, 1981–6

Such maps are fairly straightforward to produce, providing that you have accurate data and a good map with accurate divisions of area to work from.

14.8 Falsifying statistics

Although graphics of various kinds are a means of presenting statistics attractively and clearly, they can also help to distort or falsify them. The old saying that 'there are lies, damned lies and statistics' is perhaps more true of figures presented graphically than of any others. Because it is so easy to present figures in a misleading way – both intentionally and unintentionally – it is important that you are familiar with the methods used. In this way, you will not be misled by inaccurate graphic communication, and you yourself will be less likely to mislead others.

Histograms and bar charts   These can be falsified by using a scale which is not constant – that is, by altering the points on the axis so that part of the chart is represented on a larger or smaller scale than the rest. In this way, the contrast between the length of the bars will be distorted (see fig. 14.12). You should always make sure, therefore, that the scale of a bar chart or histogram is constant throughout its length.

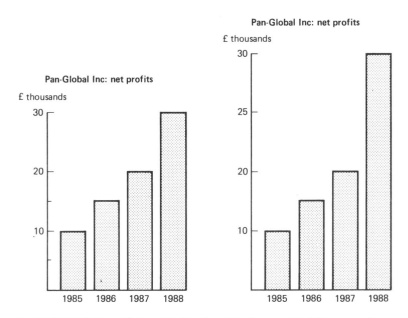

Fig. 14.12 Falsifying statistics with a bar chart. The figure on the left presents the information accurately, with the vertical scale constant. In the figure on the right, however, the vertical scale changes after £20 million so that each division is £5 million and not £10 million. This makes the net profits for 1988 seem twice as large as those for 1987, whereas in fact they are only half as much again.

Percentage bar charts   With these, the scale for one individual segment may be altered so that the segment looks larger or smaller in comparison with the other segments. Again, check the scale and make sure that it is constant.

Pie charts   Few people can judge the exact number of degrees in a particular segment of a circle without using a protractor. It is therefore easy to mislead people by adjusting the sizes of the segments. Only by careful measuring and comparison with any accompanying figures will it be possible to detect small discrepancies in representation.

Cartograms   These can easily be altered to mislead the reader by inaccurate reproduction of the boundaries between areas. In a sense, they are inherently misleading if they show a very large area. In fig. 14.11, for example, the dark shading for the South-East area suggests that house prices throughout the region rose by a similar amount. This is not so: property prices in rural areas are very unlikely to have risen at the same rate as those in developing industrial and commercial centre. Always think carefully about possible distortions of this kind rather than accepting willingly a graphic representation of data.

Graphs   Although they give a strong visual indication of the figures they represent, graphs can be manipulated in several ways. Look carefully at the three graphs in fig. 14.13. The first is a simple representation of the figures, with net profits plotted against time. It shows a clear and steady increase over the four-year period. Figure 14.13(b) shows the same graph, but on this version the vertical axis has no scale. This means that the onlooker has no idea of the range of change in the profits, or of what the company has earned in figures. The only indication is that profits have increased, apparently sharply. Notice that a slogan has been added to suggest that this increase is considerable. Without a vertical scale, however, the graph is meaningless: profits could have increased by only a few hundred pounds, for instance, if the scale were to be 1 cm = £100 rather than 1 cm = £10 000. The message is clear: never trust a graph which has no vertical scale.

A second form of distortion is shown in fig. 14.13(c). Here, the vertical scale has been 'stretched' and the horizontal one 'compressed'. This makes the line rise much more sharply, suggesting a very dramatic rise in profits, whereas a comparison with fig. 14.13(a) reveals that the rise is exactly the same. Again, the message is clear: do not be misled by the shape of a graph. Instead, verify the initial visual impression by looking at the two scales to see whether they have been deliberately set to make the change appear greater than it actually is.

When drawing a graph or any other kind of diagrammatic presentation of statistics, you should always try to avoid distortion of this kind. Labelling your axes clearly is an essential safeguard, but at the same time you should take care to calculate the scales to avoid any very steep rises – unless the range of the change is genuinely large. People often mistrust statistics: make sure that you do not justify that mistrust by presenting data in a misleading way.

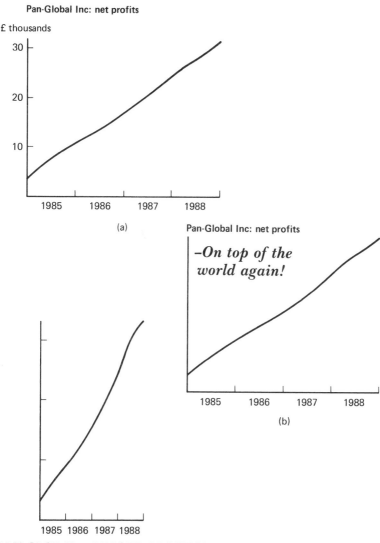

Fig. 14.13 Falsifying statistics with graphs. The first graph shows the company's net profits without distortion by using regular and clearly labelled axes. Figure 14.13(b) presents the same graph but, because the vertical axis is not labelled, the reader has only the vague idea that profits have increased. Figure 14.13(c) makes the profits seem even greater by compressing the horizontal axis and stretching the vertical. This suggests that profits have rocketed – an impression heightened by the slogan added to the graph.

14.9 Charts

14.9.1 Organization charts

As we discussed in Unit 3, every company or organization should have a clear pattern of organization. Similarly, every company should be able to produce a chart of this system, which shows the lines of authority and the chain of command it uses. The organization chart will make clear who is in charge of each department or section, and show the person to whom each worker is responsible. Organization charts are discussed in detail in Unit 3 in terms of how they affect communication: here, we are concerned solely with their construction and interpretation.

First, try to talk to someone who is involved in planning the company's structure – a personnel officer, perhaps, or a director or manager responsible for recruitment. Ask him or her for details of each separate grade of employment within the company – workers, supervisors, line managers, department managers, directors, and so on. Note down each category carefully.

Next, seek out individuals from each of these levels of the organization. For each one, get details of his or her job title, the person to whom he or she is responsible, and the people who are responsible to him or her.

Your research will be much easier if you record the data like this:

Job title	*Senior to*	*Responsible to*
Line Manager	Supervisors	Works Manager
Personnel Director	Personnel Managers	Managing Director

Once you have collected information on workers at every level of the organization, you can construct your first draft chart. Use plenty of space, and experiment with different layouts until you find the clearest. Make sure that every department is presented separately, and that lines of responsibility are clearly shown. Then prepare your finished version, which will be something like the one shown in fig. 14.14.

14.9.2 Flowcharts

A flowchart is a diagram of a sequence of decisions or instructions involved in a process. Flowcharts are used widely in business to work out the stages of writing a computer program, but they can also be valuable in highlighting the separate stages in a sequence of events. Figure 14.15 shows a simple flowchart, which uses the following international symbols:

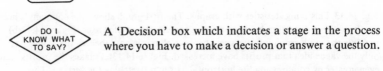

A box which means 'Start' or 'End'.

A 'Decision' box which indicates a stage in the process where you have to make a decision or answer a question.

A 'Process' box which indicates a stage where something is done, often as a result of a decision.

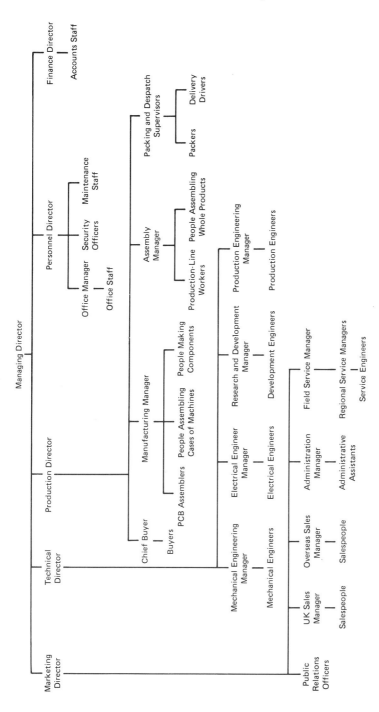

Fig. 14.14 Organization chart

Writing a memo

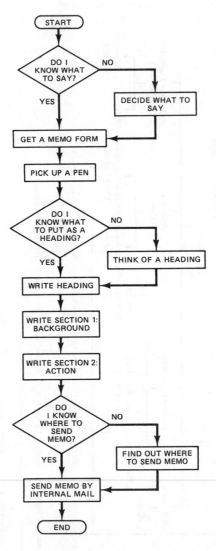

Fig. 14.15 Flowchart

To produce a flowchart, you must first separate the process concerned into separate stages. Next to each stage, note down which of the three categories above it falls into: start/finish, decision, or process. In a third column, write a brief but clear statement, question or instruction to be included inside the box. If there are alternative paths which might be followed, write them in, stage by stage, between the relevant process boxes. Now check your draft to make sure that it includes every stage of the process. Finally, draw your flowchart, making sure that you use the right shape of box at each stage.

Flowcharts can often help you to solve problems, since they force you to break a process down into stages and think carefully about what is involved at each stage. For this reason, it is often useful to construct a flowchart when you are faced with the task of simplifying an office procedure or achieving a new objective. Not only will it help you to see what is going on, but the process of constructing the chart itself also encourages logical thought.

14.9.3 Planning charts
Many business organizations use planning charts to show how different projects are progressing. Planning charts are similar to graphs in that they have a vertical and an horizontal axis, and like some bar charts they use horizontal bars. The vertical axis lists the separate stages in a process, while the horizontal one is usually a time axis. The example in fig. 14.16 shows the programme for the development of a new product. Each stage is allocated a period of weeks or months, and only those stages which can take place at the same time are allowed to overlap.

Information of this kind is too complex to commit to memory, and too unwieldy to write about. A planning chart presents all the necessary information clearly and succinctly. When reproduced in a large format and placed on a wall, it also acts as a production schedule and a spur to productivity.

Another way of recording the progress of a project is shown in fig. 14.17. This kind of progress chart is useful when a project has to go through several clear stages, each of which must be completed before the next can be started. This kind of planning chart can be used to record the progress of several projects at once and, like the chart above, can be used to encourage productivity.

14.10 Using graphics

How do you decide which kind of graphic presentation to use? The decision will depend on several factors, the most important of which are outlined below.

Purpose If you wish to present a series of figures which relate to the same topic – a company's output over several months, say, or the change in average earnings over a period of years – a histogram or bar chart will be the most appropriate method. Both of these present figures accurately and at the same time enable the reader to gain a good idea of the relationship between the different columns.

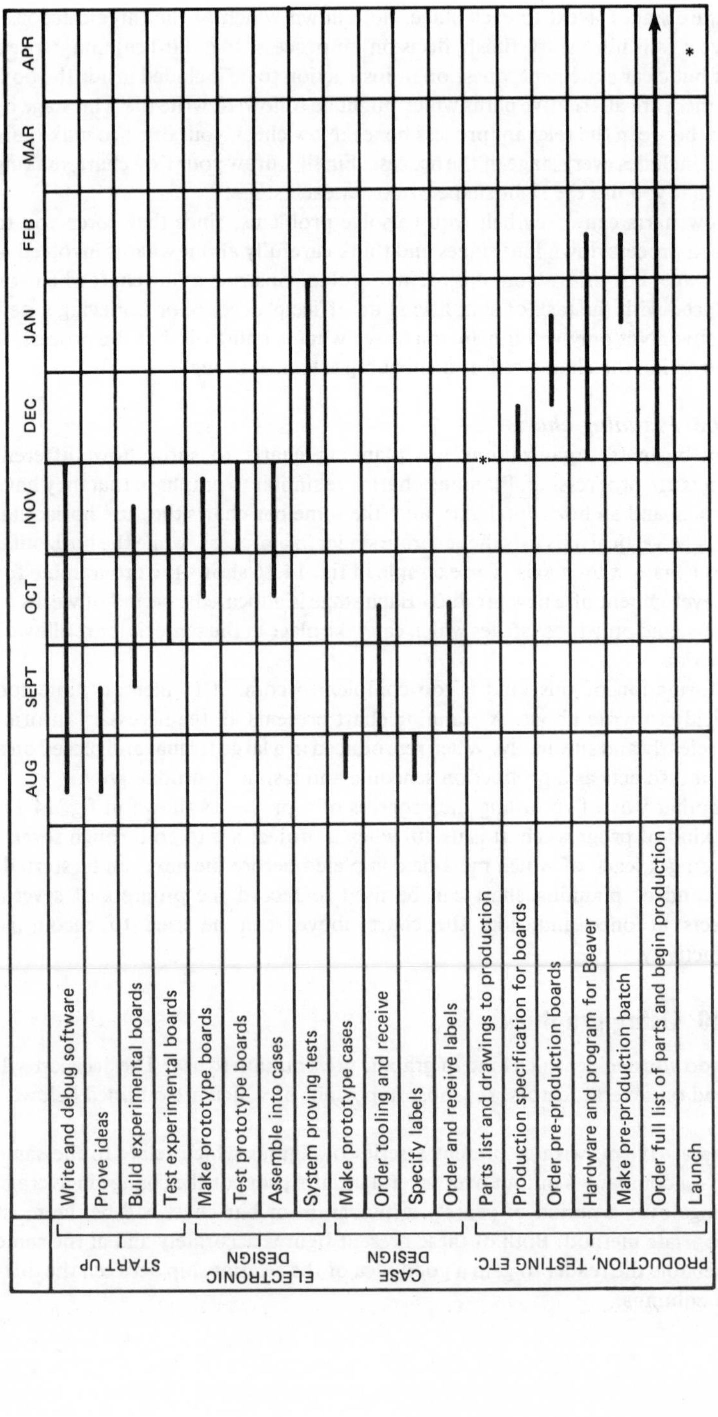

Fig. 14.16 Planning chart

Publications progress chart

	Office practice	Law	Elements of banking	British history	Information processing	World affairs	Statistics	Economics
Manuscript received	✓	✓	✓	✓	✓	✓	✓	✓
Manuscript copyedited	✓	✓		✓	✓	✓	✓	✓
Manuscript to designer	✓	✓		✓	✓	✓	✓	✓
Illustrations received	✓			✓	✓	✓	✓	✓
Copyright clearances	✓			✓	✓		✓	✓
Copy to typesetter	✓			✓	✓		✓	✓
Publicity begun	✓			✓	✓			✓
Galleys received				✓	✓			✓
Galleys checked				✓	✓			
Index copy				✓	✓			
Index to typesetter				✓	✓			
Paste-up to typesetter				✓	✓			
Pages received				✓	✓			
Pages checked				✓	✓			
Revises to typesetter					✓			
Printing					✓			
Publication date					✓			

Fig. 14.17 Progress chart

If you want to show how a large figure is divided – the expenditure of a local council on various items, for example – then a pie chart will be most suitable, as it will give a very simple visual statement of the 'slice' received by each kind of spending. Multiple-symbol pictograms give a clear visual impression too, but only in very general terms, since it is hard to calculate the exact significance of parts of a symbol. Pictograms which use single symbols are also unreliable for anything more than a general visual impression, as they too are hard to translate into accurate figures. Both forms of pictogram can be very striking, however, if used correctly.

Cartograms provide a general idea of the distribution of a particular feature over a geographical area, and in this way are very useful. But remember that there may be quite a large variation within each shaded area, and so they must not be taken as an absolute record – rather as a series of averages.

Graphs are ideal when you are dealing with two variables – two sets of figures which change constantly. They are, for example, very suitable for showing how figures of all kinds change over a period of time. But, like all forms of graphic communication, they can also be used to falsify the data they present (see section 14.8).

A different function is performed by planning charts and organization charts. They present not figures but relationships between a series of tasks to be performed in a set period, and relationships between people working in a company.

Readership   Remember that specialists will be able to understand complex graphs, tables and other diagrams much more readily than the general public. As a general rule, the greater the number of people who will read the communication, the simpler it should be, and this is particularly true of graphic communication.

Facilities   Some graphic presentations are far easier to produce than others. A table, for example, can be produced neatly and legibly with the minimum of equipment. A good graph, on the other hand, will need graph paper and a rule; a pie chart will require a pair of compasses and a protractor. Cartograms demand very precise outline maps, with divisions between different areas marked exactly – something which is not easy without specialist help.

14.11 Conclusion

All of the kinds of graphic communication mentioned in this unit have their strengths and weaknesses. Knowing which kind of presentation to use in any situation is an important skill, but not one which can be acquired overnight. This field is now becoming so specialized that many large companies employ graphic artists to select and design the presentation of their statistics in company reports and other documents. With patience and common sense, however, you will be able to produce graphics which are simple, straightforward and above all do not distort the statistical information which they convey.

14.12 Quick questions

1   (a)   What is graphic communication?
    (b)   What are its advantages?
    (c)   Give three kinds of situation in which graphic communication might be used.

2   What two aspects of a graph do you need to consider when writing a formal interpretation of its meaning?

3   Draw the right flowchart boxes for:
    (a)   decisions;
    (b)   processes;
    (c)   start and end.

14.13 Longer exercises

1 Discuss the advantages and disadvantages of three methods of visual communication.

(IPS, First certificate.)

2 Think about how you would interpret a graph. Now draw a flowchart to illustrate the process, using the correct boxes at each stage.

3 The table below shows the cost of making certain types of television programme. It also shows the number of hours that each amount of money pays for and the average cost per hour. These costs are typical for a major TV contractor such as Central Television.

(a) Present the information in diagrammatic/graphic form.
(b) Compare and contrast the effectiveness of your presentation with the way the material is presented below.

	Direct costs per year (£ thousands)	Hours paid for	Cost per hour (£)
Children's	900	120	7 500.00
Current affairs and documentary	600	280	2 142.86
Drama	220	80	27 500.00
Features	250	100	2 500.00
Light entertainment	240	125	19 200.00
Outside broadcasts	500	100	5 000.00
Religious	80	15	5 333.33
Schools	280	110	2 545.45

(Southern Examining Board, GCSE specimen question)

4 The chairman of your company has asked you to produce some informative diagrams for inclusion in a report which he is compiling.

(a) Draw pie charts to illustrate the following data.

Application of sales revenue

	Previous Year (£000s)	Last Year (£000s)
Salaries	10 650	13 278
Expenses	10 971	10 309
Profit	1 412	1 189
Materials	47 767	50 824

(b) What other methods of graphical illustration would have been appropriate?
(c) What are the advantages of using diagrams to illustrate data?

(IDPM, People, communication and information in organisations)

5   Study the figures for local authority spending in the table below. Then prepare:

(a) a graphic presentation of the spending in 1986–7;
(b) a graphic presentation of the income in 1987–8.

1986–7				1987–8		
Spending (£ million)	Income (£ million)	Net cost (£ million)		Net cost (£ million)	Income (£ million)	Spending (£ million)
182.6	32.4	150.2	Education	169.0	34.2	203.2
32.6	6.6	26.0	Social services	28.6	6.8	35.4
30.4	7.1	23.3	Transportation	22.7	7.3	30.0
30.4	16.3	14.1	Police	15.6	17.9	33.5
8.6	0.8	7.8	Public protection	8.4	0.8	9.2
5.1	0.8	4.3	Libraries and museums	4.5	0.9	5.4
1.8	1.4	0.4	Magistrates' courts	0.4	1.4	1.8
1.7	1.4	0.3	Probation	0.4	1.5	1.9
3.2	4.7	–1.5	Other services	—	3.3	3.3
296.4	71.5	224.9	Total	249.6	74.1	323.7

6   Ayco, Beeco and Ceeco are engaged in similar business. The percentage increase in their earnings per share has fluctuated as follows:

	1979	1980	1981	1982	1983	1984	1985	1986
Ayco	8	8	7	5	9	9	11	6
Beeco	10	11	10	12	14	17	20	22
Ceeco	5	5	8	12	17	17	21	23

(a) Illustrate these by means of a compound graph.
(b) Draw a bar chart to show the year by year changes in the case of Ceeco.

Ceeco is active in most branches of engineering. In 1985 it increased its range by buying up an electronics manufacturer. By 1986 the contributions to Ceeco's turnover were as follows:

Civil engineering	18%
Machine tool manufacture	27%
Electrical engineering	24%
Aeronautical engineering	9%
Electronics manufacture	22%

Illustrate these proportions by means of a pie chart. Freehand drawing is acceptable if clear.

(ABE, Business communications)

UNIT 15

Reports

15.1 Introduction

A business report is a document which investigates a specific subject according to a prescribed format and for a clearly defined readership – generally those in superior positions within a company or organization. A report may be presented on a pre-printed, single-page form or in a bound volume of several hundred pages, or anything in between.

Simple reports consist of no more than a straightforward statement recording an event, or a series of events or circumstances, with some indication of the action taken in response. Others include an explanation of the causes of such circumstances if known, or suggestions of possible causes, and recommendations for future action. More substantial reports demand personal research by the writer, involving interviews and visits to factory sites or other relevant places, and perhaps some academic research in libraries. The information obtained will often need to be presented in tabular or graphic form, and the writer should be prepared to interpret the facts to produce a clear but comprehensive set of conclusions and recommendations.

Whatever their length and purpose, reports demand certain skills of the writer, all of which are of fundamental importance to many other forms of communication. They may be summarized as follows:

(a) the ability to record facts clearly and objectively;
(b) the ability to interpret facts and attribute them to causes;
(c) the ability to formulate and present opinions – based on the facts but clearly separated from them – as to ways in which a situation may be improved or remedied.

Some organizations specify the layout to be used when writing a report, whereas others accept any layout which is clearly presented and logically structured, and allows the writer scope to demonstrate the key skills of report-writing mentioned above. Whatever form you are following, it is important to remember the purpose of a report: to give a clear statement of the facts, followed by an interpretation of possible or actual causes, in a logical and precise manner.

15.2 Report forms

The simplest kind of reports are those which are completed on pre-printed forms. They are generally used to record events of a routine nature – ones which occur so often that the organization involved has provided special forms to simplify the reporting process and to make sure that all the necessary information is included.

Report forms are completed in the same way as any other form, following the principles laid down in Unit 13. They should be designed to be as precise and attractive as possible, to encourage those who have to complete them, and to safeguard against the risk of misunderstanding.

Forms of this kind may be used to communicate upwards within an organization – to record the monthly output of a department, for instance, or the progress of a particular project, or the results of an appraisal interview. They may also communicate downwards or horizontally – for example, a manager may complete a form to let his or her workers know the required output figures for a given period, or a head of department may pass a form on training or sales activities to the head of the relevant section.

Despite their simple appearance, reports of this kind convey essential data within an organization and this should be borne in mind when designing them. If clearly designed and completed, report forms allow progress to be monitored at regular intervals, and any irregularities can then be identified and faults remedied before they become too serious. Poorly designed forms will be completed neither fully nor accurately, and irregularities may go unchecked.

Look at fig. 15.1, which shows a form of this kind. The simplicity and directness of the questions, the provision of alternative answers, and the generally attractive layout encourage the reader to respond.

15.2.1 Accident report forms

Under the Health and Safety at Work Act, all employers in the United Kingdom are required to keep records of industrial accidents which occur on their premises. The immediate record is usually made on an accident report form (see fig. 15.2). Since this needs to be completed as soon as possible after the accident, so that any necessary action can be taken, the form needs to be very straightforward – the reader may be distressed by the accident, and misunderstandings may arise unless the form is easy to follow and written in very simple language. Alternative answers should be given wherever possible to ease the task of the person completing the form.

15.3 Writing a report

Before you begin to write a report, it is essential to know why you are writing it and exactly what you are writing about. With a report form these questions will

```
HRG MOTOR COMPANY

Weekly production report for week ending Friday _____ 19__


  Department    Sheet metal          ┌───┐
                Body carpentry        │   │
                Machine shop          │   │
                Trim                  │   │
                Finishing/testing     │   │
                Paint                 │   │
                Chassis building      └───┘


  How many vehicles have been processed this week?    ____
  How many were processed last week?                  ____
  What number was fixed as the target for this week?  ____


  Why were more/less than the target number processed?
                      Staff shortages                      ┌───┐
                      Design changes                        │   │
                      Parts shortages                       │   │
                      Bank/other holidays                   │   │
                      Other reason  (please explain below)  └───┘


  What can we do to increase output? Write any ideas or suggestions in
  the space below.




  Signature _____    Date _____
  Name      _____    Position _____
```

Fig. 15.1 Production report form

be answered for you by the nature of the form itself, but in a written report you will have to define the purpose and subject for yourself.

Examine the origin and composition of the report in fig. 15.3. The situation inspiring the report is typical of the kind which might arise in a business organization: one day the office is almost empty; personal callers have to wait; the telephone goes unanswered; and routine correspondence and other business are not dealt with. The office manager wants to know why this has happened so that she can make sure that the situation will not be repeated.

Once you have established the subject and the reason in this way, you need to collect and assess the data which you may wish to include. In this case, for example, you may know that Mrs Jenkins had a day off for Christmas shopping, because she had told you where she was going and what she wanted to buy over lunch a couple of days before. You also know that Ms Walker was away ill, although you suspect that it was not flu that she was suffering from but the after-effects of a party which she had attended the night before. To this information you add the fact that Mr Fielding and Mr Walton were at a training course, which you discover while investigating the circumstances for your report.

All this information must be treated properly if it is to be of value in the report. It must be considered carefully, the facts separated from matters of opinion, and any irrelevant material rejected from the final report. Here, the details of where Mrs Jenkins was doing her shopping and what she bought can be left out as irrelevant, and your suspicions about Ms Walker's 'flu' can be dismissed as opinion and not fact. This will leave you with three pieces of factual data: that Mrs Jenkins was doing her Christmas shopping; that Ms Walker had flu; and that the two men were on a training course. From this, you will have be able to write the central section of the report.

You might be asked to take action or suggest what you think should be done if similar circumstances arise in the future. Your answer will depend on the nature of the report and of the organization for which you are writing, but you will need to use your judgment and experience to make sure that any comments are valid and appropriate to the given situation.

In this way, the complete report is built up as shown in fig. 15.3, so that it is clear, factual and easily understood. Bear in mind who is going to read the report and choose your expression accordingly along the lines set out in Unit 4. You should also use a layout which is clear and attractive, with headings to establish the main purpose and content of each section of the report.

Although we have concentrated on one specific report, the principles discussed apply equally to reports of all kinds. These principles may be summarized as follows:

(a) Know *why* you are writing the report.
(b) Know *what* you are writing about.
(c) Keep reports accurate, relevant and concise.
(d) Omit opinions from sections concerned with fact.
(e) Organize your points in a logical order.

Health and Safety Executive
Health and Safety at Work etc Act 1974
Reporting of Injuries,Diseases and Dangerous Occurrences Regulations 1985

Spaces below
are for office
use only

Report of an injury or dangerous occurrence

- Full notes to help you complete this form are attached.
- This form is to be used to make a report to the enforcing authority under the requirements of Regulations 3 or 6.
- Completing and signing this form does not constitute an admission of liability of any kind, either by the person making the report or any other person.
- If more than one person was injured as a result of an accident, please complete a separate form for each person.

A   Subject of report *(tick appropriate box or boxes) – see note 2*

Fatality ☐   Specified major injury or condition ☐ 1   "Over three day" injury ☐ 2   Dangerous occurrence ☐ 3   Flammable gas incident (fatality or major injury or condition) ☐ 5   Dangerous gas fitting ☐ 6

Box 4 appears between Dangerous occurrence and Flammable gas.

B   Person or organisation making report (ie person obliged to report under the Regulations) – *see note 3*

Name and address –

Nature of trade, business or undertaking –

If in construction industry, state the total number of your employees –

and indicate the role of your company on site *(tick box)* –

Post code –

Main site contractor ☐ 7   Sub contractor ☐ 8   Other ☐ 9

Name and telephone no. of person to contact –

If in farming, are you reporting an injury to a member of your family? *(tick box)*   Yes ☐   No ☐

C   Date, time and place of accident, dangerous occurrence or flammable gas incident – *see note 4*

Date [ ] [ ] 19 [ ]   *day   month   year*   Time –

Give the name and address if different from above –

ENV

Where on the premises or site –
and
Normal activity carried on there

Complete the following sections D, E, F & H if you have ticked boxes, 1, 2, 3 or 5 in Section A. Otherwise go straight to Sections G and H.

D   The injured person – *see note 5*

Full name and address –

Age [ ]   Sex [ ] (M or F)   Status *(tick box)* –   Employee ☐ 10   Self employed ☐ 11   Trainee (YTS) ☐ 12

Trainee (other) ☐ 13   Any other person ☐ 14

Trade, occupation or job title –

Nature of injury or condition and the part of the body affected –

F2508 (rev 1/86)   *continued overleaf*

Fig. 15.2 Accident report form (*continued opposite*)

E Kind of accident - *see note 6*

Indicate what kind of accident led to the injury or condition (*tick one box*) —

Contact with moving machinery or material being machined ☐ 1	Injured whilst handling lifting or carrying ☐ 5	Trapped by something collapsing or overturning ☐ 8	Exposure to an explosion ☐ 12
Struck by moving, including flying or falling, object. ☐ 2	Slip, trip or fall on same level ☐ 6	Drowning or asphyxiation ☐ 9	Contact with electricity or an electrical discharge ☐ 13
Struck by moving vehicle ☐ 3	Fall from a height* ☐ 7	Exposure to or contact with a harmful substance ☐ 10	Injured by an animal ☐ 14
Struck against something fixed or stationary ☐ 4	*Distance through which person fell [_____] (metres)	Exposure to fire ☐ 11	Other kind of accident (give details in Section H) ☐ 15

Spaces below are for office use only.

F Agent(s) involved — *see note 7*

Indicate which, if any, of the categories of agent or factor below were involved (*tick one or more of the boxes*) —

Machinery/equipment for lifting and conveying ☐ 1	Process plant, pipework or bulk storage ☐ 5	Live animal ☐ 9	Ladder or scaffolding ☐ 13
Portable power or hand tools ☐ 2	Any material, substance or product being handled, used or stored. ☐ 6	Moveable container or package of any kind ☐ 10	Construction formwork, shuttering and falsework ☐ 14
Any vehicle or associated equipment/ machinery ☐ 3	Gas, vapour, dust, fume or oxygen deficient atmosphere ☐ 7	Floor, ground, stairs or any working surface ☐ 11	Electricity supply cable, wiring, apparatus or equipment ☐ 15
Other machinery ☐ 4	Pathogen or infected material ☐ 8	Building, engineering structure or excavation/underground working ☐ 12	Entertainment or sporting facilities or equipment ☐ 16
			Any other agent ☐ 17

Describe briefly the agents or factors you have indicated —

[_____]

G Dangerous occurrence or dangerous gas fitting — *see notes 8 and 9*

Reference number of dangerous occurrence [_____] Reference number of dangerous gas fitting [_____]

H Account of accident, dangerous occurrence or flammable gas incident - *see note 10*

Describe what happened and how. In the case of an accident state what the injured person was doing at the time —

[_____]

Signature of person making report [_____] Date [_____]

REPORT ON STAFFING LEVELS IN THE GENERAL OFFICE, WILLIAMS ENGINEERING,
ON FRIDAY 15 DECEMBER 19--

BACKGROUND

On Friday 15 December the general office was staffed only by Ms Jones,
the other four members of staff being absent. As a result, the services
available were severely limited. I have discussed the matter in
confidence with each member of staff involved, and also with other
departments which were concerned.

FINDINGS

On the day in question, Mr Fielding, Mrs Jenkins, Ms Walker and Mr
Walton were all away from the office. This meant that Ms Jones had to
deal with all the matters usually shared between the five staff,
including reprography, typing of letters and invoices, outgoing mail,
answering the telephone, and dealing with enquiries from personal
callers. In consequence, much routine correspondence was delayed,
and for a time the telephone answering machine was used to deal with
incoming calls, while Ms Jones dealt with urgent matters including
enquiries from visiting clients.

After discussion, I have discovered that Mr Fielding and Mr Walton were
away at a staff training weekend run by the Company Training Officer.
Mrs Jenkins had a day's Christmas shopping leave, authorized by the
Personnel Officer two weeks ago in accordance with company practice; and
Ms Walker was absent with 'flu. The combination of all these
circumstances meant that only Ms Jones was present.

ACTION

I have contacted the Training Officer and suggested that, in future,
only one member of a department should be seconded to a training weekend,
and that the details of such secondments should be sent to the Personnel
Officer so that he or she may avoid arranging for staff to have time off
on the day or days concerned. This should ensure that only one person
will be away from the general office for training or other reasons at
any time. Even allowing for unexpected circumstances such as illness,
this should make it impossible for staffing levels to fall to such a low
extreme in the future.

F K Unwin
General Trainee
19 December 19--

Fig. 15.3 Short or routine report

(f) Use your judgment and experience when suggesting action or making recommendations.

(g) Use language suitable to the reader.

(h) Use clear headings for each section.

15.4 Short or routine reports

Reports of this kind cover matters which are fairly straightforward yet do not occur often enough to merit a specially printed form. They are usually no longer than a single side of A4 paper – roughly 200–250 words – and are written at the request of an immediate superior. In subject, they usually refer to a single event or set of circumstances about which there is some doubt or about which some action must be taken.

There are no absolute rules for organizing and presenting short reports as there are for, say, memos. Any structure which presents the facts directly and logically will usually be acceptable, although you should check to see whether your employer prefers a particular format.

The presentation used in the report in fig. 15.3 is acceptable for most professional uses, as it is logical and direct in the way that it puts forward information. It begins by stating the circumstances, moves to an interpretation of them and concludes with an account of action taken. This simple progression is complemented by the use of direct, everyday vocabulary.

The report is clearly divided into various sections, which may be described as follows.

Title   The title should be concise yet comprehensive. The situation is stated briefly, together with the name of the company and the date of the event. It is important that all this information is included: it establishes the subject quickly and precisely and, should other reports be read or filed at the same time, the possibility of confusing them is minimized.

Background   This section contains information of two kinds: a brief description of the circumstances under discussion and an outline of the procedure or method of enquiry used by the writer. A brief indication should be given of visits made, people interviewed, or reference works consulted.

It is usually possible to state this information in two or three sentences, especially if the title has already conveyed the essential points. In short, this section aims to establish the circumstances under enquiry as concisely as possible, to enable the reader to pass on to the next section with a sound understanding of the context of the report.

Findings   The heart of the report, this section generally contains two parts:

(a) a simple, factual account of the events and circumstances. This will amplify the information given in the background section, and should be expressed in a clear, factual style.

(b) a passage which offers an interpretation of the facts or circumstances. This usually suggests a cause for them, or makes clear why the events occurred in the way they did. It is important that this interpretation rests solely on the information given earlier in the report, otherwise the logical progression that is so important in a report will be broken and the reader will have the impression that something has been concealed.

In practice, this division is often indicated by the use of two distinct paragraphs, as in the example in fig. 15.3.

Action   In most situations where a short report is requested, you will be asked to include details of the action you have taken in response to the events under investigation. Read the details in the report carefully, think hard about exactly what you did, and be brief but thorough in your explanation.

You may be asked to add recommendations to your report, in which case you should include these in the final section. However, if you are asked to write a report with recommendations, it is likely to be a much longer report, which will contain more detail about the circumstances under investigation and the methods of enquiry used.

15.5 Longer or special reports

Longer reports are needed in an organization on occasions when a complex matter requires investigation. Comments will be required on its possible causes, along with recommendations as to how the situation might be remedied or improved and similar occurrences avoided in the future. The basic pattern and structure of a long report is similar to that of a short one, but the longer report approaches its subject in much greater depth and detail (see fig. 15.4).

Reports of this kind follow a more clearly defined structure than routine reports: they are broken into a number of sections, each of which performs a specific function. The same structure is used for full-length reports by government departments or commissions of enquiry. It is not simple, but it does provide a framework around which to organize and express complex ideas in logical progression. Once mastered, it will prove an invaluable tool.

A full-length report consists of the following sections:

(a) title;
(b) circulation list;   } only in the longest and most
(c) list of committee members;   } complex reports
(d) summary;
(e) terms of reference;
(f) procedure;
(g) findings;
(h) conclusions;
(i) recommendations;
(j) appendices;
(k) signature, position and date.

Long reports often form the basis of important decisions and actions at a high level within an organization. As a result, it is even more essential to plan them logically and express yourself precisely than when composing shorter reports.

The separate points of a report should be clearly numbered, particularly the three sections which lie at the heart of the report – findings, conclusions and recommendations. Points should be covered in the same order in all sections, and should have the same number in each so that the reader may follow the progress of one particular topic from one section to another. A common form of numbering is the alternate use of letters and numbers:

1   *Causes of road accidents*
    (a) Accidents caused by motor vehicles
       (i) Accidents between motor vehicles
      (ii) Accidents involving motor vehicles and pedestrians
    (b) Accidents caused by pedestrians

Alternatively, a purely numerical system may be used.

1   *Causes of road accidents*
  1.1 Accidents caused by motor vehicles
    1.1.1   Accidents between motor vehicles
    1.1.2   Accidents involving motor vehicles and pedestrians
  1.2 Accidents caused by pedestrians

In many ways the first system is simpler, but practice will vary according to the individual organization and its house style.

15.5.1 Title

This should be as detailed as possible, self-explanatory, and above all unambiguous. It may well extend over two or three lines and – like the title of a short report – should include dates, names of departments and any other relevant information which will convey the subject of the report accurately and concisely.

15.5.2 Circulation list

Longer reports may well be confidential. They may, for example, discuss ways in which a company is planning to change or develop, or they may record the progress of new products – information which should be kept secret from competitors. Should such reports fall into the wrong hands they might give rise to alarming rumours in the first instance and unauthorized copying of ideas in the second.

To avoid this, many longer reports have a restricted readership which is indicated by a circulation list. This is simply a list of people who are entitled to read the report. It may be headed like this:

This report is to be read only by the following people:

The list should be displayed prominently at the beginning of the report where it

---

REPORT ON THE ORGANIZATION OF THE LIBRARY, NEWTOWN COLLEGE OF FURTHER EDUCATION, WINTER 19--

TERMS OF REFERENCE
As academic representative of the Students' Union, I was asked by the President to prepare a report on the general organization and running of the college library and to make recommendations as necessary.

I was specifically asked not to cover questions of professional competence of individual members of the library staff.

PROCEDURE
I visited the library on four occasions during the week ending 14 March 19--, making notes on the layout, stock and borrowing arrangements. I also interviewed the librarian, Mrs PJ Neale, and her two assistants, Ms G Openshaw and Mr Olurenfemi. In addition, I compiled a questionnaire about library facilities and their use and circulated this among a random selection of students who use the library. A copy of the questionnaire is attached to this report as Appendix A.

The information collected from the visits and interviews was then collated and used as the basis of this report, and the responses to the questionnaire were tabulated. They are presented graphically as Appendix B.

FINDINGS

A   LAYOUT OF THE LIBRARY
The general layout of the library is shown in the plan given as Appendix C. From this it will be clear that the library is divided into three areas:
1   the enquiry and issue desk area, situated at the further end of the library, away from the entrance door;
2   the main shelving area, with the library stock housed on wooden shelves and tables for the use of those making reference to books;
3   a 'browsing area' containing works of fiction and current numbers of magazines.

Of the 25 people who returned the questionnaire:
*   11 felt that the enquiry and issue desk was well-sited;
*   22 felt the shelving area was satisfactory;
*   17 found the 'browsing area' well-sited and easy to use.

B   LIBRARY STOCK
The library has a stock of some 35 000 volumes, of which 30 000 are non-fiction - mainly related to academic courses studied at the college. The remainder are fiction, mainly in the form of paperback novels. In addition, 23 magazines are taken regularly, of which the great majority (18) are related to academic courses.

At present there are no cassette, record or video-cassette holdings.

C   BORROWING ARRANGEMENTS
Each student may borrow up to six books. Loans last for a period of four weeks. There is no system of fines for overdue books, nor is there a system for reserving books currently on loan to other borrowers. Of the 25 students who completed the questionnaire, 20 felt that this did not encourage borrowers to return books on time.

Fig. 15.4 Longer or special report (*continued opposite*)

CONCLUSIONS

A LAYOUT OF THE LIBRARY
1 The siting of the enquiry desk at the far end of the library makes it difficult for people to ask the librarians for help, and makes it difficult for librarians to check on the unauthorized removal of books.
2 The browsing area is sited so as to make the library's fiction and magazine stock easily and attractively available to readers.
3 The main shelving area has been carefully designed to help those using books for reference purposes, with reading tables close to the shelves to facilitate study.

B LIBRARY STOCK
The stock has been built up to provide a reference collection of books for the use of students. Consequently, the fiction stock has been kept low.

This proportion is also reflected in the magazine holdings. Overall, it is clear that the library stock has been developed primarily to provide a source of reference for students.

C BORROWING ARRANGEMENTS
These appear to have been organized to provide the maximum freedom for students who wish to use the library. In terms of the numbers of books which may be borrowed, the duration of loan, and the absence of fines, all arrangements are generous in comparison with local county libraries.

From the responses to the questionnaire, it is clear that many feel that the arrangements are too generous and do not allow all who wish to use the library to do so.

RECOMMENDATIONS

A LAYOUT OF LIBRARY
1 The enquiry desk and issue area should be moved to just inside the entrance, so that those seeking assistance from the library staff can do so more easily.
2 The 'browsing area' should be remain in its present form.
3 The main shelving area should also remain as it is.

B LIBRARY STOCK
The present bias towards academic works should continue, since this is clearly the main purpose of the library. Magazines of general interest should not be provided, since they are easily available in local county libraries.

An experiment should be made, however, in the form of a small collection of cassettes and video-cassettes of an educational nature, to reflect the clear demand for these revealed by the questionnaire.

C BORROWING ARRANGEMENTS
To reflect the general feeling that these are too generous, the loan period should be reduced to three weeks, with a system for readers to request books being used by other readers.

If this does not improve the use of the library, an experiment should be made with the introduction of fines. This should, however, be viewed with caution, since it might well deter readers from borrowing books.

If these measures were introduced, I feel sure that the already excellent service provided by the library would be developed and continued.

D S Thomas
Academic Representative, Students' Union   26 March 19--

cannot fail to be noticed by a would-be reader. It may not, however, be enough to prevent unauthorized people from reading the report. A 'Private and confidential' heading may help, but the best approach is to make sure that the report is only made available to those authorized to read it.

Although there are sometimes genuine grounds for a report to be confidential, it is nonetheless bad practice to produce documents of this sort as a matter of course. Employees may develop the impression that the company depends on tight security and mistrusts its members, and this might well encourage the circulation of damaging rumours. If a report is genuinely confidential, it should be treated accordingly, but in general longer reports should be made available to everyone whom they are likely to affect.

15.5.3 List of committee members

Many reports – especially those of government and royal commissions – are the work of several people acting as a committee. Such reports are generally prefaced by a list of committee members.

Usually, such committees produce a single report of their findings, but it is not unknown for disagreement to arise and for two or even more reports to be produced. In this case, there will often be a *majority* and a *minority* report.

Majority report   This is the report giving the findings, conclusions and recommendations of the majority of the committee. It will usually represent the official view of the matter under investigation.

Minority report   This is produced by a small number of committee members who interpret the information obtained in a manner different from that of their colleagues. It will be produced separately, and will only list the names of those members who share its views.

It is unlikely that you will be involved in the production of majority and minority reports, but you should be aware of the meaning of the terms and the reasons why such differences might arise.

15.5.4 Summary

A long report, which may run to several hundred pages, will sometimes include a short summary at the start to give readers an initial idea of its contents. This is written using the techniques outlined in Unit 9, with particular care being taken to avoid falsifying the information by over-simplifying it. Writing summaries of this kind is a taxing and highly skilled task which will usually be undertaken by someone in a senior position. At the same time, he or she may prepare a much shorter form of the report for wider circulation, stating the main points of the full report but leaving out much of its detail.

15.5.5 Terms of reference

The purpose of this section is to give a precise indication of the area covered by the report. More particularly, it will contain details of the following elements:

● the exact subject of the report. This will include details of dates, places and people involved in the topic the report covers.
● any matters specifically excluded from the report. This is particularly important for those who will have to act on the report's findings. It will prevent them from criticizing the writers for failing to cover certain aspects, and it will also allow them to judge the conclusions and recommendations in the context of the data on which they were based. Both are crucial to a just and unbiased assessment of the report.
● details of how the report was commissioned, and by whom. These, too, are important for those acting on the report, since they will alert them to any possible bias in its contents.

Reports written by an individual rather than a committee may also give the name and position of the writer at this point.

The terms of reference supplement the details given in the summary by showing the limitations and conditions under which the report was written, and are therefore an essential part of the report. In general, however, this section is fairly short, the information being conveyed in three or four sentences, as in the example in fig. 15.4.

15.5.6 Procedure

This section explains the methods used in the writing of the report. It does *not* explain any procedures or methods which may be the subject of the report; these are dealt with in the next section as part of the findings. Rather, it provides an overall account of how the report was compiled. It covers two main areas: methods of research and treatment of data.

Methods of research Readers of a report need to know how the data it contains was collected, so that they may have an idea of how valid its findings are. Research will usually include some or all of the following methods:

● *Research in libraries* Public, academic and specialized libraries, private archives and research collections of material both in printed form and in the form of computer databases provide the major sources of information here. Advice on using resources of this kind is given in Units 9 and 18.
● *Investigation of buildings, working spaces and other physical resources* This may be needed in a report which looks at recreational facilities, for example, or the feasibility of building a factory on a particular plot of land. Full details should be given of the number, duration and date of the visits made, and the nature of the place visited should be made clear by the use of maps and diagrams, usually included as appendices (see section 15.5.10).
● *Personal interviews and meetings* These are particularly significant in a report which deals with the best course of action for a company, as they give an indication of the feelings and opinions of those people most directly involved. Advice on organizing and conducting interviews and meetings appears in Units 5 and 16 respectively. As with site visits, full details of the date and duration of relevant meetings should be given in your report.

● *Ballots and questionnaires* Both are valuable ways of gaining the reactions of people involved in a matter, and are quicker and more confidential than large meetings.

A ballot is a means of testing opinion by asking a single question which can be answered – on paper and in secret – by all those involved. Such a question should be worded very clearly and unambiguously, as in the following example:

Are you in favour of operating a flexible working hours system in this office?

Questionnaires provide a way of canvassing people's opinions in more detail. If properly worded and attractively laid out, a questionnaire can add considerably to the data available to the compiler of a report. The main principles of designing and writing questionnaires are outlined in Unit 13.

Treatment of data As well as methods of research, the procedure section of a report makes clear how the data was treated once it had been collected. It will usually include details of some of the following:

● *Collation and interpretation of notes* This is the process of bringing together the material collected into some kind of order and making sense of what may well be a large mass of notes from written and spoken sources.

● *Tabulation of results from questionnaires* This involves totalling the number of answers of each kind for every question, and presenting the results either as a table or in some other kind of graphic form which makes them easy to grasp quickly. Any of the methods of presentation described in Unit 14 may be used here.

● *Analysis by computer* Computers are increasingly being used to analyse and interpret data. The simplest form of computer analysis consists of interpreting statistics and preparing graphic illustrations of them, but more complex systems are capable of analysing information and perhaps giving interpretations and recommending future action according to a pre-programmed model. Full details of the nature and extent to which computers have been used in compiling a report should be included under 'Procedure'.

Although this section can potentially contain many elements, in practice it is usually fairly short. It should nevertheless be quite clear and specific in explaining how the report was written.

15.5.7 Findings

In many ways this section is the heart of the report. It presents in simple, clear and unbiased terms an account of the events or circumstances which form the subject of the report.

To aid the reader, there are some basic principles that you should follow when preparing the findings section.

(a) Organize your material in sections according to subject area and present each one under a clear, descriptive heading, which should be clearly numbered. This will assist the reader in finding exactly the information he or she requires and will assist those who wish to cross-refer to the conclusions and recommendations sections.

(b) Write in a clear, simple style about the topic under consideration only. Do not use note form or numbered points beneath your headings; instead use a direct prose style similar to that which you would use for a business letter (see section 11.5).

(c) Include only those statistics which are really essential to support your points; present the full details of statistical research in an appendix at the end (see section 15.5.10). In this way you will give full support to the points you make, without interrupting the flow of the writing with long, complex tables. Similarly, maps and diagrams should be included as appendices for ease of reference while the reader is working through the report.

Remember that the findings should do no more than observe and record. They should not interpret, by attempting to find causes for the events they describe, nor should they recommend what action should be taken. Both of these tasks will be performed by later sections.

15.5.8 Conclusions

In a formal report, the term 'conclusions' does not refer to final or concluding statements. Instead, it is used to describe that section of the report which interprets the facts and observations presented in the findings. It is essential to understand this principle at an early stage, otherwise the structure and function of your reports will be seriously inaccurate.

The conclusions section, then, presents a clear and direct interpretation of the events or circumstances stated in the section immediately before it. This interpretation will usually make clear the reasons why certain events occurred or why certain circumstances came into being. It is here that your own individual thoughts and opinions can be presented, and in this respect the conclusions differ quite considerably from the impartial, factual findings.

In order for the section to appear reliable and convincing, it must follow on logically from the data presented in the findings. It must be composed of a valid and sensible series of interpretations, which in turn demands careful thought at the planning stage. In addition, it is essential that the conclusions rest only on data presented in the findings. If the statements rest on data which was not included earlier, the reader will have the impression that the report is biased and that the writer is concealing other relevant information.

Again, there are some basic principles which should be followed.

(a) Conclusions should be presented under the same series of subject headings as findings, in the same order, and with the same system of numbering. This is so that the reader can cross-refer from conclusions to findings about one particular area of the report, to refresh his or her memory and to clarify the logical progression from one stage to the next.

(b) Like the findings, conclusions should be written in simple, continuous prose. It is harder to write clearly where opinion and interpretation are concerned than it is when handling simple factual records, but every effort should be made to be quite specific when attributing events to causes. The advice on style given in section 4.10 is especially important here. For example, instead of writing

> the material decay of the upper surface of the building seems to have been occasioned by constant entry of the elements over a sustained period of time

you should say

> the dry rot in the warehouse roof was caused by rain getting in for four months.

As in this example, vague, impressive-sounding words and imprecise factual elements should be replaced by clear, direct language and precise details. Wherever possible, refer to specific causes.

(c) Do not include statistics, graphs or maps which have not been included in the findings. This will suggest that the section does not rest solely on the findings which, as we have already seen, is to be avoided.

15.5.9 Recommendations

This is the final major section of a report, used to put forward a future course of action concerning the topic under investigation. It should be written according to these principles:

(a) Each recommendation should be as specific as possible, given the information available. Instead of saying 'something should be done to remedy the poor service at the Foreign Exchange counter', for example, you should 'recommend that an extra member of staff be taken on to ensure that the Foreign Exchange counter be staffed at all times'. Only if this is done will the report succeed in fully communicating the facts, causes and likely remedies of the situation under discussion.

(b) Even when you feel that the present arrangements for a certain aspect of the topic are satisfactory, you should mention this in the recommendations section. A simple statement such as

> The current arrangements for replacing lost library tickets are satisfactory and should remain unchanged.

will make quite clear that the situation need not be changed, whereas a failure to comment on a particular aspect will leave the reader in some uncertainty as to your opinion.

(c) Recommendations should be grouped under the same headings – which should appear in the same order – as were used in the findings and conclusions. This allows readers to refer quickly to points on the same subject in different sections.

(d) Recommendations must rest on the information in the findings and the reasoning in the conclusions, so that the reader can see that the report proceeds clearly and logically, and that nothing has been concealed.

15.5.10 Appendices

As has been suggested in earlier sections, the appendices of a report contain material which is relevant to the content but which would interrupt the flow of the argument were it to be included in the main text. They may consist of the following:

- *Full statistical tables* The complete results of statistical enquiries should be given as an appendix, with full details of their source.
- *Copies of questionnaires* If a questionnaire is used to obtain opinions, a blank copy should be included as an appendix.
- *Answers to questionnaires* Full details of the responses made to questionnaires should appear as an appendix, presented in an attractive form so that they can be easily read and interpreted (see Unit 13).
- *Maps and diagrams* Unless they are fairly small, maps and diagrams should also come at the end of the report.
- *Bibliography* In reports where a large amount of library research has been undertaken, a list of works consulted should be given. These should be cited in alphabetical order of author, in the manner described in section 8.3.1.

Although reports which have been based on information of this kind should include appendices, they are not always necessary, and very few reports would call for the inclusion of all of the kinds of appendix outlined above.

15.5.11 Signature, position and date

All reports should conclude with these elements, unless they are written by a large committee, in which case a list of those involved will be included elsewhere in the report (see section 15.5.3). They make clear exactly who wrote the report and the place occupied by the writer within the company or organization – a detail which may have an important bearing on the conclusions or recommendations put forward. It is important to include the date, since the report may be consulted some time after it was written, in which case more recent research may be available to the reader than was available to the writer.

15.6 Some additional guidelines

If you follow the above guidelines for constructing a report, you should have no difficulty in writing a clear, logical document representing a carefully reasoned analysis of the situation under discussion. There are, however, a few points which you should bear in mind which may make the process simpler and still more effective.

(a) Make sure that you know exactly what aspects of a topic you are to cover, and which are to be excluded.

(b) Remember the difference between findings, conclusions and recommendations, which can be summarized as follows:

> Findings *observe*.
> Conclusions *interpret*.
> Recommendations *suggest*.

You can check that you have made points in the right section by looking at the tense of verbs used in each. In the findings, for example, you would use the present tense:

> The roof leaks.

The conclusions should say:

> Tiles *had been* missing from the roof for several months.

The recommendations section, however, should be worded thus:

> The roof *should be* repaired immediately.

Checking the tenses in this way will often make clear where each point should go in the report.

(c) Plan the three major sections together. This will ensure that there is a genuine and close connection between them, and will speed up the writing process. For example, in planning a report about parking facilities for your company's offices you might include the following:

Findings	Conclusions	Recommendations
Car park covered in dust when cars leave	Surface loose	Lay tarmac

(d) Check the report by cross-referring between the three major sections, ensuring that conclusions and recommendations about each point follow logically from the findings which describe them. Logical presentation of information is one of the major skills essential to report-writing, and checking your work in this way will make sure that you develop this skill.

(e) Make sure that you know the order of the sections of a report and are aware of the appropriate style to use (see section 4.10). Being able to construct the routine sections of the report with ease will leave more time for the three major sections, and will ensure that you can produce an accurate, thorough and useful document even under pressure.

15.7 Quick questions

1　When are report forms used?

2　How long is an average short routine report?

3　What sections would you include in a short routine report?

4 What do the following sections contain:

    (a) terms of reference?
    (b) procedure?
    (c) findings?
    (d) conclusions?
    (e) recommendations?

5 In a single word for each, describe the purpose of the findings, conclusions and recommendations of a report.

15.8 Longer exercises

1 You are Assistant Accounts Manager of JPS Electronics. Mr Jarrett, the Office Manager, has asked you to investigate a complaint from a regular customer, Brooke Industries plc. They have been told their account is £764.83 overdue, but say that a cheque for this amount was cleared through their bank on 11 August, although they were given no receipt for the amount.

    You investigate and find that the amount was credited to the account of Brook Industrial Products. In August some regular staff were on holiday and temporary workers were employed.

    Write a report explaining what happened and what action you have taken to put the matter right.

2 Write a report on the part-time job you have at weekends. Make clear what it is you do, and include recommendations about how the efficiency of what you do could be improved.

3 Write a report on the recreational and canteen facilities of a company or organization that you work for, making recommendations where necessary.

4 The Claims Manager of Goodfriars Insurance Ltd has received a claim for £200 compensation for a fire at the home of Mr C.D. Eden, 1 Oak Road, London SW3 2BW. He has asked you, as assistant to the Claims Inspector, to visit the insured and to report on the extent of the damage, suggesting the amount of compensation which you estimate should be paid to him.

    On your visit you discover: a mattress, bought five years ago for £150, and bedding damaged, i.e. two sheets, one electric blanket, one duvet and one duvet cover. All are now unusable. You think Mr Eden's claim should be paid.

    Write the necessary report.

        (Pitman, *English for business communications* (intermediate))

5   As a sales representative for Domestic Cleaning Products Ltd, you have been criticized recently for a decline in sales orders. The cost of your company's polishes, brushes and detergents is proving very high and competition is fierce; you are also receiving complaints that goods ordered are slow in arriving. Response from sales literature is poor. Write a report to your Divisional Manager, Mr G. Holroyd, explaining the reasons for the fall in orders and suggesting what could be done to improve sales.

(Pitman, English for business communications (intermediate))

6   The Managing Director has asked you to make enquiries into the services offered by a local debt collecting agency and to write a report for submission to the Board of Directors on your findings and recommendations. From the rather muddled information below, write a clear report in approved fashion:

(ICM, Business communications)

---

3 April – Mr Prophet asked for report on Best Agency Ltd. – Broad Street, Birchester.

10 April – Saw Mr Best at their offices. Long talk. Several handouts to read. See him again on 17 April.

17 April – Saw Mr Best again with queries.

All charges are fixed. Majority of what they charge paid by debtor. For letters before action they charge £1.25 plus VAT (this includes posting on by first-class mail of any cheques received – they don't bank them). Where the debt is greater than £3000, all the costs of issuing a writ are payable by the debtor. They can provide references from satisfied clients all over the country. Whenever they do issue writs, they add interest at 12% (which is the statutory rate) to the claim. They have special arrangements for dealing with debtors who make silly complaints in order to avoid payment, and say they can offer several methods of encouraging payment without unpleasantness or legal proceedings where this is preferred. Where the debt is overdue for 60 days, the interest charged to the debtor is £19.72 for £1000, £57.19 for £3000 and £98.63 for £5000. If the debt is 90 days overdue, the interest payable is £29.58 on £1000, £88.76 on £3000 and £147.94 on £5000, and where the debt is 120 days overdue this rises to £39.45 on £1000, £118.15 on £3000 and £197.26 on £5000.

Interest will more than pay their charges.

Committees and meetings

16.1 Introduction

Any organization which has a number of members needs to hold regular meetings of various kinds. It will need to bring its members together to exchange information, to solve problems, to take decisions and – perhaps most important – to make sure that each section or department knows what is going on in other areas of the organization.

As anyone who has attended a poorly run meeting will know, they can be lengthy, dull affairs, which seem to be controlled by people who like the sound of their own voice and which rarely make any impression on the day-to-day running of the organization. To safeguard against this, it is essential that everyone who is involved in a meeting has a clear idea of its purpose and contributes fully and effectively to the discussion. Before covering the conduct of meetings, however, we will first examine the nature of committees, the reasons for their formation, and the roles played by their members.

16.2 The role and rules of a committee

As Unit 5 has shown, meetings between individuals are an important part of any organization's communications. As well as interviews, however, there is often a need for regular meetings of small groups of people, and in such cases a committee will usually be formed. In some cases, this is a legal requirement: the board of directors of a company, for example, must by law meet at regular intervals. Other kinds of committee may bring together:

- representatives from several different departments – to review sales figures, perhaps, or to monitor the company's progress in different areas of activity;
- people who are working together on a new product;
- representatives from management and the workforce (often called a joint consultative committee);
- people who are organizing a social club such as a dramatic society or a cricket team.

Many organizations also hold meetings of much larger numbers of people – for example, full employees' meetings, meetings of shareholders and annual general meetings (a legal requirement for public companies). Such meetings use many of the procedures described in this unit, although they take place less frequently than committee meetings and rarely allow for full discussion between all those present.

If a committee is to function effectively, it must be well organized and properly run. Different organizations have different ways of making sure that this happens. You should make sure that you know the procedures followed by any committees with which you are involved either socially or at work, and those of larger meetings such as annual general meetings of companies or societies. Although there are some differences between individual committees, there are nonetheless many points of procedure which are common to all and which are described later in this unit. The same is true of the roles of committee officers outlined in section 16.3: they are broadly similar but may vary between different committees, and you should make sure that you know the practice of your own organization.

16.2.1 Standing orders

Most committees are formed and run according to a written set of rules known as standing orders. In some cases these are laid down by law. Standing orders cover the following matters.

Constitution   This is the actual membership of the committee. The standing orders define the number of members, give details of who qualifies for membership, and dictate how members are chosen. For example, a club's standing orders might prescribe that its social committee consist of ten members, and that every member of the club be eligible to stand for election to the committee by the vote of the members. The standing orders might also contain rules about the roles of the committee members, perhaps stating that four members should be responsible for fund-raising and the other six have no special responsibility. On such a committee, members might be elected at an annual election to serve for one year. By contrast, a joint consultative committee in a company might – by virtue of its standing orders – consist of twelve members, six to be nominated by the employer and six by the trade union, all of whom would serve for two years.

An efficient committee should have an appropriate number of members. In general, this will be between ten and fifteen, although sometimes it will be fewer. It is by no means a coincidence that most sports teams contain about this number of players, since it allows for a good spread of ideas and abilities without being so large as to be unwieldy in operation.

Terms of reference   These specify what the committee has powers to discuss, together with any particular topics which are outside its area of concern. For example, a staff sports and social committee might be empowered by its standing orders to discuss social events and outings, but have to refer to a management committee before spending sums in excess of £250 on any single event. Similarly, a joint consultative committee might be empowered to discuss changes in workers' conditions of service and to make recommendations to the · board of directors, but have no power to insist that its recommendations be implemented.

Regularity of meetings The standing orders also specify the frequency with which meetings should be held – every three months for a sports and social committee, for instance, or every month for a joint consultative committee.

Quorate attendance Before a meeting can proceed, it must be what is known as *quorate*. This means that a specified number of members must be present – known as a *quorum*. Without a quorum, a meeting cannot take place. This is because if only a small number of people attend, a full discussion will not take place, and any decisions taken will not represent the views of the whole committee. The size of the quorum will obviously depend on the size of the committee.

As individual committees vary greatly, both in the way in which they are formally constituted and in the extent to which their powers are formally recorded, it is not possible to give further details about the rules which govern their organization. Overall, however, it is important to remember that a committee will function well only if its membership, areas of responsibility, frequency of meetings and attendance necessary for a quorum are clearly defined and made known to its members.

16.3 The members of a committee

Most committees consist of a combination of members who have particular responsibilities and some who have no specific duties. The most important roles are as follows.

16.3.1 Chair

The word 'chair' is now commonly used instead of 'chairman', 'chairwoman' or 'chairperson', since it is shorter and completely avoids the question of sexual stereotyping which some find offensive. The chair of a committee has a very important role to perform, since it is up to him or her to ensure the smooth running of the meeting. The chair's duties are as follows:

● to prepare a list of items to be discussed at the meeting – known as an *agenda* (see section 16.4.2) – with the help of the secretary;
● to declare the meeting formally open at the designated time;
● to introduce each item for discussion, together with the committee member who is to talk about it, where necessary;
● to ensure that the committee works through each item for discussion at a reasonable pace;

- to make sure that no one is allowed to dominate the discussion, by seeking the views of everyone on the committee;
- to intervene if the discussion becomes heated or if personal animosity or abuse seems likely;
- to supervise voting procedures, count votes and announce the results;
- to suggest that further research or investigation is undertaken by suitable committee members if this seems necessary;
- to suggest that the committee move on to discuss other matters if it is apparent that no conclusion can be reached on a particular issue;
- to make sure that the meeting is at all times run in accordance with the standing orders, and in particular that nothing is discussed which is beyond the committee's terms of reference;
- to declare the meeting closed at the appropriate time, when all the business has been concluded;
- to make sure that a full written record of the meeting is produced by the secretary and circulated to each member for agreement at the next meeting.

Fulfilling these functions demands tact and diplomacy, as well as the ability to be firm on occasion. Notice that the chair often takes little part in the actual discussion of the committee: his or her function is that of a facilitator – to help others to make their contributions clearly and effectively. The chair does not usually vote as part of the committee. In some cases, however, he or she has what is known as a *casting vote* (see section 16.5.7).

The chair of a formal committee has various other powers. He or she can, for example, rule a member 'out of order', meaning that the member has gone against a rule of the standing orders. In extreme cases, the chair can order a member to leave the meeting, although this is only done in extreme circumstances. Some chairs also have the power to 'co-opt' members – to request people not on the committee to join it, usually because they can bring a particular area of knowledge or expertise to its deliberations. These are powers usually found only in more formal committees, however.

16.3.2 Secretary

The secretary of a committee fulfils a very different role from that of the office or shorthand secretary, and is often someone in a senior position in an organization. After the chair, the secretary is easily the most important member of a committee. He or she has many responsibilities which are essential to the efficient functioning of the committee and its meetings. The secretary's duties are:

- to send out notices of the meeting in good time to all the members (see section 16.4.1);
- to request and receive items for discussion at each meeting;
- in conjunction with the chair, to draw up an agenda (see section 16.4.2) and to send copies of it to members in good time before the meeting;
- to circulate among the members any documents which might be necessary to enable them to contribute fully to the discussion of matters listed on the agenda;

- to make arrangements for the accommodation of members who have to travel a long distance to attend meetings;
- to see that a room is available for each meeting, and that pens, paper and other requisites are made available for members;
- to draw up a special agenda for the chair, including any details which will help him or her to conduct the meeting satisfactorily;
- to record details of what takes place during the meeting;
- after the meeting, to write up these notes into a formal record of the meeting – known as the *minutes* (see section 16.4.4) – and circulate this among the members, after gaining the approval of the chair;
- to deal with any correspondence received by the committee.

From the above, it will be clear that the secretary's role involves considerable planning and organizational skills, and the ability to communicate well both orally and on paper. Note that the secretary plays no part in the discussion during the meeting, unless he or she is asked to give a report, read out correspondence or talk to the committee about 'matters arising' (see section 16.5.4). Except in small or very informal committees, the secretary has no vote: his or her chief functions are to take the minutes and to help the chair in making sure that the meeting runs smoothly and in accordance with the standing orders.

16.3.3 Treasurer

Many committees have a treasurer, whose role it is to take care of the financial aspects of the committee's operations. As a result, many committee meetings include a *treasurer's report*. This is a financial statement given by the treasurer which details the financial position of the committee or the larger organization which it represents. Often it is accompanied by the presentation of a balance sheet, detailing income and expenditure for a stated period, a copy of which is given to each member by the secretary – preferably before the meeting to allow members time to study it carefully. The treasurer usually has various powers – specified in the standing orders – concerning the funds belonging to the committee, and takes care of any payments that have to be made. Apart from his or her function as treasurer, the treasurer takes part in meetings as any other committee member, and is not restricted to discussing financial matters.

16.3.4 Other special roles

Some committees allot special roles to individual members. One or more members might be responsible for publicity, for example, or for liaison with a particular branch or department of the parent organization. Others might represent on the committee the views of a particular group of employees. These roles will vary, however, with the concerns of the individual committee and the nature of the organization within which it exists.

16.3.5 Ordinary committee members

The committee members who have no single role allotted them bear the responsibility for the full discussion of matters brought before them. The extent to which they fulfil this responsibility largely dictates the effectiveness of the committee since, however well the chair directs and the secretary plans the meeting, it will achieve little unless there is a full discussion. The proper discharge of this responsibility includes the following three major functions.

● *Talking* A major role of a committee member is to make clear his or her own views, or those of the group which he or she represents. This does not mean being domineering, however. A good committee member will make his or her points clearly and simply, and will not attempt to take over the proceedings by talking at great length. By the same token, the person who says nothing at a committee meeting and then complains bitterly about what happened – usually just after the meeting – is not fulfilling his or her role properly. The art is to find a proper balance: members should make their own views clear, but also allow others to take part in the discussion.
● *Listening* When someone is speaking, the other members should pay full attention to what he or she says, thinking carefully about its meaning and not interrupting (see section 6.2.2).
● *Facilitating* This is a rather grandiose term which means trying to help other people to express their views clearly. You may find that you disagree very strongly with what another member says, but you should still allow him or her to say it. Help others to express their ideas by using expressions such as: 'If I've understood you correctly, you're suggesting that . . .'; 'Can I just make clear what you're suggesting?'; or 'Would you please explain that in a little more detail?' This will help the speaker to make his or her ideas absolutely clear, and will also give the other members time to evaluate what is being said, rather than blundering straight in with their own points. Facilitating in this way is an important function of the chair, but it is something which other members should also do.

16.3.6 The importance of roles

You may have come across the technique of 'role-play' in your studies at school or college. People are given a particular role to adopt in a given situation, and act out their part in conjunction with others playing other roles. You might, for example, be given the role of an applicant for a job, and be asked to act out an interview with someone playing the role of the employer.

Exercises of this kind are a valuable way of gaining experience and have the additional advantage that, because you are not personally involved in the situation, you are not influenced by feelings of anger or animosity towards the other characters in the role-play.

There is an important message to be gained from this. Social psychologists have recently shown that people who regard their work as a kind of role-play – in which they have no direct personal involvement but which they nonetheless take seriously and perform professionally – suffer far less stress than those who become personally involved.

This technique can also help considerably in reducing tension and conflict in committee meetings. If you stop thinking of the other members as individuals whom you like or dislike, and see them simply as 'the office manager' or 'the accountant', and yourself as 'the training officer', for example, you will avoid potentially awkward situations. The next section on committee procedure will suggest other ways in which this may be done, but in general terms role-play has much to recommend it as a way of approaching meetings, freeing the energy which might be expended in anger or frustration for more creative uses.

16.4 Committee documents

For any committee to function effectively, a series of documents is necessary, consisting of:

(a) notice of meeting;
(b) agenda;
(c) chair's agenda;
(d) minutes.

16.4.1 Notice of meeting

All committee members must be given adequate notice of each meeting. This is usually done by the secretary, who sends out a formal *notice of meeting* in good time, with details of when and where the meeting will take place. In cases where meetings have to be held by law, the period of notice will be legally set.

The notice of meeting may include a request for items to be included on the agenda, together with a time limit by which these should be given to the secretary. Where the items for the agenda are decided by the chair, or are referred by another body, there will be no such request. The notice may also be accompanied by the minutes of the last meeting, and may be combined with the agenda for the next one. This will depend on the practice of the individual committee, as laid down in its standing orders. Figure 16.1 shows a simple notice of meeting; fig. 16.3 shows a combined notice and agenda.

16.4.2 Agenda

An agenda is simply a list of items to be discussed at a meeting. It is circulated to committee members by the secretary in good time – usually three or four weeks before the meeting. Some items on the agenda are fixed and some appear only for particular meetings.

Fixed items   Almost all agendas contain the following fixed items, in the order given here:

(a) apologies for absence;
(b) minutes of the last meeting;
(c) matters arising from the minutes;
(d) correspondence;
(e) any other business;
(f) date of next meeting.

NOTICE OF MEETING

A meeting of the company's Social and Welfare Committee will take
place in the Committee Room on Wednesday 7 May at 10.30 a.m. Items
to be included on the agenda should be sent to the Secretary to arrive
no later than 5.00 p.m. on Wednesday 16 April.

G Patel
Secretary   7 April 19--

Enc: Minutes of meeting of 5 March 19--

Fig. 16.1 Formal notice of meeting

AGENDA

For a meeting of the Social and Welfare Committee to be held in the
Committee Room on Wednesday 7 May at 10.30 a.m.

1   Apologies for absence

2   Minutes of the last meeting

3   Matters arising from the last meeting

4   Correspondence

5   Report from recreational fund treasurer

6   Staff medical insurance scheme

7   Any other business

8   Date of next meeting

G Patel
Secretary   22 April 19--

Fig. 16.2 Agenda

```
                            NOTICE OF MEETING

A meeting of the company's Social and Welfare Committee will be held
in the Committee Room on Wednesday 7 May at 10.30 a.m.

The agenda will be as follows:


1   Apologies for absence

2   Minutes of the last meeting

3   Matters arising from last meeting

4   Correspondence

5   Report from recreational fund treasurer

6   Staff medical insurance scheme

7   Any other business

8   Date of next meeting


G Patel
Secretary                                      22 April 19--
```

Fig. 16.3 Combined notice of meeting and agenda

The use of a set order gives stability to a meeting, as well as emphasizing the formal nature of the occasion.

Particular items   These are the items of business to be discussed in detail at an individual meeting, usually taken between 'correspondence' and 'any other business'. Some will be routine matters which may be dealt with quickly, whereas others will be more complex and will need more time. The chair and secretary should place routine matters first on the agenda, so that they may be dealt with quickly, leaving time for the more important business. This approach also means that the committee members can get to know each other again and the formality of the occasion can be established before the more serious issues are raised.

Particular items will generally fall into one of three categories.

● *Reports and papers*   These are items presented by one committee member, who addresses the meeting using a document he or she has prepared earlier. The most common are reports from the treasurer and other committee officers, but papers on a range of subjects – to do, say, with the development of an area of the company's activities, or a topic which the member has been asked to research in detail – may also be named on the agenda for presentation at this point in the meeting.

● *Proposals*   These are formal suggestions on which the committee will vote during the meeting. The nature of proposals is discussed in section 16.5.6.

● *Topics for discussion*   As well as reports and proposals, an agenda may simply list a topic for discussion – 'Staff training in emergency first aid', for example, or 'Possible changes to company pension scheme'. In such cases, no formal proposal on the topic will have been put forward, and no single person asked to present a report – although one person might well briefly introduce the subject to start off the discussion.

In general, it is not good practice for an agenda to contain a large number of items for detailed discussion. Some are bound to be discussed too quickly, and time may well prevent the coverage of others altogether. Drawing up an agenda which will allow time for all the necessary business to be covered in the necessary depth is a skill which a chair and secretary must develop with practice and with experience of the nature of the committee concerned.

An example of an agenda is given in fig. 16.2.

16.4.3 Chair's agenda

As the chair is responsible for directing the meeting, a special agenda is often prepared for his or her individual use, giving further details about each item. The chair will refer to this during the meeting. It may give information about who is to introduce each item; whether any further documents are available for committee members to support their discussion; and how much time is available for the discussion of each item. Chair's agendas are usually produced by the committee secretary, but whether or not they are used will depend very much on the individual committee: clearly they are most suitable for more

```
                            AGENDA

 for a meeting of the company's Social and Welfare Committee to be
 held in the Committee Room on Wednesday 7 May at 10.30 a.m.

 1   Apologies for absence

 2   Minutes of last meeting       TS will propose.

 3   Matters arising              Short report from JK on directors'
                                   discussion of new crèche facilities.
                                   Matter is still being considered -
                                   will be on agenda for next meeting
                                   so keep short.

 4   Correspondence               GP to read letter from OXFAM about
                                   fund-raising evening in March.

 5   Report from recreational fund GF to speak to paper, including
     treasurer                     balance sheet for year ending
                                   5 April 19--, circulated at meeting.
                                   10 minutes at most.

 6   Staff medical insurance scheme TS to introduce proposals from
                                   directors. Main business of meeting
                                   - get views of all members, and
                                   encourage canvassing of opinion
                                   among employees.

 7   AOB                          Keep short: put on agenda for
                                   next meeting if necessary.

 8   Date of next meeting         Must be within 2 months. Suggest
                                   Wednesday 25 June or 2 July.
```

Fig. 16.4 Chair's agenda. Notice the use of abbreviations, and the directions as to main speakers and time to be spent on each item.

formal meetings which discuss business of considerable importance.

A chair's agenda is shown in fig. 16.4.

16.4.4 Minutes

Minutes are a record in writing of the proceedings and resolutions of a committee meeting, written by the secretary from notes taken during the meeting and sent to each committee member shortly afterwards. For some committees – notably the board of directors of a company – they serve as a legal record of events, and thus must be kept accurately and mention every significant event of the meeting.

Minutes begin by stating the time and place of the meeting, and listing those present and those from whom apologies for absence have been received. They then go on to record in turn the topics discussed at the meeting, along with any resolutions passed. Minutes should always be written in the past tense, as follows:

Ms Mukerjee proposed and Mr Gruffyd seconded that . . .

The depth of detail provided by the minutes will vary considerably with the individual committee. Some require only a record of the resolutions passed and motions defeated: others require a full account of the major points advanced in the discussion, in addition to the formal decisions taken. Most minutes will include – as *appendices* – copies of reports or papers which were the basis of discussion.

Many committee meetings include heated exchanges of opinion over controversial issues. Minutes should ignore such elements of the discussion, recording only the factual basis of the points raised. Nor are minutes intended to convey the writer's opinion about the issues raised or the views of other members. They should simply record and not interpret in any way. For example, instead of a passage such as this:

> In a witty and incisive speech, Mr Finsbury argued for the institution of a flexible working scheme for all office employees, and such was his eloquence that everyone voted in favour of his motion

you should write:

> Mr Finsbury proposed that flexible working hours be implemented for all office employees. The motion was seconded by Mrs Nott and carried unanimously.

An example of a set of minutes is given in fig. 16.5, and the transcript of the discussion they report is given below.

Tom Smith: Thank you, Chair. I hope that everyone has had time to read the paper circulated last month about the new health insurance scheme which the Board of Directors has suggested. It'll work for all employees – contributions to the scheme will be deducted at source by the wages office, and everyone will pay at the same rate: the details are given in full in the paper, and I won't go over them again. There are many benefits: everyone will receive private medical care and, just as important in my view, compensation for loss of earnings through illness. I'd really like to hear people's views on the scheme. Could I ask for comments through the chair, please?

Mrs Fraser: Well, Chair, I can't speak for everyone, but I think it's an excellent idea. The deductions aren't a very great deal of money, and as they'll be taken off at source nobody will really notice them. What's particularly good, I think, is that everyone will make the same payment – none of the old business of first-class treatment for management and second-rate stuff for the workers. We've gone a long way to getting everyone on the same level and this will help take things further.

Mr Jones: That's all very well, Madam Chairman, but surely we should have the right to pay more for better benefits if we want to? Why shouldn't I have the right to pay more – it's my money, after all?

Ms Gieves: I agree. Some of us have different priorities, you know – it's all very well for Mrs Fraser to get all idealistic, Chair, but we don't all have her political opinions . . .

MINUTES

of a meeting of the company Social and Welfare Committee held in the
Committee Room on Wednesday 7 May 19-- at 10.30 a.m.

Those present: Ms H. Jackson (Chair)
                Mr G. Patel (Secretary)
                Mr G. Forbes (Treasurer)
                Mr C. Black, Mr F. Iles, Mr K. Naseby, Mr T. Smith,
                Mrs H. Fraser, Mr T. Gieves, Miss S. Holt, Ms D. Long

Apologies for absence were received from Mr T. Clarke, who is attending
a conference in Scarborough.

Minutes of the last meeting, held on 5 March 19--, were proposed as an
accurate record by Mr T. Smith, seconded by Ms Gieves and approved by
the Committee.

* * *

Staff Medical Insurance Scheme Mr Smith introduced this topic,
speaking to a paper giving full details of the scheme as suggested by
the Board of Directors and circulated to committee members (see
Appendix I of these minutes). The scheme would operate by deduction
of contributions from pay at a standard rate, and contributors would
receive a range of benefits including private health care and
compensation for loss of earnings through illness.
    Mrs Fraser welcomed the scheme, but Mr Jones had reservations,
feeling that deduction should be variable in amount, to enable those
who so wished to insure for higher rates of benefit. Mrs Fraser
disagreed strongly, seeing the scheme as a further way of breaking
down barriers between management and employees.
    After a full discussion, it was proposed by Mrs Fraser and
seconded by Mr Naseby that the opinions of all employees be sought by
means of a questionnaire. An amendment that the questionnaire
should also ask if employees would prefer a standard or variable rate
of contribution was proposed by Mr Jones and seconded by Ms Gieves.
This was passed by six votes to three, and the motion that the
questionnaire be produced and circulated was then passed unanimously.

* * *

Any other business Ms Long raised the question of maternity and
paternity leave for all staff. After a brief discussion it was agreed
that this be placed on the agenda for the next meeting.

Date of next meeting This was fixed for Wednesday 7 July at 10.30 a.m.
in the Committee Room.

The Chair declared the meeting closed at 12.07 p.m.

Fig. 16.5 Excerpts from minutes of the discussion in section 16.4.4

Mrs Fraser: Just what do you mean by that? I'm only trying to make sure that we all get fair treatment . . .

Ms Jackson (Chair):   Thank you, Mrs Fraser – I'm sure no one is suggesting anything else. This is a topic we all have our own opinions on, and I'm sure all the employees do, too.

*   *   *

Mrs Fraser: Chair, we've discussed the thing from several angles – may I suggest that we do something to get the employees' views? I propose that a questionnaire be drawn up and circulated among the workforce.

Mr Naseby: Fine – I'll second that.

Ms Jackson (Chair):   May we then move to the vote?

Mr Jones: Not yet, Chair, if you don't mind. I'd like to propose an amendment that the questionnaire also ask if employees would prefer a standard or variable rate of contribution.

Ms Jackson (Chair):   Is there a seconder for the amendment?

Ms Gieves: Certainly – I'll second it.

Ms Jackson (Chair):   Can we vote on the amendment, then? Those in favour – six – thank you: and those against – three. Thank you. I declare the amendment carried. Let's now vote on the amended proposal. Those in favour – that's everyone, isn't it, Mr Patel? Carried unanimously.

Remember that every committee will have its own conventions about how minutes should be written and presented, but fig. 16.5 gives an idea of the fundamental style to adopt. Most minutes are not intended as a word-for-word transcript.

In those cases where a definitive transcript of the meeting is required, it will usually be prepared by a secretary who is trained in shorthand and so can take a full record of what is said while the meeting is in progress.

If you are called upon to take notes and produce minutes for a meeting, follow these basic principles:

(a)   Do not write all the time. Spend plenty of time listening, following the general points which are made.

(b)   Record important points about a topic when the discussion moves to another topic, when arrangements are being made for a vote, or at other times when the discussion is less concentrated.

(c)   Always think about main points, not individual words.

(d)   Take care to record the exact wording of every motion and amendment.

(e)   Check your notes carefully after the meeting and write out in full any abbreviations you may have used before you forget what they stand for.

(f)   Go through the minutes with the chair to see if you both have the same impression of what happened at the meeting.

(g)   Write up the minutes in the simple, factual style used in fig. 16.5.

16.5 Committee procedure

Formal committee meetings follow a very strict procedure, which makes use of a number of formal terms. The degree to which these terms are used, and the procedures followed, varies with every committee. The current trend is towards informality in all but the most important meetings. Formal language does, however, have the advantage of lessening the risk of personal antagonism. It also makes sure that the committee is run in a business-like and efficient way, and in accordance with the standing orders. For all these reasons, the formal procedures and language of the committee have an important function as a form of business communication.

The account of a committee meeting which follows contains most of the common terms used, although some committees make use of others which are not included. You should make every effort to become familiar with the terms used by any committee on which you sit, so that you can make full use of the standard procedure and thus take a full part in the discussion.

16.5.1 Starting the meeting

When everyone is present for the meeting, or when the chair is satisfied that there is a quorum, he or she will *call the meeting to order*, or make sure that everyone is paying attention and ready to start. The chair will then *declare the meeting open at* whatever the time happens to be, making clear that the meeting has formally started and recording the exact time. This is important for two reasons: first, it establishes that anything said from then on will be recorded in the minutes; secondly, since a full record of proceedings is a legal requirement for some committees – notably those of a company's directors – full details must be kept of when they start and finish.

Although many meetings do not demand this degree of formality, it is none-theless important for the chair to start the proceedings in this way, since it imposes a formal structure on the meeting and makes clear to all involved the seriousness of the occasion.

16.5.2 Apologies for absence

After the meeting has been opened, the secretary will read out the names of those who cannot be present but have sent apologies for their absence. Some-times reasons for absence are given, to make clear that the members are not missing without due reason.

16.5.3 Minutes of the last meeting

The first item of business at most committee meetings is the formal agreement that the minutes of the last meeting are 'a true and accurate record' of what happened. It is important that any differences between the events of the meeting and the way they have been recorded be made clear and put right at this stage, especially if the minutes have a legal significance. If the minutes are accurate, a proposal will be made to pass them and a vote will be taken on this (see sections 16.5.6 and 16.5.7). The chair will then sign the minutes.

16.5.4 Matters arising from the last meeting

Matters which were not concluded at the last meeting, or items arising directly from that meeting, will be discussed at this stage. In general, this item is kept short, to avoid repeating ground covered in the last meeting. Here, the skill and tact of the chair are particularly important.

At this stage, too, members of the committee who have been asked to pursue matters raised at the last meeting will give their reports. A member might have been asked to write to various suppliers for estimates of particular goods or services, for example, or to investigate possible sports fixtures for a company hockey team.

16.5.5 Discussion

The main business of the meeting will be the discussion of a series of items outlined on the agenda (see section 16.4.2). The chair will invite any member who has a report to deliver to do so, perhaps briefly introducing the subject and the terms of reference given to the speaker. Sometimes, the member concerned will *speak to a paper* – discuss a paper or report which he or she has written and circulated among the other committee members before the meeting. Often a *treasurer's report* will be given at this stage of the meeting, particularly at the end of a financial year.

While items are being discussed, the following procedures are normally observed.

Speaking through the chair   When members contribute to the discussion, they should address their comments *through the chair* rather than directly towards any individual member of the committee. In the most formal committees, it is the practice to preface all remarks with a direct address to 'Chair' or 'Mr Chairman'. This may seem very formal and old-fashioned, but it has a good purpose: to make the discussion as general and impersonal as possible, and so reduce the risk of personality clashes. It also ensures that only one person is speaking at any time, preventing the formation of small groups, which can be highly destructive of committee discussion.

In less formal committees, it is possible to speak directly to other members, especially when facilitating, and, often, going 'through the chair' means no more than looking at the chair when speaking, to avoid breaking the meeting down into a discussion between two individuals.

Rulings from the chair   It is the role of the chair to make sure that the standing orders are adhered to, and to make *rulings* on possible contraventions. As well as ruling individual members *out of order* for behaving in a manner contrary to the standing orders – for introducing matters for discussion which are not on the agenda, for example – the chair can rule a matter *ultra vires* (literally, 'beyond the powers'), which means that the matter under discussion or proposed for discussion lies beyond the committee's terms of reference. At this point, the discussion must cease.

Progress   Sometimes the discussion may reach a stage at which no new points are being introduced and no further action can be taken. At this stage, various options are open to the committee. If a member requires further details, he or she can raise a *point of information*, which should be answered by the chair or any other member who has the necessary data. A point of information can also be raised if a member wishes to give information to the committee. If insufficient information is available, a member may propose to *lay the matter on the table* – in other words, to leave the topic in abeyance until further data becomes available. Alternatively, if the discussion has continued for some time and has made no progress, the chair or another member can *move progress* – propose that the committee move on to the next item on the agenda. This is also referred to as *moving next business*.

If the deadlock continues for a longer period, or if the available time is used up, the meeting can be *adjourned*. This means that it is closed for the moment, to *reconvene* or meet again at some later date. It may be adjourned until a specific date and time, or adjourned *sine die* – without a new date being fixed.

Adjournment may be proposed by any member of the committee, but in general is suggested by the chair, and usually as the result of a shortage of time or particularly serious circumstances, such as illness of members or physical danger.

16.5.6 Proposing and seconding a motion

Most committee meetings are more productive than the last section would imply so that, after discussion, a member might suggest a particular course of action. This is known formally as *proposing a motion* – putting forward an idea to be adopted as the conclusion or policy of the committee. Proposals for discussion are often listed on the agenda in the manner outlined in section 16.4.2. In a larger meeting, such as a company AGM, a shareholder who is not a member of the board can contribute to the discussion or propose a motion, in which case the action is referred to as *moving from the floor*.

A motion is usually proposed in formal language, like this:

> It is proposed that the committee investigate the possibility of engaging a communications consultant to deal with the press during the current takeover crisis.

Once a motion has been proposed, it must be *seconded*. Usually someone will offer to second the motion – give it his or her support. Sometimes, however, the chair will need to ask if there is a seconder for the motion.

16.5.7 Voting

If there is a seconder, the motion is *put to the vote*. The chair suggests formally that the committee *move to the vote*, and a show of hands is taken of those *for* the motion, followed by those *against* the motion, and finally those who wish to *abstain* or show that they are neither for nor against it.

A motion may be either *carried* or *defeated*, depending on the majority of votes. The figures should be accurately recorded in the minutes in the form:

> The motion was carried by a majority of eight votes to three.

If everyone eligible to vote votes for a motion, it is referred to as having been carried *unanimously*. If some of those eligible to vote are absent, or if all are present but some abstain and none votes against, the motion is carried *nem. con.* - short for *nemine contradicente*, meaning 'with no one disagreeing'. If votes for and votes against are equal, the chair may use his or her *casting vote*. Practice as to how this vote is cast varies with individual committees and is usually laid down in the standing orders. In some cases, the chair is free to cast his or her vote as he or she wishes; in others it is automatically cast in favour of the motion. In some committees there is a convention that the chair votes to preserve matters as they are - in other words, the chair always votes against proposed changes or abrupt departures from usual practice.

Once a motion is passed, it is referred to as a *resolution*.

16.5.8 Amendments
An amendment is a change in the wording of a proposed motion which slightly alters its meaning, often making it more specific or precise. For example, the motion above might be the subject of the following amendment:

> That the words 'for a period of no longer than one calendar month' be inserted at the end of the proposal.

Any member of a committee may propose an amendment, but it must be formally proposed and seconded in the same way as any other kind of motion. Amendments may only be proposed before a vote is taken on the motion to which they refer, however. The chair conducts a vote on the amendment and, if it is carried, the revised motion is put to the vote in the usual way.

16.5.9 Correspondence
The main business of the meeting is indicated by the agenda, and the committee works through the list of items, discussing and voting on motions as it does so. When all items on the list have been dealt with, the secretary usually announces details of any correspondence which has been received. Should any action be necessary in response to this, the committee will discuss it and vote on any resulting motions.

16.5.10 Any other business
Most agendas include this as the final item for discussion. It provides an opportunity for additional matters to be raised and discussed, but should not be used as a way of introducing important new business. Anything of importance should be placed on the agenda of the next meeting, so that members can have time to consider the subject and conduct any necessary research.

The chair is responsible for making sure that no matters of any real gravity are raised under this heading, and for suggesting that they be laid on the table or placed on the agenda of the next meeting.

16.5.11 Closing the meeting
When any other business has been dealt with, the chair moves on to fix the date of the next meeting. Often this is dictated by the standing orders, which lay

down the frequency with which meetings are to be held. When all the members are in agreement over the date, the chair then *declares the meeting closed at* the exact time when business ceased.

16.6 Conclusion

The procedures for a formal committee meeting are used to varying extents for all kinds of meetings, from those of boards of directors to full meetings of employees or shareholders. Every committee, however, has its own particular approach to the way it organizes its affairs, although the fundamental principles remain the same in most circumstances. Even meetings which are far less formal, and consist of only a small number of colleagues coming together to discuss a particular business venture, retain elements of the same structure: one person usually acts as chair, and there is a clearly defined – if unwritten – agenda and some record of the meeting, perhaps in the form of a memo or letter confirming agreements reached.

By far the best way of getting to know how committees work is to become involved in one, taking part in discussion and gaining experience in writing minutes. This will help you to learn the procedures involved, which play an integral part in the communications of organizations of all kinds.

16.7 Quick questions

1 Explain the following terms:

   (a) quorum;
   (b) *ultra vires*;
   (c) to adjourn *sine die*;
   (d) to pass *nem. con.*

2 What are minutes? Who writes them? How do they differ from a word-by-word record of a meeting?

3 Name the three functions of every committee member.

4 List four duties of a committee chair.

16.8 Longer exercises

1 Prepare a notice of meeting and a chair's agenda for a meeting of a committee with which you are familiar.

2 Farming Friends Ltd, situated in Lobham, Surrey, has just taken over another company called Dell Farming Ltd, based in Yarby, Yorshire. This takeover was financed by Finssos Yhtyma Oy., Helsinki, Finland, the parent company of Farming Friends Ltd. You work for the Managing Director of Farming Friends, Mr J. Holmes, and the General Manager, Mr

T. Harris. A special meeting for Farming Friends' staff only is to be held on Thursday 13 February at 1.30 p.m. in the Board Room at the offices of Farming Friends Ltd. The topics to be discussed are: a general outline of the takeover and the reasons for it; details of the range of products to be marketed under Farming Friends Ltd, and those which will be marketed separately by Dell Farming Ltd; the implications this will have for all staff and the effects of marketing strategies on administrative procedures; the likelihood of redundancies and possible promotions; and the likelihood of relocation of staff.

Write the agenda for the special meeting.

(RSA, Communication in business II (part))

3   At the above meeting, the following emerged as probabilities: four out of the six Farming Friends' sales staff could be made redundant and Dell Farming staff would market all products; all staff would be reporting to the Yarby office and the Managing Director of Dell Farming Ltd (Mr Andrews) might be in overall command. The Farming Friends clerical staff and administrative staff would either be made redundant or have to relocate to Yarby (although the latter possibility seemed unlikely to be offered). The administrative and clerical staff at Yarby would not be promoted but would undertake an increased workload, and the administrative staff at Lobham would like to relocate to Yarby.

It was decided, therefore, that an immediate telex be sent to the parent company, Finssos Yhtyma Oy., putting forward the staff's anxiety concerning the effects of the takeover. Mr J. Holmes would send the telex, and the names of Mr Harris and Ms T. Stephenson (Chief Sales Representative) would also appear on the telex.

These notes have been passed to you by the General Manager who has asked you to put suitably selected information in brief minutes of the meeting. He has not recorded the information in the order in which it was discussed.

Write the minutes of the meeting; you may group the ideas together as appropriate, or keep to the agenda item numbers as in your answer to question 2 above.

(RSA, Communication in business II (part))

4   Write an article of no more than 200 words for your company magazine on 'How to be a super secretary in meetings'.

5   From the chairman's agenda opposite write up the minutes of the meeting, and write a paragraph explaining who signs them and when.

(ICM, Business communications)

BELLCO MARKETING PLC

Chairman's Agenda
For the Board of Directors Meeting held at the registered
offices of the company at West Mill, Newtown, on Friday 31
October 1986 at 1100 hours.

	Items	Chairman's notes
1	Apologies for Absence Mr Green is in Kuala Lumpur, Mr Brown is in hospital.	Messrs White, Bluett, Chan, Fuad & Ray there.
2	Minutes of Last Meeting Chan intimated that he DID send apology but this was not noted in Minutes.	Altered.
3	Matters Arising. Item 4 - Mayor's Office confirms that Town Hall will be available for December 14.	Get sec to make definite booking.
4	Company Logo. Should we appoint Godfrey's Agency to design new logo?	Prop Bluett, Sec Fuad, RESOLVED.
5	Display stand at East of England Show. Should this be booked for 1987 - we missed out this year?	Prop Ray, Sec White, RESOLVED. Fee £690.
6	Award of Long Service Certificate and gifts to N Whiteside (Accounts - 20 years) and S Harris (Canteen - 25 years).	RESOLVED. At Dec 14 Staff Dance. Colour TV Whiteside and video recorder Harris.
7	Moving Western Region's offices on expiry of lease. 91 Bristol Road, Exeter, Devon - should be fully operative by end of January.	RESOLVED. Try for completion by Dec 21 though.
8	Appointment of Eastern Trading Co of Kuala Lumpur as sole agents.	RESOLVED. Green to be told by telex immediately.
9	Flexible working hours at head offices. Should we go ahead?	RESOLVED. Unions agree. Commence Feb 1, 1987.
10	Date of Next Meeting. Friday 28th November? 11.00 hours.	AGREED.
11	Any Other Business.	None.

Information technology and communication

17.1 Introduction

Information technology has been with us for longer than many people realize. The typewriter is an early example of technology applied to the processing of information – a mechanical device producing letters and other documents more quickly and more legibly than is possible by hand. As it is used today, however, the term 'information technology' has a much more precise meaning: the storage, processing and retrieval of information by means of electronic technology, in particular computers and advanced telecommunications.

Electronic devices of various kinds are already an essential part of our lives. We may be woken by the sounds of our favourite music played on a cassette-player programmed to start at a certain time in the morning. For breakfast, we might have some toast prepared to just the right shade of brown by a toaster with a sophisticated electronic monitoring device. We might do the washing, using a machine which offers a range of programs for washing, rinsing, spinning and even drying, all controlled by computer technology. Later in the day, we might pop out to the bank, where a cash dispenser will hand out money and debit it from our account on the bank's central computer system.

These are simple examples of information technology in use in the everyday world. It is in the fields of business and administration, however, that IT is having the most striking and far-reaching effects. Tasks previously done by hand, in what are known as 'manual systems', can now often be done much more quickly and efficiently by electronic means. This has changed the way people work in offices, and will doubtless cause many more changes in the future. Before looking at some of these changes, though, we will first consider the main forms of information technology in use in business communication.

17.2 Technology in the office

Most modern offices make use of computers in some way. The extent to which they are used and the purposes for which they are employed will depend on the nature of the business and the kinds of computers available.

17.2.1 Kinds of computers

The most commonly used business computers are *microcomputers*. These consist of a keyboard, a screen or visual display unit (VDU) on which data is displayed, and a central processing unit (CPU) – the heart of the computer where the actual processing is done. They are also known as *desk-top* computers since they are small enough to fit on top of a desk. Microcomputers may be used for wordprocessing as well as a variety of other activities such as financial calculations and company record-keeping. Although they are very versatile in terms of the functions they can perform, they are only capable of accommodating one user at a time.

Fig. 17.1 A microcomputer with keyboard and printer

Minicomputers are larger in size and storage capacity than micros, and can deal with up to 50 users at a time. They can be used to process volumes of information sufficient for the operations of all but the very largest companies or government departments, and for this reason are often run by medium-sized companies.

The largest computers – in terms of both size and storage capacity – are *mainframes*. These are large, complex machines which look rather like fridge-freezers from the outside. Mainframes need to be kept in a special room, with their own power supply and air-conditioning unit. They are capable of storing

Fig. 17.2 A mainframe computer with drives for exchangeable disks in the foreground

and processing vast amounts of data – the names, addresses and personal details on every driver's licence in the UK, for example. They can also run very complex programs, such as those for the design of cars and aerospace equipment. Mainframes are costly to instal and to run, and require highly qualified professional staff to maintain and operate them. Not surprisingly, such computers are usually to be found only in the very largest companies.

17.2.2 Computer software
Computer hardware – the machines themselves – depends heavily on software – the coded instructions or *programs* which tell a computer what tasks to perform. The software for microcomputers usually takes the form of *floppy disks* – circles of plastic which record data as magnetic impulses. They may hold programs which tell the computer how to work – as a wordprocessor, for example, or as a spreadsheet for recording and analysing figures – and they may also be used to store the documents or other information produced during the operation of these programs (see section 17.7). *Hard disks* can be used to enter and record information in a similar way, but have a much larger capacity. They are built into the casing of the computer, whereas floppy disks are entered into the computer's *disk drive* every time they are used. Some computers are fed data on magnetic tape – similar to that used in a tape- or cassette-recorder, but on a larger scale – but disks are now the major means of entering and storing information.

17.2.3 Input and output devices

Whether a computer uses floppy or hard disks, the main way of entering or *inputting* new data is by means of the keyboard. Some computers incorporate a device called an *optical character reader*, which enables them to 'read' printed material. In others, drawings or graphics can be produced on the screen by means of a 'mouse' – a sensor whose movements across the top of the desk are reproduced on the VDU. The most advanced computers now feature voice recognition facilities: when programmed to receive a particular voice, they will carry out simple tasks in response to certain key words.

Fig. 17.3 A microcomputer with (*clockwise*) additional disk drive, mouse and keyboard

Most computers display input data on a VDU, which is invaluable while the data is being processed, but does not provide a tangible record. To produce a printed or *hard* copy, a printer is required. Modern computer printers can output high-quality documents in seconds using laser technology, and even the cheaper daisy-wheel and dot-matrix printers can produce good quality documents very quickly. Its extremely fast printing speed is one of the greatest advantages of the wordprocessor in the modern office.

17.2.4 Self-standing computers and networks

Microcomputers can be used independently or as part of a linked system or *network*. In many offices, each executive will have an independent desk-top or personal computer (PC), with its own printer, which will perform a wide variety of functions. A more efficient use in many circumstances is to connect these individual *workstations* to form a network, which is then linked to a central store of information or *database* (see section 17.7) held in a minicomputer or a mainframe. Any network user can call up data held on the central database, taking what is needed into the memory of his or her own unit, processing it, and returning the updated or revised version to the database. In this way, duplication of data is avoided and updated or new data is instantly available to all individuals and departments who need it.

17.2.5 The integrated office

In the modern office, a computer can be used for a range of applications, such as:

- recording orders, invoices and despatch of goods;
- storing staff records;
- filing data of all sorts for instant access;
- producing letters and all kinds of business documents;
- sending messages and documents within a company;
- conducting meetings between people in different parts of the country;
- communicating with organizations in different parts of the world;
- keeping up to date with the latest business developments.

In the following sections of this unit, these and other applications are discussed separately. The great advantage of the modern office, however, is that functions previously performed by different people or departments may now be conducted by one operator at his or her workstation. Section 17.9 will provide an example of how this integrated approach to information technology might work in an office setting.

17.3 Wordprocessing

A wordprocessor is a device for the production, editing and storage of documents – in essence, a combination of a typewriter and a microcomputer. Most often, wordprocessing takes place on a microcomputer used with wordprocessing software (see section 17.2.2). To produce a document, the operator types text on the keyboard, using the keys both to create letters and to instruct the computer how to present them – as capitals or small letters, in lines of a certain length or in different typefaces, for example. The text is displayed on a VDU as it is typed, and at the same time it is stored in the computer's short-term memory. If the operator makes a mistake or wishes to change the layout, he or she can alter the text, adding to it or deleting items as necessary. When satisfied with the text on the screen, the operator presses a key to store the completed document on the computer's disk. Finally, at the touch of another key, the operator can set the printer in action to produce as many printed or 'hard' copies of the document as are needed, on the company's headed letter paper if required. The finished document can be stored on disk almost indefinitely, to be used again and again.

A wordprocessor has many advantages over a conventional typewriter.

- Errors can be corrected on screen so that – in theory, at least – there should never be any errors in the finished document.
- Many wordprocessors have a spelling–check programme, which will check the spelling of the whole document far more quickly than would be possible by reading.
- The 'find and replace' facility can be used to replace one word with another whenever it appears in a document. For example, if on rereading a document you decide against the word 'discriminating', you can locate every use of it and replace it with 'thoughtful' in an operation which takes only seconds.
- Sections of the text can be marked off to make a 'block' and moved to any part of the document.
- Words or phrases which are used frequently can often be entered into a special memory and recalled at the touch of a single key.
- Revisions of text – perhaps of a complex legal contract, or the text of a new company brochure – can be made without having to retype the whole document.

The capacity to store and edit documents saves a great deal of time. Standard letters (see section 12.10) can be composed, stored and called up on screen when needed. Slight changes can be made to make a letter more personal, and spaces can be left for addresses or other details to be inserted as appropriate. Standard openings, complimentary closures, sentences and even whole paragraphs which are used frequently may be stored and incorporated into a document at the touch of a key: one estimate has suggested that the text in some 70 per cent of all documents sent out from sales offices had been used previously.

Where the same letter is to be sent to a long list of people, the names and addresses can be entered on a *database* held on another disk (see section 17.7) and the database can be combined with the letter in an operation known as a *mailmerge*. The letter can then be printed out, with the appropriate name, address and salutation, and will look as if it is a personal letter sent only to the receiver. Few readers are taken in by such letters, but the process does have the advantage that a large quantity of identical letters can be produced quickly and accurately. The data on the database can, of course, be stored and reused on other occasions and for other purposes.

17.4 Telex and electronic mail

An increasing number of companies are now using wordprocessors or micro-computers linked to a telephone line to send messages to other companies, or to branches of their own organization in different parts of the country. This facility, known as electronic mail or EMail, will soon completely replace the older telex system, in which two keyboards are linked by telephone line to provide a typed message for the receiver.

Fig. 17.4 A telex machine with text-editing facilities

In the telex system, an operator dials the telex number of the person he or she wishes to contact and, on receiving an acceptance code – often given automatically – types a message on to his or her keyboard. The message is then transmitted in the form of electronic impulses along the telephone line, decoded and printed on the receiver's machine. Thus it is possible to send a message with the speed of the telephone and the permanence of a letter. A disadvantage, however, is that telex machines – also known as teleprinters or telewriters – have a smaller range of characters than a normal typewriter, so that documents can only be typed in upper-case (capital) letters, with the standard punctuation symbols and numbers.

Electronic mail is similar to telex, except that the telephone line links two computers. The sender types a message which is entered into the memory of the receiver's computer. It may then be displayed on the screen, and a hard copy produced by the receiver's printer if he or she wishes.

Both systems allow messages to be sent quickly to parts of the world in different time zones without the need to wait for an appropriate time or the next working day. This has considerable advantages for business organizations, saving time and money and dispensing with the need to calculate time differences. For example, a manufacturer in Sydney, Australia, can send a message to a designer in London, England, knowing that it will be waiting for the designer when he or she comes into the office the next day. Both systems also make the most economical use of telephone lines, since there is no need to track down and speak to the actual individual for whom the message is intended.

Electronic mail has one advantage over many telex machines. As the text is entered into the memory of the receiver's computer, it can be altered and edited by the receiver on screen and returned to the sender straight away. This allows complex documents such as contracts, press releases and even the texts of books to be exchanged and revised without needing to be retyped. Both parties will also have the text of the document stored on disk, in a far more permanent form than that offered by telex.

Advice on writing telexes and international telemessages is given in section 11.7.

17.5 Fax systems

Fax – or facsimile – machines work on a similar principle to telex and EMail, but they resemble two photocopiers linked by a telephone line, rather than two keyboards. The sender places a document on a fax machine, which scans it electronically and converts it into a series of electronic impulses which are fed into a telephone line. At the other end of the line, a compatible fax machine converts the impulses back into images, and a replica – or facsimile – of the original document is produced. Fax machines have two major disadvantages. First, you need to make sure that the receiver's machine will be able to accept messages from your own. As the fax system becomes more widespread, equipment is becoming standardized, but it is still possible that a machine will be unable to transmit at its usual speed due to incompatibility with the receiver's machine. Secondly, the quality of material sent by fax is sometimes less than perfect – although, again, quality is constantly improving with technical development.

Fig. 17.5 A fax machine being used to transmit a circuit diagram

This service is of especial use where drawings, maps and diagrams have to be transmitted quickly. If, for example, a fashion reporter wants to send sketches of the latest collections from Paris to London, he or she can use a fax machine and get the drawings there in time for the next edition. Some fax machines store the information they receive and will only reveal it to password-holders, which means that confidential documents – such as drawings of new components which must be kept away from competitors – can be sent by fax in the knowledge that they will be safe from unauthorized receivers. This is not always the case with telex, where messages are often sent when the receiver's equipment is unattended.

Though fax is used mainly for transmitting illustrations rather than text – since it offers neither storage facilities nor the potential for editing and returning text – it can be used instead of electronic mail where the main requirement is for a printed copy of a document.

17.6 Electronic conferencing

Many companies with regional and international offices are concerned at the time that is lost by having top employees travel hundreds of miles to attend meetings. There are more constructive things for people to do than sit in traffic jams or admire scenery from a train – and, as well as the loss of time, there is the strain of travelling to be considered.

Electronic conferencing makes it possible for meetings to be held between people at different ends of the country or even in different parts of the world, by the use of television cameras and receivers, computer technology and telephone lines. A camera at one location produces an image of one of the people present, which is then converted into electronic impulses and fed into a telephone line. At the other end of the line, the impulses are converted into their original form and fed to a monitor – a conventional television screen. There is both a camera and a monitor at every participating location, so that all concerned can see and hear one another. The quality of the picture produced is somewhat poorer than that of a regular television transmission, but it is perfectly adequate for its purpose. Holo conferencing, in which a three-dimensional holographic image of each participant is generated at each site, is currently being developed, although it may not be in use for many years.

So, is it likely that, in a few years' time, the whole business community will never move from its VDUs? The answer is, probably, no. There will always be occasions when it is more tactful or courteous to discuss something with a client or colleague in person, and it is also far more difficult to gauge someone's reactions from a poor-quality, two-dimensional image. Although conferencing is a valuable tool, it does not altogether replace the need for personal meetings.

17.7 Data storage and retrieval

Most companies make use of their computers to store information in what is known as a *database*. A database is really only another name for a large collection of information – a kind of computerized reference library. Like a reference library, a database is carefully organized so that any piece of information can be retrieved easily and quickly from a mass of details.

Companies use database to store records of:

- names and addresses of customers;
- staff career progress;
- details of suppliers and consultants;
- specifications of goods ordered;
- current stock position;
- progress of competitors;

and any other data of importance to the company's area of business.

How does a computer find an item of information on a database? Imagine a library catalogue, structured to include general subject classifications, each containing a series of subject headings, under which the titles of individual books are listed. Under the general heading of 'History', for example, you would find the subject heading 'Second World War', and under that a list of books on World War Two. In a computer database, a *file* is the equivalent of a general classification; a *record* the equivalent of a subject; and a *field* the equivalent of a book title – or the smallest piece of information in the catalogue.

To find an item of data in a database, the operator must first *access* – or call up on screen – the appropriate file and select the appropriate record. Assume that you are trying to find the National Insurance number of a former employee called Joanna Smith. You know that the database file on former employees includes the following fields:

- surname;
- initials;
- dates with company;
- position;
- employee number;
- National Insurance number.

Having accessed the file on former employees, you must find the record for Joanna Smith. First, the computer will need to know the surname. The question 'Surname?' may appear on the screen – to which you will enter the response 'Smith' – or you may simply be required to enter the information 'Surname = Smith'. The computer will search the database and might find that there are ten Smiths who have worked for the company, so you would then enter the initial – 'J' for 'Joanna'. If the database contains several J. Smiths, you will have to go to the next field – dates with company. The process will continue until Joanna Smith is firmly identified. The computer can then be asked to give her full record, and you can access the field which gives her National Insurance number.

Databases are often stored on hard disk, as part of the central store in a network. It is also possible to keep records of staff, customers, orders, stock – in fact, anything which is related to a company's business – on a series of floppy disks. One disk can hold the equivalent of a vast number of sheets of paper, and as the most commonly used disks are 5¼ inches in diameter and wafer thin, they represent an immense advantage over conventional methods of document storage. Filing cabinets and even filing departments can be replaced by a series of disks and the appropriate storage boxes.

Databases eliminate the risk of errors and increase the speed and efficiency of a company's operations. One sheet of paper inadvertently inserted into the wrong file in the wrong drawer of a filing cabinet can cause chaos in a manual records system, but this kind of error is not possible with a computer storage system.

Further advantages are apparent in those organizations which use a network with a central database. A linked system of this kind allows a large number of people to have access to the same information at the same time, instead of having to wait for a file to be returned to a filing cabinet, or a memo or report to be produced, copied and circulated. Information is instantly available, whatever the distance between departments, company branches or warehouses. If each user also has the facility to update the information in the database, the database will not only be easy to use, it will also be completely up to date.

Correctly used and maintained, a database can therefore add greatly to the efficiency of a business organization, whatever its size. Furthermore, because data is so easily available, employees can concentrate on using that information more efficiently.

17.8 Videotex systems

There are various systems in operation which allow the business user access to information held on a central database belonging to an outside organization. These are known collectively as *videotex systems*. Some – known as *teletext systems* – are broadcast television-based services. Others depend on the use of telephone lines linked to either a television screen or, in some cases, a computer terminal, and are called *viewdata systems*.

Both teletext and viewdata work in much the same way. The user has a *keypad* – resembling the remote control of a television set and often integrated with it. In the integrated office, a standard keyboard will often fulfil this function. By pressing the appropriate buttons according to an on-screen index or *menu*, he or she can call up data on to the screen. Data is arranged in sections, each of which is designed to fit the area of the screen and is called a *page*.

17.8.1 Teletext systems

These are the public television systems such as Ceefax (BBC), Oracle (ITV) and Fortel (Channel 4). They consist of vast numbers of pages of data, on subjects such as weather, news, finance, gardening and other recreational and educational matters, which are transmitted alongside the regular television signal and decoded by special equipment in the receiver's television set. Teletext systems are rather limited in scope for business organizations, as they are aimed at the home user and do not allow subscribers to respond to the data in any way. As a rapid reference source, however, they can be useful.

The main cost of teletext is in the hire or initial purchase of the receiving equipment, other than which it costs no more to use than a normal colour television.

17.8.2 Viewdata systems

Like many of the electronic devices discussed in this unit, viewdata systems depend on the use of telephone lines for the transmission of information, in this case linked to a television transmitter. The first system of this sort in the UK was British Telecom's Prestel. This provides news, information, and a business service, which allows organizations to broadcast details of their own products and services. The major difference with this type of service is that it is 'interactive' – that is, the user can make contact with the organization supplying the data shown on the screen. It is possible, for example, to call up information on flight departures and book a seat, or to compare the prices of office furniture and place an order with a particular firm, or even to make a donation to a charity, simply by using the keypad to access the appropriate subject, and then the appropriate organization, and finally the appropriate service.

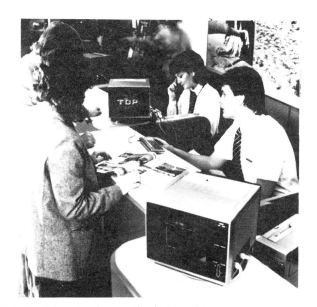

Fig. 17.6 A viewdata system in operation in a travel agency

Many professional organizations have their own viewdata systems which provide data and enable information to be exchanged. The Institute of Grocery Distribution, for example, has its own network known as FIND (Food Industry

News and Data), which provides information about the prices of food, its availability in the major markets, and related matters. The Association of British Travel Agents operates a similar system which enables travel agents to obtain up-to-the-minute information on holiday and flight vacancies and to reserve seats and hotel rooms instantly by electronic means (see ·fig. 17.6). Many national and international finance markets, too, have their own system of computerized dealing. Since 1986, organizations throughout the country have been able to buy and sell shares and securities on the Stock Exchange in London by linking in with the Exchange's central computer system.

Viewdata systems are not cheap to use, and for that reason they are mainly restricted to members of certain professional bodies or organizations in related areas of business, such as travel agents or food retailers. There are three elements involved in the cost:

(a) capital cost of the equipment – VDUs and 'dedicated' telephone lines which are used solely to receive the service;
(b) subscription to the information service – charges vary;
(c) cost of using the telephone lines – charged by time and distance like the standard telephone bill.

17.9 The integrated office: a case-study

As suggested earlier in this unit, the individual devices discussed here may be used separately in an office setting, but are more likely to be used in conjunction with each other as part of an integrated communication system. The following case-study illustrates how an integrated office might work in practice.

Ahmed works as a product development officer for a firm of electronic instrument manufacturers based in Birmingham. He has been asked to prepare a report and then address a meeting on the possible development of a sophisticated new electronic telephone. His first task is one of background research. Using his desk-top computer, he accesses the viewdata systems to which his company subscribes to see what information is available on recent developments in telecommunications and the state of the telecommunications market. His computer is also linked to his own company's network, so he can also access the company archives for information on similar products or related research projects. He recalls working on a telephone system some time previously, and locates the relevant floppy disk in his own storage boxes. He enters this into his computer and quickly scans through the data on screen.

Next, Ahmed needs to contact the firm's marketing department, which is based at the London office, for initial views on possible markets for the new telephone. Using the electronic-mail facility on his personal computer, he is able to send a detailed memo to the marketing manager, and within a short time receives a reply to his queries. The marketing manager includes with her memo several documents which she feels will be useful in drawing up a report. Ahmed reads these on his VDU, and prints out several copies of one document which he wishes to distribute at the meeting.

The questions of finance and resources have to be dealt with next. Further EMail messages are sent to the finance department and the personnel officer. The finance department is able to tell Ahmed how much remains in the research and development budget for his division. The company database of suppliers reveals a likely source of the necessary components for the telephone. Ahmed decides to find out if the supplier is prepared to offer a reduced price for bulk orders. The supplier is based in Hong Kong, and is having trouble with his own computer network, but suggests that Ahmed send a formal proposal by fax. Ahmed prepares the proposal on screen, prints it out on company headed paper and sends it to Hong Kong on the company's fax machine. A favourable reply is received within a very short time. Using the spreadsheet on his PC, Ahmed can now prepare some costings for the telephone, based on the figures from the finance department and the supplier.

Meanwhile, the personnel officer has checked the employee database and provides a list of development engineers with relevant experience. She has also used her code number to gain access to confidential files on staff wages, and is able to provide Ahmed with a rough indication of salary costs for the project. He amends his estimates accordingly.

Ahmed remembers that the meeting to discuss the project has yet to be organized. He rapidly accesses the company diary which is held on the central database and, entering the names of those who will be attending, is presented with a choice of possible times when all will be free. He then asks the computer to find a room for the meeting, and books this on the computer. Finally, he writes a short memo, indicates to the computer who is to receive it, and leaves the electronic-mail system to distribute the message.

Ahmed now turns to preparing his report. He is glad that he took the trouble to prepare a report format – with headings and frequently-used sentences – on his wordprocessor the previous week: now, he need do no more than type up the report. Since he plans to circulate copies of the report to those present at the meeting, and knows that few of them have time to read lengthy documents, he switches to the graphics function and includes some pie charts and a graph to illustrate his more complex points. He is relieved that the company has recently invested in a laser printer which enables him to produce an attractive document of this kind – it may well sway the meeting in his favour.

17.10 Electronic data and confidentiality

As we have seen, databases make possible the collection and storage of vast amounts of information, to which both authorized and unauthorized users may have instant access. In response to uneasiness about the amount of information on individuals which is kept on databases, and the serious consequences which could result from the circulation of inaccurate or incorrect data, many countries have introduced legislation to control the use of such information and to establish certain rights for the individual.

In the United Kingdom, the Data Protection Act 1984 provides that information on individuals that is kept on computer files must:

- be obtained lawfully;
- be kept for a specified purpose;
- be held no longer than is necessary for that purpose;
- be updated regularly, where necessary;
- be disclosed only to specified parties.

Those who keep such information also have a responsibility to see that it does not fall into unauthorized hands, and to divulge the data on a particular individual to him or her on request, and sometimes on payment of a fee. Any information found to be incorrect must be amended or deleted from the database, and in some cases the individual may claim compensation for associated damage.

In the context of the Act, 'information' is seen to include facts and opinions, but not statements of intent on the part of the user – for example, an employer's plans for promotion of an employee. The Act also does not cover information held on organizations.

Data on individuals must be registered with the Data Protection Registrar, to whom individuals can also refer when data is withheld from them. This legislation brings the UK into line with the Council of Europe Convention on Data Protection.

The main effect of the Data Protection Act will be to impose tighter controls on the unauthorized storage of, access to, and use of information about individuals. The effect of the Act can best be illustrated by an example. Hannah Marshall has applied for a job with IMS Production Services. At her interview she is offered the post she wants, dependent on IMS receiving a favourable reference from her present employers, ABS International. A few days later, Hannah receives a letter from IMS regretting that they are unable to confirm their offer, as the reference from ABS International is unsatisfactory.

Hannah is very surprised to learn that ABS has not supported her application: she has always received favourable reports on her work for the company, and her supervisor has already expressed regret at her leaving. Hannah approaches the personnel department at ABS International and asks permission to see a copy of the records kept on her in the company's computerized storage system. She is denied access to the data. Hannah knows that under the Data Protection Act she is entitled to see any records kept about her on computer file, and she therefore makes an official written request for access. When ABS International fails to reply within the allocated 40 days, Hannah contacts the Data Protection Registrar to lodge a complaint. The Registrar is satisfied that Hannah has sent her request to the proper address referring to the proper register entry for ABS International, and that ABS does hold information about Hannah which it ought to give her. He serves ABS with an enforcement notice requiring them to comply with her request for information. ABS decides not to appeal against the notice which takes effect 28 days after it was served. If the company now fails to supply the information it will be committing a criminal offence. Hannah finally gains access to her file, which turns out to be seriously inaccurate.

Although Hannah has now lost the chance of the job with IMS Production Services, she finds that she may be entitled to some compensation from ABS for the consequences of their actions, and she decides to pursue this through the courts.

Everyone involved in business should be aware of the Act, as it affects the ways in which electronic data is collected, stored and used. Before compiling a database on its employees, for example, a company will have to register; and once the database has been set up, any employee will be entitled, by law, to see his or her record. This not only represents an important advance in the management of information, it can also improve communication in the workplace. Giving employees the opportunity to see the information held about them and to make sure that it is correct will improve trust and understanding, and so develop an atmosphere in which communication becomes more relaxed and thus more effective.

17.11 The effects of information technology

We have already mentioned some of the most obvious effects of the revolution in information technology. It allows many tasks to be performed much more quickly and with greater accuracy, cutting costs and reducing the risk of errors; it enables personal letters to be produced simply, thus providing the receiver with a better image of the sender; it can reduce the need for travel to personal meetings; it increases the security of the transfer of confidential documents; and it means that changes in a company's financial or stock position can be recorded and circulated with the minimum of paperwork.

As these changes occur, we must be careful not to overlook two important factors: however efficient they may be, electronic devices depend on the accuracy of the data they are fed, and electronically produced documents – however rapidly printed and conveyed – depend on the precision of the language in which they are written. Unless the text on a VDU, the message in the electronic-mail slot, or the document in the fax machine are clearly written – following the guidelines in Units 4 and 5 – all the advantages of advanced technology will be wasted.

In the same way, simply because the text on a VDU can be edited, there is no reason to suppose that it always will be. Many people feel that the simplicity with which documents can now be composed and altered has led to reports and letters which are poorly planned and sloppy in expression. Everyone who uses a computer to produce even the simplest letter needs to be just as aware of the principles of good communication as the Victorian clerk who used a quill pen and a sheet of rag paper. Language and the means of communication may have changed, but the need for precision and clarity is just as strong.

One major effect of the IT revolution has been on the way in which people work. New skills are now demanded by employers. The ability to type – now grandly called 'keyboarding' – is essential for today's managers and executives, rather than being relevant only to the secretary. People without keyboard skills will be denied access to all but the simplest IT devices – that is, until a future generation of desk-top computers emerges which can produce written text from dictation. It is likely, too, that in the future many more people will be able to work from home, staying in contact with their employer and colleagues by linking in to a central computer and making greater use of communication facilities such as telex, electronic mail and answerphones. Along the same lines, the growth in the use of radiopagers and bleepers in recent years has meant that a businessperson is never out of reach of important clients or customers, and the advent of cellular carphones has carried this ease of contact still further.

Information technology has also affected the number of people who work. The demand for copy-typists has decreased, as documents can be produced far more quickly by electronic printer. The speed and efficiency of the word-processor has also meant that many jobs have been combined. Typists and secretaries now tend to take on the work of receptionists as well as their own, and sometimes some accounting tasks as well. With the advent of databases to which all members of an office have direct access, the need for filing clerks has also largely disappeared.

Information technology has certainly done away with the more menial office tasks, but it has also done away with employment opportunities for many people without providing a ready alternative. Other job functions will follow these into oblivion, as customer sales, servicing and marketing are increasingly taken over by computers, and as companies, customers and clients communicate increasingly by electronic mail.

The effects of information technology on the wider world of communication have also been considerable. With a microcomputer, a suitable software package and a laser printer, the business user can now produce high-quality printed material such as sales leaflets, company reports or political pamphlets in a process known as 'desk-top publishing'. The advent of accurate, reliable programs for producing graphics also means that business is far more aware of the advantages of graphic communication. Pie charts, bar charts and graphs can be produced very simply with the appropriate software and these, along with training and promotional videos, are having a considerable impact on business communication.

The nature of reference sources is also changing. Many specialized journals are now published on disk to save printing costs, and many directories and reference books are published in disk as well as book form, for the convenience of computer users. For example, the *Oxford English Dictionary* is now available on a series of floppy disks, which are more convenient and less expensive – albeit less imposing – than the original twelve-volume set. For the publisher, there are additional advantages: the computer database can be readily updated and it can also be used as the source for a range of smaller dictionaries, since data is more easily located and processed by computer.

Many exciting and far-reaching developments doubtless still await us. But we should also be aware of the potential dangers of information technology. Already, doubts have been raised about the health risks associated with working at a VDU for long periods. 'Sick building syndrome' is now a recognised ailment, caused by working in an environment with artificial light, fluorescent strip lighting, VDU screens and impure air. In addition, it has been suggested that the isolation of sitting alone at a workstation may have serious effects on behaviour.

Although a letter from a computer may look neater, do we really feel that it is addressed personally to us? Similarly, computers may be able to produce beautiful graphics, but are they always strictly necessary? A database may be able to store vast amounts of personal information, but how do we make sure that 'hackers' – unauthorized users – do not somehow manage to gain access to that data and use it for their own ends? Frauds such as getting a payroll program to pay money into an unauthorized account are already costing large organizations millions of pounds. How do we prevent 'computer crime' of this sort? These are questions which need to be considered seriously by everyone involved in communication. No amount of technology can prevent errors at the most important part of the system – the person who operates it.

Technology continues to develop, but the basic principles of communication remain unchanged. Knowing what to say and how to say it should remain your fundamental aims, together with ensuring that electronic technology is put to the service of those aims, rather than making users slaves to its own procedures.

17.12 Quick questions

1 Write brief descriptions of the following:

(a) wordprocessor;
(b) viewdata;
(c) electronic mail.

2 What advantages does a wordprocessor have over an electronic typewriter?

3 What advantages does a company gain from having a network of linked desk-top computers?

4 What is a fax machine, and when would you use it?

17.13 Longer exercises

1 How would you use information technology to solve the following communication problems?

(a) The directors of your company must discuss problems concerning the safety of a new product you have just launched. There are four directors, and two are out of the country at the moment.

(b) Your company frequently needs to hold departmental training courses, but it is becoming difficult to timetable these so that the trainees and the trainers are all available at a time when the company's training suite is not in use.

(c) Until recently you have employed a printer to produce your company's newsletter. Not only has this has become very expensive but the newsletter also frequently appears late. You need to produce something which is quicker and cheaper.

2 You are a trainee manager in a firm of wholesale distributors with offices in London, Birmingham, Cardiff and Southampton. Every month the managers of each office meet to discuss matters of policy and the routine running of their departments. The manager of the Birmingham branch is concerned about the amount of time spent in travelling to these meetings. She has asked you to prepare a brief report about the ways in which information technology could help to reduce travelling and improve contact between the four offices. Write the report.

3 Write an article entitled 'Developments in data storage' for inclusion in your company magazine. It should say what a database is, what it contains, and the advantages and disadvantages it has over other ways of keeping information. Use no more than 250 words.

4 Next month your company is to introduce wordprocessors to replace the old electric typewriters used in the general office. As trainee office manager, write an A4 memo to all the typists telling them when the new scheme will come into operation, reassuring them that full training will be given, and showing them how the new equipment will make their work easier and more efficient.

5 Discuss the role of modern computer technology as applied to the field of management information systems.

(IDPM, People, communication and information in organisations)

Business reference sources

18.1 Introduction

Every organization has to keep abreast of national and international affairs, in order to remain aware of the conditions affecting its workers, factors which might influence its supplies of raw materials, and any likely changes in its markets. It must also keep up to date with the latest technical developments in every area in which it operates. This may mean knowing about advances in the design of products, or in production techniques, or in the use of computers to produce an integrated database and so streamline administration.

A great array of books, periodicals, official publications and other sources of reference exists to meet this need. Although often supplemented by the data available on electronic databases (see section 17.7), the majority of such material is still presented in printed form. Knowing which source to use for each kind of information is an essential skill in business communication and forms the basis of this final unit.

18.2 Published reference sources

Publications of this kind can be classified into several groups:

(a) dictionaries and books on language usage;
(b) encyclopaedias;
(c) yearbooks;
(d) directories;
(e) official publications;
(f) newspapers and periodicals.

Although different in content and the regularity with which they appear, these sources have one thing in common: all are available to the public, either on sale or on loan through a local, national or academic library. Larger companies may well subscribe to some of these sources: smaller companies will probably rely on a library.

Two essential points need to be stressed about published reference sources. First, you should make a point of finding out where you can consult them. Spend some time simply browsing through local libraries to see what they have in stock and how it is classified, comparing various branches to see what is in each and deciding which is best suited to your needs. This will pay off when you need to find information in a hurry. Academic libraries and the collections of private companies may also be open to you, perhaps on payment of a fee or annual subscription. Once again, this will be a worthwhile investment.

Secondly, always make sure that you use the most up-to-date edition of the source in question. Using out-of-date material is not only a waste of time, it may also have serious consequences for your business. For example, incorrect data about the social policies of an overseas government to whose country you are hoping to export goods may well mean lost orders and wasted development expenditure; even an old address can mean an hour wasted trying to contact a new supplier. There is no guarantee, of course, that information in a current edition will be correct when you read it, since writing, printing and publishing the volume will have taken several months at least. But using the most recent editions of books and directories – including the loose-leaf supplements issued for many directories and annuals – will mean that such errors are kept to a minimum.

18.2.1 Dictionaries and books on language

These are fundamental sources of reference. Most efficient secretaries have a dictionary on their desk, in case they need to check what a word means or how it is spelt. Similarly, no manager or executive can afford to be without one. The standard work of reference is the complete *Oxford English Dictionary*, which runs to several volumes, but for practical purposes a smaller volume such as *Chambers' Twentieth Century Dictionary* or one of the smaller Oxford ones is adequate.

Specialist dictionaries are also available, which provide definitions of terms used in particular areas of business. A dictionary of banking or insurance terms will be useful for many businesses, and dictionaries of accounting and computer terminology almost essential. Careful use of the books relevant to your field of interest will help you to learn the specialist terms used by people in other firms with whom you will have to deal, and so make your communication more effective.

Roget's Thesaurus is widely used and differs from a dictionary in that it provides lists of words of similar or closely related meaning, classified according to subject rather than alphabetically. It is thus very useful when you wish to avoid repeating a word, or when you can think of a word which is almost what you mean but not quite right.

To use a thesaurus, you look up the word for which you need an alternative in the index at the back, which is arranged alphabetically. This will give you a numbered category or categories in which that word appears. By turning to the relevant category in the thesaurus, you can choose a suitable word from the range given.

There are numerous books on matters of expression. Fowler's *A Dictionary of Modern English Usage* gives guidance on the common problems and finer points of the language – whether to write 'syllabuses' or 'syllabi', for example. *The Complete Plain Words*, by Sir Ernest Gowers, fulfils a similar function. If you use books like these, however, do remember that language is constantly changing, and that what was written about it even two or three years ago might now be out of date.

If you are involved in editing and preparing text for printers, three publications are particularly useful. *Hart's Rules for Compositors and Readers at the University Press, Oxford* – generally known as *Hart's Rules* – is used by all professional editors. *Copy-editing: the Cambridge Handbook*, by Judith Butcher, is a clear and thorough guide. Finally, the business of checking printers' proofs can only be done properly if you use the British Standard proof-correction symbols. Butcher gives the most common ones: the full set can be obtained from the British Standards Institution.

18.2.2 Encyclopaedias

General encyclopaedias are invaluable for business research. *Encyclopaedia Britannica* gives detailed information on a wide variety of topics, and can be consulted in all public libraries. A smaller encyclopaedia such as *Pears Cyclopaedia* can be used for desk-top reference.

18.2.3 Yearbooks

Annual publications about one specific area of activity can often provide a mine of invaluable data. For example, they can tell you about the currency and main government members of any country to which you may have to export goods, or give you details of the current rates of corporation tax. You should always remember, though, that these books are revised every year. Make sure that you refer to the latest edition of the book, so that you are not working with incorrect data.

A general yearbook in wide use is *Whitaker's Almanack*. It summarizes the main events of the past year, outlines major new legislation, details the world's major countries in statistical form, and gives other information such as time zones, currencies, government departments, educational and sporting facilities, and planning regulations. It is probably the single most valuable source of instant information for the business user, apart from specialist publications.

A similar publication is *The Statesman's Year Book*. This is concerned especially with information about the major nations of the world, including their legal systems, currencies, main ministers, and other data of interest to the business user concerned with export or international trade.

Slightly different in nature are *Keesing's Contemporary Archives*. These are published weekly as well as in annual volume form, and provide a clear, unbiased summary of world news. They have the advantage that they record changes more or less as they occur, so that a revised rate of corporation tax, for example, can be noted as soon as it is introduced.

18.2.4 Directories

Unlike yearbooks, directories refer to a very specific area of activity. They, too, are updated annually and so care should be taken to ensure that the most recent edition is used. One group gives details about business organizations. The *UK Kompass Register of British Industry and Commerce* lists business organizations of every kind in the United Kingdom, along with employers' organizations and trade unions. Organized according to category of business, it is of particular use to businesses who wish to find suppliers or customers, and it also allows organizations to keep an eye on their immediate competitors in terms of size, output and profits. *Kelly's Business Directory* (formerly *Kelly's Manufacturers and Merchants Directory*) is similar, except that it lists firms alphabetically, so that it is possible only to look up companies already known to the user. Another title of this kind is *The London Chamber of Commerce and Industry Directory*.

A second group of directories covers information of value to organizations involved in international activities. The *International Year Book and Statesmen's Who's Who* and the *Year Book of World Affairs* give general information about international affairs, governmental changes and other similar matters. *Export Data: the Exporter's Year Book* gives details of import restrictions, customs practices and other matters of value for anyone wishing to export goods or services throughout the world. Finally, *Sell's British Exporters' Register and National Directory* offers details of companies involved in export trading similar to those given in *UK Kompass* and the other titles described in the last paragraph.

More specialized directories offer information specific to particular trades and industries – the *Stock Exchange Official Year Book*, the *Building Societies' Year Book*, the *Municipal Yearbook and Public Services Directory* and the *Insurance Directory and Yearbook*, for example. As soon as you become involved in communication work within an organization, you should find out which directories cover its particular areas of activity, and where you can buy or consult them. Such works contain a great deal of valuable information, and it is usually well worth your while to invest in a copy.

Perhaps not surprisingly, the communications industry produces a large number of reliable and accurate yearbooks and directories which are of value to anyone with a professional interest in communicating. *British Rate and Data (BRAD)* and *Willing's Press Guide* list newspapers and periodicals, giving addresses, circulation figures and the kind of material they publish. These provide a useful guide when you are seeking to place advertisements, to issue press releases or to gain editorial coverage of events in your organization. Press and broadcasting are both covered by the *Advertiser's Annual, Hollis Press and Public Relations Annual*, and *Benn's Media Directory*. The *Post Office Guide* gives details of current charges and practices for sending letters and parcels by post, and British Telecom publishes an annual *Products & Services* magazine.

Finally, there are the local directories which are vital to any company, but perhaps most vital to small organizations whose main trade is with other companies in the same locality. *Kelly's Directories* are available for most towns in the UK, as are *Thomson Local Directories*. Relevant volumes of *The Phone Book* and *Yellow Pages* for the local area are given to all telephone subscribers, but investing in copies for nearby regions is often worthwhile. Ordnance Survey maps, and guidebooks published by the AA, Baedeker and other leading companies may also be of use, especially in planning international business trips and conferences.

18.2.5 Official publications

So far we have considered only material published by trade organizations and commercial publishers. In addition, valuable reference material is available from government departments, either for sale or for free distribution among relevant bodies. The Government Statistical Service booklet 'Government Statistics; a brief guide to sources' outlines the major sources of official inform- ation. *Key Data* and the economic bulletins issued by the Treasury, along with publications of the Business Statistics Office, will be particularly relevant to the business reader. More complex data is provided by the *Annual Abstract of Statistics*, which gives, for example, the average income and expenditure of various sections of the population. The information it contains is of use in many ways to all kinds of business organizations. For example, it will list the number of video-cassettes sold in the past year, which will be of vital importance to a company producing video-cassettes or other video accessories.

Social Trends is a volume of essays which analyse these statistics to show how people's behaviour and attitudes are changing. It will reveal, for example, the average size of family, or the expenditure on certain items of food or drink. Data of this kind is esential when contemplating the launch of a new product, or planning cash-flow projections for the coming year.

In addition to those publications issued by the UK government, many inter- national organizations provide volumes of statistics or other data. Large bodies such as the International Monetary Fund (IMF) and the World Health Organi- zation (WHO) publish annual reports which are particularly useful to multi- national companies; the *Yearbook of the United Nations* offers data in a more easily accessible form, bringing together information on all member nations in one volume. Slightly more limited in scope are the reports and other publi- cations of the Organization for Economic Co-operation and Development (OECD) and the European Economic Community (EEC). All are available in larger public and academic reference libraries.

18.2.6 Newspapers and periodicals

Most of the sources discussed so far appear annually. This is inevitable where their preparation involves the collation of large amounts of information and statistics. For more immediate information, however, the business community can consult publications of various kinds which are produced at quarterly, monthly, weekly or even daily intervals. The main advantage with these publi- cations is that they can carry the latest information on a subject, particularly in the fields of research and development, where findings are often published as soon as they become available. A drawback in this respect is, of course, that initial reports may well be proved inaccurate if further information comes to light at a later date.

Whitaker's Almanack has an extensive list of trade, business and professional journals, in which it is possible to find periodicals covering almost every area of activity. Journals of particular interest to the business reader include *The Economist*, the quarterly reviews issued by the clearing banks, *UK Press Gazette, Campaign* (the journal of the advertising industry), *Banking World, Accountancy Age* and the *Petroleum Times*. These should be supplemented by the *Local Government Chronicle*, which covers local politics in England and Wales, and *Parliamentary Debates (Commons)* – better known as *Hansard* – which provides a transcript of the proceedings of the House of Commons.

Daily newspapers are an obvious but essential reference source. *The Financial Times* is usually regarded as the best source of daily information about the Stock Exchange, commodity markets and international exchange rates. Similar information is given by the other 'quality' newspapers – *The Times, The Daily Telegraph, The Guardian* and *The Independent*. Data from any of the daily papers should, however, be checked against other publications, since inaccuracies inevitably occur in day-to-day reporting. This does not, however, apply to statistical data such as Stock Exchange reports reproduced in them.

18.3 Private reference sources

All of the material described so far is widely available to the public. In addition, however, there is a large amount of information which is available only to members of particular trade organizations or even individual companies.

18.3.1 Publications of professional organizations

Bodies such as the Stock Exchange, the Institute of the Motor Industry and the World Bureau of Metal Statistics regularly supply data to their members. All such data is confidential, and available only to those organizations who are genuinely involved in the relevant area of activity.

Other organizations supply data to a wider range of companies on payment of a subscription. Prominent among them is the Economist Intelligence Unit, which offers data on changes in the economy which will affect markets and their growth.

18.3.2 Archival sources

This is the name given to the documents amassed by an individual company or organization during its commercial activities. Such material is usually confidential, and may be available only to be a restricted group of employees within an organization, such as those working in research and development departments. A company archive may consist of reports about new products or items under development, market research reports, files of correspondence, minutes of meetings, files of press cuttings, and abstracts of articles of interest to the company's activities.

Archival material can frequently provide very detailed and specific inform-ation. At the same time, however, it can lack the necessary breadth of per-spective for a full and objective view of a topic, and so must be approached with caution. You should always attempt to support information obtained in this way with material from more general sources.

Finally, you should remember that company abstracts are often produced from the reference sources listed in the earlier sections of this unit. The prepara-tion of such abstracts has already been covered in Unit 9, and will also feature in section 18.5. When you are consulting abstracts in an archive, make sure that you note the details of the original articles or sources they summarize, so that you can consult these if necessary. This will prevent you from relying on material which may be incomplete, and will mean that the final data which you collect is more comprehensive and reliable than that in the company archive.

18.4 Electronic data

Unit 17 has discussed how data may be obtained through electronic means, from viewdata and teletext systems and from company databases. Such sources are an important way of keeping up to date with business developments, and will come increasingly to the fore as technology grows.

18.5 The literature search

When you need to find a specific item of information – such as the name of a manufacturer of office furniture or the number of people going on winter package holidays – one or more of the above reference sources can usually help. But when you require a more general view of a whole topic – such as the production and sales of frozen foods of a certain kind, and the potential market size – you will need to consult a much wider range of sources.

Doing this in a haphazard way will be time-consuming and might mean that you overlook important facts. Instead, you should follow a systematic approach – usually known as a literature search – in which you proceed from general to specific sources of information, noting down what you find at each stage in the way described in Unit 9. In most cases, you will find that each stage leads on to further sources, so that the search unfolds naturally and becomes easier as it progresses.

The stages of an effective literature search are outlined below.

Define your topic and purpose   Unless you know exactly what you are looking for, it is easy to be misled by the sheer volume of material available, especially if you are investigating an area of national or even international significance. Thinking carefully at the start of a literature search can save a great deal of time later on. If you know, for example, that you are interested in the number of suppliers of Indian frozen foods, the sales figures for the last year for which data is available, and the likely expansion of the market, you will not need to carry out research into the way they are produced, the sources of raw material or the possible export markets. Instead, you will wish to concentrate on the nature and extent of the UK market, the factors likely to influence it in the coming months, and the number of companies involved in production.

Consult a general work   At this stage, you will need to gain a general outline of the topic you are researching. Here, a general work such as an encyclopaedia will often be helpful.

First, write down as many headings as you can under which you think your topic may be described. For example, as well as 'frozen food', list 'Indian cookery', 'curry', and even very general terms such as 'catering', 'supermarkets' or 'retail grocery'. At the same time, think of related topics, such as 'dried foods'.

When you have a list, look up the various entries. Most encyclopaedias are arranged alphabetically, so there should be little difficulty in finding each one. Read each entry carefully, to extend your general knowledge of the topic. Make a note of any books mentioned.

Consult the library catalogue   Most libraries of any size will have a catalogue which you can use to find the books mentioned by your general source. Such a catalogue will either consist of a series of small cards in a cabinet, or - increasingly - will appear on *microfiche*. A microfiche is a small piece of plastic film carrying a photographic image minutely reduced - for example of an alphabetical list of books, according to author, title, or sometimes subject (see fig. 18.1). It is read with the help of a projector which magnifies the image on to a screen (see fig. 18.2).

Some libraries have a computer database of their catalogue linked to a VDU: when the details of a book are entered, full information about the volume and its location in the library appears on the screen.

Whatever form the library catalogue takes, it will tell you where the book is located in the library. More important at this stage, it will also give you a subject heading or general classification number under which the book appears. This will enable you to consult other entries in the catalogue under the same subject or code number, and so give you several more books to consult in your search.

Consult specialist books   When you have the full reference from the catalogue, find the place on the shelves where the book is kept. Have a quick look at nearby shelves to see if there are any other titles which may be of interest. Appraise them carefully, as described in section 8.3.1, choose the most relevant and recent, and go through the most important passages in detail.

Consult relevant periodicals   A specialist book will often make references to articles which have appeared in professional and trade journals. Note down carefully any titles which seem to be important and consult the catalogue to see if the library holds them. If it does not, you will probably be able to obtain copies through the inter-library loan service. The librarian will be able to give you details.

Fig. 18.1 A microfiche

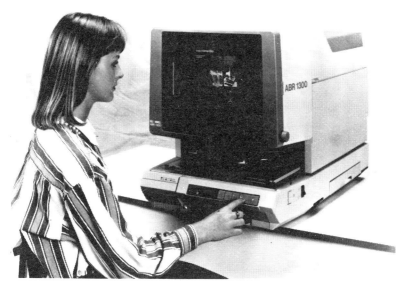

Fig. 18.2 A microfiche reader

Consult relevant directories A periodical or book may refer to a particular company or organization as being at the forefront of work in the field you are researching. Referring to directories at this stage will tell you about the nature of this company – its size or profits, for example – so that you can assess its strengths as a possible business rival. Here, you would need to consult the *Frozen and Chilled Foods Year Book* and perhaps the *Food Industry Directory* in their most up-to-date editions.

Follow up private sources Further information on companies can be sought from archival sources if you have access to them – which is unlikely if they belong to your competitors. The databases of relevant professional organizations are, however, more likely to contain the data you need, and should be checked carefully for information to supplement that already collected. In this case, the Institute of Grocery Distribution may be able to help.

Compare findings with official publications At this stage, you should try to compare your specific findings with the more general data to be found in official publications. The *Annual Abstract of Statistics* may give you data about total spending on processed frozen foods in the UK; *Social Trends* will tell you whether and to what extent a trend is emerging for eating at Indian restaurants. Putting the two together, and combining the information with that you have already collected, you might decide that the time is right for your company to begin marketing a new kind of frozen Indian food.

Run a final check When you have completed all the stages above, you will have a considerable body of information which you may then use as the basis for business decisions. Before you do so, however, you should double-check with other sources as follows:

- *current periodicals* – to get up-to-the-minute data;
- *bibliographies and publishers' catalogues* – to check for very recent publications;
- *the archives of your own company* – to see if anyone has already conducted research into the topic and made abstracts of relevant material.

Using the stages listed above, and following the advice on note-making in Unit 9, you should be able to collect all the available material about a particular research topic. Remember to record carefully details of the books and articles you consult. Sometimes you will need to look at all of the different kinds of material listed here: sometimes you will need only to look at two or three of them. Whichever is the case, a methodical approach to research is essential if you are to gather fully and accurately the material available to you.

18.6 Conclusion

The reference sources and methods of using them described above are really only the beginning of the process. Once you have collected all your data, you will need to sift through it for the most important points, weigh up conflicting evidence, and – depending on the document you are preparing – add your own ideas and interpretations. You might also need to add the results of surveys you have conducted using questionnaires and personal interviews, especially if you are involved in an important piece of marketing or production.

The report or other document you produce from this information may well form the basis of a major decision at a high level within your company, which may affect the jobs and livelihoods of many employees and contractors. What began as a simple process of consulting a book in a library or a computer database on a floppy disk may end up as a matter of considerable economic, social and personal importance. When you are next asked to write a report, bear this in mind; it highlights the need to get the right facts from the best sources, and demonstrates once again that business communication is something which affects the lives of all of us.

The skills outlined in this unit will not only be called into use when you are making a full literature search. On many occasions you will only need to look up a simple piece of data: the address of a company or the number of return air tickets to Ibiza sold in the winter months, for example. Research like this can be just as important as more extended projects, and this shows once again that reference sources are a major communication tool, and that the ability to use them accurately and quickly is an important skill for communicators at every level of operation.

18.7 Quick questions

1 What kind of publication would you use to find the following:

   (a) a local printing firm?
   (b) the world's largest exporter of coffee?
   (c) the current political leader of El Salvador?
   (d) how much the average family spends on heating?

2 Why might you consult *The Financial Times?*

3 What is a microfiche?

4 Name three electronic sources of data.

5 Put the following into the order in which you would consult them in a full literature search:

   (a) a specialist book;
   (b) a library catalogue;
   (c) a directory;
   (d) periodicals;
   (e) company archives.

18.8 Longer exercises

1   Write a set of notes instructing new members of your company on how they
should complete a literature search.

2   You have been asked to write an article for your company's newsletter,
choosing six reference books which you think are indispensable for your
business and giving reasons for your choice. Write the article in no more
than 200 words.

3   Carry out a literature search on 'The integrated office'. Note down all the
material you consult at each stage, and compile a file of notes which you can
use for reference purposes.

4   Make notes for a brief talk you have been asked to give on 'Company
archives – what and why?'

Assignments

The following pages contain four assignments which bring together many of the different aspects of communication discussed in this book. They will give you an idea of how communication is used in a working context.

You might like to work through the assignments as a way of consolidating the skills gained while studying the various units, or as preparation for an examination. They are arranged in approximate order of difficulty, starting with the simplest.

Assignment 1

Health and safety

Every school, college or firm has to have a 'Health and Safety Policy'. This is a booklet which the organization must produce and allow all students or workers to read. It's a very important document, because it tells you how you should try to prevent accidents, the names of people to contact if they do occur, and what to do in case of fire.

Activity 1

Get a copy of the policy document for your organization. Spend some time reading it carefully. Then answer the following questions.

(a) Does it tell you exactly what to do if there's an accident?
(b) Does it tell you where to go if there's a fire?
(c) Does it use clear, straightforward language which anyone could understand?

Activity 2

When you've arrived at answers for these questions, make a list of some of the ways in which the document could be improved. Try to be as detailed as you can in this. For example, your list might read like this:

1   There should be a plan showing exactly where first-aid boxes are kept.
2   The wording on page 7 should be changed. Instead of 'Officially-certified first-aid personnel are available to administer aid', it should read 'People trained in first-aid are there to help.'

Go on with your list until you're satisfied that, if all the changes were made, the document would be quite clear and easy to understand.

Activity 3

Design a notice to tell people in your room or section what they should do and where they should go if a fire should break out.

To do this, you first need to take out the necessary information from the policy document, making sure that what it says is quite correct. Referring to the document, list the points you need to include.

When you've done that, get the points in the best order, and work out which are the most important. This will help you to decide what points should appear in the biggest lettering, or be made to stand out in some other way.

Now draw a map to form part of the notice. It should show:

● the nearest fire alarm;
● the nearest fire extinguisher;
● where you should go if there's a fire.

When you've drawn the map in rough, and are sure that it's accurate, design the notice. Remember, it should be:

● clearly laid out;
● simple and direct in what it says;
● accurate in what it says.

Remember, too, that people will probably only look at the notice when there's a fire. They'll be upset and confused: you must make sure that your message gets across as quickly as possible.

Activity 4

Someone's suggested that all newcomers should be given a bookmark which will tell them what to do if there's an accident in your department or section.

First, go to the policy document and list the points you need to include – where the first-aid boxes are, who you should tell and so on. Then decide which are the most important, and get them in the best order.

Now take a piece of A4 paper. Fold it in four horizontally – so that the folds go across it. Tear along the folds, so that you have four long, thin pieces of paper, each one the size and shape of a bookmark.

Now design the bookmark, using some of the slips of paper for rough versions until you settle on the final one. Make it striking and make it attractive – but above all make it clear.

Activity 5

Use your computer system to make a health and safety database. Include:

(a) names of people to contact in an emergency;
(b) instructions for action in case of fire, accident, spillage of hazardous chemicals and other emergencies.

Design it so that it can be accessed by anyone quickly and efficiently.

Assignment 2

Situation 1

The following letter has appeared on your desk together with a note from your employer:

3 Robin Road
Swansley
SW6 3TF
Tel. Swansley 4276

10 June 1987

The Manager
Tomes & Tomes
Carter Road
Swansley
SW1 3NZ

Dear Sir,

I want to complain about the treatment I had from one of your employees. I bought a book last week from your Hepton branch. When I got it home I found all finger marks on some of the pages and one or two were dogeared, some quite bad. I'd bought it for a present, and I couldn't give anybody a thing like that. So I took it back and your man didn't seem interested. He said the customers mess them about and had I got my receipt. But I'd lost it. And he said had I bought it there and I said 'yes'. But he said he couldn't change it without a receipt. But I said I'd looked all over for that book and yours was the only place that had one 'Flowers of England'. In the end he did change it because a crowd of people were waiting. But I don't think it's good enough.

What are you going to do about it? I know the man his eyes are close together.

Yours

Mavis Thrush (Mrs)

11 June

Please prepare a reply to Mrs Thrush so that I can sign it. Tell her how sorry we are and that our policy is to please our customers. If we can identify the member of staff we shall pass on her complaints. Ask Mrs T if she would like a companion volume to her purchase, 'Weeds of England.' If she would like to call at our Swanksley branch we would be pleased to give it to her. Tell her we are distressed and glad that she told us of her treatment.

Jeremy Tomes

Prepare a reply for Mr Tomes' signature. Assume that this will be typed on headed stationery; there is therefore no need to include the firm's name, address or telephone number in your answer.

Situation 2

Mr Jeremy Tomes wants to remind all employees that the business relies on the goodwill of its customers and that customers' complaints are to be treated with great seriousness. He would like to have reports from all branches on the incidence of complaints from customers. He also requires details of types of complaint. He wants branch managers to inform all employees that from now on all complaints are to be logged in an incident book kept for this purpose.

He believes that no one wins an argument with a customer. Full-time staff are to be given training in dealing with complaints. Part-time staff are to be watched and helped if they have difficulties. Staff may not make promises but must pass complaints to management as soon as possible.

Your employer asked you to prepare the relevant memorandum to go from him to all branch managers immediately.

Prepare the memorandum.

Situation 3

Your employer wants you to devise a poster for exhibition in staffrooms at branches. It is to help in a campaign for better customer relations. He gives you these notes:

> I wish all staff to remember that the customer is the most important person in the shop. I would like you to make up a ~~handout~~ poster to put over these ideas: The aim is to serve — listen to the customer — be willing to suggest alternatives if we don't have what they want. Note the names of regular customers — be willing to take special orders. Always have references books ready to look for book titles, the customer is always welcome even at twenty-past 5. Let the customers browse — but be ready to help — know your stock + be seen to make enquiries when the customer needs info.
>
> J. Tomes

Prepare a poster in which you put over the ideas you have been given as effectively and clearly as possible. Use only one side of A4.

Situation 4

You are to reorder copies of books. You look in the sales record book and notice that the following books published by Bligh and Bounty were among those sold this week.

Author	Title	Publisher	Unit price
Johnson, J	The Golden River	Bligh & Bounty	£8.95
Brown, A	A Motorist's Guide	Shortman's	£7.85
Handy, R	The Pop Scene	Bligh & Bounty	£4.50
Rivers L	Happy Homes	Bligh & Bounty	£7.50
Davis D	Holidays Abroad	Blandings	£5.50
Deeds J	Fast Cars	Bligh & Bounty	£8.00
Williams, N	12 Great Engines	Olds	£6.50
Grace E.	Tell Your Fortune	Bligh & Bounty	£5.00

You have a Bligh and Bounty Order Form [see below]. The order number is TT. 6-2-1155. Mr Tomes Senior will decide on the quantities. They are to be delivered to the Tomes and Tomes Central Store at Horseman Road, Swansley SY4 4XL.

Fill in the order to Bligh and Bounty, for Mr Tomes' signature. List the books alphabetically by author.

(RSA, Communication in business I)

BLIGH AND BOUNTY PUBLISHING COMPANY

ORDER FORM

Author	Title	Quantity	Unit Price	Total
....	....	....	... ...	....
....	....	....	... ...	....
....	....	....	... ...	....
....	....	....	... ...	....
....	....	....	... ...	....
....	....	....	... ...	....
....	....	....	... ...	....
....	....	....	... ...	....
....	....	....	... ...	....
....	....	....	... ...	....
....	....	....	... ...	....
....	....	....	... ...	....
....	....	....	... ...	....
....	....	....	... ...	....
....	....	....	... ...	....

Retailer: ....

Address: ....

....

Delivery address (if different from above): ....

....

Date: .... Order no: ....

Authorized by:

Assignment 3

General information

Assume that you are employed as a general assistant to the Advertising Manager of a local newspaper, the *Bayfield Sirius*, which publishes weekly on Fridays. Your work includes filing, reception, answering the telephone and general office duties, but occasionally your 'boss', Ms Lizzie Kennett, the Advertising Manager, gives you some specialized work in order to improve your chances of promotion. The paper is printed by the Bayfield Press, at 78–90 Norrington Road, Bayfield; the 'deadline' for acceptance of material to be published by Friday is 16.00 hours on the previous Tuesday. The address of the *Bayfield Sirius* is Star Street, Bayfield, Kempshire BF1 K34 and the telephone number is (082 890) 3451. The Editor is Mike Linton and the Chief Reporter is Cecil Parslake.

Situation 1

The staff of the newspaper meet each week on Monday mornings at 10.30 in Mike Linton's office. The meetings are informal but records are kept quite strictly, particularly those on decisions made and any policy changes. Item number 7 on the agenda for next Monday's meeting is revenue from advertising, which has been slowly decreasing over the past year. Mike has already asked staff for ideas – the *Bayfield Sirius* has excellent circulation figures – 100 000 copies sold weekly – so there is good potential for increase of sale of advertising space. The meeting begins promptly at 10.30 and the following conversation takes place:

Mike: Good morning everyone, hope you've got some good ideas for me. Lizzie has been quite worried about the financial position of the *Sirius*, haven't you?

Lizzie: Yes I have, we're losing money now and it can't go on for much longer.

Mike: Well, let's hear from you, yes Cecil?

Cecil: What about circularizing the industrial estate again. We haven't done it for 18 months and it has really grown, you know – several new industries have moved into the area . . .

Lizzie: Yes, and many more have been established in and around Holygate and Mimpsfield too. Why didn't I think of that!

Mike: Well, that's one decision then. Your assistant can get the letters ready, Lizzie. Now, any more bright ideas?

You: Can't we use the local 'Fun Run' at all? We didn't think about it last time and we were too late but it isn't until late September this year and we've got plenty of time. Radio Kempshire are broadcasting a commentary and I intend to run again this time if I can get enough sponsors.

Mike: Did you finish last time? I can't remember?

You: I certainly did, and in 1 hour 35 minutes – not a bad time at all and I raised £400 for local charities!

Cecil: Don't count me in. I don't mind watching but running – never! The paper could sponsor people, we could give away balloons to children during the month of September and even sell specially printed teeshirts with a *Sirius* slogan. . . .

Lizzie: Hey! Cecil, what super ideas, you had better come and work for me!

Mike: Yes, sponsorship is a good idea, we'll definitely do that – we'll run an article in August . . .

You: I hope you are going to sponsor me . . .

Mike: Only if you promise to write a piece for us to publish – you know – 'The Fun Run – by one who took part in it' or something similar.

You: All right, and I'll get my two friends to make a few notes as well. They'll both be watching.

Cecil: Not too professional, mind . . . I don't want to lose my job!

Write the minutes for the part of the meeting reproduced above. Use any suitable minuting style with which you are familiar. Resolution minutes will be insufficient.

Situation 2

Immediately after the meeting Lizzie asks you to prepare a suitable letter to be circulated to all businesses within a fifteen-mile radius of Bayfield. She tells you to give them some idea of the cost of the larger sizes of advertisement and to point out that it is intended to make a feature of local firms starting with the first issue in June. She says to you: 'I'm sure that people don't realize how much business results from good advertising and that they feel that large full page ads are too expensive, but we can do them a very good deal for blocks of full or half-page. Put a return slip on the letter to be used if further details are needed – don't send the advertising rates as we want to promote the larger size adverts if we can. Use your own judgment in selecting material to use from the advertising rates. Oh, yes, in the special June issue there is to be a double-page pull-out section giving publicity to local firms and we're going to use colour highlights.'

Using material from the advertising sheet opposite, prepare the letter (which Lizzie will sign) to be produced on a wordprocessor. Assume that it will be presented on headed paper and that it will be completely contained on one sheet of A4.

Situation 3

The Fun Run took place on Sunday 28 September over 10 miles, starting at the War Memorial in Bayfield High Street and ending at the Leisure Centre in Star Street. You finished the run in 1 hour 25 minutes and your friends Julie Pettifer and Allen Walmsley took some notes for you. You also receive a press cutting

ADVERTISING RATES FOR BAYFIELD PRESS

AREA	STANDARD RATE (£)	FULL PAGE (£)	HALF PAGE (£)	FRONT PAGE (£)	BACK PAGE (£)
Bayfield Town	2.50	760	380	500	400
Millgap (2 miles from town centre)	2.00	700	320	450	330
Holygate (5 miles from Bayfield)	1.78	640	290	390	290
Mimpsfield (10 miles from Bayfield)	1.50	598	220	310	220
Ollerfield (16 miles from Bayfield)	1.33	500	190	295	198

Situations vacant page in any area: special rate for display
3" x 3" - £25.00

Name and address of firm
advertising vacancy
IN BANNER TYPE PRINT

AUDIO TYPIST

A position is now available for a full-time audio/shorthand typist to
work within the typing pool, with future prospects.

Salary negotiable depending on experience.

35 hours per week Monday to Friday with 3 weeks' holiday per year.

Applicants for the above position please forward C.V. to:

details of position - person to
write/telephone etc.

Standard rate means per line of print e.g.

Sale of discontinued lines of
men's clothing at Dearborn's
Emporium, Star Street,
Bayfield starts today. Hurry
for your bargain of the year!

This advertisement would cost £2.50 x 5 in Bayfield Syrius = £12.50

All area newspapers are named Syrius e.g. Holygate Syrius

All above rates are for one issue and special rates are available
for block bookings, minimum or three - possible 12½% off larger
space advertisements.

about Johnny McVey who was the official starter of the race. Mike is keen to have your article; he says: 'Cut the information down by about a third but don't leave anything out which makes the article interesting for the local people to read.'

Prepare the article for the paper using the press cutting, Allen's notes and Julie's.

LOCAL BOXER BECOMES EURO-CHAMP!

Johnny McVey, a local boxer, sensationally knocked out Aleppo Rossi the Italian welterweight champion to take the European Championship. At 26 years of age McVey, who has only been a professional fighter for 5 years now, has the chance to meet the American Rodriguez de Haan who is a contender for the world title.

    After the fight McVey told this reporter that he intended to return home to Britain and his fiancee Hannah Lewis who is a nurse at Bayfield General Hospital - 'We hope to marry early in 1988 and we intend to live in Bayfield'.

Allen's notes

I've never seen so many people in Bayfield before; the queue of runners was over ¼ mile long. The weather was poor, rain falling about 08.00 hours but it did clear up for the 'off' which was scheduled for 10.30 but because there were so many runners Johnny McVey couldn't get through in his car and he had to leave it in a car park and push his way through the crowd. He eventually got there at 10.48 and the starting pistol was fired at 10.55. Did you know the oldest runner was 81 years old and the youngest was only 13! What a sight when the competitors all sent off - like waves on the sea! I think that there were over 2000 but they didn't all finish. I saw you - did you see me? I was right by the War Memorial.

Allen

```
Julie's notes

I've typed them up for you as my writing is awful ! I stood
by the Leisure Centre and saw everyone at the finish,Colin Mallows
won in a time of 59 minutes - a record I think. He runs with the
Bayfield Harriers. He was covered in mud - said he had fallen over
a dog which insisted on running beside him all the way -but he still
won. He told me that he intends to try the London Marathon next.. !
All competitors finished, (Jenny Flethcer (Colin's fiancée) was
   first woman home and the last one home (not Bill Torrance the oldest
competitor) took 2hrs 35 mins. The staff of the leisure Centre all
took part I believe - so they should! I got some figures for you;
competitors included three doctors, seven nurses, ten policemen, five
dentists and eleven teachers, one of the nurse s,   Hannah Lewis won
the women's section last year .   All the sponsor money is not in
yet so I don't know how much cash was raise d. Wasn't it a great sight
to see !


p.S. Hannah Lewis w as 3rd. woman home '.
```

Situation 4

Six full months have gone by since the letters were sent out to promote advertising and some figures have been completed. Mike asks you to prepare a bar chart to be presented at the next meeting of staff. He says: 'I only want you to chart the figures from April 1987 onwards, but will you just comment on the success or otherwise of the campaign – just a couple of paragraphs which highlight the successful increase in sales of space – or otherwise of course – we want to know if we should write to businesses again just yet.'

Using the figures provided below produce the bar chart and notes for Mike.

Advertising revenue

	1986(£)	1987(£)
April	5000	5000
May	6500	8000
June	6000	19000
July	7700	11500
August	6750	10000
September	5990	5000

(RSA, Communication in business II)

Assignment 4

Shadhalts plc is a group of department stores retailing in the North-East and North-West of the United Kingdom. They sell a wide variety of their own goods including ladies' and gentlemen's fashions, cosmetics, electrical goods and home furnishings as well as a number of other manufacturers' branded goods. In addition a number of firms, retailing camera and computer equipment, rent floor space from Shadhalts. Head Office is located at 14–20 The Headway, Huddersfield, West Yorkshire HD1 1BP. It is there that you work in the group's centralized Accounts Department. You work as Accounts Supervisor dealing with accounting, financial and personnel matters. Altogether there are thirteen people working in the Accounts Department:

Mrs Anne Catcliffe	Chief Accountant
Tracey Davis	Chief Accountant's Secretary
Usha Patel	Financial Accountant
You	Accounts Supervisor
Desiree Roden Surinda Patel	} Wages Clerks
Mike Paton Harjit Rai	} Sales Ledger Clerks
Justine James	Credit Control Clerk
Lynda Moss John Micha Balvinder Rai Philippa Jones	} Charge Account Clerks

It is Thursday 18 June. You arrive at work and perform your early morning routine duties in something of a hurry as you have an appointment in your diary for 9.30. This is a meeting about the department's induction programme for new accounting personnel to which you and Usha Patel have been invited. The meeting is to be held in Mrs Catcliffe's office.

At 9.30 you arrive at Mrs Catcliffe's office. Before she starts to speak she asks you if you'll take the minutes of the meeting. She then explains that the three of you are going to constitute a task group. Your remit will be to address itself to the devising of an effective induction programme. Although you're familiar with the nature of the problems surrounding the current induction programme, Mrs Catcliffe runs over them for you. Up until now there has only been a group induction scheme which has taken the form of the group's Director of Personnel travelling around the department stores in the group and personally inducting new staff. To economize on his time employees have been inducted in batches which has resulted, on occasions, in 'new' staff being inducted up to eight months after joining the group. The group's Chief Executive is aware of the bad feeling this procedure has generated and the poor reputation for training which Shadhalts currently has. Consequently he has issued a directive instructing all departments in all of the group's stores to devise their own induction programmes. He wants departments to induct new employees on an individual basis immediately they are engaged by stores. Mrs Catcliffe now asks you and Usha for your suggestions.

After much discussion the three of you agree upon a number of elements to be included in the Accounts Department's own induction programme. You all feel a 'mentor' system (whereby a long-serving member of staff will 'look after' new employees until they are settled in) would be a good idea. Communication is something at which you feel the department doesn't excel. Accordingly, you decide to explain, as fully as possible, matters such as grievance and disciplinary procedures; holidays and sickness benefits; maternity leave; staff benefits (including staff charge cards and staff discounts); staff training; and staff progress. In addition you feel that what any new arrival to the department needs is a genuinely warm welcome. Finally, it is decided that the production of a staff induction booklet containing all of the items mentioned above would be an efficient way of packaging all this information. To make sure that this booklet starts off on a friendly note Mrs Catcliffe asks you if you'd draft a personal letter of welcome from you, a longstanding employee, to new arrivals.

Mrs Catliffe closes the meeting at 10.45. You return to your desk. You know that minutes need to be written up as soon as possible after a meeting has taken place so you do this straight away. Once they're finished you set about drafting the welcoming letter. You want to tell a new employee a little about the firm but not too much; you want to give them an idea of what you do; you want to introduce them to other staff in the department; but most of all you want to make them feel welcome. When you've completed both of these tasks you take photocopies for Usha and for your files, place the documents in envelopes on Mrs Catcliffe's and Usha's desks and then go for lunch.

1 Write up the minutes of the meeting which took place between Mrs Catcliffe, Usha Patel and you.

2 Write the draft letter of welcome, on the firm's headed paper, to new employees.

The Accounts Department staff induction programme appears to be working well, judging by the positive reaction you have received from the two new employees the department has taken on to replace Philippa Jones and John Micha who have left for other employment.

It is mid-morning on Monday 21 November when one of the general office staff brings the second delivery of post. Five minutes later Usha Patel comes over to you. In her hand she has a letter of complaint from Mrs Caroline Higgins of 'East-Lea', 26 Sowood Fold, Stainland, Halifax, West Yorkshire HX4 4AB. She complains that there is a charge on her Shadhalt's customer charge account for which she does not have a receipt. It's for an item of cosmetics costing £42.81, supposedly purchased at the Huddersfield branch. Mrs Higgins says she did not purchase this item nor does she have a receipt for this supposed purchase. Usha asks you if you'd deal with this matter. You go to Donna Clarke's desk. She is one of your new staff. She has taken over responsibility from John Micha for charge card accounts for customers with surnames E to K. You ask her to investigate this matter and to report back to you before lunch. She does so and comes back to you at 12.45. She has established that Mrs Higgins' card was not a stolen one; that all the other entries on her statement of account were valid; and that the card was used at a valid point, that is, the cosmetics counter of the Huddersfield branch of Shadhalts. You thank Donna and tell her she may return to her desk. It could still be the case that Mrs Higgins has made a mistake but a fraud could have been committed by an employee. There has never been any charge card fraud at Shadhalts, although you have recently read a newspaper article about the increasing problem of credit card fraud.

You inform Usha of Donna's discoveries. She's reluctant to bring in the police at this stage although she doesn't discount this possibility. With the assistance of the Branch Manager and one of your floorwalkers it is established that Josie Baughan, one of the cosmetics counter sales assistants, had run Mrs Higgins' charge card through on a blank sales voucher. Later she completed the voucher to reflect a sale of cosmetics to the value of £42.81.

Usha decides on a number of courses of action. She asks you to draft a letter of apology to Mrs Higgins. Secondly she asks you to attend a meeting at 4 o'clock that afternoon to decide what should be done about the fraudulent behaviour on Ms Baughan's part. Finally, she asks you to produce a notice urging Shadhalts' staff to resist the temptation to commit fraud.

3   Draft the letter of apology, ready for Miss Patel's signature, to Mrs Higgins.

4   Prepare the useful notes you would take to the meeting with Miss Patel to discuss the matter of Josie Baughan's having committed fraud.

5   Produce the notice to all staff warning them not to commit any fraud.

Although Shadhalts has never experienced employee fraud of this nature before, there have been instances of stolen or mislaid charge cards and subsequent frauds attempted or achieved. The system that Shadhalts currently operates with its charge cards is as follows. A customer presents his or her card when making a purchase; the sales assistant takes the card and imprints the information on it on to a two-copy sales voucher; the top copy is retained by the customer as a receipt and the bottom copy is passed to the centralized Accounts Department for recording and customer charging purposes. For some time now Mrs Catcliffe has felt that this system is unsatisfactory.

Accordingly Mrs Catcliffe has invited a company called International Credit Register (ICR) to make a presentation about the system it manufactures, installs and maintains. Mrs Catcliffe invites Usha Patel and you to attend this presentation which is to take place on the afternoon of Wednesday 25 November. She asks you to take notes during the presentation and to write a formal report detailing the main points made by the ICR representatives and offering your recommendations as to whether the ICR system constitutes a viable improvement to Shadhalts' current procedures. The day arrives and you attend the presentation. The ICR representatives explain that they are able to offer a number of services to organizations which buy in their systems. First of all ICR will design and manufacture sales vouchers for any firm which uses their system. These sales vouchers have four carbonized copies: the top (clear) copy is the customer's receipt; the second (green) copy is retained by the store where the sales transaction takes place; the third (red) copy and the fourth (grey) copy are forwarded to the centralized accounting function where the red copy is manually processed by accounting staff for recording and customer charging purposes, and the grey copy is filed and retained for checking purposes. In addition ICR manufactures and installs cash registers which can machine-read and check customer's charge cards thus obviating any wear and tear on plastic charge cards. Finally, ICR offers a maintenance service on the registers it installs in retail outlets.

The ICR representatives conclude their presentation. On behalf of Shadhalts Mrs Catcliffe thanks them and they leave. Over a late afternoon cup of tea Mrs Catcliffe, Usha Patel and you discuss the pertinent details of the services offered by ICR. You then gather up your notes and leave for home. That night you read over the notes you've taken from the presentation and prepare a rough draft of your report for Mrs Catcliffe. In this you compare and contrast the relative advantages and disadvantages of the system which Shadhalts currently operates with the services which ICR offers. At work the next morning you read over and revise your draft report. You then write up the final copy of your report, containing your account of the presentation, your assessment of the services offered by ICR and your recommendations as to whether or not Shadhalts should buy in ICR's services. You present this to Tracey Davis to type up as a matter of some urgency. Early in the afternoon you receive the typed copy from her, you check it over to ensure it is accurate and then take your report to Mrs Catcliffe.

6   Write your detailed formal report for Mrs Catcliffe.

(AAT, Communication)

Bibliography

- Black, S., *Practical Public Relations* (Prentice Hall, 1984)

- British Standard 5261 *Copy preparation and proof correction*. Part 1: 1975 *Recommendations for preparation of typescript copy for printing*. Part 2: 1976 *Specification for typographic requirements, marks for copy preparation and proof correction, proofing procedure* (British Standards Institution)

- Bryson, B., *Penguin Dictionary of Troublesome Words* (Penguin, 1984)

- Burchfield, R. W., *The English Language* (Oxford University Press, 1986)

- Burchfield, R. W., *The Spoken Word: A BBC Guide* (BBC Publications, 1981)

- Burgess, A., *Language Made Plain* (Collins, 1984)

- Butcher, J., *Copy-editing: The Cambridge Handbook* (Cambridge University Press, 2nd edn, 1981)

- Carey, G. V., *Mind the Stop* (Penguin, 1971)

- Elbow, P., *Writing with Power: Techniques for Mastering the Writing Process* (Oxford University Press (NY), 1981)

- Flowers, S., *Success in Information Processing* (John Murray, 1988)

- Fowler, H. W., rev. Gowers, E., *A Dictionary of Modern English Usage* (Oxford University Press, 1965)

- Gowers, E., *The Complete Plain Words* (Penguin, 1970)

- Hackett, P., *Success in Office Practice* (John Murray, 2nd edn, 1988)

- Hall, C., *Editing for Everyone* (National Extension College, 1983)

- *Hart's Rules for Compositors and Readers at the University Press Oxford* (Oxford University Press, 39th edn, 1983)

- Hayakawa, S. I., and Fletcher, P. J., *Cassell's Modern Guide to Synonyms and Related Words* (Cassell, 1971)

- Heller, L., and Humez, A., *The Private Life of English Words* (Routledge & Kegan Paul, 1984)

- Hornby, A. S., *The Oxford Paperback American Dictionary* (Oxford University Press, 1986)

- Howard, P., *New Words for Old* (Unwin, 1981)

- Howard, P., *Weasel Words* (Hamish Hamilton, 1978)

- Howard, P., *Words in Your Ear* (Penguin, 1985)

- Hudson, K., *A Dictionary of Diseased English* (Macmillan, 1980)

- Inglis, J., and Lewis, R., *Report Writing* (National Extension College, 1982)

- Kane, T. S., and Peters, L. J., *Writing Prose: Techniques and Purpose* (Oxford University Press (NY), 1986)

- De Leeuw, M. and E., *Read Better, Read Faster* (Penguin, 1969)

- *MHRA Style Book* (Modern Humanities Research Association, 1981)

- Mitchell, J., *How to Write Reports* (Fontana, 1974)

- Partridge, E., *A Dictionary of Historical Slang* (Penguin, 1972)

- Saville, J. and T., *The Business Letter Writer* (Ward Lock, 1981)

- Sillars, S., *Communication Rules OK!* (Jonquil, 1986)

- Sillars, S., *Grammar Rules OK!* (Jonquil, 1985)

- Sillars, S., *Spelling Rules OK!* (Jonquil, 1984)

- Sillars, S., and Good, M., *The Writing Course* (The Open College, 1988)

- Williams, R., *Keywords* (Fontana, 1983)

Index